Trinitarian Pneumatological Personhood *and the* Theology *of* John Zizioulas

Trinitarian Pneumatological Personhood *and the* Theology *of* John Zizioulas

RONALD L. ADKINS II

PICKWICK *Publications* · Eugene, Oregon

Pickwick Publications
An Imprint of Wipf and Stock Publishers
199 W. 8th Ave., Suite 3
Eugene, OR 97401

www.wipfandstock.com

PAPERBACK ISBN: 978-1-6667-3671-7
HARDCOVER ISBN: 978-1-6667-9544-8
EBOOK ISBN: 978-1-6667-9545-5

Cataloguing-in-Publication data:

Names: Adkins II, Ronald L., author.

Title: Trinitarian pneumatological personhood and the theology of John
    Zizioulas / Ronald L. Adkins II.

Description: Eugene, OR : Pickwick Publications, 2023 | Includes bibliographical
    references and index.

Identifiers: ISBN 978-1-6667-3671-7 (paperback) | ISBN 978-1-6667-9544-8 (hard-
    cover) | ISBN 978-1-6667-9545-5 (ebook)

Subjects: LCSH: Zizioulas, Jean, 1931–. | Trinity—History of doctrines—20th
    century.

Classification: BT767.8 .A35 2023 (print) | BT767.8 .A35 (ebook)

FEBRUARY 23, 2023 4:39 PM

To the Life and Memory of
Ryan N. Adkins
(February 22, 1974–December 14, 2013)

A son, a father, a husband, an uncle, a cousin, a friend,
A jack-of-all-trades, master-of-all: artist, theologian,
musician, mechanic, carpenter,
Most of all, my only sibling, my brother—my friend

Contents

Acknowledgments

I WOULD FIRST LIKE to thank Dr. M. William Ury for his classes in theology, where my heart and mind were first enlightened to trinitarian-personhood through the readings of John D. Zizioulas. The opening question on that first day of my seminary experience still captures my imagination: "What was the Trinity doing before creation?" It has changed my life and driven my research.

I would like to thank my PhD advisors at Asbury Theological Seminary, Dr. Larry Wood and Dr. Steven O'Malley. Upon being accepted into the London School of Theology program in partnership with Asbury Theological Seminary, Dr. O'Malley welcomed me into his book-packed office and carefully walked me through the breadth of historical pneumatology. Dr. Wood has been a constant source of encouragement and fantastic knowledge. I have been humbled not only by him as an academic resource but always a gracious host, placing his full attention on my needs. I am indebted and deeply grateful to my PhD supervisor, Dr. Graham McFarlane (London School of Theology), and his tireless work, extraordinary gift for reading details, keen theological mind, and being a man of prayer. The latter is eternally emblazoned in my memory as Dr. McFarlane prayed for my daughter.

Several institutions that made my PhD dissertation possible deserve my deepest thanks. First, I am thankful to the two churches I was privileged to simultaneously shepherd during the first half of my research and for their graciousness: Farmer and Ney United Methodist Churches. I am also grateful to the East Central Conference of The Evangelical Church denomination for seeing qualities that led me to be their Conference Superintendent. Thank you also for allowing me time to research and write. Also, I could not have accomplished this work without the financial support as a Preaching-Teaching Fellow at The Francis Asbury

Society (FAS). I would like to thank both presidents I served at FAS, Dr. Ron Smith and Rev. Stan Key. I am thankful to Mr. Tom and Mr. Caleb Turnbull, part owners of Oberlin-Turnbull Funeral Home, for supplying me with a large, furnished office. The Turnbull family is gracious, loving, genuine, thoughtful, and generally fun. Finally, my family is deeply indebted to Mr. and Mrs. David and Lisa Karlstadt, owners of Karlstadt Farms, and the beautiful apartment that they supplied my family in the closing years of my research.

I would like to thank my parents, Mr. and Mrs. Ron and Frances Adkins, for their prayers, love, and financial support. In like manner, I am grateful to my father-in-law and mother-in-law, Rev. Dr. Blake and Nancy Neff, for their prayers, encouragement, and financial support.

Finally, my most profound appreciation goes to my wife, Jan, and our four children, Ronnie, Nathaniel, Eli, and Maddie. Each of you was directly impacted sacrificially by this long and arduous work. I love you and am very thankful to you. My prayer is that you will walk in the footsteps of your Savior, Jesus Christ. My dearest wife, Jan, has been a source of strength, courage, unfailing love, and faithfulness. I love you deeply. You have much to do with the content within these pages as you live out trinitarian pneumatological personhood.

Abbreviations

CEOC *The Concise Encyclopedia of Orthodox Christianity.* Edited by John Anthony McGuckin. Chichester: Wiley-Blackwell, 2014.

ESV English Standard Version

LXX Septuagint

MT Masoretic Text

NIDB *The New Interpreter's Dictionary of the Bible.* Edited by Katharine Doob Sakenfeld et al. 5 vols. Nashville: Abingdon Press, 2007.

NLT New Living Translation

NT New Testament

ODCC *The Oxford Dictionary of the Christian Church.* Edited by F. L. Cross and E. A. Livingstone. 3rd ed. Oxford: Oxford University Press, 1997.

OT Old Testament

TDNT *Theological Dictionary of the New Testament.* Edited by Gerhard Kittel and Gerhard Friedrich. Translated by Geoffrey W. Bromiley. 10 vols. Grand Rapids: Eerdmans, 1972.

TGNT *The Greek New Testament.* Edited by Barbara Aland et al. 4th ed. Stuttgart: Deutsche Bibelgesellschaft, 1998.

TLOT *Theological Lexicon of the Old Testament.* Edited by Ernst Jenni and Claus Westermann. Translated by Mark Biddle. 3 vols. Peabody, MA: Hendrickson, 1997.

TMCE *The Modern Catholic Encyclopedia.* Edited by Michael Glazier and Monika K. Hellwig. Collegeville, MN: Liturgical, 2004.

Introduction

ZIZIOULIAN THEOLOGY

THEOLOGIAN JOHN ZIZIOULAS DESCRIBED what it means to be a person (i.e., personhood)[1] as being-in-communion first found in the Triune God and second modeled in the church as many people become one church body while sharing in the Eucharist.[2] Zizioulas argues for a theology of the Trinity that begins with the particular persons (*hypostases*) and then moves toward their unity (*ousia*). However, for Zizioulas, the Holy Spirit constitutes Christ (not Christian people), who institutes the church through the participation of the Eucharist.[3] Ironically, in Zizioulas's theology, the economy of the Trinity is at least blurred, if not lost, as is also the personal identity of the Christian who is lost in the mass gathering of the church. Therefore, an alternative presentation of Zizioulas's foundational work is that a Christian person is constituted by the Holy Spirit and drawn into a relationship with the Triune God and other Christian people, making them the church.

Zizioulas's body of work connects theology, philosophy, and the church through such proposals as freedom and communion, one-and-many, and being and relation to form a coherent contemporary theological ecclesiology in what Knight calls "an unrivaled expression of Christian theology."[4] More specifically, Zizioulas's theology consists of a Christology embedded in trinitarian thought, his philosophy is an existential ontology,[5] and his view of the church is a eucharistic-ecclesiology

1. Zizioulas, *Communion*, 9–11.
2. Zizioulas, *Being*, 54–55, 57–62, 126–36, 149–58; Zizioulas, *One and the Many*, 6.
3. Zizioulas, *Being*, 139–40; Zizioulas, *One and Many*, 14–16, 68.
4. Knight, "Introduction," 1.
5. Knight, "Introduction," 6–7.

of communion where the church is not simply an institution, but "She is a 'mode of existence,' *a way of being*."[6] Zizioulas's motivation is ecumenical to draw together Eastern and Western Christians into communion as one church in the image of God, who is Triune.[7] While Zizioulas has uniquely tied persons with communion as a pillar for his eucharistic-ecclesiology, the question remains: has Zizioulas given meaning to the human person's "'personal identity'"[8] as he set out to do, or more specifically, what it means to be a Christian person?

Zizioulas begins his paradigm with the need for a theological definition of person who is *not* defined by what they are by nature (i.e., human being, homo-sapiens, etc.), but rather by their freedom in relationship with another.[9] Person-in-relation is first applied to God, who is Father, Son, and Holy Spirit.[10] The importance of this is shown in the Eastern Orthodox description of the Trinity as described by their names: Father, Son, and Holy Spirit first, followed by the declaration that they are One. In contrast, Western theology typically states that God is One, followed by identifying the Father, Son, and Holy Spirit.[11] Furthermore, Zizioulas theologically focuses on Christ, who was conceived and later baptized by the Holy Spirit, showing that the particular person makes up the (historical) whole Jesus Christ.[12] In turn, Zizioulas's eucharistic-ecclesiology is founded on Christ, who constitutes the church by the institution of the Eucharist.[13] When people participate in the Eucharist, they become the one church which for Zizioulas is the formulation of personhood as God designed.[14] While the sacrament of Eucharist is important with its mystery and symbolic meaning to Christianity, Zizioulas's starting point of persons-in-relation has real promise for a fresh concept of personhood. However, this concept ends with the functional ceremonial act and the loss of particular people ("personal-identity") into the one church.

---

6. Zizioulas, *Being*, 15.

7. Zizioulas, *One and Many*, xix–xxiii, 309–413; Zizioulas, *Being*, 15–19.

8. Zizioulas, *Being*, 27.

9. Zizioulas, *Communion*, 18–19.

10. Zizioulas, *Lectures*, xii–xv.

11. Zizioulas, *Being*, 40; Zizioulas, *One and Many*, 10–12.

12. Zizioulas, *Being*, 110–11, 126–30; Zizioulas, "Capacity and Incapacity," 441–42.

13. Zizioulas, *Being*, 130; Zizioulas, *One and Many*, 337.

14. Zizioulas, *Eucharist*, 17–18.

TRINITARIAN PNEUMATOLOGICAL PERSONHOOD

This book engages Zizioulas's theology of personhood and suggests that personhood, specifically as persons-in-communion, is established by the person of the Holy Spirit as a specific Christian anthropology from a Wesleyan theological perspective. Zizioulas challenges theologians to engage in studies of anthropology, and in particular for studies to be done in trinitarian-personhood. [15] Zizioulas's starting point in personhood and his call for anthropological application enhances Wesleyan theology. Therefore, our working question is, "Does Zizioulas's trinitarian personhood successfully accomplish an anthropological definition?" The answer is, "No." Zizioulas is unsuccessful in offering an anthropological definition of the Christian person based on trinitarian personhood because he first has a narrow perspective on particularity of the Holy Spirit and human beings. Second, Zizioulas's understanding of the presence of God with/in humans is limited to the corporate participation of the Eucharist. Third, human participation in the life of God does not deal with the problem of sin and the remedy of spiritual recreation of the Christian person. In turn, we will argue specifically that the Christian person is each particular person who has encountered the presence of God and continues to live in that presence by participating in the life of the Trinity initiated and sustained by the Holy Spirit. Therefore the purpose of this thesis is to correct Zizioulas by affirming his starting point of trinitarian personhood, which leads to persons-in-relation, but present a trinitarian pneumatologically constituted personhood of communion as a specific Christian anthropology.

OVERVIEW

This book is divided into two parts. In part 1: "Zizioulas: Trinity, Personhood, Holy Spirit," we set up the major tenets of the topic historically and theologically while also including some contemporary thought which will aid us in correcting Zizioulas's results. Chapter 1, "Basis for Trinitarian Pneumatological Personhood and the Theology of John Zizioulas," establishes the purpose and presuppositions of this thesis along with a brief literature review from some contemporary writers who have

---

15. Zizioulas, *One and Many*, 30–31, 383. More specifically, Zizioulas calls for the need to relate the doctrine of the Trinity with anthropology (Zizioulas, *One and Many*, 6).

critiqued Zizioulas. Also included in the review are references to some current theologians of constructive pneumatologically oriented trinitarianism. While this line of thinking takes an alternative direction to what is presented in this thesis of trinitarian pneumatology, these theologians are relevant to the field of study. The purpose of chapter 2, "Trinitarian Personhood: West and East," is to historically and theologically trace the foundation of Zizoulas's central argument on personhood and the doctrine of the Trinity that supports his compendium of *being as communion*. This chapter places the person in relational terms instead of natural or materialistic terms. Furthermore, person is philosophically understood in terms of particularity and will be further developed in chapter 5. In chapter 3, "Zizioulas and Traditional Thought," we evaluate Zizioulas's methodology. In the evaluation, we critically follow Zizioulas's line of thought to determine whether or not his conclusions are correct. Since Zizioulas writes for a contemporary audience, chapter 4: "Zizioulas and Contemporary Implications," addresses Zizioulas's Dictum of trinitarian ontology as a "mode of existence" in the contemporary context. Here, we introduce trinitarian pneumatology as a solution to the outcome of Zizioulas's mode of existence, which is explicitly worked out through his eucharistic-ecclesiology. The issue at hand is whether a sacramental activity or the person of the Holy Spirit constitutes a Christian person?

Part 2, "Trinitarian Pneumatological Personhood," is dedicated to correcting Zizioulas's eucharistic-ecclesiology as constituting persons-in-relation by emphasizing the divine-human relationship, and more specifically, showing the person of the Holy Spirit constitutes the Christian person. Chapter 5, "Particularity in God and in Human Being," suggests that a theology of particularity is relevant to trinitarian theology as it gives a balance to the topics of unity, community, and oneness. Colin Gunton's work will be significant for building a case of particularity in understanding the persons of the Trinity and human persons as relational beings. Chapter 6, "Personal Presence: A Shadow of Things to Come," suggests the flaw in Zizioulas's eucharistic-ecclesiology is that while Zizioulas starts his theology by pointing out the need for a relationship to constitute personhood, humans are devoid of personhood in Zizioulas's theology as the relational element between God and humans is experienced only through sacramental acts. The result is that the relational activity remains within the Trinity for the divine and corporate gathering around the Eucharistic table for the humans. The corrective to this unacceptable result is the personal presence of the Holy Spirit into the life of every believer, making them a Christian person. The purpose of chapter 7, "Participation and Christian Anthropology," is to demonstrate that when the person of the Holy Spirit encounters a particular person, a new and dynamic relationship is developed that constitutes the human person as a Christian person resulting in new relationships with God and others (i.e., persons-in-relation). The Christian person is a spiritually recreated person whose character is transformed from sinful-selfishness toward holy-love as desired by God and whose mission and outlook on the world is aligned with God's will. This transformation supports and enhances Wesleyan soteriology in that the Holy Spirit can move a human being from their natural state (i.e., fallen, sinful, selfish) to a sanctified state (i.e., raised, holy, selfless).

PART 1

Zizioulas: Trinity, Personhood, and the Holy Spirit

INTRODUCTION

ZIZIOULAS PROPOSES A THEOLOGICAL approach to ontology and, more specifically, "personal identity."[1] According to Zizioulas, if we are going to understand what it means to be a person, we need to turn our attention first to the eternal God who has revealed himself as Father, Son, and Holy Spirit.[2] Zizioulas revisits the Cappadocian Fathers and their understanding of the Trinity to find a concept of person. Therefore, our question is, "Does Zizioulas's trinitarian personhood accomplish an anthropological definition?" The fault we find in Zizioulas's goal toward a concept of person based on a model of the Trinity is an insufficient presentation on the person of the Holy Spirit. In part 1, "Zizioulas: Trinity, Personhood, and the Holy Spirit," we will trace and expand on Zizioulas's tenets of Trinity and personhood. We will also identify Zizioulas's insufficient use of pneumatology and, at the conclusion, suggest that the Christian person is each particular person who has encountered the presence of God and continues to live in that presence by participating in the life of the Trinity initiated and sustained by the Holy Spirit.

In chapter 1, the purpose, presuppositions, and scope of this study are laid out. A brief literature review is given from significant critiques on Zizioulas's theology. The literature review also includes a brief review on constructive pneumatology that is trinitarian in orientation from

---

1. Zizioulas, *Being*, 27.
2. Zizioulas, *Being*, 40–42, 44; Zizioulas, "Holy Trinity," 46, 59–60.

1

Pentecostal theology. Chapter 2 is a historical study from a theological and philosophical perspective rather than a chronological dialectic. The purpose is to engage Zizioulas's study on personhood and Trinity to support his notion of *communion*. Chapter 3 is a study into Zizioulas's methodology. Zizioulas writes for ecumenical concerns and has been critiqued and praised by various theologians from various theological perspectives. Therefore, this chapter will theologically look at Zizioulas's Greek Orthodox roots, showing his traditionally orthodox, constructive, and novel development of eucharist-ecclesiology. Finally, chapter 4 evaluates Zizioulas's primary contribution in trinitarian ontology as modes of existence and contemporary implications. This chapter offers trinitarian pneumatology as an alternative approach to Zizioulas's persons-in-relation (i.e., being as communion).

Chapter 1

Basis for Trinitarian Pneumatological Personhood and the Theology of John Zizioulas

> "If anyone loves me, he will keep my word . . . and *we* will come to him and make *our* home with him."
>
> —Jesus the Christ[1]

PURPOSE

The purpose of this thesis is to answer whether Zizioulas's trinitarian personhood accomplishes an anthropological definition. This question arises from Zizioulas's call for more work to be done in anthropology and his attempt to link relationality with ontology and make anthropology a being-as-communion or persons-in-relation.[2] In Zizioulas's theology, a being (i.e., non-person, individual, archaeological being, Adam-like) becomes a person (i.e., personal, "de-individualized," eschatological person, Christ-like) by communion with others in the ecclesial activity of Eucharist where the Holy Spirit constitutes the church. At the same time, (the corporate) Christ (the-one-for-the-many) institutes the church.[3]

---

1. John 14:23; emphasis mine. Unless otherwise noted, all biblical citations are from the ESV.

2. Zizioulas, *Being*, 15, 18, 22, 123–24, 132; Zizioulas, *One and Many*, 6, 30–31, 383.

3. Zizioulas, *Being*, 132–38, 140; Zizioulas, "Capacity and Incapacity," 409–10, 425, 432, 436, 441–44.

Zizioulas describes anthropology as the *koinōnia* (i.e., communion, community) of the many into the one (e.g., the body of Christ).[4] Thus, for Zizioulas, the authentic person (i.e., personal, "de-individualized," eschatological person, Christ-like) is the one who overcomes the boundaries of the self and is freed from the natural self (i.e., non-person, individual, archaeological being, Adam-like) through baptism into the corporate ecclesial communion (persons-in-relation) that is maintained through the Eucharist.[5] Since human beings are simultaneously caused and created (by God) existing under the "creaturely mechanisms of cause and effect," and if freedom to be a person is through a relationship with another (*ekstasis*),[6] then why not develop a more personal-relational connection between the divine and human beings? Why not focus on the person of the Holy Spirit engaging the human person? For Zizioulas, an authentic person is ultimately free in their[7] relationship toward another.[8] The persons of the Trinity are absolutely free, while human freedom is limited.[9] Therefore, would it not be reasonable to focus on the possibility of a divine-human relationship that frees the natural human being from the self into an authentic person, or more specifically a Christian person, through the personal presence of God by the person of the Holy Spirit who has absolute personhood and who can offer authentic personhood by the eternal trinitarian relationship?

Despite Zizioulas's aesthetically attractive theological composition, our answer to the research question is that Zizioulas's theology does *not* successfully accomplish an anthropological definition. Ironically, Zizioulas's one-and-many methodological approach on the topic of personhood gives more weight to the oneness (i.e., unity), causing the topic of persons to lose its distinctiveness. However, Zizioulas's starting point

---

4. Zizioulas, *Being*, 112–13; Zizioulas, "Capacity and Incapacity," 434, 443; Zizioulas, *One and Many*, 49–60.

5. Zizioulas, *Being*, 44–65.

6. Zizioulas, *Being*, 42–44; Zizioulas, "Capacity and Incapacity," 403–9, 414, 416–17, 428–29. Farrow, "Person and Nature," 110–12.

7. The collective singular pronoun "their" is used in order to cover the spectrum of gender (male and female).

8. Zizioulas, *Being*, 44–46; Zizioulas, "Capacity and Incapacity," 407–10, 425–28.

9. Zizioulas, *Being*, 18–19, 39–50, 120–21; Zizioulas, "Capacity and Incapacity," 414. See Zizioulas's development from creation to the salvation of humans with the underlining theme of "freedom" (Zizioulas, *Lectures*, 83–119).

or hypothesis that being-as-communion, or what we will call persons-in-relation, will be tested and affirmed as a launching point through philosophy, history, trinitarian theology, and Scripture. This method is also filtered through a Wesleyan theological perspective or expression. A further problem in Zizioulas's eucharistic-ecclesiology from a Wesleyan perspective is that the person of the Holy Spirit constitutes Christ and not the Christian person. Wesleyan theology also expresses Zizioulas's proposition of the dichotomy between individual and de-individualized persons as the sin nature and sanctification. Therefore, we hypothesize that a Christian person is constituted through trinitarian pneumatology, which the Holy Spirit initiates. This thesis intends to show further that the Christian person is each particular person who has encountered the presence of God and continues to live in that presence by participating in the life of the Trinity initiated and sustained by the Holy Spirit.

This hypothesis is *not* tested solely against Wesleyan theologians but from a collection of relevant scholars in their specific fields of theology. The theological emphasis of trinitarian pneumatology will call for scholarship from the early church fathers to modern theologians and Eastern and Western thinkers. Where relevant research outside of theology is called for, like, anthropology, philosophy, and psychology, it will be referred to as needed.

PRESUPPOSITIONS

Every work in theology comes with presuppositions and personal experiences, no matter how objective the writer attempts to tackle the topic at hand.[10] This thesis is no different. Metropolitan John Zizioulas of Pergamon (1931–) is a twentieth-century Greek Orthodox theologian who has written and has worked with scholars outside of his tradition to renew an ecclesial ecumenism.[11] In comparison, I am theologically a Wesleyan following the biblical and practical theology of John Wesley (1703–91). From a Wesleyan perspective, I believe a Christian anthropology of persons-in-relation enhances soteriology, and more clearly articulates the Wesleyan *ordo salutis* from justification to entire sanctification (or

---

10. Allison and Köstenberger, *Holy Spirit*, 1–2; Atkinson, *Trinity*, 12; Volf, *Likeness*, ix–xii, 1.

11. Zizioulas, *One and Many*, xiii–xxiii.

Christian perfection; cf. *not* sinlessness).[12] A persons-in-relation ontology gives Wesleyan theology an expression that keeps it from derailing into a legalistic theology. Furthermore, the nuances of Wesleyan soteriology are not simply a work of salvation so that one might have eternal life but rather deals with the Christian life and living in the presence of God as a daily relationship.[13] At the same time, concerning Zizioulas's persons-in-relations concluding with eucharistic-ecclesiology, we find his aims toward personhood fall apart primarily because the person of the Holy Spirit is denied access to the Christian person in a personal, relational manner.[14]

The purpose and goal of this thesis are *not* a comparative study of Greek Orthodoxy versus Wesleyanism or John Zizioulas versus John Wesley,[15] but instead, we are aware of this Wesleyan presupposition and its effects on the scope of this study. Therefore, it is necessary to point out some Wesleyan theological assumptions that affect this thesis's scope and limits.

A Wesleyan theology presupposes the active and direct work of the Holy Spirit upon the human person in soteriology from convicting grace of the sinner to entire sanctification (or Christian perfection) and moment by moment presence for one to live the holy-life (i.e., cleansed from all sin and to love God and to love others).[16] Also significant un-

---

12. Wesley, "Plain Account," 383–85, 442; Wesley, "Brief Thoughts," 446; Collins, *Wesley*, 15, 82, 99, 125, 139, 146, 155–56, 163, 188, 256, 284, 286, 303, 307, 310, 329. Wesley, "Marks," 198–200.

13. Collins, *Wesley*, 124–27, 253–56; Henderson, *Wesley's Class*, 11–12, 28, 50–51, 56, 59, 60, 65, 66–69, 84, 86–112, 112–13, 117–26, 128–29; Langford, *Practical Divinity*, 17, 20, 33–42, 254–55.

14. Zizioulas, *Being*, 110–11, 126–27, 130, 131–32; Zizioulas, *Eucharist*, 15–16; Zizioulas, *One and Many*, 337.

15. The opposite might be true in that there are more similarities than differences between the two. For further reading on comparing Eastern Orthodoxy and Wesleyanism, see Kimbrough, *Orthodox and Wesleyan Spirituality*; Maddox, "Wesley and Orthodoxy," 29–53; also notice the specific point that Outler makes by suggesting that the Greek Fathers shaped Wesley's pneumatology in Outler, "Introduction," 74–76.

16. Wesley, *Holy Spirit and Power*, 16, 23, 25, 26–27; Wesley, "Way," 77, 78–79, 80–81, 86; Wesley, "Almost Christian," 137, 141; Wesley, "First Fruits of the Holy Spirit," 87–97; "Witness of the Spirit (Discourse 1)," 111–23; Wesley, "Witness of the Spirit (Discourse 2)," 123–34; Wesley, "Marks," 212–23; Wesley, "Holy Spirit," 508–20; Wesley, "Farther Appeal," 48–49, 61, 62, 65, 66, 75, 76–77, 78–111; Wesley, "Character," 341–42; Wesley, "Plain Account," 378–80, 383–84, 387, 388, 391, 393, 394, 401–2, 404, 407, 419, 420, 421–22, 424, 439, 445.

der the category of soteriology is that Wesleyan theology views sin as a two-pronged problem as the acts of sin (commission and omission; intentional and unintentional) and the sin nature.[17] Therefore, due to a two-fold sin problem, Wesleyan theology views God as offering a two-fold solution through imputed grace and imparted grace.[18] In Wesleyan theology, grace is God's transforming power through the Holy Spirit in human life.[19]

The final presupposition is that Wesleyan theology does not separate formal theology from practical spirituality. Theology is personal-relational as it is a spiritual exercise of cooperation and communion of the Holy Spirit upon and with the believer.[20] The outcome and the result of "true religion" or formal theology is the effect of the Holy Spirit upon the human heart to cause one to love God and love others.[21] Therefore, a theology that does not lead to the believer's spiritual growth resulting in a love for God and others is suspect. However, this does not negate the fact that Wesleyan theology, like most formalized theology, begins with the objective (Who is God?) and moves toward the subjective (Who am I?) in its methodology.

Since this thesis is a study into Zizioulas's theology (e.g., Trinity, pneumatology, anthropology, ontology, ecclesiology, etc.) to test his trinitarian personhood for an anthropological definition from a Wesleyan theological expression, and *not* a comparative study, Wesleyan theology will be implicit, remaining in the background, except for where relevant definitions and concepts are necessary. When Wesleyan theological thought needs to be clarified or explained, an indication will be given to the footnotes rather than the body of the text to keep the flow of thought connected.

---

17. Wesley, "Plain Account," 375, 377, 379–80, 395, 401–2, 418, 422–23, 423, 432, 444.

18. Wesley, "Minutes of Some Late Conversations," 277–78; Wesley, "Second Essay," 393–97; Wesley, "Plain Account," 378–79, 390, 443–46; Taylor, *Formulation*, 108, 142, 157–66; Maddox, "Wesley and Orthodoxy," 35.

19. Maddox, "Wesley and Orthodoxy," 37; Collins, *Wesley*, 122–23.

20. Thorsen, *Quadrilateral*, 91; Wesley, "Way," 76–86; Wesley, "Circumcision of the Heart," 202–12.

21. Wesley, "Way," 79–80; Wesley, "Catholic Spirit," 492–504; Wesley, "Difference," 263; Wesley, "Unity," 269–73.

LITERATURE REVIEW

The impact of John Zizioulas's work is demonstrated by the many notes, chapters, articles, and books dedicated by scholars who have engaged him. In 2007 a collaborative effort by twelve international scholars from various traditions was given to acknowledge Zizioulas's impact on theology in the form of a book, *The Theology of John Zizoulas: Personhood and the Church*. In dedication to Zizioulas, Knight declared, "John Zizioulas is widely recognized as the most significant Orthodox theologian of the last half-century and acclaimed advocate of ecumenism."[22] Moreover, "John Zizioulas is one of the best-known theologians of the contemporary Orthodox Church, a central figure in the ecumenical scene and one of the most cited theologians at work today."[23] With these accolades come criticisms. This section will briefly look at eleven scholars and their responses or critiques of Zizioulas's theology. Throughout the book, these scholars will engage Zizioulas where relevant. These eleven scholars are listed below in chronological order by the publication year of their book or academic article, which critiques Zizioulas's theology. Following the critical review will be a brief literature review of current Pentecostal theology in constructive pneumatologically oriented trinitarianism. This relatively new Pentecostal expression of pneumatological trinitarianism[24] is the *opposite* approach than we are taking in this thesis of trinitarian-pneumatology, although some outcomes are similar. Therefore, the scope of this thesis is *not* to formally or explicitly engage Pentecostal theology except where specific points are relevant. However, in the literature review, we will make aware that this relatively new constructive pneumatologically oriented trinitarianism is currently impacting Pentecostal circles and will undoubtedly bring a long-needed focus on pneumatology to theology.[25]

22. Knight, *Theology of Zizioulas*, i.

23. Knight, "Introduction," 1.

24. Atkinson, *Trinity*, 33.

25. Synonymous with Colin Gunton's words in the second edition of his book, *The Promise of Trinitarian Theology* (here after, *Trinitarian Theology*), six years after the first, "Suddenly we are all trinitarians, or so it would seem" (Gunton, *Trinitarian Theology*, xv), I can foresee the possibility in the near future of someone exclaiming, "Suddenly we are all Pentecostals!" The reasons for this theological forecast is threefold. First, there has long been a need in theology for an emphasis in pneumatology (Yong, *Spirit-Word-Community*, 9; Oden, *Spirit*, 3–4). Second, while theologians cringe at injecting experience and pragmatism into formal theological dialectic, it connects with people in a wholistic way (Tucker, *Preacher*, 10–21; Atkinson, *Trinity*, 12–16; Macchia, *Baptized*, 11–14). Third, current Pentecostal theologians have incorporated an academic foundation to their distinctive faith (Atkinson, *Baptism*, 19–22).

André de Halleux

French patristic theologian, de Halleux, is said to be one of the first scholars to do lasting damage to Zizioulas's trinitarian ontology.[26] De Halleux produced two large articles for *Revue théologique de Louvain* (1986) titled, "Personnalisme ou essentialisme trinitaire chez les Pères cappadociens? Une mauvaise controverse" in which he argued that Zizioulas's theological approach incorrectly read personalism into the Cappadocian Fathers.[27] De Halleux leans heavily upon St. Basil to show that contrary to Zizioulas's point that the Cappadocians separated *hypostasis* from *ousia* and in turn associated *prosōpon* with *hypostasis* revealing the primacy of relation over essence, Basil, de Halleux argues, relied on the term *koinōnia* to describe the essence of the Trinity.[28] De Halleux's point is that by looking closely at Basil, we see that the Cappadocians were arguing from an essential priority of the Trinity (i.e., what is shared within the Trinity) through the term *koinōnia* rather than grounding his thought in an extreme view of the personal (relational) with the use of *hypostasis*.[29] De Halleux says that the *koinōnia* identifies the "community of the nature" and not the "property of persons" as Zizioulas espouses.[30]

Colin E. Gunton

While de Halleux sought to balance the trinitarian views from personalists versus essentialists[31] of the Greek East and the Latin West, Gunton attempted to balance Zizioulas's monarchy of the Father and the modern emphasis of communion through social-trinitarianism.[32] Zizioulas's trinitarian theology is rooted in the *monarchia* of the Father, who causes the Trinity to exist.[33] The person of the Father rather than divine substance is the cause of the Trinity to exist (i.e., the Son and the Holy

---

26. Anatolios, "Personhood," 148.

27. De Halleux, "Personnalisme," 1:135.

28. De Halleux, "Personnalisme," 1:144–48.

29. De Halleux, "Personnalisme," 1:144–45.

30. De Halleux, "Personnalisme," 1:144.

31. De Halleux, "Personnalisme," 1:129–31; 2:265, 289–92.

32. Gunton, *Trinitarian Theology*, 195–201.

33. Zizioulas, "Holy Trinity," 52; Zizioulas, *Being*, 83–89; Zizioulas, *Communion*, 137–45.

Spirit).[34] Gunton affirms that God is personal, which he viewed through the trinitarian relationships rather than the determining factor found in Zizioulas's theology. In Gunton's critique of Zizioulas's monarchial view of the Trinity, he offers an equality-with-headship[35] model of the Trinity. This equality-with-headship model does not reduce the persons of the Trinity into impersonal definitions or in some way substance, but rather "the Son and the Holy Spirit are truly God as is the Father" all the while they subordinate themselves by "doing the will of the Father in the world."[36] In Gunton's contribution, he also shows how the particularity of persons can enhance a balanced view of the Trinity and human persons.[37] Gunton supports his trinitarian model of relations with the doctrine of *perichoresis*, where all three persons do the activity of God.[38] Gunton attempts to strike a balance between the distinctiveness of the persons of the Trinity and their oneness of essence. In Gunton's trinitarian theology, there is an equality-with-headship.[39]

John G. F. Wilks

Similar to Gunton's equality-with-headship of the Trinity, Wilks assumes a Cappadocian interpretation to be an "absolute equality of different *hypostases*," all the while, the function of the *hypostases* is *not* equal.[40] The stress on equality keeps trinitarian theology from a subordinationist view.[41] Wilks further critiques Zizioulas on a lack of patristic support concerning his interpretation of being-as-communion and the weight given

34. Zizioulas, *Being*, 39–72, 83–89; Zizioulas, *Communion*, 137–45; Zizioulas, "Holy Trinity," 50–55; Zizioulas, *Lectures*, 53, 59–62; Zizioulas, *One and Many*, 10–14.

35. "Equality-with-headship" is *my term* for Gunton's expression that the particular persons of the Trinity are equal through *homoousios* and *perichoresis*. Gunton, *Trinitarian Theology*, 197–201; Gunton, *One, Three, Many*, 152–54; 163–66, 172, 183–84, 191.

36. Gunton, *Trinitarian Theology*, 197–98.

37. Gunton, *One, Three, Many*, 157–62, 172, 181–84, 190–91, 193–94, 225, 229.

38. Gunton, *Trinitarian Theology*, 198; Gunton, "Persons," 100.

39. Gunton, *Trinitarian Theology*, xviii, 134–35, 140–41, 197–98; Gunton, *Father, Son, & Holy Spirit*, 44–45, 73–74; Gunton, *One, Three, Many*, 152–53, 163–79, 185–86, 189, 191, 204, 212, 214, 230. Gunton relies on T. F. Torrance for his development of *perichoresis* (Gunton, *Trinitarian Theology*, 197–98; Gunton, *Father, Son, & Holy Spirit*, 44–45, cf. Torrance, *Doctrine*, 102–3, 110–11, 113, 133–34, 136, 168–202).

40. Wilks, "Ontology," 72.

41. Wilks, "Ontology," 72.

to the monarchy of the Father (i.e., causative nature).[42] Wilks suggests that the causative nature of the Father was only looked at as minor in the Cappadocian writings.[43] Finally, Wilks states that the Cappadocian Fathers did not place the unity of God in the *hypostasis* of the Father, but instead, they placed the unity of God in the *ousia*.[44]

Alan J. Torrance

Torrance, like Wilks, argues for *ousia* as the unity of the Trinity rather than the Father, but more specifically, the *ousia* is the mutual indwelling of the persons: Father, Son, and Holy Spirit.[45] He stresses that the intra-divine communion of the persons of the Trinity is primordial and eternally "given" as opposed to Zizioulas's claim that the Holy Trinity is ontologically primordial while simultaneously stating the Father causes the Son and Holy Spirit; thus, the Father is the cause of the Trinity.[46] Ultimately, Torrance argues, Zizioulas commits some level of subordinationism where the Son and the Holy Spirit are contingent upon the exclusively primordial Father.[47] Finally, Torrance takes issue with Zizioulas's ecclesial and anthropological implications of the church as a "mode of existence."[48] Torrance states that this view of the church and personhood does not consider human suffering or those who remain outside of a "salvific communion."[49] The answer for Torrance is a more holistic teaching of Jesus's life and ministry that takes up the meaning of the gospel.[50]

Nonna Verna Harrison

Harrison's purpose in "Zizioulas on Communion and Otherness" further develops studies in theological anthropology. Harrison takes Zizioulas to

42. Wilks, "Ontology," 74, 77.

43. Wilks, "Ontology," 77.

44. Wilks, "Ontology," 82.

45. Torrance, *Persons*, 293–94.

46. Torrance, *Persons*, 292–93.

47. Torrance, *Persons*, 292–93.

48. Torrance, *Persons*, 295.

49. Torrance, *Persons*, 296.

50. Torrance, *Persons*, 301–6.

task on his monarchy of the Father by questioning his use of freedom as an absolute ontology of personhood.[51] Harrison's counterpoint to Zizioulas's point that the person of the Father is absolutely free (e.g., *ekstasis*) comes in the form of a rhetorical question, "Now, since the Son and the Spirit do not constitute their own essence in the same way the Father does, how, in Zizioulas's terms, are they absolutely free, which they must be since they are fully God?"[52] She answers that their divine essence relates the persons of the Trinity.[53] The essence of the Trinity is ontologically dependent upon the persons of the Trinity.[54] Harrison argues for more emphasis on the equality of the persons of the Trinity through mutual self-giving to affirm "full personhood."[55]

Miroslav Volf

Like those before and after him, Volf critiques Zizioulas's monarchy of the Father, but he further juxtaposes Zizioulas's trinitarian monarchy with Zizioulas's ecclesial hierarchy.[56] Volf also argues for a more egalitarian view (or *perichoretic* view)[57] of the Trinity (and a congregational polity/ polycentric community of the church)[58] by emphasizing the particularity of persons.[59] However, Volf, like Zizioulas, desires to steer clear of individualism.[60] Volf points to the Orthodox doctrine of *generatio* and *spiratio* as examples of the particularity of the Son (*generatio*) and the Holy Spirit (*spiratio*) being from the Father (begetter) and unique from each other.[61] Volf says, "Translated anthropologically, this means that each human being *is constituted into a person by what in each case is a different relation of God to that human being.*"[62] In other words, each human being

---

51. Harrison, "Zizioulas," 273–74, 279.

52. Harrison, "Zizioulas," 279.

53. Harrison, "Zizioulas," 279–80.

54. Harrison, "Zizioulas," 279.

55. Harrison, "Zizioulas," 289–90.

56. Volf, *Likeness*, 3, 4, 114–15, 214, 215, 217–18.

57. Volf, *Likeness*, 208–13.

58. Volf, *Likeness*, 217–20, 224, 225–27.

59. Volf, *Likeness*, 181–82.

60. Volf, *Likeness*, 3–5.

61. Volf, *Likeness*, 182.

62. Volf, *Likeness*, 182.

is created distinctively different from one another yet shares humanity with every other human being. God's call is generally to all humans and specifically to each human.[63] The proper response to God's call is faith, and for Volf, faith is the capacity to become a person. However, he points out that Zizioulas has "no role" of faith in his soteriology.[64] This life of faith opens up new multiple relationships with God, other humans, and their environment.[65]

Lucian Turcescu

Turcescu has been one of Zizioulas's most outspoken critics on interpreting the concept of person into the Trinity (i.e., persons-in-relation) by the Cappadocian Fathers. Turcescu's article, "'Person' versus 'Individual', and Other Modern Misreadings of Gregory of Nyssa,'" resulted in a rebuttal from Papanikolaou[66] and a rare response from Zizioulas.[67] The core of Turcescu's argument is that Zizioulas does not prove a Cappadocian theology of person, but rather that he has read twentieth-century theology into the Cappadocians, causing a fallacious argument between person and individual.[68] Turcescu relies almost solely on Gregory of Nyssa to argue that *the Cappadocians understood hypostasis* as "individual."[69] Furthermore, Turcescu argues that while the Cappadocians used person and individual interchangeably, they did not understand person in relational terms.[70] Turcescu's definition of individual is "a person as a collection of properties," an enumeration of individuals ("that is, individuals being subject to addition and combination"), and "indivisible" person.[71] Turcescu's arguments contrast Zizioulas's view of person, which has "the claim of absolute being" independent of qualities from other beings or substance.[72]

---

63. Volf, *Likeness*, 182.

64. Volf, *Likeness*, 95.

65. Volf, *Likeness*, 186.

66. Papanikolaou, "Existentialist?," 601–7.

67. Zizioulas, "Appendix," 171–77.

68. Turcescu, "Misreadings," 534, 536.

69. Turcescu, "Misreadings," 533–34.

70. Turcescu, "Misreadings," 532, 533–34, 536–37.

71. Turcescu, "Misreadings," 530–33.

72. Zizioulas, *Communion*, 99–100.

Douglas Farrow

Farrow's opposition to the concept of person in Zizioulas's theology resides in the charge that he uses it univocally for both the persons of the Trinity and for the human person.[73] While Zizioulas develops a trinitarian theology that speaks of the divine persons as "co-inherent" in each other (i.e., *perichoresis*), meaning the whole God is in each person of the Trinity, this theology cannot be transferred to human persons.[74] Farrow believes that there must be a distinction in the use and understanding of person as applied to divine and human persons. Zizioulas's connection of the divine person and the human person is in Christ, who is the-one-for-the-many through the Eucharist and in the Church. While Farrow does not argue Zizioulas on this point (i.e., eucharistic-ecclesiology), his concern is that Zizioulas is in danger of making the Church a *tertium quid* between God and humans as it is a mode of existence.

In contrast to Zizioulas, Farrow states that Christ is not the Church but an analogy of the Church.[75] However, according to Farrow, the problem with Zizioulas's Christology and ecclesiology is the dialectic Zizioulas creates in the development of necessity and freedom.[76] Farrow does not believe that "nature and necessity" should contradict "personhood and freedom."[77] In Zizioulas's theology, Christ rescues humans from the necessity of nature and frees humans to become authentic persons in the image of God.[78] Farrow sees this as a type of Eutychianism (i.e., one nature) supported by the univocal use of person.[79] In contrast, Farrow suggests that humans are not freed from nature or necessity but are freed within nature and given personhood from God.[80]

---

73. Farrow, "Person and Nature," 118.
74. Farrow, "Person and Nature," 118.
75. Farrow, "Person and Nature," 120.
76. Farrow, "Person and Nature," 112.
77. Farrow, "Person and Nature," 121.
78. Farrow, "Person and Nature," 111–12, 121.
79. Farrow, "Person and Nature," 121.
80. Farrow, "Person and Nature," 121–23.

Najeeb G. Awad

Awad offers two articles of critique on Zizioulas. In the first article, "Between Subordination and Koinonia: Toward a New Reading of the Cappadocian Theology," Awad argues that Zizioulas's monarchial view of the Father, interpreted through Cappadocian theology, is an unfair assessment of Cappadocian thought.[81] Awad demonstrates that Basil believed that the Godhead was designated to the Father alone, while Gregory of Nazianzus attributed the three *hypostases* together as the Godhead.[82] Zizioulas, of course, follows the Basilian thinking that the person of the Father causes the substance of God to exist.[83] Furthermore, Awad argues that since Zizioulas has mistaken the nuances of Gregory of Nazianzus's trinitarian theology, Zizioulas misinterprets Nazianzus.[84]

In Awad's second article, "Personhood as Particularity: John Zizioulas, Colin Gunton, and the Trinitarian Theology of Personhood," he critiques Zizioulas's concept of persons-as-communion as reductionistic and finds that Gunton's unity-in-particularity concept to be a better explanation because of its emphasis upon particularity.[85] Furthermore, Awad finds that Zizioulas's persons-in-communion is restrictive because God's essence is communion rather than the persons participating in communion, whereas Gunton's unity-in-particularity expresses lively movements of free persons in unity.[86]

Stephen R. Holmes

Holmes summarizes Zizioulas's theology in his book, *The Quest for the Trinity: The Doctrine of God in Scripture, History and Modernity*, with two significant critiques relevant to the modern trinitarian debate.[87] First, Holmes takes issue with Zizioulas's "stress on the personal, volitional nature of God's existence."[88] The result of this focus by Zizioulas, according

---

81. Awad, "Between," 182.

82. Awad, "Between," 182, 183–87, 191–93.

83. Awad, "Between," 187.

84. Awad, "Between," 196–98.

85. Awad, "Personhood," 1–2, 13, 16–17, 19, 20–22.

86. Awad, "Personhood," 7, 8, 19.

87. Holmes, *Quest*, 12–16.

88. Holmes, *Quest*, 13.

to Holmes, is that it implies that each *hypostasis* possesses their own will.[89] The problem with this interpretation is that it tends toward tritheism. In contrast, Holmes argues that Zizioulas's problem is his emphasis on the freedom of God, which means that the One who is free causes (*aitia*) everything else and is ontologically personal.[90] Holmes then takes issue with Zizioulas's reading of the Cappadocian Fathers and points out that Zizioulas's thesis argues that the Cappadocians' ontologically tied *hypostasis* to *prosōpon* and separated it from *ousia*, then each personal *hypostasis* becomes a source or a cause having their own will (volition).[91]

Second, and rather briefly, Holmes takes issue with Zizioulas's labeling both God and humans as "persons."[92] Furthermore, in Zizoulas's theology, a human can only be a true person (as God) eschatologically and similarly to God.[93] This view by Zizioulas correlates in many ways with the Orthodox Church's idea of deification (*theosis*).[94] Holmes's corrective is to begin theology from the *ousia* of God and differentiate it from the nature of humans.[95]

Terry L. Cross

Cross's writing is a polemic in constructive pneumatic ecclesiology.[96] Therefore, Cross's work is not explicitly a critique of Zizioulas. Opposite of Zizioulas's approach, Cross begins from the subjective (i.e., the needs of "the people of God" or the church of God) rather than the objective (i.e., the being of God, Trinity, Holy Spirit, etc.) in his ecclesiastical development.[97] Cross's primary concern is with "God's *direct presence* for individual believers" and the believing community rather than concern

---

89. Holmes, *Quest*, 14.

90. Holmes, *Quest*, 13.

91. Holmes, *Quest*, 14.

92. Holmes, *Quest*, 15.

93. Holmes, *Quest*, 15. Cf. Zizioulas, *Being*, 172–88; Zizioulas, *Lectures*, 153–61.

94. Zizioulas recognizes that his theological perspective is novel and not always consistent with Orthodoxy. On this point of eschatology, Zizioulas says, "Orthodox theology has not fully drawn its conclusions from this." Zizioulas, *Being*, 191; Zizioulas, *One and Many*, 31, 32, 34–35, 36–39.

95. Holmes, *Quest*, 13, 14, 15–16.

96. Cross, *Presence*, 7–9.

97. Cross, *Presence*, 6, 8.

on the media (signs and symbols) of religious experience.[98] This point contradicts Zizioulas's development of eucharistic-ecclesiology (signs and symbols), where humans find their personhood as persons-in-relation.

Furthermore, Zizioulas argues that the Church's unity can only come from a Christological view rather than a pneumatological view. Zizioulas specifically guards against a "pneumatocentric ecclesiology" for concern that it will result in a 'charismatic sociology' where ecclesiology would begin by viewing the community as the "body of Christians" united in the Holy Spirit.[99] Zizioulas argues that a Christocentric approach to ecclesiology views the church in an ontological manner as "the body of Christ."[100] Cross's ecclesiology is thoroughly pneumatocentric as the Holy Spirit encounters people and transforms them into a new community.[101]

We now turn our attention to five Pentecostal theologians for their specific work in constructive pneumatologically oriented trinitarianism. This theological approach is the opposite of the one we are arguing through trinitarian pneumatological personhood. Nevertheless, this relatively new theological expression in Pentecostalism offers significant thought and scholarship in pneumatology. These theologians are listed in chronological order by their significant publication or contribution on the topic of "pneumatological trinitarianism."[102]

Amos Yong

Yong's work in *Spirit-Word-Community: Theological Hermeneutics in Trinitarian Perspective* is powerfully provocative as his pneumatological trinitarianism is applied to areas of metaphysics, epistemology, and spiritual interpretation (including hermeneutics). Whereas pneumatological trinitarianism approaches theology from a subject-object ordering (i.e., experience-oriented, pragmatic approach, functional, etc.), Yong's

98. Cross, *Presence*, 10, 16.

99. Zizioulas, *Eucharist*, 16.

100. Zizioulas, *Eucharist*, 16.

101. Cross, *Presence*, 7.

102. The term "pneumatological trinitarianism" is used explicitly by Atkinson as a point of purpose and trajectory for constructive pneumatologically oriented trinitarianism (Atkinson, *Trinity*, 33). Also, the term appears as a theological category in Yong, *Spirit-Word-Community*, 18. The term "pneumatological trinitarianism" will be used to describe Pentecostal constructive pneumatologically oriented trinitarianism. However, the nuances, if any, will be briefly described by the individual theologians.

theological methodology into epistemology (i.e., how a person can know God) is developed in his concept of "pneumatological imagination."[103] Pneumatological imagination is the linchpin of Yong's theory by synthesizing passive and active encounters of the Holy Spirit with people both cognitively and emotionally as ordinary human-divine reality.[104] For Yong, the passive and active encounter with the Holy Spirit is relational, rational, and powerful (dynamic).[105] This relational, rational, and dynamic reality implies a trinitarian reading in Yong since God is indivisible.[106] Yong further tempers the imagination's effects on the affective and spiritual dimensions with the Word, or what he calls the "root metaphor."[107] Yong qualifies the notion of "normativism" of the pneumatological imagination as being moral and value-based.[108] Pneumatological imagination discerns the powers at work in the world, described as "the inter-dimensional play of powers and forces" in the non-material.[109] In Yong's pneumatological trinitarianism, we are left with a human relationship with God through the Holy Spirit, who is the (Augustinian-like) dynamic love enabling humans to live in community (inter-relationality) charismatically enabling that community to interpret the Word and spiritual experience.[110]

103. Yong, *Spirit-Word-Community*, 119–217. On the topic of subject-object approach in Pentecostal theology and current Pentecostal diversity, Studebaker says, "the current trend among scholars is to move away from defining Pentecostalism in terms of doctrine and theology and toward seeing experience or the encounter of the Holy Spirit as the characteristic mark of Pentecostalism. Pentecostal theology that takes the experience and biblical category of Spirit baptism as a fundamental starting point is legitimate because large segments of the historical and contemporary Pentecostal movement identify it as vital to their experience of God and theology, even though not all Pentecostals and charismatics worldwide understand it the same way" (Studebaker, *Pentecost*, 48).

104. Yong, *Spirit-Word-Community*, 123.

105. Yong, *Spirit-Word-Community*, 83, 84–85, 97, 100–101, 109–10, 115–18.

106. Yong, *Spirit-Word-Community*, 49–50, 57, 58, 59, 61, 63, 68, 69–70.

107. Yong, *Spirit-Word-Community*, 134, 136–39.

108. Yong, *Spirit-Word-Community*, 134, 139–41.

109. Yong, *Spirit-Word-Community*, 134, 140–41.

110. Yong, *Spirit-Word-Community*, 61–68, 222–23, 227, 230, 237, 242–43, 245, 275–76, 286–87, 297–98.

Frank D. Macchia

Macchia's work in *Baptized in the Spirit: A Global Pentecostal Theology* is formulated as a specific Pentecostal theology systematically dealing with the theology of spirit baptism[111] to unify the different factions within Pentecostalism.[112] Macchia's theology is exclusively and consistently filtered through Spirit baptism so that his trinitarian theology could be labeled pneumatological-baptismal-trinitarianism. Spirit baptism is the connection of the Holy Spirit with humans. However, Macchia's Spirit baptism has a trinitarian act or structure built into it.[113] The trinitarian act is reciprocal in that the Holy Spirit, who is the Augustinian-like bond of love, is sent from the Father through the Son and then returns through the Son back to the Father.[114] Macchia sees the importance of this act as further development of Spirit baptism in that the recipient lives in the presence of God and participates in the life of God.[115] Finally, the reality of the trinitarian act in Spirit baptism ushers in the kingdom of God as the eschatological freedom (soteriological and missiological).[116]

Steven M. Studebaker

Studebaker's bold pneumatological trinitarianism certainly begins with the Holy Spirit but further seeks to answer how the Holy Spirit fulfills the Trinity by contributing "to the identity of the Father and the Son."[117] Beginning with the Spirit of Pentecost, Studebaker identifies three characteristics of the Spirit in Scripture. The first is a liminal characteristic where the Spirit is present in a creative-redemptive act that completes a trinitarian theology in one aspect.[118] The second is a constitutional characteristic where the Spirit has a substantial role in the creative-redemptive

---

111. Macchia addresses the changing Pentecostal theology and considers whether or not "spirit baptism" is the central focus of Pentecostal theology. Macchia, *Baptized*, 28–29, 33–38.

112. Macchia, *Baptized*, 16–18.

113. Macchia, *Baptized*, 115–17.

114. Macchia, *Baptized*, 116–17, 119.

115. Macchia, *Baptized*, 117, 118, 125, 126.

116. Macchia, *Baptized*, 128–29.

117. Studebaker, *Pentecost*, 3, 5, 6–7, 9.

118. Studebaker, *Pentecost*, 53, 68–72.

act, which also, in another aspect, completes a trinitarian theology.[119] The third is an eschatological characteristic where the Spirit enables the creative-redemptive act to be fulfilled, contributing to the completion of trinitarian theology fellowship.[120] Studebaker states that the Holy Spirit's role in these three ways in Scripture supports pneumatological trinitarianism.[121] Furthermore, Studebaker applies these three characteristics (liminal, constitutional, and eschatological) to theology, demonstrating that the Spirit completes the fellowship of the Trinity by being central and essential to God's creative-redemptive work.[122]

William P. Atkinson

Atkinson explicitly constructs a pneumatological trinitarianism that views the Spirit of Pentecost as functionally/instrumentally, impersonally, and personally informing trinitarian theology in his appropriately titled work, *Trinity after Pentecost*.[123] To accomplish this construct, Atkinson systematically introduces the scriptural distinction of the persons of the Trinity, beginning with the Spirit, then the Son, and ending with the Father, showing what is shared and what is different.[124] However, the unity of the trinitarian persons is described by Atkinson through the Spirit's impersonal role in the *perichoresis*.[125] What appears to be impersonal acts of the Holy Spirit in Atkinson's *perichoretic* model result in personal, dynamic (impersonal), relational connections between humans to God and human to human.[126] This apparent result marries well with his paradox of *kenōsis* and exaltation. Atkinson shows that the loving model of the Trinity in *perichoresis* includes a series of *kenotic* and exaltative actions among the three persons of the Trinity.[127] However, Atkinson does not

---

119. Studebaker, *Pentecost*, 53, 72–75.

120. Studebaker, *Pentecost*, 53, 75–78.

121. Studebaker, *Pentecost*, 78.

122. Studebaker, *Pentecost*, 94–100.

123. Atkinson, *Trinity*, vii, 1–2, 33, 34, 35, 39.

124. Atkinson, *Trinity*, 33, 39–41, 77–79, 113–15.

125. Atkinson, *Trinity*, 35–36, 50–56, 76, 141–42, 150, 152–57.

126. Atkinson says, "Let me suggest that if the Spirit can relate personally within the Trinity, however rarely this concept may be presented, then it will be more likely than not that the Spirit will at least in rare ways relate personally to, for instance, Christians" (Atkinson, *Trinity*, 60). See also Atkinson, *Trinity*, 60–62, 162–66.

127. Atkinson, *Trinity*, 34–35, 60–71, 102–11, 130–42, 146–48.

fall into the equality trap of *perichoresis* but instead offers an explanation for dynamic trinitarian relations where there is equality-with-headship found in the Father's eternal exaltation and shared glory, the Son's eternal life, name, authority and submission, and the Holy Spirit's work of upholding the eternal existence of the Son, establishing the Father-Son relationship, and humbly being the communication of love.[128] What arises from this work is an approach of the Trinity that Pentecost initiates.

Andréa D. Snavely

Snavely offers a theology that seeks to describe Christianity as "life in the Spirit."[129] Snavely's approach to life in the Spirit is a Spirit-Christology that shows Jesus lived an obedient life to the Father made possible by the constitutive Spirit who can also transform Jesus's followers to live obedient lives in the Spirit.[130] Snavely builds his Spirit-Christology on the contribution of John Howard Yoder's post-Constantinian critique of Christian theology, claiming the Christian life has not been challenged to pattern the life of Jesus.[131] The Christian life lived correctly as the cruciform life is a non-materialistic, simplistic, peaceful, spiritual life that mimics the life of Jesus (in his trinitarian life) and can only be accomplished by the Holy Spirit.[132] Snavely argues that this Christian life begins by bearing the Spirit ("constitutive ingredient") and draws one ("other sons") into the trinitarian life of obedience and mission.[133] Snavely says, "After Christ pours out his Spirit on the day of Pentecost, Jesus's followers begin living out Jesus's life of cross and resurrection as their own, doing what they were previously unable and even *unwilling* to do before they received the Spirit."[134]

128. Atkinson, *Trinity*, 60–76, 102–11, 130–42, 150–51.

129. Snavely, *Life*, 1.

130. Snavely, *Life*, 4.

131. Snavely, *Life*, 5–6.

132. Snavely, *Life*, 28, 154–89.

133. Snavely, *Life*, 8, 28–29, 59–61, 62–65, 68–70, 93–99.

134. Snavely, *Life*, 99.

SUMMARY

The thesis of this book seeks to build on Zizioulas's initial thought of persons-in-relation beginning with God as Trinity and moving toward human personhood and a description of an authentic person as Zizioulas attempted to do, or more specifically, a Christian person. This method (object-subject) is the opposite of the Pentecostal theologians constructing a pneumatological trinitarianism (subject-object). Methodologically, we seek to determine that pneumatologically constituted personhood of communion is established within the Trinity and serves as God's design for his image-bearers.[135] However, we will show that Zizioulas's method is flawed in three ways: (1) Zizioulas's monarchy of the Father leads to a hierarchical model of the Trinity; (2) Zizioulas's eucharistic-ecclesiology serves only as a functional divine-human connection which undercuts his persons-in-relation ontological concept; (3) Zizioulas has a limited pneumatology which only secondarily applies to humans by constituting Christ and the sacraments.

The response to Zizioulas's monarchy of the Father as the source of the Trinity has stirred trinitarian theological debate. On the one hand, scholars like Gunton, Wilks, A. J. Torrance, Harrison, Volf, and Awad believe that Zizioulas's emphasis (necessity) on the communion (relation) between the three *hypostases* leads to a monistic unity and the loss of distinctiveness.[136] On the other hand, some, like de Halleux and Holmes, see Zizioulas's monarchy of the Father and stress upon *hypostasis* to lead to a tritheistic view of three volitions.[137] De Halleux, Wilks, Turcescu, Awad, and Holmes believe that Zizioulas's "Cappadocian revolution" (that separates *hypostasis* from *ousia* and then connects *hypostasis* with *prosōpon* with the intent of defining person) is a twentieth-century interpretational error of the Cappadocian Fathers.[138] While Wilks, A. J. Torrance, and Holmes view the unity of the Trinity as the *ousia*; most of these scholars see a need for a balanced approach to the Trinity but grapple with the paradox of the distinctiveness of the *hypostases* and

135. McConville, *Being Human*, 26–27; Gunton, *One, Three, Many*, 181–84.

136. Gunton, *Trinitarian Theology*, xviii–xxiv, 9, 196–97, 200; Gunton, "Persons," 97; Wilks, "Ontology," 77–79; Torrance, *Persons*, 293–94; Harrison, "Zizioulas," 273–74, 279; Volf, *Likeness*, 3, 4, 114–15, 214, 215, 217–18; Awad, "Between," 182, 183, 187–89.

137. De Halleux, "Personnalisme," 1:134–35; Holmes, *Quest*, 13–14.

138. De Halleux, "Personnalisme," 2:289–92; Wilks, "Ontology," 74, 77; Turcescu, "Misreadings," 534, 536; Awad, "Between," 182; Holmes, *Quest*, 14.

the unity of persons.[139] To explain this paradox, we will rely on Gunton's concept of unity-in-particularity[140] as a clarification of *perichoresis* that leaves room for persons-in-relation while acknowledging the unequal roles of the *hypostases*.[141] Therefore, there is within the Trinity an equality-with-headship.

A focus on pneumatology can fulfill the deficiencies in Zizioulas's methodology of persons-in-relation. My emphasis on the Holy Spirit as the primary cause of fulfilling Christian personhood as persons-in-relation is not contingent upon Pentecostal theology but mirrors it in some ways (e.g., soteriology, indwelling, Christian life). The pneumatological concepts referred to in this thesis are (implicitly and explicitly) theologically Wesleyan. However, the intention is to expand on these Wesleyan pneumatological concepts as we seek an anthropological definition from the perspective of persons-in-relation that begins with the Trinity. Therefore this thesis deals with trinitarian pneumatological personhood.

Pentecostal constructive pneumatological trinitarianism addresses the need to emphasize the Spirit in trinitarian theology. The Spirit connects humans to God by the Spirit and through Jesus Christ.[142] However, the Pentecostal (pragmatic) approach to trinitarian theology is primarily from experience and gives the Spirit precedence central to trinitarian theology.[143] Thus, the theological pendulum has swung from Zizioulas's monarchial view of the Father as the source of the Trinity to Yong's pneumacentric trinitarian vision of God.[144] Whereas Atkinson follows the Pentecostal approach to the Trinity as pneumatologically oriented trinitarianism, he comes closest to an understanding of the Trinity that strikes a balance between the extremes by using a paradox of *kenōsis* and exaltation of the persons within the *perichoretic* method that recognizes

139. Wilks, "Ontology," 82; Torrance, *Persons*, 293–94; Holmes, *Quest*, 13, 14, 15–16.

140. The term "unity-in-particularity" is assigned by Awad to Gunton's concept of "person with relational particularity." Awad, "Personhood," 16–17.

141. Gunton, *Trinitarian Theology*, 39, 128–36, 196–98.

142. Yong, *Spirit-Word-Community*, 41–42.

143. Yong, *Spirit-Word-Community*, 7, 8, 92–94, Yong argues for "experience" to function as theological object, Yong, *Spirit-Word-Community*, 246–48; Macchia, *Baptized*, 11–18; Studebaker, *Pentecost*, 15, 17–18, 23; Atkinson, *Trinity*, 12–16; Snavely, *Life*, 28; cf. Keener, *Spirit Hermeneutics*, 25–38.

144. Zizioulas, *Being*, 40–42, 44; Zizioulas, *Communion*, 137–45; Yong, *Spirit-Word-Community*, 2, 49.

the "inequalities among the persons of the Trinity."[145] Thus, he indicates that there is within the Trinity an equality-with-headship. Nevertheless, it is not our purview to engage in Pentecostal debates unless there is a pertinent point of demarcation or point of relevant support.

Chapter 2, "Trinitarian Personhood: West and East," delves into the historical, theological, and philosophical development of personhood and the Trinity as critical components to Zizioulas theology. Zizioulas's approach to *who* humans are is reflected in *who* God is. Chapter 2 begins with the development of person and the significance in grounding person in the Trinity.

---

145. Atkinson, *Trinity*, 62, 74, 107, 131, 148, 150–51.

Chapter 2

Trinitarian Personhood: West and East

> "Personhood is where the orthodox definition
> of God as Trinity is settled."
>
> —MALCOLM B. YARNELL III[1]

INTRODUCTION

THE PURPOSE OF THIS chapter is to trace and explain how Zizioulas demonstrates the concepts of *person* and *Trinity* as denoting *being in communion*[2] were first developed as unique terms by the early church fathers. For Zizioulas, the doctrine of the Trinity describes the divine persons in relationship, who are ultimately relational, and the model for human personhood. Farrow argues that this persons-in-relation approach compromises the distinction between the divine and the creature.[3] The concept of God's personhood inevitably involves an ontological statement about the reality of God's being because it includes the metaphysical identity of *who* a person is, or in this case, *who* is God?[4] In this persons-in-relation approach, person is the cause for (divine or human) being to exist.[5] Since person (*whoness*) is the starting point of being rather than

1. Yarnell, *Holy Spirit*, 78.

2. Zizioulas, *Being*, 16–19, 54–55, 57–62, 126–36, 149–58; Zizioulas, *Communion*, 9–11.

3. Farrow, "Person and Nature," 119.

4. Zizioulas, *Communion*, 99–103.

5. Zizioulas, *Being*, 39, 41; Zizioulas, *Communion*, 137–40.

nature (*whatness*), person, or personhood, has "the claim of absolute being."[6] Furthermore, when applied to trinitarian theology, personhood is the "claim of absolute metaphysical identity independent of qualities borrowed from other 'beings.'"[7] Zizioulas's use of the term "person" along with its cognate "personhood" is not the popular Boethian definition of an "individual substance of a rational nature."[8] Instead, Zizioulas envisions an emphasis on pre-Boethian personhood as found in the fourth century Cappadocian Fathers and based on the relationality of beings.[9] Two aspects of this model of personhood are presented in that being is *ekstatically*[10] and *hypostatically* constituted.

On the one hand, the *ekstatic* aspect of personhood suggests that one transcends the boundaries of the self and relates to another resulting in the activity of communion and the state of community.[11] On the other hand, the *hypostatic* aspect of personhood suggests that each person is "unique" and "unrepeatable."[12] Zizioulas uses the terms "persons" and "personhood" synonymously as illustrated here: "The combination of the notion of *ekstasis* with that of *hypostasis* in the idea of the person reveals that personhood is directly related to ontology—it is not a quality added as it were, to beings, something that beings 'have' or 'have not', but is constitutive of what can be ultimately called a 'being.'"[13] Therefore, comprehending Zizioulas's theory of personhood is to understand persons voluntarily in a relationship with another. Indeed, to define personhood other than in relational terms would lead to a more substantially (i.e., materially) oriented definition as found in the sciences categorizing

6. Zizioulas, *Communion*, 100.

7. Zizioulas, *Communion*, 99–100.

8. Boethius, "Eutyches and Nestorius," in *Theological Tractates*, 85.

9. For other interpreters along these lines, see Boff, *Trinity and Society*; Gunton, *Trinitarian Theology*; LaCugna, *God*; Turcescu, *Gregory of Nyssa*; also, while not founded in Cappadocian definitions, rather modern readings concluding in relational concept of the person, see Grenz, *Social God*.

10. Zizioulas typically uses a transliteration of the Greek word "*ekstasis*" when he spells it. This spelling will be used throughout.

11. Zizioulas, *Communion*, 213. See *ekstasis* as the Christ-event in Farrow, *Ascension*, 137.

12. Zizioulas, *Communion*, 101, 213. For a more comprehensive concept of *hypostasis*, see Zizioulas, *Being*, 49–65.

13. Zizioulas, *Communion*, 213. Also, for exocentricity in anthropology, see Pannenberg, *Anthropology*, 37, 63–65, 76, 80–83, 95, 97, 105–7, 159–60, 185, 187, 237, 265–67, 338, 397, 408, 412–13, 415, 480, 486, 490–91, 518–19, 524–25, 529–31.

personhood as an impersonal *thing*.[14] Zizioulas engages the modern secular world as well as the church to reveal the tragedy of Western theological and philosophical individualism.[15] Zizioulas's body of work is a historical and theological study in divine personhood and applied to contemporary human personhood.

According to Zizioulas, "Person" and "Trinity" are uniquely developed terms by the early church fathers, denoting *being in communion*. Zizioulas uses the word choice "person" to designate the idea of relational beings that emerged from the church's need to explain what is meant by saying that God is Father, Son, and Holy Spirit as classically expressed in the Nicene-Constantinopolitan Creed in the fourth century. Furthermore, Zizioulas argues that person as described by the early church fathers for the Triune God also is to be applied to human beings created in the image of God. This particular nuance of human beings as persons-in-relation is not found in Greek or Roman philosophy because neither understood the transcendent capacity of humans to enter into a relationship with a transcendent, Triune God who is Father, Son, and Holy Spirit. While Greek and Roman philosophy assumed that human life was controlled by fate and unable to lift itself out of the vicissitudes of nature, on the other hand, the early church fathers believed the biblical revelation showed that human life was meaningfully related to the Triune God and hence possessed a spiritual freedom beyond this natural world.

GREEK AND ROMAN[16]

Zizioulas connects the contemporary humanistic ideas regarding *being a person* of our day back to perceived flaws in ancient philosophy.[17] These

14. In the area of psychology and more specifically, in psychiatrics, the concept of "person" is classified through the "probabilistic approach" based on "central tendencies." See Kihlstrom and Hastie, "Mental Representations," 720–22. In transpersonal psychology, all elements (matter, body, mind, soul, and spirit) serve as an unbroken "chain of being" in the make-up of the whole person; see Murphy, *Return to Spirit*. While the history of science might often lead to an impersonal definition of personhood, Neteruk, *Light from the East*, shows that it does not have to be the case.

15. Knight, "Introduction," 6–7; Papanikolaou, "Existentialist?," 601–7.

16. The outline of this chapter is *not* chronological, but rather philosophical and theological.

17. Zizioulas, *Being*, 27. Zizioulas is not heavily critiqued on his use, or critique, of ancient philosophy. This is due in part because of his basic observation that classical Greek ontology identified beings by their nature (*physis, ousia*). Later Greek patristic

philosophies sought to express essential truths about God, humans, and the world.[18] The result was a closed cosmology of necessary beings bound to static substance and the fate of their gods.[19] While these philosophies continued to evolve into more complex systems, there was no answer for either human tragedy (i.e., fear, pity, and death) or the emotional side of humanity.[20] The puzzle of what a person is (i.e., body, soul, mind, nature, etc.) had to be solved, and an adequate and enlightening concept had to be formulated.

Zizioulas addresses the current identification of person as associated with (extreme) individuality.[21] This trend to identify the human being in individualistic terms results from humanism going awry and the suppression of theology.[22] In identifying the source(s) of the problem, Zizioulas revisits ancient philosophy regarding *being* a person. Philosophy could not conceive personhood, in its earliest conception, as an absolute[23] reality, like fire, water, air, and earth.[24] Personhood was viewed as

---

theologians (i.e., Cappadocians) identified beings as persons or personal (*prosōpon*). See Brown, "Criticism."

18. For examples of the ancient philosophical creation myths of Egypt, Babylon, pre-Milesian Greek, Hesiod, the Milesians: Thales, Anaximander, Anaximenes, and Parmenides, see Gregory, *Ancient Greek Cosmogony*.

19. Zizioulas, *Being*, 17–18, 27–28, 33, 35, 39–40, 48, 69–70; Zizioulas, *Communion*, 102–5; Zizioulas, *Lectures*, 58–61; Zizioulas, *One and Many*, 147; Ferguson, *Backgrounds*, 222–27; Oswalt, *Myths*, 78–81.

20. Fitzgerald, "Passions," 1–25. See Munteanu, *Tragic Pathos*.

21. For individualism based in utilitarian egoism, see Spencer, *Synthetic Philosophy*. For a human individualism that stresses rationalism and empiricism, see Kant, *Pure Reason*. For a personalist approach to existentialism, see Sartre, *Existentialism & Humanism*. For modern individualism applied to politics and economics that is focused on groups and associations, see Angell, *Great Illusion*. For a social psychological approach to the individual as creative thinker, see Wallas, *Art of Thought*. For an individualistic interpretation of the Scriptures for the purpose of introspection ("the hidden inwardness"), see Kierkegaard, *Training*.

22. Zizioulas, *Being*, 27.

23. The term "absolute" along with its cognates (i.e., absoluteness) will be used in the way Zizioulas uses the word which is associated with the metaphysical concept of completeness, totality, the thing-in-itself. Zizioulas associates absolute with "personal identity" (Zizioulas, *Being*, 35). Zizioulas says, "Personhood, in other words, has the claim of absolute being, that is, a metaphysical claim, built into it" (Zizioulas, *Communion*, 100). However, this is not a claim for self-existence (i.e., static entity), for there to be a living being means communion with another (Zizioulas, *Being*, 16). For further reference of Zizioulas's use of "absolute," see Zizioulas, *Being*, 35–40.

24. Plato, *Timaeus*, 31A–32C.

a compound of material, substances, or ingredients. Furthermore, person and being were not mutually inclusive; rather, person was an addendum to being. For Zizioulas, this materialistic, substance-based view of personhood is founded in ancient philosophy. Eventually, this philosophical approach separated from the Scripture and theology results in (extreme) individualism.[25]

Zizioulas argues that the starting point from which Greek philosophy began was flawed. Most Greek philosophy metaphysically began from the concept of "One" and moved toward particulars. Thus, "Ancient Greek thought in *all* its forms (Parmenidean, Heraclitean, Platonic and Aristotelian), despite its variations on other aspects, agreed on one thing: particularity is not ontologically absolute, a being in itself; the many are always ontologically derivative, not causative."[26] For Zizioulas, the purpose is to reveal that ontological truth is *not* found in the concrete universal One from which abstract particulars find their meaning. Instead, truth in ontology is discovered in the concrete particulars connected to/with the abstract universal.[27] In other words, from a philosophical perspective, there must be some pre-existent substance (i.e., "stuff," "material," "elements") from which all things were made (i.e., God, humans, the world). It was this general substance (i.e., "stuff," "material," "elements") that constituted the specific person (i.e., each human being).[28] Zizioulas's critique is made to challenge the modern understanding of "personal identity" rooted in ancient philosophy describes personhood as a quality added to humans rather than a human "being" a person.[29] In offering this ontological interpretation of communion,[30] which is simultaneously a plurality and interdependence of the person,[31] Zizioulas strengthens his thesis by returning to where he believes the problem began. However, in doing so, Zizioulas, on the one hand, glosses over more Aristotelian nuances where universals inhere particulars, for instance, as found in

25. Zizioulas, *Being*, 27–29, 64–65.

26. Zizioulas, *Communion*, 102.

27. Zizioulas, *Communion*, 104–5.

28. Zizioulas, *Communion*, 104–5.

29. Zizioulas, *Being*, 27; Zizioulas, *Communion*, 99.

30. This thought is founded in the Cappadocian formula for the Trinity and will be expounded on further down. Zizioulas labels the shift from the Cappadocians as a "historical revolution." See Zizioulas, *Being*, 39–40; Zizioulas, *Communion*, 157–58; Zizioulas, *Lectures*, 50–51.

31. Zizioulas, *Lectures*, 53.

arithmetic and geometry.[32] On the other, Zizioulas does not explore the specifics of ancient philosophy, like failing to mention Aristotle's god, while not a creator *ex nihilo*, is a god that is activity (substantially) within active humans, real rather than abstract, and perfect.[33] Since Zizioulas builds his thought on the works of Plato and Aristotle, it is important, at this point, to explore them further.

Plato was steeped in Eleatic teaching, as seen in *Parmenides* (*hen einai to pan*).[34] The monism of *Parmenides* is absolute so that the One cannot be particular or many.[35] This lack of particularity is due to the fact that the One is the only true, eternal, and absolute *being*. In contrast, the particulars, like humans, for instance, are *becoming*[36] because humans and creation are formed from preexistent elements (i.e., fire, water, air, earth).[37] These elements are what Plato ascribes to as forms. However, for Plato, these four primitive elements have a primary substance (*hulē*),[38] namely, space and energy.[39] Thus, for Plato, the Demiurge takes primitive, intelligible elements (Forms) and the unintelligible space and time to create the world.[40] The problem for Platonic philosophy is the definition of person. The person is not, nor can be, identified with the human being because the human being is a compound of material that will cease to exist and immortal soul, all of which is bound up in a cosmos of necessity. Such is the essence of the Greek tragedy.[41]

If the human body is material and can cease to exist, we deduce that it lacks fundamental ontology. What remains is a preexistent soul.[42] For Plato, the soul is the source of life, and being that source is thus a

---

32. Aristotle, *Metaphysics*, 1.2.

33. Mure, *Aristotle*, 163–65, 171–76.

34. Plato, *Parmenides*, 128B.

35. Plato, *Parmenides*, 137C.

36. Plato, *Timaeus*, 27D–28C. Moravcsik reveals a concept of *technē* in Plato which illustrates human *becoming* by attaining "fire" or knowledge from the One (Moravcsik, *Plato and Platonism*, 14–17).

37. Plato, *Timaeus*, 31A–32C.

38. Plato, *Dialogues*, 514.

39. Friedländer, *Plato*, 370.

40. Friedländer, *Plato*, 363–65; Clegg, *Structure*, 35–40.

41. Zizioulas, *Being*, 31–32.

42. Plato, *Laws*, 2.10, 892A–C. In contrast, Clark says, "Plato despised the bodily" and "distrusted sensory experience." Aristotle presents a higher view of the body as a living thing which has experiences as experienced by a pounding heart. Clark, *Aristotle's Man*, 197–98.

self-mover, eternal, immortal, and intelligent.[43] However, Plato presents in *Timaeus* the concept of two souls: one is mortal (*tēs psychēs thnēton*) and dwells within the abdomen,[44] and the other is immortal (*psychēs, . . . hoson theion*) and is encased within the skull.[45] This immortal soul also fails to offer an ontology of personhood as it "is not united permanently with the concrete, 'individual' man: it lives eternally, but it can be united with another concrete body and can constitute another 'individuality,' e.g., by reincarnation."[46] In this case, the One rules the particular by order of nature and necessity, and personhood is not a reality but something added. It is Aristotle who attempts to pull together this *something* with the individual.

Where Plato's dialogical approach and metaphorical language concluded truth in the Idea, Aristotle presented logical analysis in syllogism to determine truth or the "is" of a *thing* (i.e., the distinction between *Thatness* and *Whatness*). While Zizioulas views Aristotelian philosophy as unable to offer an ontology of person because of Aristotle's emphasis on the *psychē*, he sees the usefulness in Aristotle's approach that moves the discussion closer to a correct concept of personhood. Plato could only offer real being as connected to the universal One that exists independent of objects or matter (i.e., Truth, Goodness, and Beauty), later, Aristotle approached reality through empirical evidence, the physical traits found in the particular or matter, in order to arrive intellectually at the universal or intelligible form. Beginning with the particular, Aristotle had to name or categorize the particular.[47] The prerequisite in identifying a particular would be to separate it from everything else. This "separation" (*chōriston*) of "individual things" (*tode ti*) forces us to name the *thing* and thus give it an ontology of existence.[48] "In order to exclude someone or something,"

43. Zakopoulos, *Plato*, 47.

44. Plato, *Timaeus*, 69E.

45. Plato, *Timaeus*, 72D.

46. Zizioulas, *Being*, 28.

47. Aristotle, *Metaphysics*, 8.1, 1041A.

48. Aristotle, *Metaphysics*, 7.4, 1030B; 8.1, 1042A. It is not simply the "name" (*onoma*) for Aristotle that separates things from other things, rather it is their essence (*ousia*) that corresponds to the name. In *Categories*, he goes further into describing different ("corresponding") essences under the same name which he calls "*homonymous*" (ὁμωνύμα) and those things which have the same essence and name, yet two things are "*synonymous*" (συνώνυμον). Aristotle, *Selections*, 1–3, 588–89, 617. I have translated *tode ti* as "individual things" from a more literal translation of "this thing" or "a certain person" all of which isolates and defines a particular thing/one from the

says Zizioulas, "you need an 'ontology' of separation, that is, of isolating a particular being from the relations that constitute it and defining it as Aristotle's τόδε τι, an entity in itself."[49] The advantage of this Aristotelian way of describing "this individual thing" as having existence apart from "that thing" (apart from all others) is that it leads toward an ontology of person.

Contrary to Plato, Aristotle observed and categorized living things, which moved the study of being away from a generalized Idea toward a more particularized identification. Aristotle's metaphysical formula for "this individual thing" includes an essence (primary essence), which is substance.[50] While "essence will belong to nothing except species of a genus," according to Aristotle, species do not have primary substance rather secondary substance.[51] A nuance in Aristotelian philosophy is that while species are categorized as secondary substances, species are not equated with essence; rather, species *have* (primary) essence because primary essence defines "what it is."[52] Furthermore, Aristotle used the term species (*eidos*) in its compound *hylomorphic* context, meaning a species has both form and matter.[53] That is to say, objects are divided into classes of genus determined by what is in common; these are categorized further into species by their particularities, and a species is defined by both its form and matter. Of significance, at this point, is Aristotle's use of the word *hypokeimenon*,[54] which appears to mean both matter and the concrete being.

> Now in one sense we call the *matter* the substrate; in another, the *shape*; and in a third, the combination of the two. By matter I mean, for instance, bronze; by shape, the arrangement of the form; and by the combination of the two, the concrete thing: the statue. Thus if the form is prior to the matter and more

---

many. Zizioulas further defines *tode ti* as "an entity in itself" (Zizioulas, *Communion*, 73).

49. Zizioulas, *Communion*, 73.

50. Aristotle, *Metaphysics*, 7.4, 1030B.

51. Aristotle, *Metaphysics*, 7.4, 1030A.

52. See Cohen and Reeve, "Aristotle's Metaphysics," sec. 7n4.

53. Cohen and Reeve, "Aristotle's Metaphysics," sec. 7.

54. Aristotle, *Metaphysics*, 7.3, 1029A.9; 7.4, 1029B.23. Tredennick translates *hypokeimenon* as "substrate."

truly existent, by the same argument it will also be prior to the combination.[55]

Aristotle's philosophical process of distinguishing matter from shape in describing something more specifically is for Zizioulas a step in the right direction toward discovering real being (ontologically).

Zizioulas develops an ontology on the history of the terms substance and *hypostasis*, "Because of the double meaning which Aristotle seems to accord this term . . . in the period after Aristotle, the term 'hypostasis' displaces the term ὑποκείμενον because of the materialistic sense of the latter and itself assumes the meaning of concrete and independent being."[56] As will become apparent later, this development from *hypokeimenon* to *hypostasis* speaks of what defines "this thing" (or person), from "that thing" (or person).

While Aristotle may bring us closer to an ontology of person by dealing with matter and essence as a concrete reality,[57] the question remains: what happens when the person ceases to exist? It would appear that death brings an end to the individual, but Aristotle would suggest that reality lives on through the species by reproduction.[58] Truth for Aristotle is found in the "is," which could be described here as the reproduction of the species. When an individual dies, he or she "is not," therefore, truth would not be determined in the individual person, rather in the species (i.e., human). Death invalidates the syllogism of life and being.[59] In the Aristotelian paradigm, it is illogical for the goal of being to end in non-being. Thus, Aristotle appears to grapple with this issue when he says, "For when living creatures are destroyed, the knowledge or health that is in them is destroyed also. . . . It might reasonably be asked whether there is any place in which the destructible will be indestructible."[60] Therefore, for Aristotle, "life is *a quality added to being*, and not being itself."[61] The

55. Aristotle, *Metaphysics*, 7.3, 1029A.9.

56. Zizioulas, *Being*, 38n30. Zeno's Stoic School (later than Aristotle) used "*hypostasis*" as a term to describe "primal matter" or the subsistence for all things to come into existence (Köster, "ὑπόστασις," 575–76).

57. Aristotle, like Socrates before him, understood that self-consciousness or self-knowledge could not remain in the abstract and speculative realm but had to be experienced in the concrete world. See Gregor, *Anthropology*, 1–2.

58. Aristotle, *Soul*, 2.4, 415A.

59. Zizioulas, *Being*, 28; Clark, *Aristotle's Man*, 166.

60. Aristotle, *Life*, II.495A; III.465B.

61. Zizioulas, *Being*, 79.

idea, then, "that people 'have' personhood rather than being persons" is an ontological misunderstanding of the meaning of personhood.[62] That is to say, the particular unique person, which makes you, you, and me, me, is absolute. There will never be another specific you, nor will there ever be another specific me. Nesteruk explains,

> The personhood as hypostatic existence means that it cannot be communicated to another person (in contrast with the natural, for example, biological factors, which are shared by all human beings and can in principle be communicated from one human being to another, such as the transplantation of organs).[63]

In this way, personhood is absolute.[64] Zizioulas concludes, "Aristotle's concern with the particular did not lead to the survival of the concrete being for ever, except in the form of its species. The αὐτὸ passes away; what survives is the οἷον αὐτό."[65] Thus, in the same way that Plato's thoughts on being were found not in the particular, but in the One, so Aristotle could only go so far as to show that being was the participation of the particulars in unity/genus/species,[66] or in other words, the many find their being in the *Intelligible* one, that which is common, homonymous or "the account of essence."[67] Secular philosophy, thus, fails to answer the modern "personal identity" question (i.e., "What does it mean that someone *is* rather than *has* a person?").[68] As will be argued later, Christian theology fills this void by making personhood absolute, that is, the essence of being.

In addition to Aristotle's philosophical concepts of being, Zizioulas traces the etymology and evolution of words used to describe being. Two of these words are foundational in a theological perspective of ontology: *hypostasis* and *prosōpon*. Zizioulas refers to the marriage of these two

---

62. Zizioulas, *Communion*, 99.

63. Nesteruk, *Light*, 210.

64. Zizioulas, *Communion*, 101.

65. Zizioulas, *Communion*, 102. I translate and interpret Zizioulas as saying, "The *self* passes away; what survives is the/a *similar* [kind of] self."

66. Using Aristotelian philosophy, Thomas Aquinas combines matter and form to describe essence. This essence is the principle of species. The essence is the nature of the *hypostasis* of the person with all the components: both physical and spiritual. Thus, "hypostasis and person add the individual principles to the idea of essence." See Aquinas, *Summa Theologiae*, I.29.1–2.

67. Aristotle, *Selections*, 1.

68. Zizioulas, *Being*, 27–28; Zizioulas, *Communion*, 99–101.

words as *revolutionary* in the history of philosophy, for which he gives most of the credit to the Cappadocian Fathers.[69] We have already seen how Aristotle used the word *hypokeimenon* (substrate) to describe the quality of nature in substance.[70] Furthermore, matter is substance and is a concrete being, suggesting that the concrete person is also *hypokeimenon* or substance, and substance can only be defined as it is categorized with other similar substance. That is to say, the concrete person is defined by *its* species (i.e., human), which is the form (i.e., anatomy) and the matter (i.e., biology) of *its* substance. In Aristotle's philosophy, a person is a collection of basic elements into a substance called human being. However, this notion of substance has not been entirely abandoned by theologians. Instead, it has evolved as a term that cannot be neglected, especially in the discussion of the Trinity. Mackinnon has argued that rather than rejecting the concept of substance as a means to describe the relationship of the persons of the Trinity, theologians need to understand the concept more and be able to articulate it. He has suggested that the terms *homoousion* and *kenōsis* aid in this reconstruction.[71] Historically, theologians sought adequate language to describe the relationship between the persons of the Trinity and the two natures of Christ, who would borrow these terms (i.e., substance, *ousia*, *hypostasis*) from the philosophers. For instance, Stead points out that while Athanasius uses *hypostasis* and *ousia* synonymously to mean substance, he only means it in a general sense. Furthermore, Athanasius uses *hypostasis* in a way that *ousia* cannot be substituted.[72] However, the point of discussion is that no matter how detailed the semantics and etymology of the word substance in the use of *hypostasis* and *ousia*, they could never unite person with the being of a human prior to the Cappadocian formula. When *hypostasis* denotes *ousia*, it cannot be real, concrete being in the philosophical sense, because it is not self-evident in areas of phenomenon.[73] Special attention is to be

69. Zizioulas, *Communion*, 157–58; Zizioulas, *Being*, 35–39.

70. Aristotle, *Metaphysics*, 7.3, 1029A; 7.4, 1029B.

71. Mackinnon, "Substance," 279–300.

72. Stead, "Divine Substance," 31. This work is a philosophical and historical study of the semantics of "substance" as a definition of *ousia* and its concept(s) in theology. Stead contrasts its meaning in Aristotle's two works, *Categories* and *Metaphysics*, arguing that a proper understanding of the word is not a general connotation but yields several specific meanings (Stead, "Divine Substance," 41).

73. Köster, "ὑπόστασις," 575. See the use of *hypostasis* in the Gnostic writing in Bullard, *Hypostasis*, 42. There is no indication as to the meaning being either "nature" or "essence." Bullard points out that *hypostasis* in this text cannot be understood in the

taken as to the context for which *hypostasis* is used. Zizioulas suggests that the early Church borrowed Aristotle's concept of *hypokeimenon* (matter and concrete independent being) and metamorphosed it into *hypostasis* to describe the person.[74] However, before the Cappadocians and their doctrinal statements, *hypostasis* had various usages and meanings from "support (to stand under)," "conceal (to place oneself under)," 'to stand off from,' "'to deposit' (to be, to exist)," 'to promise' ('support,' 'ambush,' 'deposit,' 'sediment,' 'existence,' 'reality,' 'lease'), to more philosophical meanings like "primal matter" (i.e., "subsistence of unformed matter")[75] or verbally "to come into existence," thus 'essence' and 'reality.'[76]

The word *prosōpon* also underwent a semantic transformation from the time of Aristotle to the Cappadocians, with the most significant change taking place at the cultural level from its adoption from the Greek city-state to Roman citizenship. Aristotle's use of *prosōpon* is translated as "face." However, only human beings are described as having faces (*prosōpa*).[77] The *prosōpon* had no relational attributes; rather, it was an anatomical name given to the bregma section of the human head. Cultural changes are evident in the shift of the Hellenistic *prosōpon* to the Latin *persona*:

> In its anthropological connotation the Roman persona leaned perhaps more heavily than its Greek equivalent towards the idea of concrete individuality, but in its sociological and later on in its legal usage it never ceased to express the ancient Greek πρό-σωπον or προσωπεῖον in its theatrical nuance of *role*: *persona* is the role which one plays in one's social or legal relationships, the moral or 'legal' person which either collectively or individually has nothing to do with the *ontology* of the person.[78]

---

theological sense, rather as mythological figures or power (Bullard, *Hypostasis*, 43). For a scientific perspective of person and nature, see Nesteruk, *Light*, 209–11.

74. Zizioulas, *Being*, 36–39.

75. Jowett points out inconsistencies with Plato's use of primal matter (*hulē*) in that it is the abstract "space" for which humans cannot comprehend. See Plato, *Dialogues*, 514.

76. Köster, "ὑπόστασις," 572–79.

77. Aristotle, *Animals*, 1.1, 486A; 1.8, 491B.

78. Zizioulas, *Being*, 33–34; Zizioulas, *One and Many*, 402–13.

Both terms, *prosōpon* and *persona*, made strides in developing person-hood, but they both lacked the concept of personal freedom. Both were bound by the role they played in society.[79]

Meanwhile, in the Latin West, the term *persona* was significant and may have dated back to the sixth century BCE in the ancient Etruscan civilization of Rome.[80] Scholars debate whether the Latin *persona* is borrowed from the Etruscan *phersu* or whether the Etruscans themselves borrowed the Greek *prosōpon* to describe the mask worn by actors and mimes present at social functions like funerals, games, and theatre.[81] This bifurcation of *prosōpon* from freedom to fate and perception to concrete person is best demonstrated by the name for an actor, called "*hypocritēs*," revealing the separation from reality between the individual and the role they play in the theatric play.[82]

In technical detail, Ury shows a shift in the use of *prosōpon* by the end of the Hellenistic period. The theatric mask (*prosōpeion*) became more associated with the face (*prosōpon*). The theater actors developed characters that shifted from impersonal, objective characteristics to more personal, subjective ones. During these changes, "body" (*sōma*) was added to the connotation of *prosōpon*, thus pointing to an individual person.[83] The Latin equivalent of *prosōpon*, *persona*, had a practical connotation of one's role in the community. Culturally, a person's role in the community was determined and controlled by fate.[84] The more theoretical *persona* as an agent was found in one of the following: "(i) an instance of the species 'human being', but also as (ii) the possessor of a particular physical and mental make-up, (iii) the occupier of a particular social standing and formal rank, and (iv) the pursuer of a particular career and path to distinction."[85] These ideas and concepts, although lived out, were not fully developed in writing, although they do appear in works from Panaetus, Epictetus, and Cicero.[86] In their writings, says Trapp, "It allows for individuality—a diversity of selves for different individuals to be true

79. Zizioulas, *One and Many*, 402–4.

80. Ury, *Trinitarian Personhood*, 81–82.

81. Ury, *Trinitarian Personhood*, 81; Zizioulas, *Being*, 33n20; Lohse, "πρόσωπον," 770n7. For a classical discussion, see Boethius, *Eutyches and Nestorius*, 93.

82. Ferguson, *Backgrounds*, 90.

83. Ury, *Trinitarian Personhood*, 83–84.

84. Zizioulas, *Being*, 32–34; Zizioulas, *One and Many*, 402–3.

85. Trapp, *Philosophy*, 120.

86. Trapp, *Philosophy*, 120.

to—but without individualism."[87] The concept of human diversity as being true to self was a materialistic Stoic ethic in which the *telos* of virtue formulated the Latin *persona* in its different roles. Cicero announces that virtue and friendship are the goals of a good life, yet neither he nor any other Latin thinker could offer an ontology of personhood.[88]

As practiced in the Greco-Roman theatre, humans lack freedom as they are either under the Law of nature (Greek) or the Law of the state (Roman). The Greek did not have personhood, "his 'person' is nothing but a 'mask,' something which has no bearing on this true 'hypostasis,' something without ontological content."[89] Human freedom was limited to the mask, which ultimately means a person's identity was pure "'nature' or 'substance.'"[90] Therefore, they suffered tragedy under the fate of the laws of nature and the arbitrary rule of their gods. Likewise, the Roman *persona* could only define being as it related to the legal and social environment for which they lived. The *persona* could play more than one role as the state would allow, so their personal freedom had boundaries determined by political power.[91] This development of *persona* was an expansion from the Greek universality found in the One.[92] Humans were not described as *being*, but rather humans *had being* added to their substance, like the mask from the theatre.[93] Human personhood was either cosmically or politically constituted, and determined all of which lacked freedom and personal identity.[94] In the end, all faced the same tragic fate, death, and their only hope was that the substance of the species would continue.[95]

87. Trapp, *Philosophy*, 120.

88. Cicero, *De Amicitia*, 131–33.

89. Zizioulas, *Being*, 32.

90. Zizioulas, *Being*, 33.

91. Zizioulas, *Being*, 34–35.

92. Zizioulas consistently uses this generalization of Greek philosophy of the particulars found in the One, however, this generalization misses the nuances or even misrepresents Aristotle's philosophy as shown above. Plato's "One" is the Idea/Form of Good, whereas Aristotle's "one" is Intelligible and is found in many particular things. See Mure, *Aristotle*, 178–80.

93. Zizioulas, *Being*, 34–35; Tarnas, *Western Mind*, 87–88.

94. Zizioulas, *Being*, 35.

95. Fitzgerald, "Passions," 12–15. Zizioulas says, "Tragedy is the impasse created by a freedom driving towards its fulfilment and being unable to reach it" (Zizioulas, *Eucharistic Communion*, 168). Papanikolaou says, "'Tragedy' is an important concept for Zizioulas's understanding of personhood, especially with regard to its philosophical justification" (Papanikolaou, *Being*, 143). See also, Zizioulas, "Capacity and Incapacity," 410–12.

Human freedom and *beingness* would later be a concept found in the writings and the theology of the Jews and Christians.

JEW AND CHRISTIAN

Neither the Greek philosophers nor the Latin lawyers were able to offer an ontology of personhood separate from substance and matter. As such, the person as a particular cannot be an absolute being. Rather, the person could be categorized and theorized by nature, species, etc., indicating that the nature or species supersedes the individual person in Greek and Latin. Therefore, "the particular is never the ontologically primary cause of being."[96] In this worldview, the general/universal is the cause of the particular. For instance, it was thought that human nature was the cause of human beings and never the other way around.[97] It was the Jews followed by the Christians who challenged this concept of personhood and, in doing so, included a radically different cosmology.

Jewish theology offers insight into the concept of being. Of importance, Zizioulas illustrates the biblical account of God's revelatory identity as "I Am who I Am"[98] to be the antithesis to Greek philosophy of personhood in that the particular is the cause,[99] transcendent, free to operate, and personal. Unlike Plato's god that creates from preexistent material or Aristotle's Primary Mover who moves "things" with essence of their own (*tode ti*), the God of the Jewish Scriptures, who refers to himself as "I Am," caused the world to exist because he precedes the world. Greek philosophy offered causation from *within* the world because it was viewed as primary, eternal material.[100] Instead, Old Testament and Rabbinic teaching begin with the eternal God who creates the world, all that is in the world, and human beings.[101] Human beings are created in the image

96. Zizioulas, *Communion*, 104.

97. Zizioulas, *Being*, 28–29; Zizioulas, *Communion*, 102; Aristotle, *Metaphysics*, 1.2; Plato, *Parmenides*, 137C.

98. Exod 3:14.

99. Zizioulas, *Communion*, 104; Zizioulas, *Lectures*, 40–42.

100. Zizioulas, *Being*, 17; Zizioulas, *Communion*, 104.

101. Brueggemann, states the OT never suggests an autonomous humanity, rather the human person is such only in relation to God. However, he also warns that "*the notion of humanity in the 'image of God' plays no primary role in Old Testament articulations of humanity*; it does not constitute a major theological datum for Israel's reflection on the topic" (Brueggemann, *Theology*, 450–53).

and likeness of God himself, thus the Jewish concept of God as Father.[102] However, this Fatherhood motif is unlike the epic, *Enuma Elish*, with its dysfunctional family in a mirror drama of human activity,[103] rather as a simile for the way that God relates to human beings, his children, Fatherhood is demonstrated through his communication, walking with or leading, showing and teaching, and most of all, his love for them.[104] The Old Testament offers a concept of *corporate personality*, where a particular being is united to the many, and the many are identified in the particular being.[105] This approach is a shift from Greek philosophy, where particular individuals are derivatives of One. To the adherents of the Old Testament theory of *corporate personality*, or sometimes called *social solidarity*, it is more than a personification or ideology; it is a concrete concept of the Old Testament social identity and the key to unlocking the literature, life, and thought of the Old Testament Scriptures.[106]

Brown refers to this Jewish concept of an individual's identity found in the group as "family solidarity," but does not limit it to the Jews alone, but rather finds similarity within Greek literature.[107] Furthermore, Brown views the ancient Israelite and ancient Greek cultures as complementing each other throughout history.[108] The focus of his study is the continuity of freedom, literature, and democratic leanings between Jewish and Greek societies compared to other surrounding societies. Historically, other nations in the region had versions of freedom, literature, and governmental authority within their society, but these other societies rose

---

102. Cohen, *Everyman's Talmud*, 20–22, 67.

103. Brown, "Gender and Power," 1–45.

104. Cohen, *Everyman's Talmud*, 21–22.

105. It is H. Wheeler Robinson who is identified as presenting the theory of "corporate personality" (Leach, *Corporate Personality*). Rogerson has argued that Robinson's theory is ambiguous and lacks individual responsibility (Rogerson, "Corporate Personality").

106. Leach, *Corporate Personality*, 21, 107. Interestingly, Leach notes a connection that he finds between the Jewish understanding of personality of a people group and the soul of the individual. The primitive individual's identity is found in the group, thus the soul existed before the individual person was born through the people group. Leach says this is a type of pre-existent soul or spirit that he equates as similar to Platonic philosophy (Leach, *Corporate Personality*, 30–32).

107. Brown, *Ancient Israel and Ancient Greece*, 201–2.

108. For another perspective of Greek and Hebrew thought complimenting each other, see Oswalt, *Myths*, 25–26.

and fell, while the Greeks and the Jews remained for a more extended period of time.[109]

The Jews, in contrast to the Greeks and the Romans, present a pre-existent, eternal, and transcendent God who is free to act and chooses to act personally toward humans whom he created in his image.[110] Unlike Aristotelian physics that logically needs an unmoved mover or a First Cause, Jewish theology offered a Creator who is "the absolute source of this world."[111] Indeed, Eichrodt expresses the uniqueness of the Old Testament as the connection of this Creator God with his creation. The Creator reveals himself as "I," and the creature refers to the Creator as "Thou," which Eichrodt calls the greatest gift to humanity.[112] It is God's absolute will to create such a community as he operates from his freedom. In this freedom, the community has received a promise from God's Spirit that it can reach his goals.[113]

Along with the freedom of Israel's God, Balentine shows that this God is also transcendent and separated from the material world. His work is a comprehensive semantic and theological study on the phrase "hide the face," with the majority of the work focusing on "hide" or the concept of the "hiddenness of God."[114] God sometimes hides himself from humans; other times, he hides humans, and there are times it could be an inanimate object that God hides (i.e., plans, thoughts, words, etc.).[115] There appear to have been idioms within the cultures of the An-

109. Brown, *Ancient Israel and Ancient Greece*, 49–54. Flanagan, suggests Israel's sociopolitical development and stability should be considered through the cultural evolutionary theory that Israel made the necessary changes in contrast to their neighbors (Flanagan, "Chiefs in Israel," 311–34). Demand, emphasizes the Greek "trading bases" made possible by maritime efforts (i.e., expanding commerce and culture) followed by the implementation of polis ideals with all of its structures, added to the long history of Greece (Demand, *Mediterranean Context*, xi–xvi). On the influence of Greek freedom, see Osborne, *Greek History*, 85–100.

110. Kaufmann, *Israel*, 240–41; Kinlaw and Oswalt, *Lectures*, 29–32; Oswalt, *Myths*, 64, 69–70, 81–84; Zizioulas, *Communion*, 41–43, 104–5, 108–9; Zizioulas, *Lectures*, 40–41, 89, 91–98.

111. Eichrodt, *Man*, 60. On God as the "Cause," see Basil, *Letters*, 38.4.

112. Eichrodt, *Man*, 30. See also this concept developed in modern existential thought in Buber, *I and Thou*.

113. Eichrodt, *Man*, 75–76.

114. Balentine, *Hidden*.

115. Balentine, *Hidden*, 2. Cf. Kinlaw, *Jesus*, ch. 4, "The Human Problem: Why Is Identification with God Impossible?" Here Kinlaw argues that at the core of sin in human beings, there is the heart of humans curved in on itself (*cor incurvatus ad*

cient Near East which spoke of divine aloofness. These were just as important etymologically of the word "hide" to understanding the meaning that God, the Creator, hides from his creation.[116] The theological nuance of hiddenness is relevant to understanding the connection between God and humans as presented by the Hebrew Old Testament because, in God's transcendence, he sometimes offers himself to be known and, at other times, cannot be found. Hamilton, for example, explains that the phrase "face-to-face" in reference to Jacob naming the place where he wrestled with God, Peniel (Gen 32:30), does not need to be limited to a literal understanding but that the idiom can refer to a "manifestation of presence" as in person-to-person contact.[117] Balentine proffers several reasons for this divine hiddenness from humans, along with their many consequences.[118] However, these causes and consequences, while remaining God's absolute decision, are based on humans failing to adequately relate to him.[119] Balentine also shows that context and genre reveal specific patterns. Thus, "sentences in the Psalms show a noticeable lack of words having reference to sin or divine anger, whereas in prophetic passages words having this reference appear to be relatively common."[120] However, the meaning remains the same. When God decides to hide his face, it is an analogy of divine punishment and abandonment for humans.[121] The

---

se, Martin Luther), and it is humans who have turned their face away from God and toward each person's own desire based on Isaiah 53:6 and the verb *panah* (turned) from the root word *pānīm* (face) (Kinlaw, *Jesus*, 112–13).

116. Balentine, *Hidden*, 44.

117. Hamilton, *Genesis: 18–50*, 336.

118. Balentine notes that both community and individuals lament or petition God for "hiding His face." These are expressed through "condemnation of enemies," "assertion of innocence," and "confession of sin." However, most often God hides his face as a result of "sin" even though the sin is typically inexplicable and the events, especially in the Psalms, are ambiguous (Balentine, *Hidden*, 50–51, 56). Balentine's thesis is that more than these negative approaches to understanding God's hiddenness as a result of disobedience or sin, there is a positive approach which simply is found in God's nature to be simultaneously elusive and present (Balentine, *Hidden*, 174–76). The recipients of God's hiddenness may find themselves a reproach to God or others, near death, defeated in battle or having a physical ailment (Balentine, *Hidden*, 53–55).

119. See Oswalt, *Isaiah: 40–66*, 513–14, 623–26 and the issue of sin as separation between God and humans. Balentine, *Hidden*, 50–63.

120. Balentine, *Hidden*, 47. In a rare turn of events the extreme opposite occurs in Psalm 13:1 where the Psalmist is actually accusing God of "*active* sin of commission" by hiding his face and withholding salvation. See deClaissé-Walford et-al., *Psalms*, 160.

121. Balentine, *Hidden*, 68. Brueggemann, appears more passive in interpreting

worshipper of God laments as a means "to cope" with their immediate experience, which is directly connected to the absence of God.[122] Therefore, for a human to exist, he or she must have a connection with this Creator. Oswalt explains the profound meaning through a series of questions and answers in reference to Isaiah 54:8.

> What was the way in which the people experienced God's anger? It was in the hiding of his face from them. Was it not in the terrible cruelties of the siege and destruction? Was it not in being dragged from their homes and being forced to settle in a strange place? Yes, it was all of these and more. Yet those are all expressions of something deeper and more important: the absence of the presence and favor of God. Those things happened to Israel and Judah because God refused to look at them, and that is what this part of the book (chs. 49–50) is about. Restoration to the land is really not the principle issue—restoration to the loving glance of God is.[123]

The supplicant in these "hiddenness" passages "does not raise his [human] complaint about the incongruities in his personal circumstances apart from the awareness that these are in turn reflections of his [human] relationship with God."[124] Notwithstanding, Levison connects God's face with life and life with God's Spirit, who is the breath of life.[125] Therefore, when God turns his face away or hides his face, there is death, and "Death also portends spiritless or breathless existence; thus the creative inbreathing of Gen 2:7 is reversed in a negative image of the first creation, in

---

the siege of Jerusalem in that the face of God is connected to the presence of God and that there is a vacuum left in Jerusalem by the absence of God through the hiding of his face (Brueggemann, *Jeremiah*, 313–14).

122. Balentine, *Hidden*, 167.

123. Oswalt, *Isaiah: 40–66*, 421.

124. Balentine, *Hidden*, 167. While Balentine connects the "face" (lit., פָּנִים [*pānîm*]) of God in OT theology to the attribute of being a "personal God" in comparison to idioms found in Akkadian and Sumerian texts (e.g., Prayer of Ishtar) (Balentine, *Hidden*, 30, 32–35), he stops short of explicitly connecting the face of God with the being of God. In Eichrodt, *Theology*, God's *pānîm* is his countenance as his self-revelation (Eichrodt, *Theology*, 111n2). Eichrodt finds divine transcendent-immanent tension in the OT description of God's *pānîm* (Eichrodt, *Theology*, 214). The personhood of God or beingness is described by the idiom "face of God" in the OT; see Jenni and Westermann, "פָּנִים" in *TLOT* 2:IV 3 (d)–IV 4 (a).

125. Levison, *Filled*, 14–16, 26.

which God's face pressed intimately against *adam's* to breathe life into lifeless dust."[126]

Jewish biblical scholar, Yochanan Muffs, suggests that the God of Israel is unique in that, unlike other religions, including ancient philosophy, God is not an ideology or stuck in the "metadivine" realm.[127] Instead, he is personal and is motivated by love which gives him the freedom to cross boundaries. As such, he argues, any "model of divinity that does not partake of personhood can hardly be expected to cultivate personhood in [humans]."[128] Human beings are created to be relational in the same way that God is relational. Muffs suggests that human beings, in an act of "bravery" and faith, must extend their focus outside of themselves and reach out to others through communication and love.[129]

> The God of Israel is not a slave to nature or to matter; rather, He creates the world of nature by His sovereign will. . . . His personality finds its true expression in love for another personality, independent and outside itself. It is a great love that cannot be contained by the boundaries of the self, a love that seeks involvement of the divine heart with its human counterpart.[130]

The motivation of love found in the God of Israel to create was not like the love of the other cultures that surrounded Israel. The pagan myths of creation did not only begin with preexistent *stuff* (i.e., the primordial waters in the *Enuma Elish*) but in many cases, creation was birthed as a result of *eros* and was an emanation of these gods (e.g., Erebus and Nyx). In contrast, the God of Israel expressed love as *agape*.[131] In

---

126. Levison, *Filled*, 26.

127. Cf. Kaufmann, *Israel*. Kaufmann differentiates the Israelite religion to paganism in that it fundamentally does not include a "metadivine" realm where there is a primordial power that supersedes the divine (Kaufmann, *Israel*, 23–24, 60–63).

128. Muffs, *Personhood*, 192.

129. Muffs, *Personhood*, 17.

130. Muffs, *Personhood*, 13.

131. Muffs, *Personhood*, 58. At this point, Muffs engages modern Christian theology and the theological term *Heilsgeschichte*, which is "salvation history" or more literally "blessed immanence." In so doing, Muffs uses the Greek terms *eros-agape* that were being referenced by late nineteenth and twentieth-century scholars to express the divine-human relationship. Muffs suggests the core issue is "biblical anthropomorphism" which is used to reveal the immanence of God. Scholars have attempted to explain how a transcendent God can simultaneous be described as having humanlike qualities. Those who have espoused *Heilsgeschichte*, according to Muffs, have failed to show God's personhood, while correctly showing his saving activity. The result is an

creation, the first principle is not matter; rather, the Spirit of God is the source of everything.[132] God created the world *ex nihilo* and humans in the image of God (*imago Dei*), giving them dignity and potential. This view of humanity is considered among Jews as the essential biblical truth of humanity.[133] May counters this point by saying that there is no definitive evidence in Hellenistic Judaism for the formula of *creatio ex nihilo*.[134] The definitive dogma of *creatio ex nihilo* comes from second-century Christian apologists like Tatian, Theophilus of Antioch, and Irenaeus, to name a few, in combating Gnosticism and Platonic philosophy dealing with preexistent matter.[135] The *creatio ex nihilo* formula postulates God's transcendence and will to cause the world and all that is in it to exist. He is the source of all that exists. The difference is that his being is that of a personal God who both relates and desires to know his creation and to be known by his creation. The desire of God to relate to his creation, as demonstrated through *imago Dei*, reveals that God is also immanent.[136]

---

eros-agape pagan-like paradigm that states humans are drawn to God by *eros* and God responds by *agape*. See Nygren, *Agape and Eros*. Muffs's point is that God's transcendence is linked to a "condescending monarch" whose will for a delegated people to carry out his plan is hampered by their failure to do so. The result is God's anger over their failure revealing also a personal God with humanlike emotions (Muffs, *Personhood*, 59–60). Muffs engages the theology of Wright, *God Who Acts*, who suggests that history is the loci for God's salvific activity and biblical theology is a recital in which humans recite and confess their faith in God's work (Muffs, *Personhood*, 38). Furthermore, to confess God simply means to tell (recite) the biblical story and express it's meaning (Muffs, *Personhood*, 85). In Rad, *Old Testament Theology*, the agents of the salvation history are the prophets. However, history is not understood as linear, rather is a record of God's activity with his people, Israel leading toward an eschatological event expressed as the Day of Yahweh (Rad, *Old Testament Theology*, 99–125, 362). In these OT theologies there are presented the works of God, but not the personhood of God (Muffs, *Personhood*, 60).

132. Oswalt, *Myths*, 66–67; Gen 1:1–2.

133. Hertzberg, *Judaism*, 236.

134. May, *Creatio Ex Nihilo*, 6–7.

135. May, *Creatio Ex Nihilo*, 39, 148–78.

136. While keeping in mind a paradoxical balance of the transcendence and immanence of God, it is through God's immanence that God reveals himself as personal. The danger of a lopsided transcendent-immanent dialectic can lead to either deism (an emphasis of God's transcendence over immanence) or pantheism (an emphasis of God's immanence over transcendence). God is transcendent in that he is distinct from his creation and independent of it. However, God is also immanent as he is involved in his creation as it is dependent upon him (Grudem, *Systematic Theology*, 267). Moreover, the Scripture reveals the transcendent God interacting with his creation through meetings, speaking, listening, expressing emotions, and having feelings

God the Father is immanent in his essence, as seen in the way he relates to human beings. Zizioulas calls God the Father's creativity to design human beings in his image (*imago Dei*), "man's personhood."[137] This image of God by which humans are created, Zizioulas, identifies as "freedom." It is not only the design of humanity, but for Zizioulas, God

---

(Oden, *God*, 81, 82, 84). The danger of being overly captivated by the immanence of God can lead toward a blurring of the divine and material lines making material things (Matter) a necessity for God or to an extreme where God obeys the laws of Matter because it is viewed as eternal (Tertullian, *Against Hermogenes*, chs. 17–30; also, Athenagoras, *A Plea for the Christians*, chs. 15–16). Before one speaks of God, they should first consider the details of the created world, for even the angels do not fully know God the Father, only the Son knows the Father because he is transcendent in his holiness (Cyril of Jerusalem, *Catechetical Lectures*, 6.4–7). For the survival of the doctrine of Christianity, it was necessary for the Ancient Church to strike a balance between God's transcendence and immanence. Therefore, God being transcendent is not only separated from Matter (material world) but is the Creator of Matter and all material things (Athanasius, *Incarnation*, §1–3), moreover God interacts with creation, He incarnates creation and "takes" on a human body (Athanasius, *Incarnation*, §8–9) for the purpose of redeeming humans (Athanasius, *Incarnation*, §10) and that they may know their Creator (Athanasius, *Incarnation*, §11). The Ancient Church Age ended with an Christological definition at the Council of Chalcedon (451 CE) which essentially holds simultaneously the transcendent-immanent dialectic in the personhood of Christ (Schaff, *Creeds of Christendom*, 29–34). The Medieval Age with its scholasticism in the West swung the pendulum to focus more on transcendence as demonstrated in Aquinas' "First Mover" (*Primum Movens*) (Aquinas, *Compendium Theologiae*, chs. 2–7). The Medieval Age closed with the Renaissance of humanism opening up the Modern Age to a new Enlightenment. The optimistic rationale of human enlightenment caused the pendulum to swing toward a more immanent God as demonstrated in Schleiermacher's "inward truth" toward a self-conscious fulfillment (Schleiermacher, *Christian Faith*, 76–78). Following World War 1, theologians sought something concrete and again the pendulum swung to transcendence in the form of neo-orthodoxy. The shift was to recapture what was missing, that is, God can be objectively known by the Church through the Word of God (Barth, *CD* 2/1:3–4). By the 1960s there arose dissent toward fundamentalism and as a result there was a call for theology to be contextualized or applicable to the "situation" of society (an immanent approach). The answer was an "apologetic theology" that would answer the needs and the questions of the present day (Tillich, *Systematic Theology*, 3–11). However, this stress on the immanence of God toward the "situation" of society failed and on April 8, 1966, the cover of *Time* Magazine read, "Is God Dead?" In light of this hopelessness entered Moltmann's *Theology of Hope* and Pannenberg's truth in Christian doctrine as a swing toward transcendence. Truth was presented as found in God as described in the doctrinal content of the Scriptures and is to be believed on in faith. Furthermore, truth is discovered through human reason as found in history which is universal truth, the truth of revelation (Pannenberg, *Systematic Theology*, 1:1–61).

137. Zizioulas, "Capacity and Incapacity," 424. On the topic of *image* and *likeness*, see Zizioulas, *One and Many*, 32–33; Zizioulas, *Being*, 18, 39–41.

exists because the Father is free to operate, and "the free person, constitutes true being."[138] Zizioulas qualifies this freedom given to humanity,
as "*to refuse his existence*: this is the proof of the fact of freedom. Man
is thus free to refuse his personhood, i.e., the difference between person
and nature: he can choose to become a thing."[139] Zizioulas ties together
the concept of *freedom of persons* with the concept of *relationship toward
one another* as defining *personhood* that eventually supports his *ontology of being*. Brueggemann agrees that the Old Testament is about life
and its "interactive relationships" but separates it from an ontological
claim.[140] McConville shows that the image of God in humans held both
the function for humanity to represent God through dominion or rule
(*rādāh*) over nonhuman creation and the multifaceted interrelational
value made possible by the "presence of God" found in the connection of
God, human, and nonhuman creation.[141] So important is the concept of
imago Dei in Jewish literature that the rabbis speak of the supremacy of
human beings in the economy of the Universe as "'One man is equal to
the whole of Creation' (ARN xxxi).'"[142] Nevertheless, the Old Testament
reveals that human beings are the crowning jewel of God's creation. The
Psalmist writes,

> what is man that you are mindful of him,
> and the son of man that you care for him?
> Yet you have made him a little lower than the heavenly beings
> and crowned him with glory and honor.
> You have given him dominion over the works of your hands;
> you have put all things under his feet.[143]

In Jewish culture, the name (*shēm*) was significant in knowing the
characteristics and personality of a person.[144] The name characterized the
whole being, including the person's very soul.[145] In Genesis 2, which deals
primarily with the creation of man and woman, God's personal name

138. Zizioulas, *Being*, 18.

139. Zizioulas, "Capacity and Incapacity," 428.

140. Brueggemann, *God*, 21.

141. McConville, *Being Human*, 11–29.

142. Cohen, *Everyman's Talmud*, 67.

143. Ps 8:4–6 [Ps 8:5–7 MT].

144. Barth, *God with Us*, 47–49. Rad suggested that the divine name is "an objective existence" which foreshadows "Christ" in the NT as the "Glory of God" (Rad, *Old
Testament Theology*, 356).

145. Pedersen, *Israel*, 245.

is revealed as "*Yᵉhwāh* *ᵉlōhîm*" (Lord God) ten times. The use of God's personal name in Genesis 2 stands in stark contrast to Genesis 1, where "God" (*ᵉlōhîm*) is primarily used in the creation of the six days. Green rehearses a lesson on Genesis 2 from Abraham ben Eliezer of Bohemia,

> Then Adam was called forth, and he gave an appropriate name to each of the beasts. Once he had succeeded at this task, God asked: "And what is your name?" to which Adam answered: "I should be called Adam, for I was taken from adamah, or earth." God asked once again: "And what should I be called?" Adam answered: "You are Adonay, for You are Lord over all Your works."[146]

Later, it is the name of the Lord God that dwells in the temple (Deut 12:11; 1 Kgs 8:17) as a sign of the personal presence of God. Furthermore, "the name is the soul in its full capacity."[147] When speaking of God's name, it is to know and/or express his nature as often found in the Psalms.

> The psalmist met God, and God said, "I would like to be in a personal relationship with you. I want to tell you my name. I want to be on that kind of basis with you, a first name basis." But when the psalmist gets to know who God is and what His nature is, he is astounded to discover that this Yahweh cares about the people nobody else cares about.[148]

Even more personal and intimate than the name within the Old Testament literature is the "face." At the end of Psalm 16, the psalmist is full of joy (*śōbă̆' śᵉmāḥôt*) because the Source of life has promised him life rather than abandonment. The space or place for which this fullness of joy occurs is "in your presence" (v. 11) which is literally "with your face" or "before your face" (*'ĕt pānĕykā*).[149] Ratzinger builds on the promise from Deuteronomy 18:15, "'The Lord your God will raise up for you a prophet like me from among you, from your brothers—it is to him you shall listen.'" This he connects with Deuteronomy 34:10, "And there has not arisen a prophet since in Israel like Moses, whom the Lord knew face to face." This is the announcement for the nation of Israel to look forward for a *new* Moses or a *second* Moses. The uniqueness and the sign of this *second* Moses are that he communicates with Yahweh face to face as a

---

146. Green, *Face*, 33.

147. Pedersen, *Israel*, 259.

148. Kinlaw and Oswalt, *Lectures*, 37.

149. Kinlaw and Oswalt, *Lectures*, 69.

man (i.e., human) speaks to his friend (Exod 33:11). Ratzinger reminds us that this sets a standard for prophets in the Old Testament that rather than being "soothsayers" they are to present to the people "the face of God."[150] However, his thesis is that Moses had his failings and was denied to see the face of God (Exod 33:20, 23). While Moses was the greatest prophet in Old Testament Scriptures, there is an expectation for a *second* Moses who will be granted not only to communicate with God face to face[151] but "is the radiance of the glory of God and the exact imprint of his nature."[152]

Therefore, seeking the face of God is an intimate connection and relationship between the human and the Divine.[153] Green rejects the interpretations that the image and likeness of God found in human beings is defined as rationality, intelligence, or freedom.[154] Hamilton warns

---

150. Ratzinger, *Jesus of Nazareth*, 4.

151. Ratzinger, *Jesus of Nazareth*, 2–7.

152. Heb 1:3. For further thought on the presence of God with humans, see chapter 6, "Personal Presence: A Shadow of Things to Come."

153. Green, *Face*, 28; White, *Exodus*, 278–82. Middleton, finds within the context of the ancient Near East, and more specifically Mesopotamia, there being a royal understanding of the image of God, so much so, that the image of the god is found in the king himself as a representative of his office (Middleton, *Liberating Image*, 121). However, Middleton does not simply connect the relationship between the divine and human by way of royal representation, but further suggests the *imago Dei* in Genesis 1 is a "democratization" of the image of God in that all humans, unlike the other ancient Near Eastern cultures with their elite classes, have this royal image of God (Middleton, *Liberating Image*, 204, 207, 214, 227–28, 254).

154. For Calvin, the image of God in humans is the mind and heart which has been marred by sin, and yet permeates the rest of the human being (Calvin, *Genesis*, 15). Arnold and Beyer, *Old Testament*, suggest that the theological significance behind the *imago Dei* is inexhaustible. However, they offer at the very least it means that humans have dominion over creation and represent God (especially Adam and Eve contextually speaking), and that the human image bearer specifically means that humans were created for relationship with God, unlike the rest of creation (80). In addition to this view, Davidson, "Origins," adds the resemblance of God in humans is both an "outward form and inward character" (Arnold and Beyer, *Old Testament*, 128). The "image of God" for McConville is interpreted not simply by biblical exegesis, but also within the context of Ancient Near East religions. In doing so, McConville can point to an element of human dominion over creation, but further, that humans are a representation of God in creation intrinsically as well and thus giving significance and emphasis to relationships (McConville, *Being Human*, 16–29). For Pannenberg, the image of God is fulfilled in the resurrected Jesus Christ, who is a prototype of the *imago Dei*, and thus, all humans are to bear this image which is exocentric in nature (Pannenberg, *Anthropology*, 74–79).

against a subjective rather than objective exegesis for the meaning of "in our image" and "as our likeness": "Any approach that focuses on one aspect of man—be that physical, spiritual, or intellectual—to the neglect of the rest of man's constituent features seems doomed to failure."[155] Green unabashedly suggests that the human face is a copy or a reflection of the face of God.[156] Humans relate to God as relating to another person. It is for this reason that the graven image is an abomination to God, for it cannot rightly capture "every living, breathing human being." "To take an inanimate object—something less than human—and attempt to fashion a god out of it—that is indeed idolatry, a lessening of the true divine image within you."[157] Thus, intimate knowledge of and relationship with God is achieved by opening up one's self to another human being, who is created in the image of God.[158]

Finally, the Jew seeks truth through the "signs" of God in history.[159] These "signs" are God's revelatory truth to his people, who are expected to respond to the truth by carrying out God's will and abiding by his laws. The truth of God and the word of God become synonymous. Zizioulas summarizes, "According to this way of understanding truth, it is God's promises which may be considered as ultimate truth, and these promises coincide with the goal of fulfilment of history."[160] This truth in history is carried out through a transcendent God described anthropomorphically. The God of the Jews speaks in a familial tone and adopts a people to fulfill his will and mission.[161] This Jewish view is quite different from the Greek view of truth and history where the "intelligible world," "the thinking mind," and "being" were linked together in the concept of the cosmos, which held the truth and superseded history.[162] This concept is associated

155. Hamilton, *Genesis: 1–17*, 137. The purpose is that human beings are presented as a unity. "No part of man, no function of man is subordinated to some other, higher part or activity" (Hamilton, *Genesis: 1–17*, 137).

156. Green, *Face*, 28.

157. Green, *Face*, 27.

158. Green, *Face*, 27, 35. Examples of intimate knowledge of God being lived out are found in the family structure (patriarchal religion), neighbor relationships, and caring for strangers; see Albertz, *History*; Neusner and Avery-Peck, *Judaism*, 157–86; Hertzberg, *Judaism*, 33–37, 66–70, 73–75, 88–100, 109–11.

159. Kaufmann, *Israel*, 91–93; Zizioulas, *Being*, 68.

160. Zizioulas, *Being*, 68.

161. Muffs, *Personhood*, 60.

162. Zizioulas, *Being*, 69. See also Wood's discussion on Pannenberg's definition of "truth" taken from a Hebrew concept of *emeth* (reliability, firmness, faithfulness,

with the overarching Jewish understanding that truth is lived-out morals that indicate integrity.[163]

As we shift from Jewish to Christian thought for the development of personhood, it is with an awareness that Christianity did not emerge onto history as a uniquely distinct religious institution other than its rule of faith and central focus on Jesus Christ.[164] "The identity" of Christianity was a "process of definition" as it was challenged at every turn.[165] Christianity grew out of Judaism pre-70 CE in its embryonic phase.[166] The formulation of Christianity's identity was the period from 70 to 180. However, during this period, the history of Christianity underwent immense "tension and struggle between competing ideas/faiths/practices."[167] These competing ideas included Judaism on one end of the spectrum and Hellenization in the form of Gnosticism on the other end.[168] However, the unifying center that identified Christianity during the first two centuries was the Jewish Jesus, who presented the moral code to love God and others, the fellowship and initiation of the Lord's Supper and baptism, and faith and trust in the crucifixion and resurrection of Jesus Christ.[169]

---

truth) in contrast to the Greek *alētheuein* (truth, unconcealment, unchanging reality) in Wood, *History and Hermeneutics*, 93–96. Frank argues that there is no Jewish Philosophy in the classical definition, rather a philosophy of Judaism because it is a way to understand tradition and not a branch of classical philosophy (Frank, "Jewish Philosophy," 4).

163. Jacobs, *Jewish Religion*, 282.

164. Dunn, *Neither Jew Nor Greek*, 40–41, 802. Dunn's approach to the difficult time period in Christianity of 70 to 180 CE (due to a lack of historical data) is to begin at the time of the historical Jesus and move toward the future. Typically, the approach has been to reconstruct the Jesus tradition from the future (Dunn, *Neither Jew Nor Greek*, 41).

165. Dunn, *Neither Jew Nor Greek*, 40–41.

166. Dunn, *Neither Jew Nor Greek*, 12–13.

167. Dunn, *Neither Jew Nor Greek*, 40.

168. Dunn, *Neither Jew Nor Greek*, 14–39.

169. Dunn, *Neither Jew Nor Greek*, 824. It is interesting to note that Dunn does not include the resurrection of Jesus Christ in his unifying identity of early Christianity (824), especially since he has definitively stated that the unifying aspect of the Synoptic Gospels and John's Gospel is the passion narrative (207, 803). In other places he mentions the resurrection in conjunction with the crucifixion (e.g., 190, 811–12). While the absence of Jesus Christ's resurrection might be an oversight in the final summary, one of Dunn's objectives is to trace the distinctive features of Christianity from the Jesus tradition, oral tradition, and written tradition (185–311). Furthermore, the resurrection of Jesus Christ is recorded in the Gospels (Matt 28:1–10; Mark 16:1–8; Luke 24:1–12; John 20:1–18) and in Paul's letters (Rom 6:5; 1 Cor 15:12) and in Peter's

Dunn concludes that if the simplicity of the unified center of Christianity in the second century is correct as presented, we discover different expressions of Christianity, giving both a unified and diverse history and experience.[170] An ontology was developed in this unified yet diverse community called the Christian church. Christian ontology, that is, the development and definition of "person," begins first with the personhood of God and is then projected on the Christian person.[171]

In the second century, the philosophical concept of *Logos* described the personhood of Jesus Christ. Justin appears to be the originator of Christ as *Logos*, but later, Clement and Origen expanded the thought. Converted from Platonism, Justin nevertheless bridged Greek philosophy and Christianity. He appeared to offer a monistic God who is known through the human mind.[172] Furthermore, it is within the human capacity to know God and his truth. This truth capacity is from God in the "spermatic word" within humans, and this Word (*Logos*) has become human while maintaining his divine essence.[173] Here, Justin has suggested a preexistent *Logos* in the world before Christ. Therefore Justin expressed Christ as the manifestation of the truth and *Logos* of God the Father. He took care in showing that the *Logos* was ontologically distinct in number from God the Father by being the incarnate Son, while demonstrating they share the same essence as "the light and the sun" or as a torch can be lit from a fire and both the original fire and the torch fire being distinct, yet of the same essence and nature.[174] While Justin made strides in communicating to Greek thinkers who Christ was and the truth of God, his theology, like himself, was contextual and heavily influenced by the philosophies of the day.[175] Not surprisingly, Justin's connection of truth with the "spermatic word" led some to conclude that Socrates and Plato

---

letter (1 Pet 1:3; 3:21).

170. Dunn, *Neither Jew Nor Greek*, 816–19, 824.

171. Zizioulas, *Being*, 18–20; Zizioulas, *Communion*, 140–45.

172. Justin Martyr, *Trypho*, 196.

173. Justin Martyr, *Second Apology*, 193.

174. Justin Martyr, *Trypho*, 264.

175. See Keener, chapter 4, "Global Reading: Contexualization and Scripture," in *Spirit Hermeneutics*. Based on an historical and experiential understanding of Pentecost (Acts 2), Keener reminds biblical interpreters of the various cultures and contexts that are integral to biblical hermeneutics. "God contextualized his message, and we must also contextualize our interpretation for new settings, while remaining faithful to the original message" (Keener, *Spirit Hermeneutics*, 76).

were Christians.[176] Of interest here is Zizioulas's point that this notion of fixed truth—which connects God, humans, and the world—is mediated by the *Logos* of God. The battle, then, is in the realm of the mind (*nous*).[177] Justin's attempt to personalize the Greek *Logos* in the incarnate Christ led to an aesthetic Christian philosophy where all that is good, true, and beautiful is connected to God.

In the late second century, the church attempted to describe and understand the Father-Son relationship of God. For Noetus, there is no real Father-Son relationship since they are one-and-the-same being. According to Hippolytus, Noetus promoted a modalistic view of God, "'When indeed, then, the Father had not been born, He *yet* was justly styled Father; and when it pleased Him to undergo generation, having been begotten, He Himself became His own son, not another's.'"[178] In Noetus's view, there are not two divine persons existing in holy communion, let alone three persons. He espoused a change simply in nomenclature, which begs the question, "If there is one God and only one person, then who died on the cross?" God must be dead! Noetus did not maintain that Jesus died on the cross, but only that it appeared that he died.[179] Hippolytus connects Noetus's thoughts with the philosophy of Heraclitus, who held to a monistic view of reality.[180]

At about the same time, Praxeas arrived from Asia to Rome with similar arguments as Noetus, yet further explained modalism. Praxeas reserved nothing in his presentation of modalism. Jesus Christ was not only one person, that is, the one God became Jesus Christ, but the very substance of his being was a compound of divinity and humanity becoming a *tertium quid*.[181] Praxeas offered, in essence, a hybrid being. Tertullian was so enraged by this heresy and that Pope Victor had given an ear to his doctrine that he said, "By this Praxeas did a twofold service for the devil at Rome: he drove away prophecy, and he brought in heresy; he put to flight the Paraclete, and he crucified the Father."[182] Olson points out

176. González, *Story*, 1:56.

177. Zizioulas, *Being*, 73–74, 78.

178. Hippolytus, *Refutation*, 127–28.

179. Hippolytus, *Refutation*, 128.

180. Hippolytus, *Refutation*, 126.

181. Tertullian, *Praxeas*, 623–24.

182. Tertullian, *Praxeas*, 597.

that Tertullian was the first to use the term *patripassianism* to describe the result of the modalistic heresy.[183]

The rationalistic *Logos* theology seems to have come to a head in the fourth century with Arius. As Olson has pointed out, Arius and the Antiochene School under Lucian emphasized the humanity of Jesus Christ rather than the deity, which led to an adoptionist heresy.[184] This explanation of the incarnation and person of Jesus Christ subordinated the Son under the Father in essence and dignity. Some who espoused the *Logos* theology viewed equality of divinity between the Father and the *Logos*, while others held a personal distinction between the Father and the *Logos*.[185] Ironically, this bifurcation flowed from Origen's Christology, which one perspective was adhered to in the school of thought in Alexandria and another at the school in Antioch where Arius sat under the tutelage of Lucian. Olson clearly explains the origination from the dueling schools of thought this way:

> On the one hand, Origen strongly affirmed an equality of the Logos with God the Father. Without any doubt Origen believed that the Logos is God's eternal emanation, shooting forth like a ray of the sun from God and sharing eternally in his glorious nature. On the other hand, Origen also affirmed a subordination of the Logos to the Father in order to account for his mediatorship between the immutable divine nature of God and the corrupt world of nature and history. The Logos, according to Origin, is somehow less than the Father, although he never explained exactly what that means.[186]

183. Olson, *Story*, 95.

184. Olson, *Story*, 142.

185. Hefele, *Christian Councils*, 231.

186. Olson, *Story*, 142–43. Later, the Cappadocian Fathers, specifically, Basil of Caesarea, attempted to clarify not only the Christological debate but the Trinitarian debate on equality and distinction of persons by offering an analogy of monarchy. In Basil, *Spirit*, 18.45, p. 28, "Worshipping as we do God of God, we both confess the distinction of the Persons, and at the same time abide by the *Monarchy*" (Basil, *Spirit*, 18.45, p. 28). Ironically, the monarchy of God debate is found in both Jürgen Moltmann and Wolfhart Pannenberg. For Moltmann, the uniqueness and particularity within the Trinity can be found in the definition of monarchy, however Moltmann warns of the danger in subordinating the persons (Moltmann, *Trinity*, 188–90). For Pannenberg, support for Jesus's unity with God is his eternal essence with the Father without subordination of persons as Jesus is the revelation of God the Father. However, Pannenberg guards against modalism as Jesus himself reveals the Father and maintains his own sonship (Pannenberg, *Jesus-God and Man*, 133, 150, 158–60).

The Alexandrian School took from Origen the theological point that Jesus Christ as the *Logos* was united to God the Father. The *Logos* was the reasonable character of God who shares in his glory and power.[187] As seen above, an extreme presentation of the unity of God had led earlier to modalism or Sabellianism, which ironically led to Subordinationism (i.e., one mode of being is less than another mode of being).[188] Arius was on guard against Sabellianism, thus upon hearing Alexander, Bishop of Alexandria, Arius believed him to be promoting an extreme divinity of Christ that would lead to Sabellianism. However, Alexander and others from the Alexandrian school were attempting to stress the unity of the *Logos* with the Father while also showing diversity. Athanasius of Alexandria referenced Origen to show that he held to the eternal co-existence of God the Father and the *Logos*, yet diverse as the names would indicate (i.e., Father and Word of the Father).[189]

In contrast, the Antiochene School initiated their theology with the attributes of God's immutability and impassibility. These theological attributes caused a problem with their explanation of the *Logos* and Jesus Christ. The Antiochene School and its thinkers (Paul of Samosata, Lucian, and Arius) also referred to Origen, but they viewed Origen's subordination of the *Logos* to God the Father as a particular emphasis. Origen viewed the *Logos* as from the same *substantia* as the Father, but less than the Father like the sun's rays are of the same substance, yet less than the source of light, the sun itself.[190] Emphasizing the immutable impassibility of God along with a subordination of the *Logos* to God the Father, Arius concluded that Jesus Christ, the embodiment of the *Logos*, could not be divine because God cannot change. Jesus Christ must therefore be an "exalted creature," the first among equals, thus a created being with a beginning.[191] Only God the Father is uncreated and unbegotten (*agenētos*). Quasten explains:

> The logical sequence is that the Son of God, the Logos, cannot be truly God. He is the first of God's creatures and like the others was brought out of nothingness (ἐξ οὐκ ὄντων), not from the divine substance. He differs essentially from the Father. He is a

187. Origen, *Gospel of John*, 1.42, 319–22.

188. Hefele, *Christian Councils*, 234.

189. Athanasius, *Nicene Definition*, 6.27. See also Origen, *Against Celsus*, 8.12.

190. Origen, *De Principiis*, 1.2.6–8.

191. Olson, *Story*, 143–44.

secondary God. There was a time when the Son of God was not (ἦν ὅτε οὐκ ἦν). He is the Son of God not in the metaphysical, but in the moral sense of the word. The title of God is improperly given to Him, because the only true God adopted Him as Son in prevision of his merits. From this sonship by adoption results no real participation in the divinity, no true likeness to it. God can have no like. The Logos holds a middle place between God and the world.[192]

The urgency for Christianity to correctly articulate the being of God the Father and God the Son, Jesus Christ, was that human personhood was also at stake undergirded by the fundamental doctrine of salvation. Humans, left in their natural state of sin and corruption, will dissolve into nothingness through death; therefore, salvation that leads to life can only come from One who is outside of human corruption, immortal, divine, and good.[193] The theological implication for the Alexandrian and Antiochene schools concerning the understanding of the *Logos* and the nature of Jesus Christ was a soteriological definition.[194] Was the Son truly divine and eternally connected to the Father, or was he a created being who was perfect in obedience and will? The battleground was a definition of soteriology that stemmed from God's divine mercy and grace upon sinful creatures or a definition based on a moral decision to obey a set of standards. For Alexander and the Alexandrian School, the crux of God's saving activity was found in the unity of the Father and the Son. The key to salvation for Arius and the Antiochene School was a human Christ who identified with the creature. It became evident that the personhood of God, the personhood of humans, and the event of salvation are tied together in Christian identity.

---

192. Quasten, *Patrology*, 8.

193. Athanasius, *Incarnation*, §§4–6. For Athanasius the salvation from sin and death that God offers through Jesus Christ is directly connected to the personhood of God and for the personhood of humans. He is speaking of the quality of personhood when he says, "For man is by nature mortal, inasmuch as he is made out of what is not; but by reason of his likeness to Him that is (and if he still preserved this likeness by keeping Him in his knowledge) he would stay his natural corruption, and remain incorrupt; . . . but being incorrupt, he would live henceforth as God, to which I suppose the divine Scripture refers" (Athanasius, *Incarnation*, §4.6). Athanasius connects being with life made available through God's grace and not as something added to the human being, like we find in Aristotle (Athanasius, *Incarnation*, §5).

194. Olson, *Story*, 145. For "salvation" as the true core of the Arian debate, see Kärkkäinen, *Trinity*, 33.

Clarity into the Father-Son relationship of God directly impacted the God-human relationship and the event of salvation. Soteriology has a two-fold definition. First, it has a forensic legal definition (i.e., "atonement," "justification," "transgressions," "law," etc.), and second, it has a relational definition (i.e., "propitiation," "reconciliation," "grace," "adoption," etc.). Furthermore, soteriology in total speaks of truth as simultaneously "being and life" unlike the Greek philosophers, vis-à-vis Aristotle who suggested, "life is *a quality added to being*, and not being itself."[195] In Jesus's conversation with Nicodemus, he speaks of the quality of a person's being illustrated by being born of "water and the Spirit."[196] Jesus goes further and connects this human *beingness* with life and salvation when he says, "For God so loved the world, that he gave his only Son, that whoever believes in him should not perish but have eternal life. For God did not send his Son into the world to condemn the world, but in order that the world might be saved through him."[197] Zizioulas connects the heart of the Cappadocian paradigm (three *hypostases* and one *ousia*) with Jesus's salvific purpose of being and life:

> This identification of being with life is so decisive for the history
> of Christian theology that, in our opinion, it is solely upon this
> basis that the great achievements of Trinitarian theology of the
> fourth century can be judged to their full value.[198]

Therefore, Zizioulas connects the soteriological definitions with the personhood of the Triune God exemplified through Jesus Christ. Referring to Ignatius and Irenaeus, Zizioulas does not point to their soteriology that led to this achievement, rather the Eucharist or, more broadly, the "eucharistic community."[199] Thus, there was a practical need for an orthodox statement of faith, the Trinity, and the Son of God. The person of God is not found in a monism, rather in the Trinity, from which an understanding of human personhood is derived. This trinitarian statement came in the form of the Nicene Creed and later the Constantinopolitan

195. Zizioulas, *Being*, 79.

196. John 3:5. Burge, *John*, 126, 130.

197. John 3:16–17.

198. Zizioulas, *Being*, 80. Zizioulas also makes this remarkable statement on the meaning of salvation in connecting life and being, "The eternal survival of the person as a unique, unrepeatable and free 'hypostasis,' as loving and being loved, constitutes the quintessence of salvation, the bringing of the Gospel to man" (Zizioulas, *Being*, 49).

199. Zizioulas, *Being*, 80–82.

Creed.[200] However, to arrive at this point, theological debate had to be sifted through the regional nuances of the Roman Empire. The Christian West, characterized by its Roman roots and Latin language, approached theology analytically, while the Christian East, characterized by its Hellenistic roots and Greek language, approached theology philosophically.[201]

WEST AND EAST

There were two theological approaches in articulating the Holy Trinity, which led to the creedal statements of Nicaea and Constantinople. In Zizioulas's historical interpretation of Nicaea and Constantinopolitan councils, there is a clear bifurcation between the church fathers in the West and those in the East. Zizioulas critiques the Western methodological approach to the Trinity in terms of essence, economy, morality, and rationality.[202] This methodological approach, he suggests, has led to Western scholasticism and the rationalization of the faith.[203]

Trinitarian theology often begins with the vocabulary and writings presented by Tertullian of the Latin West.[204] In Tertullian's writing *Against Praxeas*, we discover the word trinity being applied to the Godhead for the first time in history.[205] Hill notes that "Tertullian is also the first to describe the three members of the Trinity as 'persons' and the first to talk of their unity of 'substance.'"[206] Tertullian argues for the distinction of the three persons of the Trinity by use of their names and procession.[207] This argument was used to combat the heresy found in Praxeas of modalism. Tertullian then asks, if the one God simply changes modes of existence, then who suffered on the cross?[208]

200. Zizioulas, "Holy Trinity," 50–52; Schaff, *Constantine to Gregory*, 670–83.

201. Webb, *Triune God*, 295–326.

202. Zizioulas, *Being*, 19–26, 60; Zizioulas, *Communion*, 113–18, 150–54, 180–82, 187–90; Zizioulas, *Lectures*, 69–82; Zizioulas, *One and Many*, 3–16.

203. Zizioulas, *One and Many*, 102, 115–17, 350.

204. Zizioulas begins his historical development of trinitarian theology with Tertullian as a back drop to presenting the Cappadocian contribution. See Zizioulas, *Being*, 36–37; Zizioulas, *Communion*, 115, 157; Zizioulas, *Lectures*, 49–50; Zizioulas, *One and Many*, 402.

205. Hill, *Christian Thought*, 37.

206. Hill, *Christian Thought*, 37.

207. Tertullian, *Praxeas*, 605–6.

208. Tertullian, *Praxeas*, 625–26.

Tertullian appears to be writing and thinking on orthodox trinitarian theology well before his time.[209] In Tertullian's teaching, we have
very orthodox statements which, if read 150 years later, would have held
together the two great churches before they had a chance to go their separate ways. Olson explains,

> according to Tertullian the God Christians believe in is *one
> substance and three persons* (*una sustantia, tres personae*), and
> by *substance* he meant that fundamental ontological being-ness
> that makes something what it is, while by *person* he meant that
> identity of action that provides distinctness. The basic, underly-
> ing idea is "distinction without division."[210]

While Tertullian's thoughts on the Trinity were orthodox and well
ahead of his time, there are instances he presented a subordinationistic
view of the Trinity while explaining the procession of the Son and the
Holy Spirit from the Father.

> Now the Spirit indeed is third from God and the Son; just as the
> fruit of the tree is third from the root, or as the stream out of
> the river is third from the fountain, or as the apex of the ray is
> third from the sun. Nothing, however, is alien from that original
> source whence it derives its own properties. In like manner the
> Trinity, flowing down from the Father through intertwined and
> connected steps, does not at all disturb the Monarchy, whilst it
> at the same time guards the state of the Economy.[211]

Tertullian goes to great lengths to establish his point that the three persons of the Trinity are "inseparable, undivided yet distinct persons with
the Father," he also is careful to balance his statements with the idea that
the Father is continually the monarch overall.[212] Until Tertullian, the
monarchy of God was associated with monotheism. In chapters three
and four of *Against Praxeas*, Tertullian argues that monarchy is the type

209. For instance, the whole *filioque* debate, which began sometime around 589 at
the synod of Toledo and eventually was a major factor that led to the Great Schism of
1054 between the Roman Catholic Church and the Eastern Orthodox Church, very
well could have been avoided if someone would have read Tertullian's quote on the
procession: "The same remark (I wish also to be formally) made by me with respect to
the third degree *in the Godhead*, because I believe the Spirit *to proceed* from no other
source than from the Father through the Son" (Tertullian, *Praxeas*, 599).

210. Olson, *Story*, 96.

211. Tertullian, *Praxeas*, 603.

212. Olson, *Story*, 96.

of government by which God the Father rules. This divine government does not take away from the Trinity of God or God's "Dispensations."[213] The more literal use of "Son" compared to "Father," in addition to his premise of dispensations, appears in Tertullian's writings to show that Jesus Christ is less than the Father in some way, and the Holy Spirit is less than the Son. Also, in his attempt to show the oneness of the Holy Spirit to the Father and the Son, he gets caught in the classical discussion of the one who sends and the one who is sent as he understands John 14:16.[214] This send-sent discussion often negates equality and ends with the sender appearing superior to the one who is sent. God the Father is the sender who sends the Son and appears to be associated with the sending of the Holy Spirit.[215]

The above quote shows Tertullian's nature metaphors comparing the Trinity to a river, a tree, or the sun also fail to show true equality. The question might be asked, "How is the fruit equal to the root?" Tertullian would most definitely answer, "Essence." Thus, the Holy Spirit is the same substance as the Father, who is the supreme divine being. The distinctiveness is found in Tertullian's use of the *Economy* or *Dispensation* of God. Both words are a translation of Tertullian's use of *oikonomia*.[216] The *Economy* or *Dispensation* of God is the salvation plan of God. Therefore, Tertullian was straining to show both the oneness of God by describing the essence of the three persons under one monarchy and distinguishing their threeness as seen in the Father's will, the Son's sacrifice, and the sanctification of the Holy Spirit.[217] Finally, what is the Holy Spirit's role in this monarchy? Tertullian describes this role as connected to salvation history:

> . . . the Holy Spirit—the Third Name in the Godhead, and the Third Degree of the Divine Majesty; the Declarer of the One *Monarchy of God*, but at the same time the Interpreter of the *Economy*, to every one who hears and receives the words of the new prophecy; and "the Leader into all truth," such as is in the

---

213. Tertullian, *Praxeas*, 598–600. Tertullian uses the kingdom of God concept found in 1 Cor 15:24–8 and Ps 110:1 as scriptural basis.

214. Tertullian, *Praxeas*, 604.

215. Cf. John 14:15–17, 26; 15:26.

216. Tertullian, *Praxeas*, 598n9; 599n1; 603n14.

217. Tertullian, *Praxeas*, 598–600.

Father, and the Son, and the Holy Ghost, according to the mystery of the doctrine of Christ.[218]

Later, the Greek Fathers believed they were hearing Tertullian, and those of the West after him, to advocate "one *hypostasis*" in Greek from the Latin "one *substantia*."[219] This interpretation would advocate Sabellianism. However, the Latin Fathers believed the Greek-speaking East to be espousing a multiplicity of *hypostases*, thus tritheism.

It was the fourth century, and a close-knit group of bishops, pastors, and theologians from a small region of modern-day Turkey who, according to Zizioulas, *revolutionized* the debate with their specific and technical language concerning the Holy Trinity.[220] These were the Cappadocian Fathers, and their work eventually led not only to a clarification of the triunity of God but a definition of the two natures of Christ "particularized in one person" and a definition for the divinity of the Holy Spirit.[221]

In order to understand Zizioulas's contribution to trinitarian personhood, we have to turn to the Cappadocian Fathers who shaped Christian doctrine and in whom Zizioulas anchors much of his thought.[222] He relies primarily on the church fathers of the East while rejecting the trinitarian approach of the West as substance over persons stemming from

218. Tertullian, *Praxeas*, 627.

219. Chadwick, *East and West*, 13.

220. Zizioulas, *Lectures*, 50–51; Zizioulas, *Communion*, 118–24, 150, 155–56, 161–70. In Gunton, *One, Three, Many*, the language is not as strong as Zizioulas's "Cappadocian revolution" in reference to the Trinity and personhood, but Gunton accords the Cappadocians for "desynonymizing" *ousia* and *hypostasis* (Gunton, *One, Three, Many*, 191, 197). For the significant contribution of the Cappadocians, see Kärkkäinen, *Trinity*, 34–42. For the Cappadocian use of language in theological thought as it applies to *diastema* and *kinesis* (space and time) which led to the trinitarian formula, see Douglass, *Theology of the Gap*, 6–7, 195–204. The "heroes" of the ecumenical faith that led to the trinitarian faith were the Cappadocians, see Ware, *Father, Son, & Holy Spirit*, 39. Torrance gives special emphasis to the Cappadocian contribution on distinction between "Paternity," "Filiation," and "Spiration" within the Trinity (Torrance, *Trinitarian Faith*, 236). The Cappadocians moved the debate away from philosophy of Aristotle and back to the practice of faith lived out in the life of the Church (Florovsky, *Bible, Church, Tradition*, 108–9). However, Zizioulas's emphasis on "the Cappadocian revolution" toward an ontological statement is highly criticized and will be dealt with in chapter 3, "Zizioulas and Traditional Thought."

221. Zizioulas, *Communion*, 109, 179, 190–95.

222. For a critical review of Zizioulas's interpretation of the Cappadocian Fathers, see chapter 3, "Zizioulas and Traditional Thought."

Greek philosophy.[223] However, McFarlane reminds us that it is advantageous to hold the different traditions, East and West, in "harmony" rather than in "opposition" to one another, and in discovering truth, "we do not discover homogenized unity but mysterious diversity."[224]

Known as "one of the most imposing figures in ecclesiastical history" and "the most outstanding of all Alexandrian bishops," Athanasius has unquestionably influenced orthodox theology.[225] Much of Athanasius's theology was shaped by his refutation of Arius, who had espoused Origen's subordination of the Son to the Father and developed a created Son Christology.[226] At the core of Athanasius's response to Arius's theology was a need to connect the *Logos* with the Son making him part of the Trinity.[227] Athanasius built on Ignatius and Irenaeus's eucharistic theology to construct an "ontology of communion."[228] This "ontology of communion" was accomplished in two ways: (1) Athanasius "made a clear distinction between substance which he regarded as ultimate, and will, attributing to being the same ultimate character which it had always enjoyed in Greek thought,"[229] and (2) he "demonstrated that ontological otherness is an inevitable result of the distinction between will and nature" by presenting the existence of the world as a result of God's will rather than substance.[230] The magnitude of this distinction was that it broke the ancient Greek cosmology characterized as an ontological monism. With Ignatius and Irenaeus's emphasis on *life* in connection with *being* as established in the Eucharist, there is the identification with "immortality" and "incorruptibility" through the communion within the life of the Triune God.[231] Therefore, Athanasius connected the Son to the substance of God, and the world was created from the will of God. He says that the *hypostasis* is the *ousia* and exists (*hyparchis*) as being.[232] This

223. Zizioulas, *Being*, 40.

224. McFarlane, *Christ and the Spirit*, 28.

225. Quasten, *Patrology*, 20.

226. Origen, *De Principiis*, 1.2.6–8; Athanasius, *Against the Arians*, 1.4–6.

227. Zizioulas, *Being*, 83; Athanasius, *Heathen*, §§40–41; Athanasius, *Incarnation*, §§17–20; Athanasius, *Arians*, 1.4–6.

228. Zizioulas, *Being*, 83.

229. Zizioulas, *Being*, 83; Athanasius, *Arians*, 3.30.58–62.

230. Zizioulas, *Being*, 86–87; Athanasius, *Incarnation*, §3.

231. Zizioulas, *Being*, 82–83; Schaff, *Ante-Nicene Christianity*, 237–38, 241, 242–43.

232. Athanasius, *Historica* 1036 B.

etymological shift defined God as ultimately a free being. Furthermore, Athanasius gave a relational quality to substance as found in the *homoousion* of the Father and the Son. God the Father and the Son are in an eternal communion by definition of the one substance.[233]

The Nicene Creed (325 CE) defeated the tenets of Arianism for a time by making the Son consubstantial with the Father (*homoousion* and not *homoiousion*).[234] However, since Athanasius failed to distinguish between *ousia* and *hypostasis*, there was a need to further articulate the three persons' inter-relationship.[235] Arianism later resurfaced because of the stress on the *homoousion*. There was a tendency to give way to Sabellianism. Following the Nicene Creed, fourth-century Christianity was highly speculative as theologians, specifically, those of the Cappadocian region, engaged the issues of the Church not only with Scripture but also with Greek and Roman philosophy.[236] Furthermore, to accomplish this task of clarifying a truly trinitarian definition, there needed to be some linguistic redefinitions.

Basil's *On the Spirit* provides us with a comprehensive doctrine of the Holy Spirit along with a glimpse of the opposing views in his day (i.e., Arianism, Eunomianism [a form of Arianism], Sabellianism, and pneumatomachianism).[237] He began by critiquing the use and understanding of Greek prepositions by his opponents when describing the person and work of the Holy Spirit. This pneumatology was a lesson in exegesis and theology. He illustrated his point by describing the reaction he received when he recited the doxology in two different forms on two separate occasions. On one occasion, he quoted the doxology as, "God the Father *with* [μετά] the Son *together with* [σύν] the Holy Spirit," and on another occasion, "God the Father *through* [δία] the Son *in* [ἐν] the Holy Spirit."[238] The adverse reaction to the use of the preposition *with* revealed to Basil that there was a deeper issue among preachers, teachers, and bishops. Many viewed the persons of the Trinity as subordinate to

---

233. Zizioulas, *Being*, 84–86; Athanasius, "Letter LIX, To Epictetus," 574. Athanasius points out that the Son is not from the will of the Father, but that he is eternally begotten, *Arians*, 1.3–4.

234. Athanasius, *De Synodis*, 478–79.

235. Lonergan, *Way to Nicaea*, 104.

236. See, Olson, *Story*, 180; Wood, *God and History*, 39–40.

237. McConnell, *Illumination in Basil*, 1–8; Jackson, *Prolegomena*, 1.

238. Basil, *Spirit*, 1.3, 3.

one another.[239] Basil further argued that these opponents have neither the correct understanding of prepositions nor biblical metaphors. These opponents, Basil shows, associate the Holy Spirit with created matter and the Son with an instrument or tool in the hand of the craftsman, the Father.[240] Then leaving the argument on the Holy Spirit for a time, Basil discussed how the Son comes after the Father. Scripture proves that the Son is neither subordinate in time nor space. He is begotten, but that does not indicate that he was created or procreated. The Son always was, unlike the Arians, who proclaimed there was a time when the Son was not. A correct understanding of the biblical use of *begottenness* and Greek prepositions will lead one away from a subordinate view of the Son in time. Likewise, the Son is neither subordinate in space as Basil's opponents mishandled the metaphor of Hebrews 1:3, "he sat down at the right hand of the Majesty on high." Those who misunderstood this metaphor and other scriptural metaphors missed the equal glory and dignity of the Son with the Father as was indicated.[241]

Basil, Gregory of Nazianzus, and Gregory of Nyssa viewed their trinitarian formula through Platonic philosophy and the higher world of Ideas. Therefore they separated the terms *ousia* and *hypostasis*, which was causing such confusion. The term *ousia* was defined as divine substance or essence which is from *above*, while *hypostasis* became associated with *prosōpon* and the world of particulars as designated for individual identity.[242]

Zizioulas points out that this shift in terminology specifically made *hypostasis/prosōpon*/persons a relational term designated in expressing the "*Who*" of the Trinity. In other words, the Cappadocians were not saying that the trinitarian God *has* personhood; instead, God *is* person *a priori*, which precedes *beingness*.[243] "Personhood . . . has the claim of absolute being, that is, a metaphysical claim, built into it."[244] Zizioulas states his position on personhood this way:

> Personhood is not about qualities or capacities of any kind: bio-logical, social or moral. Personhood is about hypostasis, that is,

239. Basil, *Spirit*, 2.4, 4; 6.13, 8.

240. Basil, *Spirit*, chs. 3–4.

241. Basil, *Spirit*, ch. 6.

242. Basil, "Letter 38," 137–41.

243. Zizioulas, *Being*, 87–88; Zizioulas, *Communion*, 99–100.

244. Zizioulas, *Communion*, 100.

the claim to *uniqueness* in the absolute sense of the term and this cannot be guaranteed by reference to sex or function or role, or even cultivated consciousness of the "self" and its psychological experiences, since all of these can be *classified*, thus representing qualities shared by more than one being and not pointing to absolute uniqueness.[245]

Thus, the connection of personhood to *hypostasis* in this definition is to be discovered in the question of "Who I am?" rather than "What I am?" when speaking of a being.[246] At this point, Zizioulas has been accused of advancing an existential philosophy toward social trinitarianism, which he vehemently denies.[247] In Zizioulas's defense, these are philosophical concepts cast upon theology. He clarifies, "The theological concept of the person is drawn from the givens of the revelation of God in Christ, the revelation that presents to us 'how God is,' meaning His personal existence, without of course telling us anything about 'what God is,' meaning His nature or essence."[248] The "how God is" approach by Zizioulas begins with God as Father who is the cause of the "personal divine being" and thus the cause of the "personal divine existence" (the Trinity).[249] The accusations of personalism by Zizioulas's opponents are denied based on subjectivism and sociological roots. At the same time, his denial of existentialism reduces the person to a "thinking subject," leaving no room for love.[250] Both concepts raise communion to a third concept between nature and person.[251] Since humans are created in the *imago Dei*, the answer of human personhood must be connected to the *hypostasis* of the Triune God as was worked out at Nicaea and Constantinople (381) in the fourth century. Furthermore, Christology explicitly holds the key (Chalcedon 451), as Zizioulas demonstrates, giving us a particular priority in ontology.

---

245. Zizioulas, *Communion*, 111.

246. Zizioulas, *Communion*, 99–101, 110–12.

247. See Brown, "Criticism," 35–78; Zizioulas, "Appendix," 270–85; Zizioulas, *One and Many*, 17–40.

248. Zizioulas, *One and Many*, 38.

249. Zizioulas, *One and Many*, 39.

250. Critics accusing Zizioulas of personalism and existentialism include: De Halleux, "Personnalisme," parts 1 and 2; Turcescu, "Misreadings," 527–39; Wilks, "Ontology," 63–88.

251. Zizioulas, *One and Many*, 20–21.

SUMMARY

This chapter has traced and explained the theological and historical development behind Zizioulas's concepts of *person* and *Trinity* as denoting *being in communion*. In this concept, the Trinity is the model for personhood as being in communion/persons-in-relation. Zizioulas's trinitarian personhood model correlates and enhances Wesleyan theological anthropology that views the natural (original) human beings who were created in God's image (i.e., God is Spirit,[252] God is Love[253]) as (embodied) spirit and love[254] endowed with understanding, will, and liberty.[255]

The concept of personhood has developed and will continue to develop as long as humans ask and answer questions concerning life and the environment. In researching Zizoulas's basic theological tenets of *being in communion*, we traced the development from persons as substance to persons-in-relation in this chapter. We have seen from ancient philosophy these principles being developed, included was *beingness* and the connection to the One in primal matter of Platonic thought. However, the particulars were absorbed into the universal, where no meaning remained for the uniqueness of individual things. Aristotle attempted a slight reversal by investigating the particulars, which discovered concrete being through its matter and form. The concrete being denoted the nature trapped in substance. Being was an addition to the substance, but being was not absolute. For the Greeks, being was confined to the laws of nature, while for the Romans, it was bound by the laws of the state. The Jewish Old Testament set being free and gave it personal characteristics. Here, God is referred to as "I am who I am," revealing his personal freedom from the confines of the material world. In God's freedom, he created humans in his image and likeness and gifted them freedom.

Furthermore, the Jews recorded their personal existence as found in connection with this God and their community showing their identity was relational with God and one another. Christianity built on this foundation by presenting this personal God's devotion to his creation by incarnating the material world and entering human history with a message

252. Wesley, "Deliverance," 438; Wesley, "What Is Man?," 22–23.

253. Wesley, "New Birth," 188.

254. Wesley, "New Birth," 188.

255. Wesley, "Deliverance," 438–41; Wesley, "New Birth," 188; Wesley, "On the Fall of Man," 409. For more on this topic, see chapter 7, "Participation and Christian Anthropology."

and act of salvation. This message and act of salvation revealed the personhood of God as personal-relational. The personal-relational character of God and the salvation event for humans is not discovered by asking "What is God?" and "What is humanity?" God and humanity are discovered by asking "*Who* is God?" and "*Who* is humanity?"[256] In tracing the answers to these questions, one finds that God has revealed himself in a personal way as Father, Son, and Holy Spirit. While they are unique personally as Father, Son, and Holy Spirit, they are unified in their will and essence. Athanasius helped distinguish the substance of God from the will of God, thus offering a concept of otherness. Distinguishing the substance from the will of God toward an otherness focus established the early trinitarian doctrine and has become a model for personhood. God is three relational persons (*hypostases*) while simultaneously united in communion (*koinōnia*) by the Father's monarchy.[257] However, Zizioulas's presentation of the Father's monarchy is a debatable topic that we delve into throughout this book. Therefore, Zizioulas's definition of trinitarian personhood will, thus far, be examined against his use of patristic sources in chapter three and applied to contemporary thought in chapter four to develop a definition of trinitarian pneumatological personhood. After all, this is Zizioulas's typical approach, and that dogma must be understood first historically and secondly interpreted and applied to our modern-day.[258]

---

256. Zizioulas, *Communion*, 100–1.

257. Zizioulas, *One and Many*, 10–14. See Zizioulas, *Being*, 44–45n40.

258. Zizioulas, *Being*, 15–26; Zizioulas, *Communion*, 99; Zizioulas, "Preface," in *Lectures*, ix–x; Zizioulas, *One and Many*, 18.

Chapter 3

Zizioulas and Traditional Thought

> "Tradition is the witness of the Spirit;
> the Spirit's unceasing revelation
> and preaching of good tidings."
>
> —GEORGES FLOROVSKY[1]

INTRODUCTION

THE PURPOSE OF THIS chapter is to investigate Zizioulas's methodology. While Zizioulas is thoroughly Eastern Orthodox, being ordained as Metropolitan of Pergamon and bishop of the Ecumenical Patriarchate of Constantinople and Orthodox Co-President of the Joint International Commission for Theological Dialogue between the Catholic Church and the Orthodox Church, the more interesting fact is that he is critiqued for distorting Eastern Orthodoxy and misrepresenting the Tradition, especially the use of the early church fathers.[2] Therefore, the purpose of this chapter is to show more specifically the various ways in which Zizioulas remains theologically and methodologically aligned with the Orthodox Church while also showing the novelty of his theological approach. Zizioulas's critics and supporters refer to him as an Orthodox thinker and argue his theological points compared to Orthodoxy.[3] This chapter

1. Florovsky, *Bible, Church, Tradition*, 46.

2. See Turcescu, "Misreadings," 97–109.

3. E.g., Harrison, "Zizioulas," 273–300; De Halleux, "Personnalisme," 1:129–55; 2:265–92; Holmes, *Quest*, 12–16; Papanikolaou, *Being*; Papanikolaou, "Divine

takes an alternative approach by beginning with Orthodox thinking and showing how Zizioulas's theology has developed.

For the Western reader of Zizioulas's writings, the equality given in support of his thought to Scripture, the patristic fathers, and Conciliar Creeds is glaring in contrast to the typical Western Protestant, theological approach. In traditional Western Protestantism, these three are held in tension at times but most often are categorized in a hierarchy of relevance based on the inspiration of the Holy Spirit.[4] The Eastern Orthodox Church, on the other hand, equates Scripture and Tradition as one source of faith in one revelation of the One God who is Father, Son, and Holy Spirit.[5] For example, Basil defends the divinity of the Holy Spirit by substituting the pronoun "with" for "in" to express the communion of the Father, Son, and Holy Spirit.[6] In so doing, Basil confesses that this preposition ("with") concerning the Holy Spirit is *not* found in the Scriptures yet is harmonious with the Scriptures. Furthermore, he defends this action as consistent with the oral tradition or the mystery (*mystērion*) or "the tradition of the apostles."[7] Basil continues to speak extensively of this "unwritten authority" in the Church as significant so that if removed, it could "unintentionally injure the Gospels."[8] Therefore, the Eastern Orthodox Church hears Scripture and Tradition univocally: while they can be distinguished, they cannot be separated.[9] McGuckin helpfully describes tradition as "the gateway to the theology of revelation."[10] As such, tradition is not a museum display of the past; instead, it is the continuity of the Holy Spirit's inspiration of the whole Christian faith.

Energies," 357–85; Turcescu, "Misreadings," 527–39.

4. Dietrich, *Table Talks*, 93–95; Luther, *Genesis*, 297; Luther, *Penitents*, 226–27; Zwingli, *Word of God*, 49–95; Calvin, *Institutes*, 1.1–9; Outler, "Quadrilateral," 7–18; Rack, "Deed of Declaration," 92; Oden, *Scriptural Christianity*, 55–99; Wesley, "On Sin in Believers," 144–56.

5. Papadopoulos, "Revelatory Character and Holy Tradition," 98, 102.

6. Basil, *Spirit*, 1.3, 3.

7. Basil, *Spirit*, 27.65–66.

8. Basil, *Spirit*, 27.66.

9. Lossky, "Tradition and Traditions," 127.

10. McGuckin, *Orthodox*, 90.

ZIZIOULAS IN "THE HOLY TRADITION"

The Eastern Orthodox speak much of the Holy Tradition, and Zizioulas refers heavily to Tradition. What is the Orthodox understanding of Tradition, and what makes it *holy*? It is important to note that the Eastern Orthodox concept of Tradition is complex by their admission.[11] For example, McGuckin calls the Tradition "central" "for Orthodox theological life,"[12] and Meyendorff says it is "unalterable and universally binding."[13] Florovsky describes life learning in the Church as not accomplished so much *from* Tradition as one learns *in* Tradition.[14] This Tradition of the Eastern Orthodox Church is vitally important because it is inseparable from the Person and the Work of the Holy Spirit. However, McGuckin has been careful to point out that some within the Eastern Orthodox Church unintentionally mistake Tradition for "the customs of men," which Jesus himself so often railed against in the Gospels.[15] Others argue strongly that the customs or traditions of men or people groups, in general, are dead traditions while the Tradition of the Church is *living* and *holy* because the Holy Spirit constitutes it.

No one writer within Eastern Orthodoxy proposes a comprehensive understanding of Tradition because it signifies "every ecclesiastical custom."[16] McGuckin further explains,

> The Orthodox Christian doctrine of tradition is thus an ancient and richly complex idea, which is no less than an investigation of the inner roots of Christian consciousness in history; and indeed more than this—for it is the tracing of the presence of the Divine Spirit in Christ's church across the ages.[17]

An example of the vast extent and complexity of Orthodox Tradition is influenced by John of Damascus's *Orthodox Faith* which contains one hundred topics dealing with doctrine, creation, Christology, and

---

11. Lossky, "Tradition and Traditions," 126; McGuckin, "Tradition," 489; Zizioulas, *One and Many*, 126–35, 136–46.

12. McGuckin, "Tradition," 487.

13. Meyendorff, *Orthodox*, 190.

14. Florovsky, *Bible, Church, Tradition*, 46.

15. McGuckin, *Orthodox*, 90; *TGNT* uses the word *paradosis* which McGuckin translates "custom" and most English versions translate "tradition" (Matt 15:2, 3, 6; Mark 7:5, 8, 9, 13).

16. McGuckin, "Tradition," 487.

17. McGuckin, "Tradition," 489.

Christian worship.[18] The purpose here is not to present such a definition as it is to offer a basic concept by which we can interpret and evaluate Zizioulas's work. The Eastern Orthodox deeply appreciates the issue of time and space.[19] Thus Tradition is understood as the truth of God to the Church (space, i.e., *loci*), which supersedes time yet is lived out in one's context. Papadopoulos emphasizes the dynamic character of Tradition.

> Holy Tradition is a divine process; it is not ours but God's, reaching out from the *soma* to the fulness of the *pleroma*. Holy Tradition is not something static, to be safeguarded by dogmatic formulas; it is the dynamic movement of God in history, in which man shares as part of the perfect humanity of Christ. It is in this sense that we care to speak of the tradition as *Holy*. For in the light of the resurrection and the mystery of Pentecost we come to recognize, in spite of our sin, the holiness of God, Who, by the action of His love in sending to us His Son, has made us once for all His children by adoption. This is the core of our faith, the solid rock of the apostolic kerygma.[20]

The Eastern Orthodox view of Tradition is best understood as the *dogma* and *kērygma* of the Church. As seen in the quote above, *dogma* in the Orthodox sense is *not* understood as a doctrinal formula or definition; rather, it is understood as the oral apostolic teaching handed down from generation to generation, which is the charism (gift) of truth.[21] Lossky, referring to Basil, describes *dogma* as the "secret tradition" handed down and publically preached (*kērygma*) to the Church. It is the faithful Church

---

18. John of Damascus, *Faith*, 1–101.

19. For the subject of space and time in creation, see Basil, *Hexaemeron*, 1.5–6, 54–55; see also Gregory of Nyssa, *Eunomius*, 1.26; Meyendorff, *Orthodox*, 193–94; For space and time applied to creation, salvation, and the Church, see Lossky, *Mystical Theology*, 102–3. For a presentation of the issues and problems of space and time as first demonstrated in the Nicene-Constantinopolitan Creed illustrating that God incarnated the created world for salvation, see Torrance, *Space, Time, and Incarnation.* For space and time applied to the language of the Cappadocians and the trinitarian formula, see Douglas, *Theology of the Gap*, 6–7. For space and time in Orthodox worship, see Ware, "Earthly Heaven," 19. For space and time applied to the Eucharist, see Zizioulas, *Eucharist*, 114–15.

20. Papadopoulos, "Revelatory Character and Holy Tradition," 101.

21. Basil, *Spirit*, 27.66; Florovsky, *Bible, Church, Tradition*, 57, 86–87, 106, 107, 109; Lossky, "Tradition and Traditions," 128–29; Meyendorff, *Orthodox*, 190–207. Also on the phrase "*charism* (gift) of truth," see Irenaeus, *Heresies*, 4.26.2; McGuckin, *Orthodox*, 91.

who understands the "mysterious meaning" of the proclaimed word.[22] Florovsky indicates that the continuity of the message in Tradition is "the witness of the Spirit."[23] That is to say, the Holy Spirit reveals the truth and the truthfulness of the proclaimed word to the Church, not simply historically but eternally encompassing the future as well. Two things can be unclear at this point within the Eastern Orthodox Tradition: (1) the truth and (2) knowledge or the ability to know the truth.

Again, for traditional Western Protestantism, whose theological propositions begin with *sola Scriptura*, in comparison to Orthodox Tradition, there is yet anything to hang one's theological hat on. In other words, the Eastern Orthodox emphasis on Tradition sounds abstract and fluid to Western Protestantism. The difference is that the Eastern Orthodox Church does not separate Scripture and Tradition; rather, each supports and constitutes the other.[24] While the Holy Tradition of the Orthodox Church includes many instruments, outlets, or rays from one light source by which to express the Christian faith similar to the refraction of light through stained glass, the Scriptures remain superior to other expressions of the Tradition.[25] "The Scriptures," says McGuckin, "stand as far greater in moment, and richness, than any writing of the saints. However, there is not a profound difference in order, and not a dissonance of quality, for it is the same Spirit who inspires his saints in each generation, and inspires in them the same mind of the self-same Lord."[26] Furthermore, McGuckin argues that Scripture is inseparable from the Tradition. Thus, "Scripture . . . is one of the purest manifestations of tradition. It is constitutively within sacred tradition, not apart from it."[27] Therefore the truth or truthfulness in Tradition is located in the continuity of these outlets whether they be the "secret tradition" (*dogma*), proclamation of the word (*kērygma*), written (*grapha*) or unwritten (*agrapha*).[28] Truth is equated with the Word of God. As such, then, the Tradition contains the Word of God, but the Word of God is expressed in different venues, and yet, is one consistent truth. Therefore,

22. Lossky, "Tradition and Traditions," 129.

23. Florovsky, *Bible, Church, Tradition*, 46.

24. McGuckin, *Orthodox*, 101.

25. See Ware, *Orthodox Way*, 109–11.

26. McGuckin, *Orthodox*, 101.

27. McGuckin, *Orthodox*, 101.

28. Lossky, "Tradition and Traditions," 129–30. See Irenaeus, *Heresies*, 4.26.2.

the purpose of a standard of truth is to combat and clarify distorted and heretical teaching. Irenaeus knew the importance of a standard of truth: most of his ministry was spent fighting Gnosticism. While he spoke of this unwritten truth from the Apostles handed down to the Church, he also understood the dangers of secret or "strange doctrines" that were inconsistent with the *dogma* and *kērygma* of the Church.[29] Furthermore, Irenaeus stressed the importance of correct handling of the Scriptures to clarify the "canon of truth."[30] Therefore, it is not surprising that Florovsky and other Eastern Orthodox writers use Irenaeus's analogy of a master artist who creates a mosaic of jewels to depict a *beautiful* portrait of a king. Then comes an observer who removes the jewels and rearranges the pieces of the portrait to depict a *crude* resemblance of a dog and declares that this new mosaic is the correct likeness of the king.[31] However, it is not a methodology or a paradigm that gives Tradition its truthfulness. Since the truth is God's truth and the words of Scripture are God's words, it is then the Holy Spirit, the Spirit of Truth, who reveals all the truth and inspires the truth.[32] Who, then, may receive the truth?

Many groups before and after Christ have staked a claim as sole proprietors of truth. However, it is Jesus Christ who claimed not simply to own truth, but rather he claimed to *be* the truth.[33] Following Jesus's ministry on earth, Jesus promised that the Church would receive the Spirit of truth.[34] Therefore, the truthfulness of the Holy Tradition, for the Orthodox Church, is inspired by the Spirit of truth expressed in various ways (e.g., Scripture, Tradition, patristic writings, Conciliar Creeds, Orthodox symbolic books, Pedalion/Holy Canons, liturgy, etc.).[35] The Spirit of truth gives the charism of truth to the Church and the knowledge and ability to discern and know the truth. Irenaeus has pointed out that while the Church is scattered throughout the world, she is held together in her catholicity by a uniting truth manifested in the person of Jesus Christ.[36] This harmonic truth is known as the "rule of faith" (*regula fidei*), which

29. Irenaeus, *Heresies*, 4.26.2.

30. Florovsky, *Bible, Church, Tradition*, 77–79.

31. Irenaeus, *Heresies*, 1.8.1.

32. Lossky, "Tradition and Traditions," 132; McGuckin, *Orthodox*, 101–2.

33. John 14:6; cf. Exod 3:14; John 1:1; 8:31–32, 58; Heb 10:20; 2 John 1.

34. John 14:16–17; 15:26; 16:13.

35. McGuckin, *Orthodox*, 100–115; Papadopoulos, "Revelatory Character and Holy Tradition," 102–3.

36. Irenaeus, *Heresies*, 1.10.1–2.

Florovsky describes as the "intent" and "design" of the Scriptures, and Irenaeus calls the unchanged and immovable truth received at baptism.[37] Athanasius, in turn, built his arguments on the "rule of faith" and called for the Church to also use the "scope (*skopos*) of faith" when interpreting the Scriptures.[38] Here again, in fighting heresy, Athanasius refers to the *intention* of the Holy Scriptures as a means of knowing the truth. When defending the faith, this knowledge of truth was often spelled out in creedal language by the church fathers.[39] McGuckin further explains that this knowledge of truth is the mind of Christ as the charismatic life within the Orthodox Church.[40]

Finally, the Holy Tradition for the Eastern Orthodox is a *Living* Tradition. The Tradition is simultaneously mystical and concrete. The mystery of the Tradition is found in its pneumatologically constituted manner. Without the inspiration of the Holy Spirit, there is no Holy, Living Tradition; there would only be cold, dead customs of humanity. Furthermore, the Holy Spirit brings life in abundance through the transformation of people's lives.[41] This transformation is not achieved "simply by reading the Word of God or through a knowledge of dogmas, but by dying and rising again with Christ in Baptism, by receiving the seal of the Spirit in Confirmation, by becoming members of the actual body of Christ in the Eucharist, and finally by making progress in ever greater knowledge, until we attain the 'stature of the man-made in Jesus Christ' (Eph. iv.13)."[42] Here lies the complexity of Tradition, which Lossky presents as the intersection of the horizontal line and the vertical line.[43] The new, transformed life offered by the Church is human participation in the life of God through the Holy Spirit.[44]

Human participation in the divine life of the Holy Trinity is a paradox of absurdity and profoundness; nevertheless, this is Lossky's "intersection." He describes the horizontal line as Tradition with all of its oral and written features. The vertical line is the communion of the Holy

---

37. Florovsky, *Bible, Church, Tradition*, 79; Irenaeus, *Heresies*, 1.9.4–5.

38. Florovsky, *Bible, Church, Tradition*, 80–82. Also, Leithart, *Athanasius*, 39–41.

39. Athanasius, *Arians*, 1.3.8–9; Irenaeus, *Heresies*, 1.10.1; Basil, *Spirit*, 9.22.

40. McGuckin, *Orthodox*, 91–92. The Church is the *true* Church made possible by the Holy Spirit; see Behr, "Trinitarian Being," 174–76.

41. Rom 12:1–2.

42. Meyendorff, *Orthodox*, 192.

43. Lossky, "Tradition and Traditions," 130.

44. Lossky, *Mystical Theology*, 188.

Spirit and the moment of intersection is the "gnosis of God" through the "sacramental initiation."[45] The sacraments are the concrete "quantifiable reality," while the pneumatologically constituted Tradition is the mystical grace.[46] This dynamic reality is life in the Spirit, experienced in the Church, through the Holy Tradition.

Zizioulas uses the Orthodox Tradition in his methodology as found in his references to the Scriptures, church fathers, Conciliar Creeds, and liturgy. However, his use of Tradition cannot be taken for granted as he challenges the Orthodox consciousness and understanding of Tradition. The core of the Holy Tradition is the inspiration of the Holy Spirit witnessed in the continuity of the apostolic succession (i.e., the transmission of the message). This pneumatologically constituted continuity witnesses to the truthfulness of the word of God (*dogma*) and is that which is to be proclaimed (*kērygma*). Zizioulas's concern is with the outcome of this concept which may lead to a dualism being a traditionalist mindset and the practices of triumphalism.[47] Consequently, Zizioulas challenges traditional Orthodox concepts regarding *continuity of the apostolic succession* by saying that hidden within the Scriptures and the patristic writers are two distinct approaches. The first concerns the "historical" approach, and the second concerns the "eschatological" approach to "apostolic continuity."[48] Both are equally relevant.

The "historical" approach to "apostolic continuity" understands the classical understanding of apostle (*apostolos*) as the "sent one" into the world with a mission and a message. The stress of this concept, says Zizioulas, is upon the apostle as a person or individual making it applicable and authoritative to all missionaries who have the *charisma* to preach the gospel.[49] This apostolic-charisma is the picture that we get from the New Testament.[50] The picture and the purpose of Pentecost in

---

45. Lossky, "Tradition and Traditions," 130–31. Zizioulas also uses this diagram of the horizontal and vertical lines intersecting at the moment of Eucharist (Zizioulas, *Eucharist*, 18).

46. McGuckin, *Orthodox*, 92.

47. Zizioulas, *Being*, 171. These potential issues are a concern with others in Eastern Orthodoxy. See Bratsiotis, "Fundamental Principles," 23–31.

48. Zizioulas, *Being*, 172–75. See also Congar, "Appendix: Two Theologies," in *Holy Spirit*, 50–51.

49. Zizioulas, *Being*, 172–73. For further development on mission see the subhead "Participation in the Mission of God" under chapter 7, "Participation and Christian Anthropology."

50. Newbigin, *Gospel*, 116–27.

Acts 2 are that Jesus's disciples "become the place where the Spirit speaks and acts."[51] Therefore, the mission is not so much the disciples' mission or our mission as it is God's mission through his faithful followers made possible by the presence of the Holy Spirit in a new reality.[52] However, it is a scriptural presentation and one that is expounded upon by the church fathers. Zizioulas quotes 1 Clement, "'God sends Christ—Christ sends the apostles'" this "becomes the basis for the notion of continuity in terms of historical process: 'The apostles have announced to us the good news from Jesus Christ. Jesus Christ was sent by God. Thus Christ comes from God and the apostles from Christ. This double mission therefore, with its order comes from the will of God.'"[53] The "historical" approach has been the acceptable understanding toward the continuity of apostolic succession within the Holy Tradition.

Zizioulas adds a second approach to "apostolic continuity," the "eschatological" approach. This approach understands the apostles scripturally as not only "the sent out ones" but also as a "college" of apostles "gathered" around the throne of God in his Kingdom initiating the holy "convocation" "of dispersed people."[54] The "eschatological" approach stands in paradox to the "historical" approach. However, Zizioulas is careful in qualifying his use of "eschatology," explaining that there is a difference between "eschatology conceived as *orientation*" and "eschatology conceived as a *state* of existence."[55]

> As orientation, eschatology appears to be the *result of historical process* as the climax of mission . . . , whereas as a state of existence it confronts history already now with *a presence from beyond history*. In the latter case an "iconic" and liturgical approach to eschatology is necessary more than it is in the former. It is the understanding of eschatology as this kind of *presence* of the Kingdom here and now that requires convocation of the dispersed people of God and of the apostles. As such this image *presupposes the end of mission*. This proleptic experience of the presence of the eschata here and now—and not simply the

51. Newbigin, *Gospel*, 118.

52. Newbigin, *Gospel*, 119.

53. Zizioulas, *Being*, 176.

54. Zizioulas, *Being*, 174–75.

55. Zizioulas, *Being*, 174n11.

orientation towards this end—was there from the beginning (Acts 2:17) and was realised mainly in the eucharist (*Didache*).[56]

Zizioulas draws on Ignatius of Antioch for one who represents the view that the Church enters into an eschatological state when participating (i.e., the "coming together") in prayer and the Eucharist around the altar and bishop.[57]

Using McGuckin's categories in which the Tradition is both mystical and concrete, Zizioulas also suggests the same in his synthesis of the historical and eschatological approach to "apostolic continuity."[58] Mystical grace, thus, for Zizioulas is observed in the truth of continuity as demonstrated in the "historical" approach of the apostolic succession. Such an approach deals with "transmission" of authority and power in the "normal" way of copied (or rehearsed) Tradition, which "creates the basis of a *retrospective* continuity with the past."[59] The mystical grace is understood as the inspiration of the Holy Spirit making possible the continuity of *dogma* in linear history. In contrast, Zizioulas proposes a concrete image found in the eschatological approach that views the future in "anticipation of the end, the final nature of the Church that reveals her apostolic character."[60] In this view, "all of history is consummated," and the "real *presence* of the eschata is here and now."[61] Thus, the concrete view of Tradition is realized in the community of faith around the Eucharist.[62]

Theologically, both the historical and the eschatological approaches are necessary for an apostolic continuity of the Church.[63] The historical approach, argues Zizioulas, "provides the structure of continuity."[64] The

---

56. Zizioulas, *Being*, 174n11.

57. Zizioulas, *Being*, 176–77. See Ignatius, *Ephesians*, ch. 5; Ignatius, *Magnesians*, ch. 7.

58. McGuckin, *Orthodox*, 92. It should be noted that for Zizioulas the synthesis of the mystical and concrete categories along with the synthesis of the historical and eschatological approaches to Tradition are inseparable from the Eucharist. He says, "Transmission of priesthood, or *the consolidation and continuation of the canonical unity of the Church outside the Eucharist was and has remained inconceivable*" (Zizioulas, *Eucharist*, 18–19).

59. Zizioulas, *Being*, 178.

60. Zizioulas, *Being*, 178.

61. Zizioulas, *Being*, 179.

62. See Zizioulas, *Eucharist*, 16–19, as Zizioulas spells out his eucharistic-ecclesiological methodology toward theology.

63. Zizioulas, *Being*, 181.

64. Zizioulas, *Being*, 179; Zizioulas, *Lectures*, 7.

structure is centered in Christ (Christology) *who* "transmits" the Holy Spirit upon the apostles in order that they may accomplish their mission; the Holy Spirit is "the *agent* of Christ," and "vivifies *pre-existing* and *self-existing events* and relates them to different times and circumstances."[65] In this historical approach, Zizioulas articulates an *ordo operandi*. That is, the Tradition of the Church finds its significance in the continuity of the apostolic succession. However, Zizioulas points out that the Holy Spirit does a new thing in the eschatological approach by bringing the future into history. "By bringing the eschata into history, the Spirit does not vivify a pre-existing structure," says Zizioulas, "He *creates* one; He changes linear historicity into a *presence*."[66] Since the Holy Spirit is not bound by history, but instead operates in a boundless and free manner, even revealing the future in the present[67] when synthesizing the eschatological with the historical approaches to the understanding of Tradition, the Spirit of truth is able to empower the Church to have a "*memory of the future*."[68]

It is of interest to note that at the root of Zizioulas's historical and eschatological approaches to Tradition lies a methodological practice in paradox.[69] Thus, Zizioulas views the segmented theological world as narrow in its theological reasoning. Therefore, as seen above, he believes Tradition is more than "historical" but simultaneously "eschatological." This motivation is partially due to Zizioulas's ecumenical participation in the World Council of Churches.[70] Thus, while Zizioulas makes use of the paradox in several different applications (e.g., unity and diversity,[71] uni-

---

65. Zizioulas, *Being*, 179–80.

66. Zizioulas, *Being*, 180.

67. John 3:8.

68. John 14:26; 16:13; Zizioulas, *Being*, 180.

69. The methodology of paradox in theology is not seminal with Zizioulas. The Eastern Orthodox use paradox quite frequently as found in Florovsky, *Bible, Church, Tradition*, 115, on God as knowable versus "incomprehensible." In Bratsiotis, "Fundamental Principles," the "human element" and the "divine element" or "freedom and authority" (Bratsiotis, "Fundamental Principles," 24). In Meyendorff, *Orthodox*, "divine grace" and "freewill" (Meyendorff, *Orthodox*, 193), also "personal piety" (*hesychasm*) and "corporate liturgy" (Meyendorff, *Orthodox*, 201). In Lossky, "essence and energies" (Lossky, *Mystical Theology*, 67–90). In Ware, God's "Otherness" and "Nearness" (Ware, *Orthodox Way*, 11–13). In Schmemann, "Heaven on earth" as a fundamental concept of the Church (Schmemann, "Missionary Imperative," 197–99).

70. See Zizioulas, *One and Many*, 309–413.

71. Zizioulas, *One and Many*, 54, 73, 84, 260, 261, 265, 310, 326, 333–48.

versal and local,[72] "in-stitute" and "con-stitute,"[73] personal and catholic,[74] mystical and concrete,[75] created and uncreated,[76] human capacity and human incapacity),[77] there is none more central to Zizioulas's theology than "the one and the many." Therefore, we will observe Zizioulas's use of "the one and the many" as a prototype in his methodological practice of paradox.

The concept of "the one and the many" is profound to Zizioulas's thought.[78] Zizioulas uses this theological paradigm to address the Trinity, humanity, Jesus Christ, the Church, the Eucharist, and Church Polity. At the core of the-one-and-the-many is a question rooted in ancient philosophy as investigated in chapter 1, which inevitably asks, "What came first, the general or the particular?" In other words, "Does human nature precede individual people or do individual people precede human nature?" This question deals with origin. As a theologian answering this question, Zizioulas begins by discussing God and *how* God is Triune.[79] Therefore, to transpose the question to the topic of the Trinity, "Does the Threeness (Persons) of God precede the Oneness (Essence) or does the Oneness (Essence) precede the Threeness (Persons)?" We find that

72. Zizioulas, *Being*, 134–35, 257–60; Zizioulas, *Eucharist*, 107–28, 149–62; Zizioulas, *Lectures*, 140–45; Zizioulas, *One and Many*, 52–57.

73. Zizioulas, *Being*, 140; Zizioulas, *Eucharistic Communion*, 67–73; Zizioulas, *One and Many*, 14–16.

74. Zizioulas, *Eucharist*, 108–10, 112–15, 117; Zizioulas, "Informal Groups," 284, 293, 295.

75. Defined by Zizioulas as historical and eschatological (Zizioulas, *Being*, 178–79); Zizioulas, *Communion*, 286–307; Zizioulas, *One and Many*, 30, 129.

76. Zizioulas, *Communion*, 14–32, 250–69; Zizioulas, *Lectures*, 91–98.

77. Zizioulas, "Capacity and Incapacity," 401–48; Zizioulas, *Communion*, 206–48.

78. Zizioulas, *Being*, 136–39; Zizioulas, *Communion*, 107, 145–46; Zizioulas, *Eucharist*, 54–58, 67; Zizioulas, *Eucharistic Communion*, 12–19; Zizioulas, *Lectures*, 50–54. Cf. Gunton, *One, Three, Many*, who sees "the one and the many" concept as a theological engagement with modernity and the presentation of trinitarian transcendentalism beginning with a relational definition of the *imago Dei* (Gunton, *One, Three, Many*, 188–96). For a canonical history and hermeneutic dealing with the similar thought and methodology of "the one and the many," see Dunn, *Unity and Diversity*; Dunn, *Neither Jew Nor Greek*, 816–19. In *Eucharist*, Zizioulas says, "Through this link with the consciousness that in Christ the 'many' are united in the One, the Eucharist appeared as the highest expression of the Church as body of Christ" (Zizioulas, *Eucharist*, 67).

79. Zizioulas is very clear that the "What" question concerning God refers to *ousia* of being, while the "How" question refers to *hypostasis* of being. Both are equally relevant on the *beingness* of God. See Zizioulas, *Communion*, 125, 129.

ancient philosophy would state from a monistic view that the absolute One precedes the particulars[80] or that the species (what is common) precedes the individual thing.[81] Referencing the Cappadocian Fathers, Zizioulas emphasizes the "revolutionary move" to separate essence and *hypostasis* so that on the one hand, essence would be synonymous with "substance" and "nature" (*ousia*). On the other hand, *hypostasis* would be synonymous with the (unique) person making *hypostasis* an "ontological category."[82] Therefore, God's being is simultaneously spoken of as "being" as essence (i.e., divinity) and "being" as particular beings (i.e., Father, Son, Holy Spirit). "Being" as essence/nature is to speak of what is common/general in God. To speak of God's essence as being what is common in God is to imply that there are many (more than one).[83] Basil reminds Amphilochius that believers must confess God's "one essence or substance" and "confess a particular hypostasis" through an act of faith and practice as found in the creedal phrases: "I believe in God the Father," "I believe in God the Son," "I believe in God the Holy Spirit."[84] While Zizioulas confesses, that both the "substance" of God and the "person" of God are "co-fundamental" and "neither is prior to the other"; he also states "In God, too, it is not divine nature that is the origin of the divine persons. It is the person of the Father who 'causes' God to exist as Trinity."[85] Here it appears that Zizioulas has contradicted his argument by placing the "One" above the "many," however, he is stressing the point that ancient philosophy is irrational in that "there is no bare essence."[86] The way that Zizioulas justifies his point of the Father as the cause of God to exist as Trinity is also to say that the particular person does not exist outside of community. The "Father" can only be such if there is a "Son," and without the "Son," there is no "Father."

> This plurality and interdependence of the persons is the basis of
> a new ontology. The one essence is not the origin or cause of the

---

80. Plato, *Parmenides*, 137C.

81. Aristotle, "Categories," in Aristotle, *Selections*, 1.

82. Zizioulas, *Lectures*, 50–51; Zizioulas, *Communion*, 103–6, 111, 118–20, 124–26.

83. Zizioulas, *Lectures*, 51.

84. Basil, *Letters*, 236.6.

85. Zizioulas, *Lectures*, 52–53. This thought is found in Basil and his use of "Monarchy" to describe "the one and the many" with his phrase "unity and multitude" or "one and plurality" (Basil, *Spirit*, 18.44–45).

86. Zizioulas, *Being*, 41; Zizioulas, *Communion*, 125; Zizioulas, *Lectures*, 52; Zizioulas, *One and Many*, 22.

being of God. It is the person of the Father that is the ultimate agent, but since "Father" implies communion he cannot be understood as a being in isolation. Personal communion lies at the very heart of divine being.[87]

Therefore, the new ontology is also described by this phrase, "persons in communion," indicating not that the three persons in communion move simultaneously directed by the one essence, rather the one Father moves himself, the Son, and the Holy Spirit by his one will, one power, one mind, revealing the movement of God is by a person rather than an essence.[88] In other words, the Triune God moves or works toward humanity not because of his essence, which means he has to, but because of his will, which means he wants to—his love is toward another.

"Love," says Zizoulas, "is this communion of relationships which give us our existence."[89] In Zizioulas's theology, human origin can be articulated from his paradoxical axiom of the-one-and-the-many resulting from love that actually precedes human existence and is the outgrowth of the *imago Dei*. All of this occurs in the one unity of the three persons of the Holy Trinity and is stated as "God is love."[90] Therefore, it can be said that relationship and communion are initially motivated by love defining the Holy Trinity's interpersonal communion (i.e., holy communion).

In addition to the Trinity as the source of love and communion, since person precedes essence in Zizioulas's theology, humanity must point its existence back toward a particular one, which is Adam.[91] It is not the nature of humanity that is the human origin, rather the one Adam who is divisible into the many, which makes the nature/species of humanity. Adam was created by the will of the one God who spoke within the holy communion (i.e., divine inter-communication) of the three persons and said, "Let *us* make man in *our* image, after *our* likeness."[92] However,

---

87. Zizioulas, *Lectures*, 53.

88. Zizioulas, *Communion*, 131. This is the theological explanation of "Monarchy" which is used by the Cappadocian Fathers. See Basil, *Spirit*, ch. 18; Gregory of Nazianzus, *Orations*, "On the Son," 29.2. See also the concept of the submission of the Son to the will of the Father, Gregory of Nazianzus, *Orations*, "On the Son," §5.

89. Zizioulas, *Lectures*, 53.

90. Zizioulas, *Lectures*, 53. See also Johnson, *She Who Is*, 227–28; Kärkkäinen, *Trinity*, 52, 60–61.

91. Zizioulas, *Lectures*, 52.

92. Gen 1:26; emphasis mine. Notice the first person plural of נַעֲשֶׂה (first person, common plural, cohortive, qal, imperfect: "Let us make"), בְּצַלְמֵנוּ (first person, common plural, masculine singular construct: "in our image"), כִּדְמוּתֵנוּ (first person,

the freedom of the one Adam resulted in the violation of God's will and communion, leading to ex-communion with God and selfishness among other humans, which Zizioulas refers to as "boundaries of the 'self.'"[93] This act separated the many humans from the one God. Furthermore, the other-oriented love that originated from the Trinity and was the motivation for creating human beings became curved in upon the self in Adam's disobedience which broke communion and relationship between God and humans and is the cause of discord between humans and humans.[94] Thus, the answer to mend the communion between God and humans is found in the one Suffering Servant of God who takes upon himself the many sins of the multitude.[95] Jesus Christ identifies with the many; thus, he is the one-for-the-many.

For Zizioulas, Jesus Christ is the "catholic" man in that he is "one" in his "schesis" with God the Father in the Holy Spirit, and "many" in the same "schesis" "in that the same 'schesis' becomes now the constitutive element—the *hypostasis*—of all those whose particularity and uniqueness and therefore ultimate being is constituted through the same filial relationship which constitutes Christ's being."[96] Zizioulas is saying that for a particular person to exist, persons must exist in relationship. In like manner, human personhood is obtained through relationships, and more specifically, a relationship with Jesus Christ.[97] This approach to Chris-

---

common plural, feminine singular construct: "after our likeness").

93. Zizioulas, *Communion*, 213, 214.

94. Zizioulas, "Capacity and Incapacity," 407–33; Kinlaw, *Mind*, 101–4.

95. Isaiah 40–53; Zizioulas, *Eucharistic Communion*, 12. This view of Christian anthropology is further developed in part 2, "Trinitarian Pneumatological Personhood," and summarized in chapter 7, "Participation and Christian Anthropology."

96. Zizioulas, "Capacity and Incapacity," 438. Zizioulas defines "schesis" as "relation" or "relationship" and is connected to personhood, rather than the Koine Greek: condition, habit, nature, or disposition (Zizioulas, "Capacity and Incapacity," 436–37; cf. Zizioulas, *Communion*, 131–32). Zizioulas synonymously refers to Jesus Christ as the "corporate person" (Zizioulas, *Eucharistic Communion*, 105).

97. In McConville, *Being Human*, the human aspect of being created in the image and in "godlikeness" is a relational one in connection with God and with humans (McConville, *Being Human*, 11–29). For Pannenberg, the fulfillment of the "image of God" in humans is found in the resurrected Jesus Christ where human beings are to bear Christ's image as a Christian anthropology (Pannenberg, *Anthropology*, 79). Furthermore, Pannenberg, states, "The correspondence between the image of God in human beings and the trinitarian life of God is in fact fulfilled in the human community and specifically in the community of God's kingdom (Pannenberg, *Anthropology*, 531). Sanders, *Deep*, 131–53.

tology through relations of persons is quite the opposite of beginning from the substance or natures used by the Latin Fathers or Greek philosophers.[98] Furthermore, the one person Jesus Christ bridges the gap between the created and the uncreated through the historical event of the Resurrection.[99] That is to say, on one end of the spectrum, Jesus Christ, the Son of God, who is eternal, "becomes history" for the sake of humans by entering human history.[100] In this way, Jesus Christ becomes the-one-for-the-many. On the other end of the spectrum, Jesus Christ is also "the eschatological man" by speaking the words of the kingdom of God and connecting the Church with the kingdom of God through the participation of the Eucharist.[101] For Jesus Christ to be both the historical man and the eschatological man, he must be pneumatologically constituted in that the ontological personhood of Christ is a communion of relations with the Father, in the Spirit.[102]

This ontological personhood of Christ as a communion of relations is demonstrated in the one-and-many concept applied to the Church. This concept means the Church is not understood individualistically (i.e., as autonomous; cf. individual person or local church), rather relationally— in this manner it is literally a *com-unity* of persons in *com-union* with one God and with others. Furthermore, the Church "of Christ" is simultaneously the symbol of history and eschatology.[103] That is to say, the "symbolism in the Church is based on historical events" (the Christ event) along

98. Zizioulas, *Being*, 54–59. See Pope Leo I's "Tome" to Flavian for which he condemns Eutyches's view of two natures of Jesus Christ. Leo's argument, while effective, is an argument from substance or nature rather than relations of persons, which is Zizioulas's critique. Leo, "Letter XXVIII," 28.2.

99. Zizioulas, *One and Many*, 104–6.

100. Zizioulas, *Being*, 130, 160–61, 184–86.

101. Zizioulas, *Being*, 183–88.

102. Zizioulas, *Being*, 130, 185–86; Zizioulas, "Capacity and Incapacity," 439–42; Zizioulas, *One and Many*, 95, 138. Zizioulas says, "The Spirit is the *beyond* history, and when he acts in history he does so in order to bring into history the last days, the *eschato*. . . . The Spirit makes of Christ an eschatological being, the 'last Adam'" (Zizioulas, *Being*, 130). It is precisely this work of the Holy Spirit in the Christ event that reveals Christ is the one-and-the-many.

103. Zizioulas, *One and Many*, 52–53, 132, 133. See Zizioulas's discussion on the notion and meaning of sign and symbol as defined by Paul Tillich and Alexander Schmemann (Zizioulas, *One and Many*, 102–4). Zizioulas opts for "symbol" by his definition "symbol" links the created with the uncreated in the person of Jesus Christ (Zizioulas, *One and Many*, 103–4).

with the reality of the future event (the kingdom of God).[104] The Church is the (one) body of Christ, made up of many members. This dynamic is realized in what Zizioulas terms the "eucharistic community."[105] The eucharistic community is the many who "come together" (*sunerchomenōn*) as the one "church" (*ekklēsia*), or when the many become united as "the church of God" (*tēs ekklēsias tou theou*) around "the Lord's supper" (*kyriakon deipnon*).[106] In this act, the many are unified in communion or fellowship (*koinōnia*) with God and with each other.[107] Thus the Church becomes the image of the Triune God who is one in communion.[108] In this way, the Church is *koinōnia*.[109]

This servant of God, Jesus Christ, who by the institution of the Eucharist demonstrates through the elements of bread and wine the one salvation for the many with the words "for you" or "for many."[110] Speaking of the Christological dynamic of the Eucharist, Zizioulas says, "It is *Christ's* unity [one] and it is *His* catholicity [many] that the Church [one] reveals in her being catholic [many]."[111] The clearest biblical description of this for which Zizioulas relies upon is found in Paul's rhetorical questions to the Corinthians, "The cup of blessing that we bless, is it not a participation in the blood of Christ? The bread that we break, is it not a participation in the body of Christ? Because there is one bread, we who are many are one body, for we all partake of the one bread."[112] In these words, Paul is calling the many into participation (*koinōnia*) through the one bread, thus becoming one body of Christ—the Church.[113] Zizioulas's emphasis can be summarized in Paul's phrase, "we who are many are one body."[114] The one body is the Church, and it is made up of the many who have gathered in *koinōnia* around the eucharistic table.

104. Zizioulas, *One and Many*, 105; Zizioulas, *Being*, 132–33.

105. Zizioulas, *Being*, 22, 80–81, 148. Also, Zizioulas, *One and Many*, 61–74.

106. 1 Cor 11:18, 20, 22. Zizioulas, *Being*, 148; Zizioulas, *One and Many*, 62.

107. 1 Cor 1:9; 10:16–17; Zizioulas, *Being*, 145.

108. Basil, *Spirit*, 18.46, 29; Zizioulas, *Being*, 134.

109. Zizioulas, *One and Many*, 52. Also, Behr, "Trinitarian Being," 166–67.

110. Matt 26:26–29; Mark 14:22–25; Luke 22:17–22; 1 Cor 11:24–25; Zizioulas, *Eucharistic Communion*, 12.

111. Zizioulas, *Being*, 159.

112. 1 Cor 10:16–17.

113. Zizioulas, *Being*, 145, 147–48.

114. 1 Cor 10:17 (ἓν σῶμα οἱ πολλοί ἐσμεν). Cf. Zizioulas, *Eucharist*, 53–58. Cf. the chorus of Foley, *One Bread, One Body*, #620 in *United Methodist Hymnal*: "One

These definitions of the Church and eucharistic community connote the Church's institution and polity. In these final examples, the one-and-many dialectic is applied to the Church as she reflects God. The Church is one in its catholicity, expressed by many local churches in communion.[115]

> The institution that is supposed to express the unity of the Church must be an institution which expresses *communion*. Since there is no institution which derives its existence or its authority from anything that precedes the event of communion, but from the event of communion itself (this is what it means to make communion ontologically *constitutive*), the institution of universal unity cannot be self-sufficient or self-explicable or prior to the event of communion; it is dependent on it. Equally, however, there is no communion which can be prior to the oneness of the Church: the institution which expresses this communion must be accompanied by an indication that there is a ministry safeguarding the oneness which the communion aims at expressing.[116]

The institution of the Church is spelled out this way: the Church is *in*-stituted by Christ and *con*-stituted by the Holy Spirit.[117] The Church reflects Christ, who is not thought of as an individual in that he is pneumatologically constituted; he is simultaneously one-and-many. Christ is the one head of the Church, and his body is the community of believers—the many. This paradigm is also applied to the ordained minister or bishop who simultaneously acts as one-and-many. At this point, Zizioulas stresses the importance of the Eucharist for the unifying act of the many. There must be one leader who unites the many. "The Divine Eucharist is closely bound up *with the Bishop* as he is in turn with 'the whole Church.'"[118] In this act, the one bishop is identified with the many,[119] the Church, and the one Christ.[120] Furthermore, "This principle is that the 'one'—the bishop—cannot exist without the 'many'—the

---

bread, one body, one Lord of all, one cup of blessing which we bless. And we, though many throughout the earth, we are one body in this one Lord."

115. Zizioulas, *Being*, 134–35.

116. Zizioulas, *Being*, 135.

117. Zizioulas, *Being*, 140.

118. Zizioulas, *Eucharist*, 115.

119. Zizioulas, *Eucharist*, 115, 117–19.

120. Zizioulas, *Eucharist*, 116–17.

community—and the 'many' cannot exist without the 'one.'"[121] There is no ordination of a bishop outside of the community in that the community must be present in the ordination act/ceremony of the bishop. Likewise, there is no community (i.e., episcopacy) without the bishop who ordains the community (identifying them) through baptism.[122] What follows is an ideological application to Church polity in that the (one) bishop cannot do anything without the community (the many), and the community (the many) cannot do anything without the (one) bishop.[123]

The concern with Zizioulas's presentation of the-one-and-the-many is that while his theology is often referred to as "personalism" because of an emphasis on the particular persons of the Trinity,[124] he appears to stress the one over the many when applied anthropologically. His stress of the one over the many is undoubtedly a result of context as he presents his theology to a modern and post-modern audience whose thinking leans heavily toward individualism.[125] However, the one-and-many paradox concludes with the many enveloped into the one (i.e., the corporate, community, whole, etc.). Thus, Zizioulas's argument for particularity, beginning with a critique of Greek philosophy up to the "Cappadocian revolution," does not entirely fulfill his intention as the particular becomes almost lost in the general, or the individual becomes lost in the crowd (i.e., ecclesial being, eucharistic community).[126] The

121. Zizioulas, *Being*, 136–37; Zizioulas, *One and Many*, 236–53.

122. Zizioulas, *Being*, 137.

123. Zizioulas, *Being*, 135.

124. Cf. Gunton, "Persons," 97–107; Turcescu, "Misreadings," 527–39; Papanikolaou, "Existentialist?," 601–7; Zizioulas, "Appendix: *Person and Individual*, 171–77; Awad, "Personhood," 1–22. See also Behr's critique of reading *personalism* into Gregory of Nyssa's theology in Behr, *One of the Holy Spirit*, 420–27.

125. Zizioulas, *Being*, 15, 27.

126. Cf. Zizioulas, *Being*, 15, 67–122. Holmes argues that Zizioulas's theology ends in three centers of consciousness with the stress on the personal, volitional existence of the Triune God (Holmes, *Quest*, 12–16). Thus, a stress on the many-ness of God over the oneness of God. This appears to be true of Zizioulas when speaking of God, but not of humans. Holmes does not address Zizioulas's use of "the one and the many" nor the implications upon humans except to critique Zizioulas on deification, which results in the personal nature of the Trinity by grace being applied to humans (Holmes, *Quest*, 15). In Volf, *Likeness*, there is a twofold absorption: "just as in the constituting of a person the particularity of that person is lost and the individual is absorbed into Christ, so also the church itself is threatened with being absorbed into Christ" (Volf, *Likeness*, 100). Farrow, "Person and Nature," is concerned about the Eucharistic community wherein the distinction between the divine and creaturely becomes lost, making the

many are so closely united in Zizioulas's eucharistic community (both the individual person and the local church) that they become the "whole Church" in their gathering because Christ is present.[127] The only way to rectify Zizioulas's thoughts and defend against a loss of individual human identity is to define the oneness for humanity (and the local Church) by connecting communion[128] to freedom and freedom to personal existence in relation (ecstatically) toward others and to the Holy Trinity.[129] These philosophical and theological connections very well could be Zizioulas's *sine qua non* in his ecumenical endeavors.

ZIZIOULAS'S USE OF THE CHURCH FATHERS

At the root of Zizioulas's theology is his interpretation and definition of the Trinity described by the church fathers. However, his interpretation and use of patristics has brought sharp criticism accusing Zizioulas of a personalist presentation on the doctrine of the Trinity in contrast to

---

Church a "*tertium quid* between God and man" (Farrow, "Person and Nature," 119). A socio-political concern comes from Olson and Hall, *Trinity*, in that they wonder if the persons-in-communion thesis along with the historical monarchy of the Father might lead some to consider "benevolent despotism," "communitarianism," or "egalitarianism" (Olson and Hall, *Trinity*, 114–15).

127. Zizioulas, *Being*, 60–61, 148. See Zizioulas's connection of "catholic Church" and "eucharistic community" in the writings of Ignatius of Antioch as a contrast between the "local church" and the "universal church" (Zizioulas, *Being*, 148–49). Cf. Zizioulas, *Eucharistic Communion*, 16; Rom 16:23; 1 Cor 14:23; Cf. Volf, *Likeness*, 89n90. In Behr, "Trinitarian Being," he warns that the over emphasis placed on "eucharistic ecclesiology," while positively has awakened ecclesiological studies, has negatively subordinated the sacrament of baptism to the sacrament of the Eucharist for which he refers to as the "eucharistic revival." The warning is that the sacrament of the Eucharist alone cannot define the boundaries of the Church (Behr, "Trinitarian Being," 177–78). Harrison has a similar concern in Zizioulas's theology in that the one-and-the-many inevitably leads to an inequality of the many as illustrated in his ecclesiology and bishop role. She claims that Zizioulas's one-and-many dialect is not trinitarian, rather Christological (Harrison, "Zizioulas," 289). In another place she refers to the laity in the Eucharistic Liturgy as presented by Zizioulas as "an undifferentiated herd" (Harrison, "Zizioulas," 298).

128. Volf analyzes that Zizioulas's goal to deindividualize the human person requires immediate relationship (Volf, *Likeness*, 94).

129. Zizioulas, *Being*, 120–22. Both Volf, *Likeness*, 87, and Awad, "Personhood," 9–10, state that Zizioulas surrenders the particularity of persons for communion, thus succumbing to a conclusion that he himself fights when he says, "Truth as communion does not lead to the dissolving of the diversity of beings into one vast ocean of being" (Zizioulas, *Being*, 106).

essentialist interpretation. That is to say that, Zizioulas views the patristic trinitarian formula of "one *ousia* and three *hypostases*" from a perspective of persons-in-relation as distinguished from their essence. This approach is opposite from the view of the three persons' unified divine substance or common nature.

The first person to assign to Zizioulas's theology the description "personalism" in his reading the patristic sources,[130] specifically the Cappadocians, was André de Halleux, where he examined the two approaches of personalism and essentialism in the Cappadocian trinitarian formula.[131] De Halleux leans heavily on Basil's *On the Spirit* in his critique of Zizioulas, showing Basil preferred the word *koinōnia* to express what was common in the *hypostases*.[132] De Halleux further argues that Basil used *koinōnia* as synonymous with consubstantiality, demonstrating that his understanding of the community of God is a "community of nature" of the three divine persons as opposed to a "community of personal relations."[133] This theory is viewed as the purpose of the second ecumenical council, where the nature of the Holy Spirit was defended against the Pneumatomachian assault that claimed the Holy Spirit was a created being. However, de Halleux concludes that the Cappadocians did present a personal interpretation of the Trinity, but not as a radical bifurcation from essentialism as presented by Zizioulas. De Halleux claims the Cappadocian Fathers understood and defended equality of personalism and essentialism in the Trinity as seen through the formula, "one *ousia* and three *hypostases*."[134]

Turcescu has contended that Zizioulas read the Cappadocians through a modern lens, developing a personalist theology based on the Greek Fathers, which is not there.[135] Using primarily the writings of Gregory of Nyssa, Turcescu sets out to show that Gregory and the other Cappadocians understood "enumeration of individuals" as a concept of person and used this concept to distinguish between substance and

---

130. Both Zizioulas and de Halleux use the broader study of patristics (late first century to the close of the eighth century) to support their arguments on the Cappadocian Fathers (late fourth century theologians, St. Basil, Gregory of Nazianzus, and Gregory of Nyssa).

131. De Halleux, "Personnalisme," 1:129–55.

132. De Halleux, "Personnalisme," 1:137. Cf. Basil, *Spirit*, 18.45.

133. De Halleux, "Personnalisme," 1:143–44; 2:289. Cf. Basil, *Spirit*, 13.30.

134. De Halleux, "Personnalisme," 2:289–92.

135. Turcescu, "Misreadings," 527–39.

person. Zizioulas denies that a person is an individual because an individual is incomplete and is subject to "addition and combination," which for Zizioulas binds the person up in the self.[136] In *On "Not Three Gods,"* Gregory states that individuals share the same nature illustrated by Peter, James, and John, three individuals who share one human nature.[137] There is then a distinction between substance (nature) and person. There can be a multitude of people, but that does not mean there is a multitude of substances (natures). They share in one nature.[138] Turcescu uses this argument of Gregory's to counter Zizioulas's understanding of individual as isolated from others. Turcescu simplifies Gregory's thought in that his use of *hypostasis* is synonymous with individual and not substance. The term substance is equated with species. These words for Gregory are also applied as an analogy to God in "that the three divine persons have the same common substance and that the relation between the substance and the persons is the same as that between a species and its individuals."[139]

Wilks criticizes Zizioulas's lack of emphasis on the *ousia* of Trinity in comparison to the Cappadocian Fathers.[140] Wilks argues that the Cappadocians understood and used the term *ousia* as a concrete reality rather than an abstract concept of beings-in-relation as described by Zizioulas. The concrete being of God (*ousia*) is a "single undifferentiated substance" that is revealed equally in all three persons (*hypostases*) of the Trinity.[141] Referencing Gregory of Nazianzus, Wilks argues for a more closely related definition of *ousia* and *hypostasis*, "'No sooner do I conceive of the One than I am illumined by the Splendour of the Three; no sooner do I distinguish them than I am carried back to the One.'"[142] Wilks reads the Cappadocians as presenting the "unity in the Godhead" as found in their use of *ousia*, where he accuses Zizioulas of "disdain" for *ousia* and the unity of God as found in the *hypostases*.[143] This approach of *hypostasis* over *ousia* naturally leads to person over nature and places Zizioulas very close to tritheism. The person of the Father then becomes

136. Turcescu, "Misreadings," 531.

137. Gregory of Nyssa, *Gods*, 335–36; Turcescu, "Misreadings," 532.

138. Gregory of Nyssa, *Gods*, 335; Turcescu, "Misreadings," 527, 532, 533.

139. Turcescu, "Misreadings," 534.

140. Wilks, "Ontology," 63–88.

141. Wilks, "Ontology," 69.

142. Wilks, "Ontology," 70.

143. Wilks, "Ontology," 78, 79.

the source and the cause of the Trinity.[144] It is at this point of the Father as the unity and the cause of the Trinity that Wilks attaches to Zizioulas an Aristotelian "second *ousia*" or "*homoiousian*" (meaning "like substance," rather than *homoousia* meaning "same substance") interpretation of the Nicaean Creed.[145] However, Wilks also admits that Basil did have *homoiousian* tendencies and that Zizioulas does speak about *ousia* but in relational terms, which he rejects.[146] Finally, Wilks takes up the *De Deo Uno*, which is to say that the substance never exists in a "naked" state; instead, the "mode of existence" is "being-in-relation" or that the *hypostasis* of the Father precedes the *ousia* of the Trinity.[147] While Wilks dismisses this principle point of Zizioulas's theology, he does not show patristic support; instead, he references Rahner to say that separating the unity and persons of God into two doctrinal statements suggests that persons have been added to *ousia*.[148]

In an article called "Person and Individual—a 'Misreading' of the Cappadocians?"[149] Zizioulas specifically address Turcescu's critique, but his defensive points may also be applied to de Halleux and Wilks's concerns. Zizioulas's case includes the analogy problem of trinitarian theology, trinitarian enumeration, the person and nature topic, and the application of personhood. Zizioulas begins with an overarching clarification of his use of "person" as he interprets from patristic sources and, more specifically, the Cappadocians as not synonymous with "individual."

> For the persons of the Trinity, according to the above Fathers, are not "individuals," either in the psychological sense of a centre of consciousness, or in that of a combination and concurrence of natural or moral qualities, or in the sense of a number that can be added or combined.[150]

---

144. Wilks, "Ontology," 77. See also Basil, *Spirit*, 18.45; Gregory of Nyssa, *Eunomius*, 1.36; Gregory of Nazianzus, *Orations*, "On the Son," 29.2; Gregory of Nazianzus, *Orations*, "On the Holy Spirit," 14; John of Damascus, *Faith*, 1.8; LaCugna, *God*, 248–49; Lossky, *Mystical Theology*, 58–64; Zizioulas, *Being*, 40–41.

145. Wilks, "Ontology," 77.

146. Wilks, "Ontology," 78–80.

147. Wilks, "Ontology," 81.

148. Wilks, "Ontology," 81.

149. Zizioulas, "Appendix," 171–77.

150. Zizioulas, *Communion*, 171.

The purpose for Zizioulas to defend his reading of the Cappadocian Fathers is that Christian personalism flows out of divine personhood.[151]

First, Zizioulas refers to Gregory of Nyssa's warning that human analogies to interpret and understand the Trinity are deficient and incomplete: humans are mortal, humans multiply and die, humans are subject to change over time, and humans have different parents who have caused their existence. Such factors apply only to human personhood and not to God. For these reasons, Zizioulas argues that the Cappadocians abstained from using human analogies to interpret the Trinity, rather divine personhood was used to define human personhood.[152] Thus, Gregory of Nyssa uses the analogy of Peter, James, and John to describe three persons and one nature called "human." He then acknowledges the weakness in using a human analogy to describe the nature and personhood of the Trinity. Therefore, Gregory explains that the distinction of the persons of the Trinity is viewed by "cause."

> By our belief, that is, that one is the Cause, and another is of the Cause; and again in that which is of the Cause we recognize another distinction. For one is directly from the first Cause, and another by that which is directly from the first Cause; so that the attribute of being Only-begotten abides without doubt in the Son, and the interposition of the Son, while it guards His attribute of being Only-begotten, does not shut out the Spirit from His relation by way of nature to the Father.[153]

In this illustration by Gregory, "cause" is attributed to persons and not nature. Therefore, to Zizioulas's point, "*divine persons*, in contrast with human ones, *cannot be regarded as a concurrence of natural or moral qualities of any kind*; they are distinguished only by their relations of ontological origination."[154] The result is a separation of nature and person, and if allowed to begin with God, rather than with human personhood, divine personhood is a "mode of being" rather than "a collection of properties."[155]

Zizioulas's second point of defense concerns whether the Cappadocians numbered the persons of the Trinity in their theology and the

151. Zizioulas, *Communion*, 171.

152. Zizioulas, *Communion*, 172.

153. Gregory of Nyssa, *Gods*, 336.

154. Zizioulas, *Communion*, 173.

155. Zizioulas, *Communion*, 173.

thought behind the practice. Turcescu interprets the Cappadocians, and generally the larger body of Greek Fathers, as presenting the concept of person as a complex collection of properties and not as unique. He suggests that both Basil and Gregory of Nyssa used Porphyry's definition of individual qualities, individual relations, and individual substances to describe the persons of the Trinity.[156] For example, when Gregory describes Job as first "a man" and is qualified in Scriptures as a "certain man" having certain qualities and relationships, the text speaks of an individual person.[157] Gregory uses this analogy to illustrate the *ousia* and *hypostasis* of the Trinity. Of this interest, too, Zizioulas does not deny that the Cappadocians at times applied numbers to the persons of the Trinity, yet he suggests that it was minimal. Basil, for example, in a lengthy letter to the Caesareans, never numbers the persons of the Trinity but instead uses their names as they relate to one another (i.e., Father, Son).[158] The point of numbering is to indicate otherness or distinguish one from another. Zizioulas agrees that this is the purpose when the Cappadocians number the persons of the Trinity. Zizioulas more specifically articulates that persons cannot be numbered in a way that indicates "*addition* and *combination*."[159] It is at this specific point that he states, "Numbering persons in the sense of adding or combining them with each other would be absolutely inadmissible with regard to the divine persons, not only for the Cappadocians but for the entire Greek patristic tradition."[160] The addition or combination of persons of the Trinity has the possibility of aligning with the Arian heresy.[161] Zizioulas finds support in Basil when he writes, "In delivering the formula of the Father, the Son, and the Holy Ghost, our Lord did not connect the gift with number." And further down he says, "Number has been devised as a symbol indicative of the quantity of objects. . . . We proclaim each of the hypostases singly; and, when count we must, we do not let an ignorant arithmetic carry us away to the idea of a plurality of Gods."[162] Thus Zizioulas concludes,

156. Turcescu, "Misreadings," 530–31.

157. Basil, *Letters*, 38.3, 138. There is a dispute as to whether this letter is from Basil or Gregory of Nyssa as it is found in the works of both authors. See Basil, *Letters*, 38.

158. Basil, *Letters*, 8.

159. Zizioulas, *Communion*, 174. Zizioulas, *Being*, 79.

160. Zizioulas, *Communion*, 174.

161. Athanasius, *Arians*, 1.40.

162. Basil, *Spirit*, 18.44.

> Uniqueness is something absolute for the person. The person is so absolute in its uniqueness that it does not permit itself to be regarded as an arithmetical concept, to be set alongside other beings, to be combined with other objects, or to be used as a means even for the most sacred goal. The goal is the person itself; personhood is the total fulfilment of being, the catholic expression of nature.[163]

The uniqueness of a person, therefore, is a *hypostasis*, and the *hypostasis* is not an addition or combination of properties, natures, or substances.[164]

The third point Zizioulas addresses is Gregory of Nyssa's use of the term "individual" (*atomon*), or more particularly understood as "indivisible." Turcescu's critique of Zizioulas included Gregory's uses of (and enumeration of) the term individuals. Turcescu's primary point in interpreting Gregory is that he made a distinction between substance and person, resulting in the adding and subtracting (enumeration) of persons in distinction of their nature, while Gregory used the terms *atomon*, *prosōpon*, and *hypostasis* interchangeably.[165] That is to say, when we name Peter, James, and John, there are not three humanities; rather, one humanity is found in three different people (persons), showing what is common among the three persons. Zizioulas does not deny this interpretation of Gregory of Nyssa but points explicitly to Gregory's use of *atomon* in connection to *prosōpon* as it relates to personhood describes an "indivisible existence of *ousia*."[166] The point to note here is that Gregory of Nyssa and other Greek Fathers did use the term "*atomon*" at times to describe *human* existence, but it was never applied to the three persons of the Trinity because it would lead to tritheism.[167] Instead, the words *prosōpon* and *hypostasis* are applied to the divine persons portraying an aspect of relationality to ontology, making it a "*relational ontology*" while opposing an idea of individual ontology as Turcescu argues.[168]

Finally, in Turcescu's criticism of Zizioulas's personal-relational interpretation of the Cappadocian theology concerning the Trinity, he attempts to show that Gregory of Nyssa, along with Basil, were both

---

163. Zizioulas, *Being*, 47.

164. Zizioulas, *Being*, 47–48.

165. Turcescu, "Misreadings," 532–34. Cf. Gregory of Nyssa, *Gods*, 335.

166. Zizioulas, *Communion*, 175. Cf. Gregory of Nyssa, *Ex Communibus Notionibus*, 177, 180.

167. Zizioulas, *Communion*, 175.

168. Zizioulas, *Communion*, 176; Turcescu, "Misreadings," 533–34.

familiar with the language of Porphyry and used the term "*atomon*" as an "individual" in the sense of a collection of properties.[169] Furthermore, for Turcescu, the concept of person would align more with the modern existential development of personalism not found in Cappadocian theology.[170] At this point, Zizioulas argues that what is at stake is a fundamental issue of faith and this interpretation of the Cappadocians by Turcescu is illogical.[171] The concept of persons and personhood, for theology, must begin with God, and the Cappadocians, argues Zizioulas, had an overarching concept of persons-in-relationship fundamentally in the divine persons being named, Father, Son, and Holy Spirit, revealing their "mode of existence" as primarily relational rather than substantive in the case of a collection of properties.[172] This definition begins with the divine, and only after this can it be applied to human personhood.[173] Furthermore, it is this point of separation from modern existential philosophy that Zizioulas raises, and is accused of, where true personhood is discovered in God as a "mode of existence" relationally within the Trinity. In contrast, modern existential philosophy is a study in human ontology beginning with subjective individualism and applying its concepts back to the subjective individual human with no reference to the divine.[174]

Zizioulas's use of patristic sources supports his theology of the Father as the eternal and personal cosmological cause by being the Creator. Moreover, Zizioulas sees the outcome of the Father as being Creator in

169. Turcescu, "Misreadings," 530.

170. Turcescu, "Misreadings," 534–37; Papanikolaou, "Existentialist?," 601, 604–5.

171. Zizioulas, *Communion*, 176.

172. Zizioulas, *Communion*, 174–75.

173. Zizioulas, *Communion*, 177. Zizioulas, *Being*, 40–41, 84–85n60.

174. Sartre, *Existentialism & Humanism*, 24–25, 67–68. See also Papanikolaou, who states, "Notwithstanding the charge of influence by modern personalism, Zizioulas is self-consciously attempting to give expression to this core of theology, which is the realism of divine-human communion. For Zizioulas, the 'ontological revolution' is not so much the change in the meaning of the words 'person' and 'hypostasis', but in the Christian affirmation that God in the person of Christ has 'become history' and, hence the need to articulate an ontology in which the notions of history, time, change, particularity, otherness, relationality are integrated. In the end, according to Zizioulas, this can only be done through the Christian doctrine of the Trinity that affirms the monarchy of the Father" (Papanikolaou, "Existentialist?," 604). See Zizioulas, *Communion*, "Existentialist philosophy can only help us to appreciate the limitations, the antinomies and the tragic experience of personhood, and this in itself is important in order to make it clear to us that, as human beings, we are not content with what we actually are as persons, and long for true personhood" (Zizioulas, *Communion*, 141).

that the Father generates the concept of otherness and freedom as ontological consequences to being a person. To unpack this thought, we begin
with the creeds and the connection of God as Father, not "as a speculative reflection about God, but emerged from ecclesial experience."[175] The
Apostles' Creed begins, "I believe in God the Father Almighty; Maker
of heaven and earth."[176] Zizioulas questions whether the name "Father"
is to be attached to "Almighty" or to "God," thus reading, "'I believe in
God who is Father almighty,' or as "I believe in God the Father, who
is almighty"?'[177] In building his case, Zizioulas offers evidence that "almighty" is connected biblically to "God" and not with "Father."[178] Therefore, by properly attaching "almighty" to "God," we have an ontological
statement concerning God and the Father rather than a moral statement
of divine Fatherhood.[179] The Fatherhood of God for the Greek East is
connected to the Sonship of God, describing the relationship between the
first and second persons of the Trinity, and is not the description of the
relationship (Fatherhood) of God to humans. In support of this theological point, Zizioulas relies on Cyril of Jerusalem, Rufinus, and Athanasius,
who connect the Father's relationship with the Son rather than the Father
to humanity. Athanasius says, "let no one be startled on hearing that the
Son of God is from the Essence of the Father," meaning the word "God"
describes the essence of the Father and the Son.[180] Cyril writes, "God then
is in an improper sense the Father of many, but by nature and in truth
of One only, the Only-begotten Son, our Lord Jesus Christ; not having
attained in course of time to being a Father, but being ever the Father
of the Only-begotten."[181] More specifically, Rufinus says, "God is called
Almighty because He possesses rule and dominion over all things. But
the Father possesses all things by His Son" and then sites Colossians 1:16
and Hebrews 1:2.[182] The point is that almighty (*pantokratōr*) is a property

175. Zizioulas, *Communion*, 113.

176. Schaff, *Greek and Latin Creeds*, 45.

177. Zizioulas, *Communion*, 113 ("Almighty" in Latin: "*omnipotentem*"; in Greek: "*pantokratora*." Schaff, *Greek and Latin Creeds*, 45).

178. Zizioulas, *Communion*, 114.

179. Zizioulas, *Communion*, 114.

180. Athanasius, *Nicene Definition*, 165.

181. Cyril of Jerusalem, *Catechetical Lectures*, 7.5.

182. Rufinus, *Apostles' Creed*, 545. "For by him all things were created, in heaven
and on earth, visible and invisible, whether thrones or dominions or rulers or authori-
ties—all things were created through him and for him" (Col 1:16). "But in these last

common to all three persons of the Trinity and not one specific person (e.g., the Father). Therefore, the moral quality of God is found in the common unity of God and not in the economy of the Father only.

In contrast, Augustine reminds us that Jesus taught us to pray in the name of the Father, saying, "Remember then, that ye have a Father in heaven."[183] Furthermore, Jesus is reported to have said to Mary Magdalene, "'Do not cling to me, for I have not yet ascended to the Father; but go to my brothers and say to them, 'I am ascending to my Father and your Father, to my God and your God.'"[184] However, more specifically, the Apostle Paul explains that the human role of sonship in relation to God the Father and being co-heirs with Christ is through adoption in contrast to nature or essence.[185] Nevertheless, Zizioulas interprets a distinction when connecting "almighty" with Father, further connecting Father as humanity's Father, resulting in a moral rather than ontological consequence. In this approach, there is a separation between God and Father, with the divine substance of God preceding the Father and becoming the expression of divine unity.[186] In this case, almighty is connected to Father, who wills and acts along even in creating the world. In contrast, if almighty is connected to God, the Father creates through communion with the Son.[187] Again Zizioulas reveals a divide between the Latin West and the Greek East. The West describes God's freedom through his "power to *act*" (*omnipotentem*), while the East view God's freedom through "the capacity *to embrace and contain*" or "*to establish a relationship* of communion and love" (*pantokratōr*).[188] To illustrate the point, Zizioulas's well-known phrase and title, *Being as Communion*, is a theological paradigm that begins with God as Father as interpreted from the Cappadocian Fathers. Thus, Zizioulas's point of emphasis on God the Father as the source of otherness and freedom for human beings to ontologically be persons is significant in that "This way of being is not a moral attainment, something that man *accomplishes*. It is a way of *relationship* with the world, with other people and with God, and event of

---

days he has spoken to us by his Son, whom he appointed the heir of all things, through whom also he created the world" (Heb 1:2).

183. Augustine, *Selected Lessons*, 275.

184. John 20:17.

185. Rom 8:12–17.

186. Zizioulas, *Communion*, 118.

187. Zizioulas, *Communion*, 116.

188. Zizioulas, *Communion*, 116.

communion, and that is why it cannot be realized as the achievement of an *individual*, but only as an *ecclesial* fact."[189]

Zizioulas begins with God as Father. While the Cappadocians do not deny the one substance of God in connection with unity (i.e., divine oneness), an accurate discussion of unity starts with the Father. Gregory of Nazianzus explains the unity of the Trinity through the primacy of persons this way, "And the Beginning is not, because it is a beginning, separated from that which has no beginning. For its beginning is not its nature, any more than the being without beginning is the nature of the other."[190] Furthermore, Gregory adds,

> Now, the name of that which has no beginning is the Father, and of the Beginning the Son, and of that which is with the Beginning, the Holy Ghost, and the three have one Nature—God. And the union is the Father from Whom and to Whom the order of Persons runs its course, not so as to be confounded, but so as to be possessed, without distinction of time, of will, or of power.[191]

Zizioulas emphasizes what Gregory and the other Cappadocians say is that the substance of divinity (i.e., God) does not exist by itself. Rather, there is within the substance of divinity a "cause," and the "cause" is neither "incommunicable" nor a "structure" of necessity; instead, the "cause" of the being of God (i.e., divine unity) is from a person, and that person is the Father who is known through communion with others.[192] Basil explains that one cannot conceive of Father without comprehending Son; therefore, the "mode of existence"[193] found in God is his *hypostasis*.[194] Basil is conscientious about showing that while there are three *hypostases*, they exist in perfect communion without "void of subsistence, which can make a break in the mutual harmony of the divine essence."[195] Gregory of Nyssa attacked Eunomius for his ambiguous teaching on the Trinity by referring to God as first "Absolute Being" rather than expressing the names Father, Son, and Holy Spirit.[196] To suggest the substance of God

---

189. Zizioulas, *Being*, 15.

190. Gregory of Nazianzus, *Orations*, "The Last Farewell," 42.15.

191. Gregory of Nazianzus, *Orations*, "The Last Farewell," 42.15.

192. Zizioulas, *Being*, 16–18.

193. Zizioulas, *Being*, 41.

194. Basil, *Letters*, 38.4.

195. Basil, *Letters*, 38.4.

196. Gregory of Nyssa, *Eunomius*, 1.13. Gregory reveals that Eunomius's doctrine

to the Father, who is the cause of all, is also to suggest a communion of persons indicating an ontological category of true being.[197] The communion of God is established in hypostatic-love, that is, Father, Son, and Holy Spirit, and extended to the creature.[198] Therefore, "The Holy Trinity is a primordial ontological concept and not a notion which is added to the divine substance or rather which follows." The substance of God is communion of persons with the Father who is the cause of the Son and Holy Spirit before and outside of time so that there is no subordination of the persons.[199] As substance or unity of God, communion is a hypostatic-love that indicates freedom rather than necessity. In this way, freedom (i.e., choice) is an ontological concept, rather than a moral necessity, initiated by the Father to love another.[200]

SUMMARY

We have shown in this chapter that Zizioulas, being a Greek Orthodox Christian, aligns with his Church's thinking but expands it and challenges it in certain areas. For instance, while Holy Tradition is a sacred concept and theological methodology, Zizioulas further expands the understanding of Spirit-led transmission through apostolic succession not only "historically" but also "eschatologically."[201] In a moment of time in participation around the eucharistic table, the historical truth is witnessed through the continuity and truthfulness of the apostolic succession (i.e., word of God, liturgy, hymnody, etc.) and the eschatological truth of the future hope made present. Both the historical and the eschatological approaches to Holy Tradition are pneumatologically constituted.[202]

---

is heretical in that he ascribes to God as ungenerated supreme substance (*Agennētos*, called Father) who has created "subjects" similar to himself (the Son and Holy Spirit). Gregory of Nyssa, *Eunomius*, 1.13, 16.

197. Zizioulas, *Being*, 16–18.

198. Gregory of Nyssa, *Eunomius*, 1.24.

199. Zizioulas, *Being*, 17; Zizioulas, *Communion*, 119, 121–22. Cf. Gregory of Nazianzus, "Theological Oration," 2.29.2. Zizioulas believes that the intent of the Cappadocian Fathers was to offer a "third way" theology between the Alexandrians and the Antiochenes. This is seen quite possibly in their emphasis of divine nature and will (See, Zizioulas, *Communion*, 123–24).

200. Zizioulas, *Communion*, 121–22.

201. Zizioulas, *Being*, 174–75.

202. Zizioulas, *Being*, 179–80.

Zizioulas also takes the traditional Greek Orthodox methodology of paradox and, while focusing on the concept of "the one and the many," expands it into theological areas of the Trinity, humanity, Jesus Christ, the Church, the Eucharist, and Church Polity. Zizioulas justifies this expansion through what he calls the "Cappadocian revolution," where he interprets the Cappadocian Fathers for the first time in history, separating the essence of God (*ousia*) from the persons of God (*hypostasis*).[203] God is simultaneous "One" and "Many." However, it is at this point that Zizioulas's theology appears to weaken. In his application of the-one-and-the-many in ecclesiology or eucharistic personality, the many become absorbed into the one. The one body representing the church or the one catholic church representing the worldwide Christian faith seems to supersede local churches and individual people so intermingled that uniqueness seems lost.[204] At the same time, Zizioulas is accused of personalism leading to existentialism by focusing on the uniqueness of the persons of the Trinity. While much has been made of this critique, it lacks solid evidence since Zizioulas repeatedly announces that a definition of person must be found in God and applied to humanity for proper anthropology.[205] The opposite, beginning with humanity and prescribing it upon God, is illogical to Zizioulas. An existential definition of personhood would be founded in the human person, which Zizioulas vehemently denies.[206]

In chapter 2, we identified Zizioulas's historical and theological concept of trinitarian personhood. Here in chapter 3, we examined Zizioulas's paradoxical methodology as demonstrated in the-one-and-the-many as a way to reflect upon both God and the church. In all of these theological concepts, Zizioulas relies on the writings of early church fathers and, more specifically, a rereading of the Cappadocian Fathers in what Zizioulas describes as the "Cappadocian revolution." Now, by taking this foundation of trinitarian-personhood theology and one-and-many methodology, we turn our attention specifically to Zizioulas's oeuvre of trinitarian ontology, expressed as mode of existence, as found

203. Zizioulas, *Being*, 35–41, 83–89; Zizioulas, "Capacity and Incapacity," 409–10; Zizioulas, *Communion*, 185–86; *Lectures*, 50–51.

204. Zizioulas, *Being*, 145–49; Zizioulas, *Communion*, 286–89; Zizioulas, *Eucharist*, 112–17; Zizioulas, *One and Many*, 264–68.

205. Zizioulas, *Communion*, 177; Papanikolaou, "Existentialist?," 604–5; Zizioulas, *One and Many*, 17–24.

206. Zizioulas, *Communion*, 177; Zizioulas, *One and Many*, 21–22, 23–24.

in his eucharistic ecclesiology and ask if he accomplishes what he set out to do by presenting a (Christian) anthropology?[207] Finally, Chapter 4 will draw together these concepts of trinitarian personhood and one-and-many from Zizioulas and examine how these concepts help develop his dictum of "mode of existence."[208] We will then ask if Zizioulas's "mode of existence" is adequate or if there might be a deficiency, and if there is a deficiency, what, or *who* is the remedy for Christian personhood?

207. Zizioulas, *One and Many*, 6, 30–31, 383.

208. Zizioulas, *Being*, 15.

Chapter 4

Zizioulas and Contemporary Implications

"It is possible for us to participate in the other-oriented, self-giving love, which is the inner life of God himself."

—Dennis F. Kinlaw[1]

INTRODUCTION

IN THIS CHAPTER, WE hone in on Zizioulas's primary contribution to theology and the significant implications of trinitarian ontology, understood as modes of existence. The importance of trinitarian ontology, modes of existence, is that the result of Zizioulas's work, known colloquially as being as communion or persons-in-relation, affects all areas of theology as it is a study in personhood. Zizioulas expresses the outcome of his work seeks an answer in (human) personal existence.[2] Our question here is: does Zizioulas's Dictum accomplish a meaningful understanding of human personal existence? The answer is "no" based on his pneumatological presentation in light of the Trinity. However, much can be gleaned from Zizioulas's provocative trinitarian theology and historical interpretation.

---

1. Kinlaw, *Jesus*, 45.

2. Zizioulas, *Being*, 27; Zizioulas, *Communion*, 99–100; Zizioulas, *One and Many*, 30–31.

Twentieth-century trinitarian theology has been described as trinitarian "renewal,"[3] "rebirth,"[4] "revival,"[5] and "renaissance."[6] The rise of trinitarian theology in the twentieth century was a result of nearly three centuries of neglect due either to the idea that the doctrine was settled as orthodoxy, thus no need to rehash it,[7] or it was the reaction to the Anti-Trinitarian movement which itself reacted against Medieval Scholasticism and speculative non-biblical teaching.[8] For example, early nineteenth-century theologian Schleiermacher concluded his influential writing, *The Christian Faith*, with a relatively small section on the Trinity. He stated that the doctrine of the Trinity is assumed through the Christian self-consciousness where the Divine Essence is "united to the human nature" through redemption.[9] Despite this approach and placement of the Trinity in his theological work, Schleiermacher calls the doctrine of the Trinity "the coping-stone of Christian doctrine."[10] As Schwöbel has pointed out, the uniqueness of trinitarian theology is that it is "not restricted to specific issues of the Christian doctrine of God" but "effects all aspects of the enterprise of doing theology in its various disciplines."[11] Unlike other segments of theology, trinitarian theology is the interconnected tissue for the whole body of Christian theology and supersedes specific schools of thought, intellectual traditions, denominations, and theological camps.[12] What is more, trinitarian theology in modern history has claimed as a foundation a wide range of contemporary implications, such as feminist theology,[13] liberation theology (in-

---

3. Holmes, *Quest*, 2.

4. Grenz, *Rediscovering*, 1.

5. Olson and Hall, *Trinity*, 95.

6. Schwöbel, "Introduction," 1–30.

7. Olson and Hall, *Trinity*, 67.

8. Holmes, *Quest*, 170–80. Holmes describes two separate camps of Anti-Trinitarians during this period, one being the "Biblical Anti-Trinitarianism" beginning with Michael Servetus and Faustus Socinus (Holmes, *Quest*, 170–75) and the other being the "Rational Anti-Trinitarianism" beginning with Edward Stillingfleet, John Toland, and Lord Herbert Edward (Holmes, *Quest*, 176–80).

9. Schleiermacher, *Christian Faith*, 739.

10. Schleiermacher, *Christian Faith*, 739.

11. Schwöbel, "Introduction," 1.

12. Schwöbel, "Introduction," 2.

13. LaCugna, *God*, 266–305. Also from an analogous trinitarian approach toward community, see Johnson, *She Who Is*, 191–223.

cluding socio-political implications),[14] process theology,[15] Christology,[16] politics (i.e., political science/philosophy),[17] social-personalism (e.g., anthropology),[18] ecclesiology,[19] ecology,[20] eschatology,[21] evangelicalism,[22] eucharistic theology,[23] missiology,[24] and art (as a human expression of creation),[25] to name a few.

Therefore, it should come as no surprise that Zizioulas's trinitarian ontology in the latter part of the twentieth century has profoundly impacted theology and the implications of contemporary thought.[26] The purpose in part 1 of this chapter is to offer a critical evaluation of Zizioulas's trinitarian theology and three contemporary implications under the auspice Trinitarian Ontology: "mode of existence." The three contemporary implications of high value to Zizioulas are Eucharistic-Ecclesiology, Ecumenical Vision, and Ecological Concern. Part two of this chapter will offer an alternative theological perspective to Trinitarian Ontology called

---

14. Boff, *Trinity and Society*, 11–13.

15. Jüngel, *Trinity*; Pittenger, *Triunity*.

16. Coppedge, *Triune*, 13–19.

17. Moltmann, *Trinity*, 192–200, 203–9.

18. Grenz, *Social God*, 3–14. Grenz's purpose is to move the many (modern individualism) toward the one (community) by defining the self through the *imago Dei* and presenting a Global Soul (Grenz, *Social God*, 20).

19. Volf presents an ecumenical ecclesiology constituted by the trinitarian model (Volf, *Likeness*, 25, 191, 204–8, 259–76).

20. Dunham, *Trinity and Creation*.

21. Moltmann, *Trinity*, 90–96, 209–12. Referencing Fiore's *Doctrine of the Kingdom*, Moltmann attempts to create a trinitarian-eschatology which is God's openness to the future of an established kingdom on earth as opposed to a traditional dualistic kingdom (i.e., a temporary kingdom of God on earth until the parousia establishes an eternal heavenly kingdom).

22. Sanders, *Deep*, 14–17. Sanders argues from the aspect that evangelicals by name are gospel people and that the Trinity is the gospel and the gospel is the Trinity.

23. Daly, "Eucharist and Trinity," 15–38. Daly shows evidence that early in Christian history (Didache 9, 10) Eucharistic prayers were binitary rather than trinitary. This practice rapidly changed post-Nicaea. However, the greater point is the implication today that it is a corporate participation into the one act (Daly, "Eucharist and Trinity," 15–16, 37).

24. Newbigin, *Gospel*, 118–27.

25. Horne, "Art," 80–91.

26. Grenz, *Rediscovering*, 133–34, 142–43; Olson and Hall, *Trinity*, 112–13; Knight, "Introduction," 1–4; Papanikolaou, *Being*, 1–2; Anatolios, "Personhood," 147–48; Torrance, *Persons*, 290; Fox, *God as Communion*.

Trinitarian Pneumatology. The implications of Trinitarian Pneumatology will be Trinitarian Pneumatological Personhood which is laid out in part 2 of this book in the following chapters.

TRINITARIAN ONTOLOGY: "MODE OF EXISTENCE"

The previous chapters have shown Zizioulas's reliance on the early church fathers; however, contemporary context and modern theology also helped shape Zizioulas's theology. Barth's christocentric theological concept of the self-revealed Word of God is rooted in the trinitarian doctrine of Christianity. Barth writes, "The doctrine of the Trinity is what basically distinguishes the Christian doctrine of God as Christian, and therefore, what already distinguishes the Christian concept of revelation as Christian, in contrast to all other possible doctrines of God or concepts of revelation."[27] Barth's emphasis is that one cannot separate "God, the Revealer" from the effects of God; therefore, the revelation of God is eternally connected to persons or "modes" of God as indicated through the trinitarian concept.[28] The significance of Barth's starting point for theology is heightened for Zizioulas as he indicates Barth's initial question, "Who is God in His revelation?"[29] This question gave the doctrine of the Trinity an ontological primacy in modern Western theology.[30] However, Zizioulas's critique of Barth is that while he asks the question in search for the God behind the revelation through biblical names, Barth falls in line with Western Augustinian and Thomistic thinking of the Trinity by which he means Barth begins with the One divine substance of God and then describes God's three modes of being.[31]

---

27. Barth, *CD* 1/1:7.

28. Barth, *CD* 1/1:1–2, 4, 66. Barth makes clear that he prefers the term "modes" when speaking of the Threeness of the Trinity rather than "persons" (Barth, *CD* 1/1:66). The reason for Barth's distinction was that he did not want to confuse "person" for "personality" (Barth, *CD* 1/1:56).

29. Barth, *CD* 1/1:2–3; Zizioulas, *Communion*, 164; Zizioulas, *One and Many*, 4.

30. Zizioulas, *One and Many*, 4. Wood explains that Barth's theology of revelation is always based on God's free grace toward humans (Wood, *God and History*, 197). For, Zizioulas this point is significant in that to ultimately be a person means freedom from the self toward another, see Zizioulas, "Capacity and Incapacity," 414, 428–33.

31. Zizioulas, *Communion*, 150–51. See Barth, *CD* 1/1:53–55. Barth's analogy for the triunity of God as "the revealed Word of God," "the written Word of God," and "the preached Word of God" (Barth, *CD* 1/1:118–19) sounds very similar to Augustine's analogy of the Trinity being the mind, love (Word), and knowledge, see Augustine, *Trinity*, 9.2–12.

Rahner, who was a significant contributor to the documents of Vatican II,[32] entertained the option of an alternate starting point of either beginning trinitarian theology from the One and moving toward the Three or beginning from the Three and moving toward the One?[33] Barth attempted to do this with his topics of "Unity in Trinity" and "Trinity in Unity," but he gave greater weight to the unity of God in both cases.[34] Zizioulas has called Rahner's approach "one of paramount importance" as he recognized the significance of beginning trinitarian theology by "identifying God with the Father rather than with the divine substance."[35] In contrast, if God is identified with the divine substance of the Trinity, then the divine substance is primordial to the persons of God, resulting in a "quaternity" rather than a Trinity.[36] Next, Rahner expressed the importance of connecting the Trinity with humans through salvation[37] by stating, "*The 'economic' Trinity is the 'immanent' Trinity and the 'immanent' Trinity is the 'economic' Trinity.*"[38] That is to say, what God is outside of himself he is within himself, and what God is within himself he is outside of himself.[39] While Zizioulas acknowledges the truthfulness of Rahner's axiom, he warns that the immanent Trinity is not exhausted in the economic Trinity.[40] If it were the case, then God's eternal being would include a nature of suffering as reflected by the Incarnation:

> For [God] transcends suffering which Man hopes also to transcend, not by virtue of His being, but by some kind of becoming which means that He is in constant need of historical reality (involving suffering) in order to be what He *will* be, true God.[41]

32. Grenz and Olson, *20th Century Theology*, 239.

33. Rahner, *Trinity*, 58–60.

34. Barth, *CD* 1/1:53–75. Under "Trinity and Unity," Barth says, "it is of the essence of the revealed God to have these attributes, in His essence they, too, are indistinguishably one, and they cannot, therefore, be distributed ontologically to Father, Son and Spirit" (Barth, *CD* 1/1:69).

35. Zizioulas, *One and Many*, 4.

36. Rahner, *Trinity*, 60. Zizioulas, *One and Many*, 10–12.

37. LaCugna calls Rahner's trinitarian development of soteriological history a trinitarian theology "from below" because of the unity between theology and economy, God's self-revelation inevitably reveals God's nature (LaCugna, *God*, 216, 221).

38. Rahner, *Trinity*, 22.

39. Rahner, *Trinity*, 23–24.

40. Zizioulas, *One and Many*, 9.

41. Zizioulas, *One and Many*, 9.

Nevertheless, Rahner made important strides in moving modern discussions of trinitarian theology away from a priority of substance toward a priority on persons.

In the mid-twentieth century, Florovsky called for modern thinkers to remain faithful to the Church's traditions when addressing contemporary issues while still exercising creative freedom.[42] Florovsky suggested a *"neopatristic* synthesis" to call for modern theologians to engage with the patristic sources and not simply reference them.[43] He hoped that this approach would lead to ecumenical studies in theology to participate in contemporary issues.[44] Zizioulas heeded the *neopatristic* call of Florovsky by grounding his theological thought in patristics for the purpose of engaging contemporary life.[45] Zizioulas's primary concern has been to rescue trinitarian theology from a Western rationalism and de-individualize personal identity by identifying personhood through relationships as demonstrated in community (*koinōnia*).[46] To do this, Zizioulas begins with the Trinity and more specifically revisits the Cappadocian approach to the Trinity, in which his emphasis begins with persons in community.[47] Thus Zizioulas proposes, "The person both as a concept and as a living reality is purely the product of patristic thought. Without this, the deepest meaning of personhood can neither be grasped nor justified."[48] Through this trinitarian ontology, Zizioulas suggests a mode of existence where the *hypostatic* and the *ekstatic* coincide.[49]

To capture Zizioulas's starting point, one might ask, "Does God precede the Trinity, or does the Trinity precede God?" Asked in another way, "Does the word 'God' refer to the divinity (i.e., substance) of the Trinity or

42. Florovsky, "Orthodox Theology," 69.

43. Florovsky, "Orthodox Theology," 70. Even Barth saw the need to return to the historical texts, "We need not regard the achievements of the older theology at this point as just an idle game, no matter how trifling much of what is adduced may undoubtedly seem to be" (Barth, *CD* 1/1:44).

44. Florovsky, "Orthodox Theology," 70–71. See Zizioulas, *One and Many*, 345.

45. Papanikolaou, *Being*, 1, 9.

46. Zizioulas *Being*, 36–41, 109; Zizioulas, "Capacity and Incapacity," 403–7; Zizioulas, *Communion*, 243–45; Zizioulas, "Holy Trinity," 56–60; Zizioulas, *One and Many*, 7–8, 19–24, 28–33, 402–3. Also, Gunton, *Trinitarian Theology*, 1–2, 9–10, 30–33, 94–96; Grenz, *Social God*, 51–53.

47. Zizioulas, *Being*, 16–19, 41; Zizioulas, *Communion*, 111, 121–23, 150–54; Zizioulas, "Holy Trinity," 52, 56–57; Zizioulas, *Lectures*, 53.

48. Zizioulas, *Being*, 27.

49. Zizioulas, *Being*, 106; Zizioulas, *Communion*, 112.

to the Person named God 'the Father'?" Zizioulas's approach of persons-in-relation as a defining point of being is unlike Macquarrie's separation of "God" from "Being" for the purpose that God would indicate a type of being, a "holy being."[50] Illustrating God's revelation to Moses as "I AM WHO I AM,"[51] Gregory Palamas states, "Thus it is not the One Who is who derives from the essence, but essence which derives from Him, for it is He who contains all being in Himself."[52] This approach of beginning with persons-in-relation, then moving to substance, is opposite in comparison to Augustine's approach of person as a self-conscious individual[53] ("let me know myself, let me know [God]"),[54] or Boethius's "individual substance of a rational nature,"[55] or Aquinas's intradivine life of relative properties as the divine essence of the Trinity,[56] or even the inevitability that a person is simply an introverted consciousness as Descartes emphasized.[57] For Zizioulas, the being of God is not a result of impersonal substance (*ousia*) called "divinity." Quite the contrary, the being of God, is found in persons, specifically, persons-in-relationship, which makes God Triune. However, what has confounded some concerning Zizioulas's trinitarian theology of persons-in-relation is that he begins his theology with the Person of the Father as "the cause of personhood in God's being."[58]

> The one God is the Father of Jesus Christ and the Spirator of the Holy Spirit; the Trinity *depends ontologically on the Father* and is not in itself, that is, *qua* Trinity, the one God. If the Trinity is God, it is only because the Father makes it Trinity by granting it *hypostasis*.[59]

50. Macquarrie, *Christian Theology*, 115–22.

51. The phrase, אֶהְיֶה אֲשֶׁר אֶהְיֶה (Exod 3:14), can also be translated "I AM WHAT/WHO ' *ăšěr* I AM," or "I WILL BE WHAT/WHO '*ăšěr* I WILL BE," because ' *ĕheyĕh* (אֶהְיֶה) is a first person qal imperfect of *hyh* (היה), "to be."

52. Palamas, *Triads*, III.2.12.

53. Augustine, *Confessions*, bk. 10. See Zizioulas's critique in *One and Many*, 403.

54. Augustine, *Soliloquies*, 2.1.

55. Boethius, *Eutyches and Nestorius*, 85.

56. Aquinas, *Faith of the Church*; LaCugna, *God*, 150–52; Rahner, *Trinity*, 10–15.

57. González, *Story*, 2:186–88; Grenz and Olson, *20th Century Theology*, 19; Olson, *Story*, 522–23; Zizioulas, *One and Many*, 403.

58. Zizioulas, *Communion*, 141. For opposition, see Grenz, *Rediscovering*, 142–47; Gunton, *Trinitarian Theology*, 196–97; Harrison, "Zizioulas," 279; Torrance, *Persons in Communion*, 290, 289, 292, 293, 294; Volf, *Likeness*, 78–79.

59. Zizioulas, *Communion*, 154.

Grenz labels this mode of existence in God as the "Zizioulas Dictum," equating its impact and familiar axiom (i.e., "being is communion") on contemporary theology to the level of Rahner's Rule (i.e., "The 'economic' Trinity is the 'immanent' Trinity and the 'immanent' Trinity is the 'economic' Trinity"), and Pannenberg's Principle (i.e., "God's being is his rule").[60] How does Zizioulas develop this theology, and what are the implications?

Zizioulas's trinitarian ontological theology is based on fourth-century Cappadocian Fathers' work, specifically, Basil of Caesarea, Gregory of Nazianzus, Gregory of Nyssa, and Amphilochius of Iconium.[61] According to Zizioulas, these theologians overturned centuries of Greek philosophy on the meaning of person through their work in trinitarian theology in what he calls a "historic revolution."[62] This historical revolution resulted from the term "*hypostasis*" becoming identified with "person" making *the person the cause of being*.[63] Until this point, Greek philosophy identified person with essence.[64] This new perspective on the Trinity resulted from the theological vigor of the fourth century and the need to clarify Christian orthodoxy. Zizioulas highlights two significant heresies in the fourth century, Sabellianism and Eunomianism, in which the Cappadocian Fathers reacted to and, in turn, helped solidify orthodox trinitarian theology and freed the concept of *person* from a *substance*.

The fourth-century theological landscape was plagued by Arianism which stated the Son was created by God before the world, thus making him inferior and not co-equal with God the Father.[65] Marcellus of Ancyra of the Nicene Party and friend of Athanasius wrote a polemic against Arianism so strongly connecting the Son to the Father in consubstantiality that he was accused of Sabellianism by Eusebius.[66] The Council of Constantinople 335/6 deposed Marcellus.[67] Sabellianism was a heretical

---

60. Grenz, *Rediscovering*, 57–71, 96–97, 142–43, 218. For an original description of the "Pannenberg Principle," see Olson, "Pannenberg's Doctrine," 199.

61. Zizioulas, "Holy Trinity," 44. Amphilochius is not as significant as the other three Cappadocians primarily because only fragments of his writings survived.

62. Zizioulas, *Being*, 36–41; Zizioulas, "Capacity and Incapacity," 409; Zizioulas, *Communion*, 185–86; Zizioulas, "Holy Trinity," 47; Zizioulas, *Lectures*, 50–51.

63. Zizioulas, *Being*, 39.

64. See chapter 2, "Trinitarian Personhood: West and East."

65. Behr, *True God of True God*, 123, 138.

66. Behr, *True God of True God*, 74–75; Schaff, *Constantine to Gregory*, 651–52.

67. Schaff, dates Marcellus's deposition 335 CE (Schaff, *Constantine to Gregory*,

view of the Trinity that adhered to only one person of God, revealing himself in three different modes of being: Father, Son, *or* Holy Spirit.[68] These three modes of being were described as the *prosōpon* of God[69] based on the one being of God acting on the stage of history, sometimes as the Father, sometimes as the Son, and other times as the Holy Spirit. If the substance of God changes roles, then humans have no authentic dialogue or relationship with the persons of the Trinity.[70] God cannot really be known in Sabellianism because God can only be experienced through one of his stage names or characters: Father, Son, *or* Holy Spirit. For these reasons, the Cappadocians abandoned the word *prosōpon* when speaking of the three persons of God and instead used *hypostasis*, which initially was synonymous with *ousia*, meaning essence.[71] Therefore, in God, nature does not precede persons, rather persons precede nature.[72]

Following the Sabellian controversy, an advanced form of Arianism, named for its proponent, Eunomius, stirred the Cappadocians to define more carefully between persons as *hypostasis* and nature as *physis*. Gregory of Nyssa admitted that he inherited the fight against the Eunomian heresy after the death of his brother Basil.[73] Gregory reveals in his writings that Eunomius taught an Aristotelian philosophy of *genus*. The Son cannot be God because his nature (*physis*) is different from God the Father's nature. Therefore the Son is subordinate to the Father, and the Holy Spirit is subordinate to the Son simply by nature.[74] Since God the Father alone is God, in Eunomianism, the Son (by being begotten) and the Holy Spirit are not like God the Father in his essence/nature, which means they lack divinity and the essential characteristics to be God by their nature.[75] The task of the Cappadocians was to identify clearly between person and nature; the many and the one. The term *homoousion* used in the Nicene Creed, unlike *monoousion* or *toutoousion*, signaled an

---

651), but Cross and Livingstone date Marcellus's first deposition 336 (later he was expelled in 339) (Cross and Livingstone, "Marcellus" in *ODCC*).

68. Olson, *Story*, 92, 95, 142.

69. Behr, *One of the Holy Trinity*, 299.

70. Zizioulas, "Holy Trinity," 46.

71. Zizioulas, "Holy Trinity," 46; Behr, *One of the Holy Trinity*, 299; Schaff, *Constantine to Gregory*, 675–78, esp. 675n1.

72. Zizioulas, "Holy Trinity," 48–49.

73. Gregory of Nyssa, *Eunomius*, 1.33.

74. Gregory of Nyssa, *Eunomius*, 1.13.

75. Gregory of Nyssa, *Eunomius*, 1.15.

"equality of essence" rather than a "numerical identity."[76] God is not three essences or natures, rather three persons (*hypostasis*) and one essence/nature (*ousia/physis*). The terms *ousia* and *physis* philosophically suggest *genus* or *species*.[77] Therefore, the Nicene Creed affirms that all of the One God's attributes are found in each person of the Trinity.[78] Zizioulas raises the point that when God is called Father by the Cappadocians, they were *not* speaking of God's essence; instead, they said something about God's personhood.[79] Zizioulas further explains:

> In a more analytical way this means that God, as Father and not as substance, perpetually confirms through "being" His *free* will to exist. And it is precisely His trinitarian existence that constitutes this confirmation: the Father out of love—that is, freely—begets the Son and brings forth the Spirit. If God exists, He exists because the Father exists, that is, He who out of love freely begets the Son and brings forth the Spirit. Thus God as person—as the hypostasis of the Father—makes the one divine substance to be that which it is: the one God. This point is absolutely crucial. For it is precisely with this point that the new philosophical position of the Cappadocian Fathers, and of St Basil in particular, is directly connected. . . . Outside the Trinity there is no God, that is, no divine substance, because the ontological "principle" of God is the Father. The personal existence of God (the Father) constitutes His substance, makes it hypostases. The being of God is identified with the person.[80]

Basil illustrates this point by looking at the narrative of Job in the Scriptures. The introduction begins with the phrase, "There was a man."[81] This phrase only describes his nature. However, the writer further develops the characteristics of this man, thus making him a certain or a particular man as differentiated from all other men or human beings. Basil argues that this illustration can be cast upon God to understand both the *ousia* and the *hypostasis* of God as trinitarian: "Whatever your thought suggests

76. Schaff, *Constantine to Gregory*, 672.

77. Schaff, *Constantine to Gregory*, 672.

78. Schaff, *Constantine to Gregory*, 673. Schaff points out that John Philoponus, an Aristotelian and Monophysite, (sixth century) was charged with the heresy of tritheism because he did not distinguish between *physis* and *hypostasis* in describing the Threeness of the Trinity (Schaff, *Constantine to Gregory*, 674).

79. Zizioulas, "Holy Trinity," 49.

80. Zizioulas, *Being*, 41.

81. Job 1:1.

to you as to the mode of the existence of the Father, you will think also in the case of the Son, and in like manner too of the Holy Ghost."[82]

The modes of existence for Zizioulas or persons-in-relation are not based on substance or nature but, rather, begin with a person. However, one might ask, "What person?" If substance is not the cause of God, "what or who is the cause (*aitia*) of God?" Zizioulas answers, "the person of the Father and not divine substance . . . is the source and cause of the Trinity."[83] This approach to trinitarian theology is called Monarchianism, which says that the person of the Father is the source of the Trinity.[84] The Father is only the Father because of the existence of the Son and the Holy Spirit. However, there is no starting point; rather, the Father eternally causes (*aitia*) the being of the Son and Holy Spirit.[85] Therefore the persons of the Trinity are not described by their nature but can only be conceived in their relationship (*schesis*) with one another.[86] Gregory of Nazianzus says God the Father is the name of the One who eternally causes the Son and Holy Spirit and is not the name given to divine substance.

> But it is the name of the Relation in which the Father stands to the Son, and the Son to the Father. For as with us these names make known a genuine and intimate relation, so, in the case before us too, they denote an identity of nature between Him That is begotten and Him That begets.[87]

Even at this, it appears that Zizioulas's monarchial view of the trinitarian persons-in-relation is saying more than the Cappadocians were espousing.

While Zizioulas's Dictum[88] being "the one substance of God coincides with the communion of the three persons"[89] has given a solution to the existential despair concerning the nature of personhood, his

---

82. Basil, *Letters*, 38.3.

83. Zizioulas, "Holy Trinity," 52.

84. Basil uses the term "Monarchy" in reference to the Trinity's unity as opposed the distinctions of persons within the Trinity. The three persons of the Trinity serve as One Monarchy by the will of the Father (Basil, *Spirit*, 18.45). On the topics of *monarchia* and *aitia* of God, see Gregory of Nazianzus, *Orations*, "On the Son," 1–3, 15–19, 301–2, 306–8.

85. Gunton, "Persons and Particularity," 100. See Zizioulas, *One and Many*, 10–12.

86. Zizioulas, "Capacity and Incapacity," 436.

87. Gregory of Nazianzus, *Orations*, "On the Son," 16.

88. Grenz, *Rediscovering*, 142–43.

89. Zizioulas, *Being*, 134.

explanation of the Father as the cause of the Trinity is problematic.[90] In offering a trinitarian theology that describes persons-in-relation as caused by the Father, Zizioulas has framed his argument as relational (i.e., personhood) over functional (i.e., immanent trinity), monotheistic over tritheistic, Eastern (i.e., persons based) over Western (i.e., substance-based), and freedom over necessity.[91] By distilling the trinitarian problem down to these categories, one is inevitably faced with questions about whether there is One substance called God from which the three persons share, or are there Three persons who are One in communion? While the latter paradigm seems to be Zizioulas's approach, he actually says "that *what causes God to be is the Person of the Father.*"[92] Therefore, Zizioulas's framing of the issue from the personhood of God, as opposed to the starting point of substance, leads him to ask, "What is the cause of persons-in-relation?" Zizioulas concludes that the Oneness in God is not solely substance but personal relations, and for there to be personal relations, there must be persons, and persons act in freedom rather than necessity, and to freely exist means being/personal existence is caused by a person. Therefore, the cause of the Trinity is a singular person, God the Father.[93] Zizioulas's Dictum ironically undercuts three co-equal persons in mutual communion.[94]

Zizioulas confesses a hierarchy of persons within the Trinity.[95] On the one hand, Torrance sees in Zizioulas causality in that the Father becomes a "primordial reality."[96] On the other hand, Fiddes believes that this emphasis on persons leads to tritheism through individualizing the persons.[97] Instead, Fiddes takes a Thomistic approach of "subsistent relations," which he proposes as the starting point for the participation of three persons of the Trinity.[98] Ultimately, the difference between Zizoulas's argument and the Western approach to the Trinity, while valuable as it may be for developing a personal ontology, is that Zizioulas begins with

90. Wilks, "Ontology," 83–84. See McCall, *Which Trinity?*, 189–215.

91. Zizioulas, *One and Many*, 10–14.

92. Zizioulas, "Holy Trinity," 54.

93. Zizioulas, *Being*, 39–72, 83–89; Zizioulas, *Communion*, 137–45; Zizioulas, "Holy Trinity," 50–55; Zizioulas, *Lectures*, 53, 59–62; Zizioulas, *One and Many*, 10–14.

94. Gunton, *Trinitarian Theology*, 196.

95. Zizioulas, *Communion*, 143–44; Zizioulas, *Lectures*, 59.

96. Torrance, *Persons*, 292–93.

97. Fiddes, *Participating*, 17.

98. Fiddes, *Participating*, 34–46.

person over substance. Both Western theology and Zizioulas begin with the One in trinitarian thought, that being Western theology with One substance and Zizioulas with One Person.

The premise of Zizioulas's argument on the substance and person of God is to understand it as a debate of priority against the Western theological view, which gives priority to substance. That is to ask, "Was there One divine substance/nature, called God, from which three persons derive and hold their unity? Alternatively, was there One divine person, called Father, from which the Son and Holy Spirit derive and hold their unity?" For Zizioulas, the former question gives too much emphasis to substance making divinity precede the three persons.[99] The latter question begins with a person as the originator of substance.[100] Therefore, Zizioulas does not hold to a substance of unity as a priority of God's being. Instead, the substance in God is subordinated by the idea that the person of the Father is the cause of all that exists, including the substance of trinitarian unity.[101] Furthermore, in Zizioulas's presentation of the *aseity* of the Father causing the Trinity to exist, the Son and the Holy Spirit are subordinated not simply in a functional way but in an ontological way.[102] However, a surface reading of Zizioulas will conclude that person precedes substance in trinitarian theology.[103] On the contrary, Zizioulas goes to great lengths to argue that the substance (i.e., being or nature) of God is equal and simultaneous with the relationship in God as found in the concept of the-one-and-the-many.[104] The question is whether or not the Zizioulian Dictum of being-as-communion is convincing based on the fact that for Zizioulas to make his point that substance and person are simultaneous,[105] he gravitates toward an emphasis of person over

---

99. Zizioulas, *One and Many*, 13–14.

100. Zizioulas, *One and Many*, 13–14; Zizioulas, *Lectures*, 91–98.

101. Zizioulas, *Being*, 44; Zizioulas, *One and Many*, 4, 7, 10, 11, 12–14, 20, 43, 55, 265, 336–38. Zizioulas argues the Father is the cause of the Holy Trinity (Zizioulas, *Communion*, 137; Zizioulas, *Lectures*, 53).

102. Zizioulas, *Being*, 17, 41. See Torrance, *Persons*, 292–93; McCall, *Which Trinity?*, 197–202, 207, 210.

103. Zizioulas, *Being*, 43–46.

104. Knight, "Introduction," 2; Zizioulas, *Being*, 145–49; Zizioulas, *Communion*, 131–32; Zizioulas, *Lectures*, 50–51.

105. Zizioulas, *Being*, 84–85n60; Zizioulas, "Holy Trinity," 48–49; Zizioulas, "Capacity and Incapacity," 410–12, 438; Zizioulas, *Lectures*, 53.

substance,[106] the Father as the cause of the Trinity,[107] and the monarchy within the Trinity.[108]

Athanasius indeed used the term *archē* when speaking of God the Father's role in the Trinity.[109] Furthermore, Basil refers to God's *monarchia* when arguing the Holy Spirit's divinity.[110] However, it is also important to place patristic arguments in context as to their purpose. They were stressing the unity of the three persons of the Trinity.[111] This stress on unity is not necessarily the case in the modern context. Fundamental orthodox Christianity holds that the Triune God is One *ousia* and Three *hypostases*. Zizioulas offers freedom rather than necessity as a corrective to existential philosophy by beginning with persons rather than substance in trinitarian theology. The Father, through ontological freedom, causes divine being to exist.[112] The Father causes (constitutes) the being of the Son and the Holy Spirit who also bear all of the divine essence through relationship (*schesis*), and in relationship (*schesis*), the interdependent fellowship (*koinōnia*) makes the Father who He is (i.e., the Father cannot be Father without a Son).[113] Harrison asks, "Now, since the Son and the Spirit do not constitute their own essence in the same way that the Father does, how, in Zizioulas's terms, are they absolutely free, which they must be since they are fully God?"[114] "*Freedom*," says Zizioulas, "is the 'cause' of being for Patristic thought."[115] That is to say, divine essence is eternally constituted by freedom in its *ekstasis*, making it *hypostatic*, and this is the trinitarian mode of existence.[116] Zizioulas's paradigm described as freedom eternally causing being to exist relationally by causing *hypostasis* to be *ekstatic*, thus becoming the mode of existence has been shortened

---

106. Zizioulas, *Being*, 39–41; Zizioulas, "Holy Trinity," 56; Zizioulas, "Capacity and Incapacity," 403–4, 407–10; Zizioulas, *Lectures*, 53, 61.

107. Zizioulas, *Communion*, 137–40; Zizioulas, "Holy Trinity," 46; Zizioulas, *Lectures*, 60–61; Wilks, "Ontology," 80–81.

108. Zizioulas, *Being*, 44–45n40; Zizioulas, *Communion*, 131–34; Zizioulas, "Holy Trinity," 51; Wilks, "Ontology," 81.

109. Torrance, *Trinitarian Faith*, 312. Cf. Zizioulas, *Communion*, 118–23, 126.

110. Basil, *Spirit*, 27–30.

111. Basil, *Spirit*, 27–28n3.

112. Zizioulas, "Holy Trinity," 51.

113. Zizioulas, "Capacity and Incapacity," 436–37; Zizioulas, *Lectures*, 53.

114. Harrison, "Zizioulas," 279.

115. Zizioulas, "Holy Trinity," 54.

116. Zizioulas, "Capacity and Incapacity," 408–9.

to the expressions "persons-in-relation" or "being-as-communion."[117] Zizioulas's proposal of persons-in-relation is beneficial for personal ontology; however, Zizioulas's Eastern Orthodox theology and critique of Western theology have skewed certain aspects of his approach to trinitarian theology and the implications of pneumatology. An understanding of Zizioulas's trinitarian implications, along with the role of the person of the Holy Spirit, can be found in Eucharistic-Ecclesiology, Ecumenical Vision, and Ecological Concern.

Eucharistic-Ecclesiology

The event of Holy Eucharist is, for Zizioulas, the culmination of trinitarian theology as persons-in-relation. He argues that the Eucharist constitutes the Church and not the Church that constitutes the Eucharist.[118] First, a "concrete gathering of the local community" is required for the eucharistic event to occur.[119] The Church is the corporate gathering of individuals into one place for one purpose. Zizioulas remains true to his methodology of "the One and the Many" by simply describing the Church as the many gathered as one in community.[120] He further differentiates between two ways of describing the unity of the many as one. The first approach is to view the unity of people as the Church by being unified in the Holy Spirit. Zizioulas warns that this "pneumatocentric ecclesiology" can lead to a "charismatic sociology."[121] In this case, the Spirit-led community precedes the Eucharist. "This position forms part of an ecclesiology which views the Church as the Body of Christ that is *first* instituted in itself as a historical entity and *then* produces the 'means of grace' called sacraments among them primarily the Eucharist."[122] The second approach to understanding the unity of the Church for which Zizioulas advocates, begins with Christology being "the notion of the person of Christ as the Incarnate Word who also contains within Himself

---

117. Zizioulas, *Being*, 15–16, 87–88; Grenz, *Rediscovering*, 138–39, 142; Anatolios, "Personhood," 147–64.

118. Zizioulas, *One and Many*, 67–73.

119. Zizioulas, *One and Many*, 73.

120. Zizioulas, *Eucharist*, 54.

121. Zizioulas, *Eucharist*, 16.

122. Zizioulas, *One and Many*, 68.

the 'many.'"[123] This starting point for Zizioulas answers how human beings are incorporated into the person of Jesus Christ manifested in space and time?[124] Christians are incorporated into the life of Jesus Christ because he is a "corporate Personality," who does not precede the Holy Spirit but instead is himself constituted by the Holy Spirit (e.g., Isa 11:2; 61:1; Matt 1:18; 3:16; 4:1; Luke 1:35; Rom 8:11; Heb 9:14) thus indicating that the life of Jesus Christ is communal with the Holy Spirit.[125] This definition of "corporate Personality" contradicts Zizioulas's opposition to the unity of people in the Church made possible by the Holy Spirit, for which he negatively called it "pneumatocentric ecclesiology" leading to a "charismatic sociology."[126] Zizioulas further argues at this point that the body of Christ cannot be separated in the manner of his individual body and Christ's corporate body. Instead, the body of Christ is simultaneously one (individual Christ) and many (corporate/community Christ), and the only historical instance of this mutual cohesion occurring is in the Eucharist.[127] "*Therefore, the ecclesiological presuppositions of the Eucharist cannot be found outside the Eucharist itself.*"[128]

Second, the Eucharist event is the participation of the "eschatological community" into the "eschatological Christ."[129] While the Church exists in history, its identity is in its eschatological hope.[130] However, this future reality is present in the world in one way and is still yet to come in another way.[131] The future happens in the present through the Eucharist by partaking in the eschatological Christ along with the eschatological community. The eschatological community is the laity who constitute the event by their presence and response.[132] The eschatological community has a "charismatic nature" made possible through the indwelling of the

---

123. Zizioulas, *Eucharist*, 16.

124. Zizioulas, *Eucharist*, 16.

125. Zizioulas, *One and Many*, 68; Leach, *Corporate Personality*, 21, 107.

126. Zizioulas, *Being*, 126–32, 139; Zizioulas, *Eucharist*, 16.

127. Zizioulas, *One and Many*, 69; Zizioulas, *Eucharist*, 57. Zizioulas discusses this in terms of "catholization of the Church" (Zizioulas, *Eucharist*, 115–18). Zizioulas makes reference to this as "the whole Christ," in Zizioulas, *Being*, 157.

128. Zizioulas, *One and Many*, 69. For a historical perspective, see Zizioulas, *Being*, 80–81.

129. Zizioulas, *One and Many*, 69.

130. Zizioulas, *Lectures*, 127.

131. Zizioulas, *Lectures*, 129.

132. Zizioulas, *One and Many*, 69.

Holy Spirit through baptism and chrismation.[133] Zizioulas contends that there is no hierarchy with the church; rather, there is an order and gifted-ness, including deacons, presbyters, and bishop. At the same time, the deacons and the presbyters are given specific roles and duties (with)*in* the community; it is the bishop, while equal, who is ordained to lead the community from the *outside* and *inside* as part of the community.[134] By virtue of ordination, only the bishop gives the Holy Spirit to the community through the offering of the Eucharist and leading in liturgy (i.e., *Epiclesis*, the invocation of the Holy Spirit in the Eucharistic Anaphora).[135] The symbolism of the bishop is rich for Zizioulas.

> There is the paradox in the office of the bishop that is the very paradox of Christ's position in the Eucharist. In the Eucharist, Christ represents the community to the Father. He offers the Eucharist as the first-born of the brethren, as *part* of the community. At the same time, he addresses the community, especially by giving it the Holy Spirit, the charismata. In this sense, he stands above the community. The bishop does the same paradoxical work. He offers the Eucharist as part of the community and as its head.[136]

In this way, the bishop, himself, is the manifestation of unity, a type of Christ in his corporate personality made possible by his ordination in the Holy Spirit.[137] For example, in Ignatius of Antioch's letter to the Church of Magnesia, he speaks concerning church unity (i.e., "divine harmony") and in so doing reminds the congregation that the bishop "presides in the place of God" while the presbyters are "the assembly of the apostles."[138] McGuckin explains the bishop's role as primarily "the icon of Christ in the local church" and "the servant-lord of the people of God."[139] There-fore, for Zizioulas, the Church resembles the Trinity by its unity of the many made possible through the Divine Eucharist and led by the bishop.

---

133. Zizioulas, *One and Many*, 69.

134. Zizioulas, *One and Many*, 71.

135. Zizioulas, *One and Many*, 71; Zizioulas, *Communion*, 296–98. Cf. Cyril of Jerusalem, *Catechetical Lectures*, 23.7. Burgess, *Holy Spirit*, 112, 147–48; McGuckin, *Orthodox*, 289, 297, 298–99; Thiselton, *Holy Spirit*, 188; Ware, *Orthodox Way*, 89–90.

136. Zizioulas, *One and Many*, 71.

137. Zizioulas, *Being*, 136–37; Zizioulas, *Eucharist*, 218–27, 247–56.

138. Ignatius, *Magnesians*, 61.

139. McGuckin, *Orthodox*, 329.

Ecumenical Vision

A second implication to the trinitarian persons-in-relation, as demonstrated by Zizioulas, is an Ecumenical Vision. For Zizioulas, Eucharist and Ecumenism are inseparable because the end goal of the ecumenical movement is eucharistic communion.[140] The Eucharist constitutes the Church as the people of God gather as the body of Christ and the temple of the Holy Spirit.[141] Similar to Zizioulas, Cattoi writes from a Roman Catholic perspective concerning Ecumenism which he suggests is equality-with-headship. Cattoi, referencing Gregory of Nyssa, points to the Father's intra-trinitarian cause (*aitia*) as a social trinitarian model, which is also demonstrated in ecclesial networking.[142] Each local Church is distinct but undividedly serves the same purpose for salvation of souls.[143] However, Cattoi argues for authority within Ecumenism which is exercised in love.[144] Zizioulas is not blind to this perspective and offers a unity with diversity concept based on trinitarian theology for Ecumenism.[145] The Church embodies the unity of many people along with their particular diversity. Here again, is the model of the-one-and-the-many. On the one hand, the three distinct *hypostases*, Father, Son, and Holy Spirit, are *homoousion*. Moreover, on the other hand, Christ himself is also one-and-many. "If we accept the Holy Spirit *constitutes* the Christ-event . . . , we are led to the conclusion that Christ is inconceivable without this body, i.e., the 'many' who form His body by the operation of the Spirit."[146] This one-and-many theology is actualized in participation of the Eucharist in that the many diverse people are united in one act and by one Holy Spirit becoming the one church.

For Zizioulas, eucharistic-ecclesiology is evident in a truly "catholic" Church and the unity of each episcopal Church because the body of Christ cannot be divided.[147] A church cannot exist independent of

---

140. Zizioulas, *One and Many*, 317.

141. Zizioulas, *One and Many*, 310–11. See Oden, *Spirit*, 179.

142. Cattoi, "Catholic-Orthodox Ecumenical Dialogue," 185–86, 191, 192–98.

143. Cattoi, "Catholic-Orthodox Ecumenical Dialogue," 195.

144. Cattoi, "Catholic-Orthodox Ecumenical Dialogue," 196. Of course for Cattoi, it is the Roman Catholic Church who should preside over an ecumenical movement (Cattoi, "Catholic-Orthodox Ecumenical Dialogue," 196).

145. Zizioulas, *One and Many*, 333–48.

146. Zizioulas, *One and Many*, 337.

147. Zizioulas, *Eucharist*, 260, 261.

another. Thus, Zizioulas demonstrates a correlation of relationships between human personhood, the baptized believer, and eucharistic-ecclesiology. In viewing this correlation, Collins sees a new paradigm for ecclesial authority for which he says Zizioulas misses due to Zizioulas's rhetoric toward a democratic approach of the Reformed church and traditional polity.[148] Collins affirms Zizioulas's one-and-many concept for ecumenical purposes. However, rather than limit the concept to interpret Scripture and patristics, Collins suggests the-one-and-the-many concept be used for dialogue between different church traditions on the topic of ecclesial authority.[149] Furthermore, Collins would like to see Zizioulas's concepts of persons-in-relation as *koinōnia* and the-one-and-the-many connected with his concept of *college* as the operating motif toward an ecumenical goal.[150]

Zizioulas's additional concept of "college" to describe the "one Catholic Church" is a denial of the concept that the church is a "unity of parts."[151] The manner in which Zizioulas uses the collegial principle mirrors the image of Jesus's apostles as successors of his ministry. The apostle Peter was preeminent, yet each apostle had a significant role in the ministry. Peter's role was foundational and collective of the whole.[152] Likewise, each bishop and each church has a role in the kingdom of God, but they are not simply a part of the whole because there needs to be one who is "head" representing the many.[153] Each bishop and every church is a collection of all the apostles and Peter as a college.[154] Here again, philosophically, the-one-and-the-many concept is utilized in the church toward ecumenical means.

148. Collins, "Authority and Ecumenism," 156.

149. Collins, "Authority and Ecumenism," 156.

150. Collins, "Authority and Ecumenism," 157–58. While Zizioulas has written much on ecumenicalism, it is typically from an Orthodox Church theological and ecclesiological polemic. For example in an article titled, "Uniformity, Diversity, and the Unity of the Church," Zizioulas introduces a concept of "unity and diversity" as a paradigm toward ecumenicalism. However, he denies the ecumenical unity of the "confessional Church" because it introduces into ecumenicalism a diversity of confessions (Zizioulas, *One and Many*, 341–44). Therefore, Zizioulas would not be open to Collins's treatment on the topic. See Zizioulas, *One and Many*, 309–413.

151. Zizioulas, *Eucharist*, 260.

152. Zizioulas, *Eucharist*, 261; cf. Matt 16:17–19.

153. Zizioulas, *Eucharist*, 262; Zizioulas, *Being*, 168, 174, 177, 196, 200–4.

154. Zizioulas, *Eucharist*, 262–63.

Ecological Concern

A third implication of the trinitarian persons-in-relation, as demon-strated by Zizioulas, is an Ecological Concern. One of the consequences of viewing human beings as substance rather than persons-in-relation is that human beings become individuals, and when humans are defined by their individual substance and rational nature, they separate themselves from creation, developing an indifference toward creation resulting in pollution and destruction.[155] This devastating consequence upon cre-ation and all people globally for Zizioulas is "sin," which theology, rather than ethics, must answer.[156] Therefore, Zizioulas offers a concept of "man as the priest of creation" to tackle "ecological evil."[157]

Historically, Irenaeus defended and articulated that God the Father created the world from his free will against the views of the Gnostic Val-entinus as an absolute doctrinal foundation.[158] Irenaeus explained that God only used his will to create and that God's will is his substance.[159] As a result, the early church believed that the world was created by God as stated in the baptismal creeds,[160] thus indicating that the material world is good and not evil by nature which the Gnostics held.[161] By stating that God created the world indicates it is good, but also that it is *not* eternal. The world has a beginning. If the world has a beginning, then, logically, the world has an end.[162]

Christians hold to a view that the world was "created out of nothing" (*creatio ex nihilo*), meaning God as Creator did not form the world from preexistent material but simply spoke the world into existence from his

155. Zizioulas, "Capacity and Incapacity," 406n3.

156. Zizioulas, *Eucharistic Communion*, 143–44. Cf., Johnson, who refers to the "environmental problem" as "ecocide" (Johnson, *Women*, 7).

157. Zizioulas, *Eucharistic Communion*, 143, 145.

158. May, *Creatio Ex Nihilo*, 166–67, 168–69, 174.

159. Irenaeus, *Heresies*, 2.30.9, 406.

160. It is well known that the early baptismal creed was kept by memory rather than being written down so to protect it from unbelievers who might profane it. The earliest recorded forms were found in the writings of Rufinus (390 CE) in the Latin West and Marcellus of Ancyra (336 to 341 CE) in the Greek East. Although there are minor variations, the point here is that each began with the acknowledgement of God the Father being the Creator of the world, "I believe in God the Father Almighty Maker of heaven and earth" (Schaff, *Creeds of Christendom*, 18–21).

161. Zizioulas, "Creation (vol. 12)," 42.

162. Zizioulas, "Creation (vol. 12)," 43.

creative free will.[163] The first person recorded to have mentioned that the world was made from nothing was Theophilus of Antioch (late second century).[164] However, May indicates that Theophilus's formalized and clear doctrine of *creatio ex nihilo* signifies an established tradition that likely pre-dates Theophilus.[165] There is evidence of the connotation of *creatio ex nihilo* in Basilides (early to mid-second century) and the Jewish prayers in the *Apostolic Constitutions* (350 to 380 CE).[166] The conflict for some Christians is that while they believe the world has a definite and absolute beginning, they also think the world was created to be eternal. If the world was created to be eternal, then it can be said that God created "another God by nature."[167] Therefore, *creatio ex nihilo* indicates a clear beginning and a definite end.[168]

God's free will to create the world from nothing also signifies that both time and space are creations and thus have a beginning and an end.[169] Zizioulas concludes, "All this means that creation *taken in itself . . .* constitutes an entity surrounded and conditioned by nothing. I came from nothing and will return to *nothing.*"[170] All creation reveals a beginning and an end experienced in "the space-time structure of the universe."[171]

> Death is experienced as a return to nothingness, in spite of the fact that new entities may emerge out of the old ones that have died. For neither the fact that species procreate can change the fact that a concrete progenitor no longer exists after his death as a particular identity, nor, worse even, can the return of a corpse to the earth in order to become the basic natural elements for other forms of life be a consolation for the loss of a particular

163. Genesis 1. Hasel and Hasel, "Unique Cosmology," 12, 29.

164. Theophilus, *Autolycus*, 90.

165. May, *Creatio Ex Nihilo*, 156.

166. May, *Creatio Ex Nihilo*, 21–22, 53–54, 156–57.

167. Zizioulas, *Eucharistic Communion*, 161–62.

168. Doukhan offers an exegetical study of Gen 1–3 to propose that death was not part of the original biblical creation narrative in that (1) creation was described as good (*ṭōb*) without evil, (2) the writer knows the effects of evil and qualifies the creation event with "not yet" (*ṭerem*), (3) death is a direct result of sin and not God's original intent for creation, and (4) the fact that biblical evidence shows a future re-creation of heaven, earth, and an environment with the absence of death (Doukhan, "Death," 329–42).

169. Zizioulas, "Creation (vol. 12)," 43.

170. Zizioulas, "Creation (vol. 12)," 43.

171. Zizioulas, "Creation (vol. 12)," 44.

being. Death amounts to the extinction of particular beings precisely because the world, having come out of nothing and being penetrated by it, does not possess any means in its nature whereby to overcome nothingness.[172]

A relatively weak rebuttal to Zizioulas's "from nothing to nothing" axiom, yet a rebuttal nonetheless, is that since Zizioulas uses the word "nothing" to mean non-material, it is found in God's curse to Adam after the fall, "till you return to the ground, for out of it you were taken; for you are dust, and to dust you shall return."[173] In a literal sense, Adam is formed from the ground and dust (*ᵓdāmāh* and *ᶜāfār*), and he is dust, and he will return to the dust. Dust is material and *not* nothing. God formed Adam from the dust of the ground.[174] Thus God formed Adam from something, and that something was dust. At the same time, God's creative free will produced dust, ground, and earth through his spoken word for which it did not formally exist.[175] It was previously nothing. All of this is to say; the world is neither self-existent nor self-sustaining. The world has a beginning as it was created out of nothing, and the world has an end which is a return to nothing.[176] The world is not eternal. What then is the hope for the world?

The answer is found in the trinitarian persons-in-relation. Irenaeus reminds us of the two hands (the Son and the Holy Spirit) of God the Father who formed Adam into his likeness.[177] To say that humans were created in the image of God (*imago Dei*) opens up a plethora of meaning, but for Zizioulas, the key to the image of God is *freedom*. However, human freedom is distinct from God's freedom. God in his freedom created the world from nothing ("absolute freedom").[178] Human beings in their freedom can only create by using the materials in the created world ("relative freedom").[179] Therefore, human freedom is a decision between *given* possibilities.[180] The key to understanding Zizioulas's point is to

172. Zizioulas, *Eucharistic Communion*, 161.

173. Gen 3:19; Doukhan, "Death," 336.

174. Gen 2:7. See May, *Creatio Ex Nihilo*, 21–22, 49, 134, 175.

175. Gen 1:9–10. For an exegetical and theological argument on the creation narrative, see Davidson, "Origins," 59–129.

176. Zizioulas, "Creation (vol. 12)," 43.

177. Irenaeus, *Heresies*, 5.6.1.

178. Zizioulas, "Creation (vol. 13)," 2.

179. Zizioulas, "Creation (vol. 13)," 2.

180. Zizioulas, "Creation (vol. 13)," 2.

understand the difference between divine and human freedom. Divine freedom is absolute in that there is no necessity and no boundaries. Human freedom is relative to necessity and operates within boundaries. Zizioulas refers to these necessities and boundaries in human freedom as *given* or *givenness*.[181] Everything humans have, the world, the animals, other human beings, etc., are given to them by the uncreated and absolutely free God. The problem Zizioulas argues is when humans, who are created in the image of God, try to exercise their freedom in a way that is equivalent to God's freedom (i.e., boundless).[182] The result of a finite, mortal being attempting to exercise absolute freedom is *tragedy*.[183] Zizioulas quotes Dostoevsky on how a human being can symbolically attain absolute freedom for which humans are so prone to desire:

> Every one [*sic*] who wants to attain complete freedom must be daring enough to kill himself. . . . This is the final limit of freedom, that is all, there is nothing beyond it. Who dares to kill himself becomes God. Everyone can do this and thus cause God to cease to exist, and then nothing will exist at all.[184]

This human problem of desiring to execute absolute freedom and not be confined by the "givens" was actually a result of being created in the image of God.[185] Gregory of Nyssa speaks of the image of God in humanity as being the beauty and the free will, which mimics the Creator's free will.[186] He speaks of it so strongly that human free will is like that of a king who wields his will-power to rule because this will is like God's will and is good and righteous "in all that belongs to the dignity of royalty."[187] Why did the Creator place within human beings this insatiable appetite toward absolute freedom while placing them in the boundaries of time and space along with the command not to eat from a specific tree?

The answer to the ecological problem and its solution are both found in one answer. Human beings are both the answer and the problem. Zizioulas points out that the Triune God created this world and

181. Zizioulas, *Eucharist Communion*, 167.

182. Zizioulas, *Eucharistic Communion*, 168.

183. Zizioulas, *Eucharistic Communion*, 168; Zizioulas, "Capacity and Incapacity," 410–12; Fitzgerald, "Passions," 12–15.

184. Zizioulas, *Eucharistic Communion*, 168, from Dostoevsky, *Devils*, 126.

185. Zizioulas, *Eucharistic Communion*, 168–69.

186. Gregory of Nyssa, *On Virginity*, 357.

187. Gregory of Nyssa, *Making of Man*, 3.1–2; 4.1; cf. 16.1–18.

placed the human being in the world as the-one-*for*-the-many. "Person-hood in man demands that he should at all times embody in himself the totality of creation."[188] The world's survival was placed in the hands of human beings who were given limited freedom within the *givens* of their environment to be exercised for the world.[189] God's design was that human beings were to be the priesthood of the creation. However, the result is that human beings have separated themselves from creation in a utilitarian fashion, using freedom for the self and destroying the created world.[190] Zizioulas calls this misplaced freedom and its consequences the failure of Adam and the sin of all human beings for which a Savior of the whole world was needed and found in Christ.[191] The soteriological problem is when Christ is viewed simply as an individual rather than a corporate personality. Human beings have focused on individuality and have failed to connect to God's creation, inevitably abusing it because freedom becomes misplaced upon the self, and creation has no natural means of survival outside of human beings.[192] In other words, freedom through the *imago Dei* is designed to be other-oriented as illustrated in the Trinity, and human beings are to love others and be responsible for creation because human beings form "an organic part of the material world."[193] Johnson also ties together the problem of misplaced human freedom, which focuses on the individual and results in an ecological problem and the need for salvation, but she illustrates it in an extreme analogy. Johnson's soteriological-ecological approach equates the earth with Jesus Christ, and as his (Earth's) hour approaches, he (Jesus/Earth) enters into his passion and death while the disciples (humans) hideaway in the upper room.[194] Her answer is found in the conversion of humans (i.e., Earth's disciples) to the Earth by the Creator Spirit.[195] The act that Zizioulas calls people into as priests of creation is the Eucharist, where the bread and the wine are symbolic elements of creation and unites

188. Zizioulas, *Eucharistic Communion*, 174. For Zizioulas the "totality of human nature" is the doctrine of the Trinity as each particular person is unique and irreplaceable.

189. Zizioulas, *Eucharistic Communion*, 170–71.

190. Zizioulas, *Eucharistic Communion*, 171–72.

191. Zizioulas, *Eucharistic Communion*, 174.

192. Zizioulas, *Being*, 109; Zizioulas, *Eucharistic Communion*, 170; Gen 2:15.

193. Zizoulas, *Eucharistic Communion*, 171.

194. Johnson, *Women*, 9.

195. Johnson, *Women*, 62, 66.

people into communion with one another and communion with the Triune God.[196] This priesthood of creation will bring peace, unity, and ecological healing.

TRINITARIAN PNEUMATOLOGY

While Zizioulas's trinitarian ontology has positively impacted theology, contemporary thought, and existential philosophy, there remains a deficiency in his presentation of pneumatology and anthropology. Zizioulas warns against developing an economy of the Holy Spirit because it threatens the unity of God.[197] However, the results of this measure by Zizioulas leave a two-fold negative effect: (1) The Holy Spirit is reduced to an adjective, a means, or an act. This reductionism in Zizioulas's economy results in a minimal understanding of the Spirit's personhood, reducing the Spirit to constituting the Christ event or the Church through the Eucharist;[198] and, (2) the Holy Spirit's role with/in humans becomes too rationalistic rather than relational.[199] The anthropological deficiency with Zizioulas's application of trinitarian ontology starts with the human need for relationality but ends virtually with a loss of the personal for the unity in a ceremonial act of Eucharist.[200] The particulars (distinct persons) are absorbed into the one eucharistic-ecclesiology in a homogenized whole.[201]

As a correction to Zizioulas's pneumatological deficiency, this thesis seeks to qualify the economy of the Holy Spirit as trinitarian pneumatological personhood; which means, there are three distinct, particular, divine persons who are united through their interrelatedness, mutual indwelling, self-giving love, and oneness of will. Thus, to receive the Holy Spirit is to receive the grace of the Son and the will of the Father as the

196. Zizioulas, *Eucharistic Communion*, 174.

197. Zizioulas, *One and Many*, 77.

198. Zizioulas, *Being*, 111–12, 126–27, 130; Zizioulas, "Capacity and Incapacity," 441–42; Zizioulas, *Communion*, 244; Zizioulas, *Eucharist*, 15–16; Zizioulas, *One and Many*, 7, 16, 337; Knight, "Introduction," 10; Turner, "Eschatology and Truth," 21, 26–27.

199. Zizioulas, *Being*, 114; Gunton, *Trinitarian Theology*, 115.

200. Zizioulas, *Being*, 61–62; Zizioulas, *Eucharist*, 17–18, 53–58; Volf, *Likeness*, 100; Farrow, "Person and Nature," 118–19; Olson and Hall, *Trinity*, 114–15.

201. Zizioulas, *Eucharist*, 16–18, 53–58, 67–68, 92–93, 108–28. In Zizioulas terminology "catholic" (*kath' olou*) is the sum of the particulars (Zizioulas, *Eucharist*, 109).

presence of God.[202] Therefore, all three persons of the Trinity are involved in extending reconciliation toward humans, although each has a specific work in the process.[203] However, the work of the persons of the Trinity is not a cold, functional activity; rather, there is a warm, relational connection between the triune God and his creation to and with whom God communicates corporately and individually.[204] This warm, relational communication is actualized because God does not simply offer imputed righteousness (what God does *for us*, i.e., justification),[205] but also imparted righteousness (what God does *in us*, i.e., sanctification).[206] As such, then, the Holy Spirit is intimately involved in people's lives, not creating a Christian homogeneity, not dehumanizing, and not trapping people in a legalistic asceticism. Instead, the Holy Spirit dynamically enhances the particularity of the Christian person while simultaneously drawing each into a peaceful relationship with God and a self-giving understanding of love with others.[207] Christian anthropology is then the result of this human relationship with the Holy Spirit, who is intimately connected with the Father and Son. Christian anthropology will transform human personhood because human beings receive and live an abundant life through the Holy Spirit while also being incorporated into a new relationship with the Father, Son, and Holy Spirit.[208]

202. Isa 32:15; Ezek 39:29; 43:9; Joel 2:28; Zech 12:10; John 7:37–39; 13:20; 14:16–17, 25–26; 15:26; 16:7, 12–13; 20:22–23; Acts 1:4–5; 2:1–4, 32–33, 38–39; 1 Cor 6:11, 19–20. See Gregory of Nazianzus, *Orations*, "On the Holy Spirit," 26–27, 326–27; Burge, *Anointed Community*, 43, 98–99; Carter, *Holy Spirit*, 157–90; Thiselton, *Holy Spirit*, 4, 12–14, 72, 498; Turner, *Holy Spirit*, 79–81. The topic of God's Presence is dealt with in chapter 6, "Personal Presence: A Shadow of Things to Come."

203. See Coppedge, *Portraits*, 300–31; John of Damascus, *Faith*, 1.13, 15–17.

204. Gunton, *One, Three, Many*, 215–16.

205. Eph 2:8–9. Wesley, "Minutes of Some Late Conversations," 277–78; Wesley, "Second Essay," 393–97; Oden, *Spirit*, 124–25; Wiley and Culbertson, *Christian Theology*, 280–82, 313; Purkiser, *Exploring*, 297. For a study on the difference of biblical interpretation and theology between Lutherans and Orthodox, see Meyendorff and Tobias, *Salvation in Christ*, 17–24.

206. Matt 1:21 ("for he will save his people from [*apo*] their sins"); Rom 8:9–11; 1 Pet 1:15–16. Wesley, "Plain Account," 378–79, 390, 443–46; Flechere, "Portrait of St. Paul," 170, 173, 179; Oden, *Spirit*, 124–27; Wiley and Culbertson, *Christian Theology*, 302–3, 312–13; Kinlaw, *Jesus*, 149–53; Kinlaw, *Mind*, 25–27, 99–104; Purkiser, *Exploring*, 316–17; Taylor, *Formulation*, 108, 142, 157–66. Cf. Aelred of Rievaulx's desire and love spirituality in Mursell, *English Spirituality*, 126–28.

207. Gunton, *One, Three, Many*, 181–82; Purkiser, *Exploring*, 349–50.

208. Lossky, *Mystical Theology*, 161; John of Damascus, *Faith*, 3.1; 4.10; Congar, *Holy Spirit*, 2.1. Cf. Zizioulas, *Communion*, 42–43.

Zizioulas's aversion to an economy of the Holy Spirit is not without merit.[209] His purpose is to contrast Western, modern individualism by emphasizing community through the corporate personality of Christ, who is one-and-many.[210] Zizioulas offers a eucharistic-ecclesiology that is a participation in the body of Christ that is pneumatologically constituted.[211]

> A fundamental presupposition in this case is the understanding of the Person of Christ in close and unbreakable relationship with that of the Holy Spirit, as the very term "Christ" indicates, i.e. the one "anointed" with the Spirit. If we accept that the Holy Spirit *constitutes* the Christ-event (Christ is born of the Spirit, *anointed* by Him, *accompanied* by Him *in His passion* and *raised* by Him from the dead), we are led to the conclusion that Christ is inconceivable without this body, i.e. the "many" who form His body by the operation of the Spirit.[212]

Zizioulas's point for which we emphasize and build on, is an intimate interrelatedness of persons that causes being to exist.[213] Macmurray says as much in recognizing the problem of the personal in a post-World War 2 era where Modern philosophy came to be characterized through *egocentric* thought.[214] In contrast to the Kantian Self who *thought*, Macmurray offers a Self who *acted*.[215] The acting Self, or Agent, is to interrelate with others, thus showing existence.[216] For there to be unity in the movement of the Agent and the Other, they must be "persons in relation" dependent on one another, constituting their existence.[217] Macmurray offered a "heterocentric" philosophy in contrast to the "egocentric" philosophy, which inevitably becomes the structure of personal community.[218] Therefore, to discuss the economy of the Holy Spirit is not to isolate the person of the

209. Zizioulas, *Eucharist*, 14–16; Zizioulas, *One and Many*, 14–16, 75–77.

210. Zizioulas, *Being*, 27; Zizioulas, *Communion*, 1–3, 79; Zizioulas, *Eucharistic Communion*, 12–14; Zizioulas, *Lectures*, 148–53.

211. Zizioulas, *Being*, 15–16, 145–54; Zizioulas, *Eucharist*, 45–53.

212. Zizioulas, *One and Many*, 337.

213. Zizioulas, *Being*, 39.

214. Macmurray, *Self*, 29–38.

215. Macmurray, *Self*, 86–88, 134–35. This is in reference to Kant's "supreme principle of knowledge," the "I think" (Macmurray, *Self*, 50–51).

216. Macmurray, *Self*, 174.

217. Macmurray, *Self*, 188, 220.

218. Macmurray, *Persons*, 71, 122, 123, 158.

Holy Spirit from the Father and the Son, as Zizioulas contends. Instead, we view an emphasis on the person of the Holy Spirit enhances the revelation of the *intimate* Trinity and *economy* of the Trinity. The Holy Spirit is unique in that he is *from* God and *of* Christ.[219] While Zizioulas believes that there is equality in the essence of the persons of the Trinity and that personhood is based on *schesis*, persons-in-relation, it is not balanced trinitarianism.[220] He further declares that the Father cannot be a Father without the Son and vis-à-vis.[221] The same can be said of the person of the Holy Spirit as a person-in-relationship and trinitarian mode of existence.

Furthermore, the intimate and concrete *schesis* and *koinōnia* are found in two other names sometimes given to the Holy Spirit: "Spirit of God"[222] and "Spirit of Christ."[223] As such, we can conclude that personhood is determined upon relations, but this neither subordinates personal particularity to community nor makes it superior to community. The uniqueness of particulars and their similarities can have equal value in paradoxical observation or the *perichoretical* (i.e., relational) approach of trinitarian theology[224] compared to a more classical trinitarian (i.e., substance) approach.[225]

Zizioulas is unwilling to allow for neither an economy of the Holy Spirit nor observe the particular work of the Holy Spirit, which uniquely identifies Him within the Trinity. In opposition to Zizioulas's pneumatology, the Holy Spirit's work is uniquely his (e.g., sanctifying, Rom 15:16; teaching, John 16:12–13; indwelling, Rom 8:9, convicting, John 16:8, etc.) yet always intertwined in trinitarian relationship moving in the same direction motivated by the one same will.[226] At the same time,

219. Gregory of Nyssa, *Spirit*, 315. See also John 13:20; 14:16–17, 26; 15:26; 16:12–13.

220. Zizioulas, "Capacity and Incapacity," 436.

221. Zizioulas, *Being*, 41.

222. E.g., Gen 1:2; Matt 12:28. Here we are associating "God" with "Father" and not divine substance revealing a more balanced trinitarianism. See Congar, *Holy Spirit*, 1.1.1, 4, 12; Turner, *Holy Spirit*, 4–5; Pinnock, *Flame*, 50, 60–61; Carter, *Holy Spirit*, 38–41.

223. E.g., Rom 8:9; 1 Pet 1:11; see Congar, *Holy Spirit*, 1.2.3; Turner, *Holy Spirit*, 119–21; Pinnock, *Flame*, 162–66; Carter, *Holy Spirit*, 234–35, 264.

224. John of Damascus, *Faith*, 1.3, 11. See also McCall, "Relational Trinity," 117–18, 121, 123; Fiddes, "Relational Trinity," 159–60, 161.

225. Holmes, "Classical Trinity," 70, 72; Torrance, *Doctrine*, 32–36, 82–83.

226. Sanders, *Deep*, 134–37, 142.

the Holy Spirit is so interrelated within the trinitarian relations with whom he shares in divinity, worth, and dignity.[227] Consequently, the Holy Spirit's relation and communication toward humans is based on mutual trinitarian communication.[228] This communication is illustrated by the hearing and speaking of the Spirit when Jesus said, "When the Spirit of truth comes . . . he will not speak on his own authority, but whatever he hears he will speak."[229]

An economy of the Holy Spirit was developed early in church history as illustrated by Irenaeus, who said, "For where the Church is, there is the Spirit of God; and where the Spirit of God is, there is the Church, and every kind of grace; but the Spirit is truth."[230] Lossky, in turn, echoes Irenaeus as he develops an economy of the Holy Spirit who shares in the divine will of the Trinity and is equally involved with Christ in the establishment of the Church.[231] Therefore, it is surprising that Zizioulas openly rejects Lossky's economy of the Holy Spirit as applied to ecclesiology, calling it "personal" or "subjective" toward each human person and their personal spiritual life.[232] In turn, Zizioulas opts for a pneumatologically constituted Christology that narrows the definition of ecclesiology.[233]

In Zizioulas's theology, the Holy Spirit is the ontological priority causing Christ to *be*, and likewise, the Holy Spirit is the ontological priority causing the Church to *be*.[234] The pneumatological activity is primarily one of constituting. In Zizioulas's belief, Christ is pneumatologically constituted, making him a corporate being, the-one-for-the-many,[235] and the Church is pneumatologically constituted, incorporating the many into the one.[236] Zizioulas further suggests eschatology and communion (*koinōnia*) are the two aspects of pneumatology.[237] Since the Holy Spirit

---

227. Gregory of Nyssa, *Spirit*, 316–17.

228. Torrance, *Doctrine*, 165.

229. John 16:13. See Burge, *Anointed Community*, 203, 213, 214–17.

230. Irenaeus, *Heresies*, 3.24.1.

231. Lossky, *Mystical Theology*, 156–57.

232. Zizioulas, *Being*, 124–25. Also see Papanikolaou, *Being*, 32–38.

233. Zizioulas, *Being*, 130–32.

234. Zizioulas, *Being*, 132; Volf, *Likeness*, 98–99.

235. Zizioulas, *Being*, 126–30; Zizioulas, *Communion*, 37–38; Zizioulas, *Lectures*, 101–5; Zizioulas, *One and Many*, 77–79.

236. Zizioulas, *Being*, 132–36; Zizioulas, *Communion*, 38–39; Zizioulas, *One and Many*, 79–90.

237. Zizioulas, *Being*, 131.

makes way for Christ to incarnate the world through the immaculate conception, so too the Holy Spirit makes way for the Church to exist by incorporating the many (people) into the one (Church) through communion (*koinōnia*) at the Christ-event of Eucharist.[238] Then, the connection here is that Zizioulas sees eschatology and communion as the fundamental aspects of both pneumatology and Eucharist; therefore, they are the two fundamental aspects of ecclesiology.[239]

The problem with Zizioulas's argument here is that, on the one hand, he proposes a debate of priority between Christology and pneumatology for a foundation of the Church.[240] On the other hand, he stresses unity, or the one body over persons[241] (or the many), and finally ends with a Holy Spirit who works primarily through the eucharistic event and toward the corporate body in Christ.[242] In doing so, the result is that while Zizioulas offers a potent and novel argument for eucharistic-ecclesiology and the role of the Holy Spirit, he does so at the expense of believers never being able to relate to their Creator through the Son and in the Holy Spirit except in a formal and corporate ceremonial act. Thus, while Zizioulas offers a vision of the eschatological kingdom,[243] it is one that human beings can live out realistically on this side of eternity. There is a sense that Zizioulas tries to get around this problem when he suggests that while the Church is an *institution* with all of its tradition, organizational aspects, and symbolism of Christ as the body,[244] it is *constituted* by the Holy Spirit, making the Church a mystical notion of the body of Christ.[245] However, what is missing is a clear picture of the *particular*.

Help to overcome this problem may be gleaned from alternative theological anthropologies. For instance, Buber suggests genuine relationships begin with the *I* opening itself up to the *Thou* and seeing the

---

238. Zizioulas, *Being*, 130–32, 139–42.

239. Zizioulas, *Being*, 130–31.

240. Zizioulas, *Being*, 128–30. This beginning point is also demonstrated in Zizioulas, *One and Many*, 75–77.

241. Zizioulas, *Being*, 131.

242. Zizioulas, *Being*, 138. See also Zizioulas, *Lectures*, 137–38; Zizioulas, *One and Many*, 80–90.

243. This is for Zizioulas, "the icon of the Kingdom of God." Zizioulas, *Being*, 99–101, 114; Zizioulas, *Lectures*, 135–39; Zizioulas, *One and Many*, 182.

244. Zizioulas, *Being*, 135–38, 140, 177.

245. Zizioulas, *Communion*, 286–307.

world in the "boundless" *Thou* as pure relation.[246] Macmurray pointed out that the Self cannot exist in isolation but finds its existence in the dynamic *action* of relation with the Other.[247] Pannenberg, in turn, offers a theory of exocentricity (*Exzentrizität*) that is to say the center of each human being is found outside of his or herself in the life of another.[248] Lastly, Degenkolb's thesis on "participatory personhood" deals with the issue of nature versus person as illustrated by the person in a vegetative state and the helpless fetus, thus offering an *existential participation* through the personal presence of Jesus Christ ("ultimate locution") made possible by the "primary locution" of the Holy Spirit.[249] Each of these theological anthropologies recognizes that a person's existence is found in another. Christian anthropology views explicitly human beings as God's creatures, created after God's image (*ṣĕlĕm*) and likeness (*dᵉmût*).[250] For Zizioulas, the image of God in human beings is the ontological concept of personhood acting in freedom.[251]

Admittedly, Zizioulas's trinitarian theology applied to anthropology does not emphasize the person and the work of the Holy Spirit. However, these are significant because human beings' only connection to God has been made possible by the trinitarian formula: by the Father's will, through the work of the Son, and by the indwelling of the Holy Spirit.[252] If authentic personhood is found in another, as Zizioulas has claimed,[253]

246. Buber, *I and Thou*, 78–79, 89.

247. Macmurray, *Persons*, 17.

248. Onah, *Self-Transcendence*, 21; see 43n72.

249. Degenkolb, "Participatory Personhood," 9–12, 17, 24–26, 83, 238.

250. Gen 1:26; Vatican II, *Documents*, 1.1, 133; Grenz, *Social God*, xi; McConville, *Being Human*, 11–29.

251. Zizioulas, "Holy Trinity," 55–58.

252. Scripture: Exod 29:45; Lev 26:12; Isa 4:2–6; 32:15; Ezek 36:26–27; 37:14; 39:29; Joel 2:28–32; Zech 12:10; Matt 3:11; Luke 11:13; 24:49; John 4:10; 7:37–39; 13:20; 14:16–17, 26; 15:26; 16:7, 12–13; Acts 1:4–5; 2:2–3, 31–33, 38–39; 20:28; Rom 8:9–11, 14, 16–17; 1 Cor 3:16; 6:19; 2 Cor 13:14; Gal 4:4–7; Eph 3:14–17; Heb 9:14; 1 Pet 1:1–2; 1 John 2:23–25, 27; Jude 20–21. Apostolic Writings: *Didache*, ch. 7; Clement, *Corinthians*, chs. 1, 58, 59; Justin Martyr, *First Apology*, ch. 65; Ignatius, *Magnesians*, ch. 15; Irenaeus, *Heresies*, 5.6.1; Tertullian, *Praxeas*, ch. 2. Nicene and Post-Nicene Fathers: Athanasius, *Arians*, 1.2.9; 1.12.46–52; Athanasius, *To Serapion*, 1.2; Hilary, *Trinity*, 4.1; 4.13; 4.21; Basil, *Spirit*, 1.3; 7.16; 12.28; 14.31; 16.37; 18.45, 47; Gregory of Nyssa, *Spirit*, 315–16, 318, 319; Gregory of Nyssa, *Trinity*, 328; Gregory of Nazianzus, *Orations*, "On Holy Baptism," 41, 375; Ambrose, *Holy Spirit*, 2, Intro. 1–4; 2.20; 3.26; Augustine, *Trinity*, 5.8.9; 5.11.12.

253. Zizioulas, *Being*, 86–89.

then there must be a particular to a particular (person to person) connection that happens in time prior to the particular becoming absorbed into the community. However, at the same point, it must be noted that there can be no naked individuality (substance), and the essence of a person is always connected to another for good or for ill.[254] Of course, human beings are connected to another at the most basic stage of biology. Naturally speaking, each individual person is a product of two others. However, a person is more than a collection of cells or gathered earth formed in the hands of Creator God. Admittedly, Genesis reveals to us that "the LORD God formed the man of dust from the ground and breathed into his nostrils the breath of life, and the man became a living creature."[255]

By way of illustrating that human beings receive personhood from God, McConville points out that the breath (*neˇšāmāh*) of God blown into Adam, making him a living being, is similar to the "right spirit" (*rûăḥ nākôn*) and "your Holy Spirit" (*rûăḥ qādesekā*) in its "physiological connotations" of Psalm 51:10, 11.[256] However, he is quick to point out that the Psalmist does not use a definite article, which would indicate the person of the Holy Spirit. Therefore, the Psalmist's prayer is a request for a holy character like that of God.[257] The point being is that while human beings share a similar physiological make-up, each person is also unique and that the Creator God does not only commune and indwell the corporate gathering of humans in the eucharistic event, but also, and equally so, communicates and indwells the unique person in a personal-relational way through the Holy Spirit.[258]

Since in Zizioulas's theology, Christ is constituted by the Holy Spirit, making Christ the corporate person (i.e., the *hypostasis* of Christ being

254. Zizioulas, *Being*, 17–19, 41.

255. Gen 2:7. Compare Gen 2:7 "breath of life" (נִשְׁמַת חַיִּים) with Gen 7:22 "breath of spirit-life" (שְׁמַת־רוּחַ חַיִּים). The life of a person is connected to the breath of God, and the breath of God is connected to the Spirit of God. See Hamilton, *Genesis: 1–17*, 158–59, 297.

256. McConville, *Being Human*, 52.

257. McConville, *Being Human*, 52. Yarnell, disagrees with the interpretation of "right spirit" and "your holy spirit" as psychological connotations or simply character traits in Psalm 51, but rather he argues that David is praying for a "personal transformation" by which he needs the presence of God's Spirit (third person of the Trinity) to indwell his human heart, see Yarnell, *Holy Spirit*, 35–54. See subsection, "Participation in the Character of God," in chapter 7, "Participation and Christian Anthropology."

258. For further reading on particularity, see chapter 5, "Particularity in God and in Human Being." See Thiselton, *Holy Spirit*, 175–76, 212, 294, 314, 401, 413.

a person-in-relationship)[259] and therefore constituting the eucharistic event, thus leaning heavily on the many becoming one, the particular is blurred if not lost. If the particulars are lost, and the person of the Holy Spirit can only be experienced in and through the eucharistic event, then the personal presence of God through the Holy Spirit is skewed. Can there be a personal presence of God with humans if the economic Trinity is abandoned? While God can reveal Godself to the church community in a personal way, can God relate to the particular person in a way that demonstrates personhood as persons-in-relation?

As noted above, Zizioulas does speak of the particular, saying that the particular receives its ontological personhood from freedom. That is to say, the particular person, the Father, is the cause of the divine existence rather than substance (i.e., divinity) being the cause of the persons, Father, Son, and Holy Spirit, to exist which would otherwise result in necessity and not freedom.[260] Since the Father causes the Trinity to exist, the Trinity is ontologically free and not a necessity of substance (i.e., divinity).[261] In this explanation, the particular person (subjective) is only understood objectively. The objective understanding is that a person's existence depends on relationship, persons-in-communion. If, as Zizioulas concludes, a relationship is permanent and unbreakable,[262] why not then take the next step and say that to truly be a complete human being, one finite being must find their relationship in an infinite being? While Zizioulas certainly speaks of communion between God and humans, it is only experienced through the ceremonial acts of baptism and the Eucharist.[263] This ontological personhood of freedom and participation of the sacraments is extremely difficult for the one who lays in a vegetative state, the unborn, one in an unresponsive state, or the severely mentally disabled person.[264] On the one hand, Zizioulas's conclusion would render these as non-persons because they cannot participate in the Eucharist;

259. Zizioulas, "Capacity and Incapacity," 438; Zizioulas, *Communion*, 131–32; Zizioulas, *Eucharistic Communion*, 105.

260. Zizioulas, "Holy Trinity," 51; Zizioulas, *Communion*, 141. See McCall, *Which Trinity?*, 199–201.

261. Zizioulas, "Holy Trinity," 51; Gregory of Nazianzus, *Orations*, "On the Son," 2–5, 301–2.

262. Papanikolaou, *Being*, 146.

263. Zizioulas, "Capacity and Incapacity," 437–38; Zizioulas, *Eucharistic Communion*, 99–111.

264. Degenkolb, "Participatory Personhood," 238.

therefore, they are denied communion with the Holy Spirit. On the other hand, Zizioulas would explain that the ordained minister as the "mediator" would stand between God and human beings while the Holy Spirit would act as the agent, but admittedly the ordained person acts only as "representation by participation."[265] Thus, Zizioulas's personhood excludes certain, particular people because he ties freedom (from "self") to the will (to "love" another because they are other), making the *hypostatic* being *ekstatic*, or, in other words, to be a person, one must be in communion with God and others, ultimately through the participation of the Eucharist.[266] Those who are incapable of participation along with the collective *many* in the *one* Christ through the Eucharist are deficient in personhood (e.g., the "pneumatic life" is found in the Church—"revealed *par excellence* in the Eucharist").[267] Zizioulas only offers an objective approach to personhood and not a subjective one.[268]

We believe that a relational approach to creation and God's motivation to place his image in humans reveals an intimate interconnectedness between God and his creation. McConville states, "the 'image' implies the presence of God within the creation through humanity, in a way that affirms his ongoing intimate involvement with it. At the same time, the image depicts the human in a relationship of freedom with the creator and in intrahuman relationships."[269] Furthermore, humans have the capacity to grow in their relationship with God, including God's moral principles.[270] For Wesleyans specifically and evangelical Christians generally, growth in relationship with God is often understood as hearing the voice of God through Bible reading as a means of grace.[271] Another possible example of a burgeoning relationship for humans with God, rooted in

265. Zizioulas, *Being*, 230.

266. Zizioulas, "Capacity and Incapacity," 408, 409–10, 414, 425, 446–47; Zizioulas, *Being*, 145–49, 158–62; Zizioulas, *Eucharist*, 17–19; Zizioulas, *Communion*, 108–12, 119–20, 121–22, 144; Zizioulas, *One and Many*, 12, 14–15, 104–5, 404; cf. Gregory of Nazianzus, *Orations*, "On the Son," 6–7, 302–3. See Knight, "Introduction," 1–2.

267. Zizioulas, *Eucharistic Communion*, 12–14, 20–22; Also see Zizioulas, *Being*, 20–23, 80–82, 163–65; Knight, "Spirit and Persons," 183–86, 191–93.

268. Gunton, "Persons and Particularity," 104.

269. McConville, *Being Human*, 25. Cf. "Human Persons Serve as a Cosmic Microcosm," in Groppe, *Congar's Theology*, 91–92.

270. McConville, *Being Human*, 35, 37–38, 43–45. Zizioulas, "Capacity and Incapacity," 435–39. Carter, *Holy Spirit*, 224.

271. Sanders, *Deep*, 201–3.

Thomistic theology, would see the human capacity to grow spiritually as a state of grace.

> In Christ and the Spirit, we not only live through the proper capacities of our created human nature but also share a divine principle of life and action that is commensurate with our new divine destiny; we know and love with the very knowledge (the Word) and love (the Spirit) of God.[272]

McConville goes on to argue that a human being's growth in relationship with God is in the *realization* that their embodied character, which is a complexity of interrelationships affected by their heart, soul/mind, spirit, and love, is God's image embodied within them to be God (i.e., godlikeness) in the world toward other humans and for the created material world (ecologically speaking).[273]

We see this intimate connection between God and Christian believers made possible by the Holy Spirit in the epistle to the Romans.[274] This connection is described as an "indwelling" presence of the Holy Spirit in (*oikei en humin*) the believer(s) as assurance and warning to the evidence of one's place either belonging to Christ or not.[275] Paul's anthropology is based on the fact that human beings cannot exist independently but require the indwelling Holy Spirit to live eternally.[276] While the overwhelming tendency in pneumatological studies is to focus on the corporate gathering[277] where the Holy Spirit may dwell "among" or "with" the believers made by the use of the second person plural pronoun "you" (*humeis*, Rom 8:9a) or the first person plural "us" (*en hēmin*, Rom 8:4), there is clear evidence that Paul also teaches that particular persons possess the Holy Spirit. Paul warns the singular person, "Anyone (*tis*) who does not have the Spirit of Christ does not belong to [Christ]."[278] Based on the biblical accounts, Thiselton argues for a description of the Holy Spirit who is "the Beyond who is within," indicating a balance of the Holy

272. Groppe, *Congar's Theology*, 95.

273. McConville, *Being Human*, 52–58, 190. The idea of human participation in the character of God is expanded in chapter 7, "Participation in the Character of God."

274. See Rom 8. See Wedderburn, "Pauline Pneumatology," 153–55.

275. Jewett, "'Apportioned Spirit,'" 195–96.

276. Käsemann, *Romans*, 219.

277. See Zizioulas's argument in pneumatology against an individualistic concept in *Being*, 110–14.

278. Rom 8:9c, The pronoun *tis* is singular indicating a warning to each particular person. See Jewett, "'Apportioned Spirit,'" 196.

Spirit's work that is both transcendent and immanent, and for both the corporate and the individual believer.[279] Käsemann indicates the key Pauline phrase "in Christ" neither emphasizes community over individual, nor individual over community, instead "He is present in the medium of his Spirit, both in the lives of individual believers and in the community, and through both the world at large."[280]

There is no room in Zizioulas's theology for holy individuals. Holiness, for Zizioulas, is defined as "freedom" or "liberation" given by the Holy Spirit whom himself blows where he wishes (John 3:8), and "where the Spirit of the Lord is, there is freedom" (1 Cor 3:17).[281] As the Holy Spirit blows where he wishes, bringing freedom, he also creates *community* experienced in the "Eucharistic ethos."[282] Zizioulas emphasizes that the Holy Spirit's sanctifying work liberates the community from the past, itself (egocentricity), social injustices, death, and gives the freedom to love others.[283] The problem remains that community cannot occur without the particular, unique persons coming together. For what purpose would particular people be drawn together in unity as a Church to celebrate the Eucharist if not the Holy Spirit's work in the particular people?[284] Furthermore, Paul's words in Romans 8:9 appear to echo Jesus's words to Nicodemus, "unless one [*tis*, singular] is born again he cannot see [*ou dunatai*, singular] the kingdom of God" (John 3:3) and "unless one [*tis*] is born of water and the Spirit, he cannot [*ou dunatai*] enter the kingdom of God" (John 3:5). Therefore, while the Holy Spirit *constitutes* Christian personhood, at the same time, no individual person has exclusive possession of the Holy Spirit.[285] Furthermore, Zizioulas is correct in saying, "The only way for a true person to exist is for being and communion to coincide."[286] Since there appear two contradictory views, first being, God's communication and saving work beginning with particular human beings giving authentic personhood and transforming

---

279. Thiselton, *Holy Spirit*, 470–71.

280. Käsemann, *Romans*, 222.

281. Zizioulas, "Come Holy Spirit," 2.

282. Zizioulas, "Come Holy Spirit," 2.

283. Zizioulas, "Come Holy Spirit" 2–3.

284. Jer 31:3; Hos 11:4; John 6:44; 12:32; Acts 2:38–39; 10:44–45; 11:16–18; 1 Cor 12:12–13; 2 Cor 13:14; Eph 4:3–4. Also see Gunton's discussion on particularity and relatedness in the notion of *perichoresis* in *One, Three, Many*, 152–54.

285. Thiselton, *Holy Spirit*, 475.

286. Zizioulas, *Being*, 107.

them into an ecclesial community, or second, God's communication and saving work toward the ecclesial community, giving authentic person-hood through the sacraments, specifically the Eucharist; how then can we rectify the economy of the Holy Spirit with the Trinity, the particular with the community, and anthropology with theology?

For Zizioulas, Christ is the "corporate personality" as he is constitut-ed pneumatologically and is in relationship with his body, the Church.[287] Zizioulas's "de-individualizing" of Christ is ontologically motivated to-ward a "personal" definition applied to God and humans as existential truth, thus persons-in-relation.[288] However, as a result, the Holy Spirit's personhood is lost, and his powerful (*dunamis*) work qualifies Christ as the Savior and *corporate personality*, liberating humans from individual-ity through the Eucharist event.[289] The stress on the corporate personality by Zizioulas creates a homogenized body of worshippers. However, care must be taken not to lose the particular within the corporate, since a paradox of truth exists:[290] the corporate personality concept of Christ has validity, but so too does the corporate personality of the Holy Spirit. If true personhood is found where being and communion coincide, as in Zizioulas's Dictum,[291] then the Holy Trinity is a communion of persons in mutual self-giving love, each person loving the other, not for what they receive from the relationship, rather for what they can give to the other and simply for the fact that the other exists.[292] Therefore, in these terms, the Trinity can be described as persons-in-relation: the Father loves the Son and the Holy Spirit; likewise, the Son loves the Father and the Holy Spirit, and likewise, the Holy Spirit loves the Father and the Son.[293] This balanced trinitarianism is unlike Augustine's trinitarian theology, where

287. Zizioulas, *Being*, 109, 110–11, 130–31.

288. Zizioulas, *Being*, 107–9.

289. Zizioulas, *Being*, 110–13, 130, 138; Zizioulas, *Eucharist*, 15–16; Zizioulas, *One and Many*, 7, 80.

290. See Murphree, *Divine Paradoxes*.

291. Zizioulas, *Being*, 107.

292. John of Damascus, *Faith*, 4.18 ("perichoresis"); Hilary, *Trinity*, 3.1–4 ("re-ciprocally contain One Another"); Richard, *Trinity*, 3.2–4 ("love directed toward an-other"); Congar, *Holy Spirit*, 2.2.3.2; Kinlaw, *Jesus*, 34–37, 66, 68, 70, 75–79; Torrance, *Faith*, 234; Torrance, *Doctrine*, 102.

293. Gregory of Nazianzus, *Orations*, "On the Son," 16; Maximus, *Love*, 2.29, 50; Hugh, *Three Days*, 2.21.1–5; Richard, *Trinity*, 3.2–3; 3.7–8; 3.11–12; McCall, *Which Trinity?*, 64–73; Sanders, *Deep*, 156–60; Ware, *Orthodox Way*, 27–29, 32; Zizioulas, *Being*, 41; Zizioulas, *Communion*, 166–67, 260.

only the Holy Spirit is love which binds the Trinity in love.[294] Instead, the Father cannot be conceived without describing the Son and the Holy Spirit, likewise the Son cannot be conceived of without describing the Father and the Holy Spirit, and likewise, the Holy Spirit cannot be conceived without describing the Father and the Son.[295] As such, the immanent Trinity is a communion of reciprocal love, each finding their life in the other.[296] However, there is headship within the Trinity as distinguished in the names and activities of the sender and the ones sent. This concept of the Trinity indicates an equality-with-headship.[297] If Christ is a corporate personality containing within himself the-one-and-the-many as suggested by Zizioulas, the Holy Spirit can also be described as a corporate personality containing within himself the-one-and-the-many. This being the case, the Holy Spirit's corporate personality will be demonstrated by the various names given, his eternal procession, and unifying work. An example of those names and descriptions given include: "Spirit of God"[298] (e.g., Gen 1:2), "My Spirit" (e.g., Gen 6:3), "the Spirit"[299] (e.g., Num 11:26), "His Spirit" (e.g., Num 11:29), "the Spirit of the LORD" (e.g., Judg 3:10), "good Spirit" (e.g., Neh 9:20), "Your Spirit"[300] (e.g., Neh 9:30), "Holy Spirit"[301] (e.g., Ps 51:11), "the Spirit of wisdom" (Isa 11:2), "the

294. Augustine, *Trinity*, 6.5.7; 9.12.18; 15.17.27–28.

295. Ignatius, *Ephesians*, ch. 9; Basil, *Spirit*, 16.37–4; 18.44–47; Gregory of Nyssa, *Gods*, 335–36; Maximus, *Our Father*, 106, 110–11; Sanders, *Deep*, 137–40; Zizioulas, *Being*, 129–31.

296. Basil, *Spirit*, 18.47; Gregory of Nyssa, *Spirit*, 324.

297. Notice also the biblical notion of equality-with-headship within the family unit (Eph 5:21–33) and within the functions of the church (1 Cor 12:4–31).

298. For a discussion on the alternative interpretation "an awesome gale" rather than "Spirit of God," see Hamilton, *Genesis: 1–17*, 111–17.

299. When the definite article qualifies "Spirit" (either *rûaḥ* or *pneuma*) and no other qualifiers or prepositional phrases are used, then context becomes the key to interpretation of "the Spirit" at times by showing either continuity or discontinuity with the character and will of God (e.g., Mark 1:10; cf. Mark 9:20) and other times revealing the difference between "the Spirit" as the "Spirit of God" to that of the spirit of a human being (e.g., Ezek 2:2; cf. Prov 15:13).

300. Contextually, in Mal 2:15–6 "your spirit" is an address to the people of Israel and their immorality. When the pronominal suffix is attached to the noun *rûaḥ* in the Hebrew text addressing God, the genre is that of prayer (cf. Ps 51:11).

301. Levison says that this reference (Ps 51:11) cannot be understood as the person of Holy Spirit as it would be anachronistic, rather "holy" is an adjective for "spirit" which can also be "clean" and "right" (51:10) as well as "broken" like the "heart" (51:17) (Levison, *Filled*, 30–31).

Spirit of the LORD God" (e.g., Isa 61:1), "Spirit of grace"[302] (e.g., Zech 12:10), "the Spirit of your Father"[303] (e.g., Matt 10:20), "Spirit of truth"[304] (e.g., John 14:17), "Spirit of Jesus" (e.g., Acts 16:7), "the Spirit of holiness" (e.g., Rom 1:4), "Spirit of life" (e.g., Rom 8:2), "the Spirit is life and peace" (e.g., Rom 8:6), "Spirit of Christ" (e.g., Rom 8:9), "one Spirit" (e.g., 1 Cor 12:9), "the Spirit of the living God" (e.g., 2 Cor 3:3), "the Lord is the Spirit" (e.g., 2 Cor 3:17), "Holy Spirit of God" (e.g., Eph 4:30), "Spirit of Jesus Christ" (e.g., Phil 1:19), "eternal Spirit"[305] (e.g., Heb 9:14), "Spirit of glory" (e.g., 1 Pet 4:14), and *Paraklētos*[306] (e.g., John 14:16). While the

302. In this expression, there is no article given in the Hebrew text from Zech 12:10, so while some English versions include the definite article (e.g., New American Standard Bible), others interpret it with the indefinite article, "a spirit of grace" (e.g., English Standard Version). Greathouse says that we must look at the connection of "a spirit of grace" in Zech 12:10 with the effects of the people in this prophetic verse toward the crucified Messiah, and the later fulfillment as described in Heb 10:29 in order to receive a more complete understanding. See Greathouse, "Zechariah," 393–94. In Heb 10:29 the definite article is supplied and the expression "the Spirit of grace" is again connected to the crucified Messiah, "Son of God." Cockerill describes the original audience of the Book of Hebrews as having an attitude of "brazen insolence" of apostasy as they began to view the blood of Christ as "common" or "unclean." In so doing, they have likewise rejected the Holy Spirit who is "the presence and power of God" (Cockerill, *Hebrews*, 487–91).

303. This unique phrase is a quotation from Jesus to his disciples as to how one should bear witness of Jesus before authority figures. France says this phrase, "the Spirit of your Father," is the practical illustration from John the Baptist's promise in Matt 3:11 that Jesus would baptize the people with the Holy Spirit. Here in Matt 10:20 is "a particular gift or ability said to come to disciples through the Spirit 'in you'" (France, *Matthew*, 392–93).

304. For Brown, the title "Spirit of truth" heightens the understanding of who the *Paraclete* is in John's Gospel. Brown sees the understanding of the Holy Spirit in John's Gospel as the *Paraclete*, where Jesus, being the first *Paraclete*, the Holy Spirit is second or "another *Paraclete*" (John 14:16). Therefore, the *Paraclete* can be described as the "Spirit of truth" because he remains with the disciples in truth, bears truthful witness, and guides in truth (Brown, *John*, 2:643–44, 698–701, 714–17). Bultman further connects the Spirit of truth with the *Paraclete* but not as truthfulness in the world of ideas, culture, or history, rather Bultmann limits "truth" (*alētheia*) and "the Spirit" to the area of faith (Bultmann, *John*, 617). However, Köstenberger connects more closely the Holy Spirit, the *Paraclete*, and the Spirit of truth through five aspects in John's Gospel "truthfulness as opposed to falsehood," an "eschatological dimension," "an identifiable body of knowledge," "a sphere of operation," and "relational fidelity" (Köstenberger, *John's Gospel and Letters*, 397–98).

305. Witherington points out that while some scholars have indicated "eternal Spirit" could mean Christ's divine nature, it is unlikely a reference to Christ's nature but rather the agency of the Holy Spirit (Witherington, *Jewish Christians*, 270–71).

306. For a comprehensive analysis of *Paraclete* in John's Gospel, see Brown, *John*,

Son became human and thus can incorporate all believers into himself, the Holy Spirit is capable of indwelling humanity, all who "set their minds on the things of the Spirit."[307] Furthermore, the corporate personality of the Holy Spirit is found in both his *ad intra*, the interrelationships and identity within the persons of the Trinity, and the Holy Spirit's *ad extra*, his work within the divine-human relationships.

SUMMARY

This chapter has examined Zizioulas's Dictum of being-as-communion, or persons-in-relation, as a mode of existence to describe the ontological Trinity.[308] In this mode of existence, the person is the cause of being; therefore, the Father causes the Trinity to exist.[309] Zizioulas's theological explanation for his trinitarian mode of existence is the-one-and-the-many where Christ is the corporate person who is willed by the Father and constituted by the Holy Spirit.[310] Human persons are incorporated into the Church through the participation of the Eucharistic event.[311] We found that this caused a two-fold problem of reducing the Holy Spirit to an ecclesiological activity and was too rationalistic toward a divine-human reconciliation. The corrective to Zizioulas's Dictum while building on the trinitarian concept of persons-in-relation is first a theology of particularity as presented in chapter 5.

Zizioulas's Dictum does not accomplish a meaningful understanding of human personal existence because his pneumatological presentation in light of the Trinity constitutes the Church gathering around the Eucharist and not the particular persons who are assembled. Presented in chapter 5, particular persons are more complete through their relationships with another while simultaneously neither losing their particularity nor reverting toward individualism. Second, chapter 5 seeks to free Zizioulas's limited concept of the Holy Spirit from a monolithic work constituting the Church in eucharistic-ecclesiology, as shown here in

---

2:1135–44.

307. Sanders, *Deep*, 143. Rom 8:5.

308. Zizioulas, *Being*, 15, 106; Zizioulas, *Communion*, 112; Zizioulas, *One and Many*, 15, 31, 52–53, 155.

309. Zizioulas, *Being*, 39; Zizioulas, "Holy Trinity," 54–55.

310. Zizioulas, *One and Many*, 68; Zizioulas, *Eucharist*, 16.

311. Zizioulas, *One and Many*, 69; Zizioulas, *Eucharist*, 57.

chapter 4, by correcting and building on his trinitarian ontology of persons-in-relation. God reveals himself in three particular persons (Father, Son, and Holy Spirit), created humans in his image with particularity, and redeems humans in a personal particular encounter.[312] Meanwhile, God's particularity is understood in Wesleyan theology by God's oneness in holy-love, freedom, and will.[313] Therefore, the significance of Zizioulas's trinitarian ontology and theological-historical development of *hypostasis* will be further developed in our concept of trinitarian pneumatological personhood as constituting a Christian anthropology.

The person of the Holy Spirit constitutes Christian anthropology by drawing the human person into a relationship with God[314] and with others making the Spirit-indwelled person a complete person.[315] This pneumatologically constituted personhood of communion is established within the Trinity and serves as God's design for his image-bearers.[316] If personhood is found in relation with another, as developed by Zizioulas's Dictum, being-as-communion, then Christian personhood resides in a new set of relationships; as a new creation (*kaine ktisis*), or redeemed and reconciled in Christ.[317] As a result, a specifically Christian person does not have something added to their being as found in Greek philosophy,[318]

---

312. E.g., Wesley, "On the Trinity," 199–206; Wesley, "Marks," 212–13.

313. Collins, *Wesley*, 145–49; Coppedge, *Triune*, 131–35. See chapter 7, "Participation and Christian Anthropology."

314. 1 Cor 2:12–16; 6:17–20; 2 Cor 1:22. See McIntyre, *Pneumatology*, 172–83.

315. Eph 4:1–16. See McConville's OT concept of "double embodiment" as the individual person in particular totality, and the individual person embodied in society (McConville, *Being Human*, 47–59). Also see McIntyre, *Pneumatology*, 183–85.

316. Gen 1:26, 27. McConville, *Being Human*, 26–27.

317. 2 Cor 5:17; Gal 6:15; also Rom 6:4; Eph 4:22–24. "Therefore, if anyone is in Christ, he is a new creation. The old has passed away; behold, the new has come. All this is from God, who through Christ reconciled us to himself and gave us the ministry of reconciliation; that is, in Christ God was reconciling the world to himself, not counting their trespasses against them, and entrusting to us the message of reconciliation" (2 Cor 5:17–19). The significance of the phrase "new creation" echoes the creation narrative where darkness precedes light and life. Barnett says, "While Paul's reference to a new creation (verse 17) summarizes the changes which occur within the life of any believer (if anyone), these changes are dramatically focused within his own life. Love was now the controlling motive (verse 14) in place of hate. Serving the one who died for him had taken the place of selfishness (verse 15). True understanding of Jesus, his identity and achievement, have replaced ignorance and error (verse 16)" (Barnett, 2 *Corinthians*, 113). Kinlaw, *Jesus*, 139.

318. Zizioulas, *Being*, 39; also John 14:15–16.

but rather a new relationship with God (and others) made possible by the blood[319] of Christ and the indwelling of the Holy Spirit.[320] In turn, and as a result, the apostle Paul is able to contrast the wisdom of the Spirit of God in a person to that of the natural person as far more superior and intimately connected with Christ.[321] Therefore in critical response to Zizioulas, the person and work of the Holy Spirit cannot be reduced solely to the Christ-event or Eucharist only. The Holy Spirit is a person in the sense of being in relationship with the Father and the Son, and by virtue of the Spirit's own being-as-communion with Father and Son, is able both to give and sustain abundant life to those who constitute the body of Christ, his Church.[322]

---

319. Heb 9:11–28. For a discussion on the significance of the "blood" sacrifice and the Jewish Christian tension of animal sacrifice and the Christ sacrifice in the early church, see Cockerill, *Hebrews*, 386–411.

320. John 14:17. In Pinnock's words the "Spirit is present in the struggle to make creatures whole" (Pinnock, *Flame*, 62).

321. Keener, *Spirit Hermeneutics*, 176; 1 Cor 2:6–16; Rom 8:1–11.

322. Oden, *Spirit*, 31–32.

PART 2

Trinitarian Pneumatological Personhood

INTRODUCTION

IN REFLECTING UPON PART 1 of this thesis, "Zizioulas: Trinity, Personhood, Holy Spirit," we dealt with these three pillars in Zizioulas's theology from a historical, philosophical, and theological perspective. In chapter 2, Platonic philosophy suggested that a true particular being is absorbed into the primal One. As such, it was noted that the uniqueness of the particular is lost in the universal. Next, Aristotelian philosophy discovered the concrete being through particulars, but the particular in this philosophy was trapped in substance. Thus, being is not an absolute category. The Jewish Scriptures liberated being from substance and gave it personal characteristics based upon the God of Israel, YHWH. YHWH, the Creator who reveals his personal freedom from the confines of the material world, created human beings in his image and likeness with personal freedom. Finally, Christianity revealed the fulfillment of the Jewish Scriptures by showing this personal-relational God (YHWH) as motivated by love through the event of incarnating the material world (i.e., the Creator visiting creation) by means of a particular human body, being a particular person, namely, Jesus Christ,[1] who saves human beings from sin and death.[2] However, Christianity went even further and

1. Schaff, *Creeds of Christendom*, 32.

2. Rom 8:1–3. See Käsemann who argues the Spirit functionally rules in the sphere of Christ and is the giver of life, therefore the Spirit is the one who separates those from sin and death and those to life. Furthermore, while Käsemann does comment on

described God in a foundational creed as Trinity: Father, Son, and Holy Spirit, three distinct persons (*hypostases*) and one essence (*ousia*) operating in one will.[3]

In chapter 3, Zizioulas's methodology focused on discovering his theological perspective concerning the Trinity, personhood, and the Holy Spirit. Zizioulas has taken the Greek Orthodox methodology of paradox and further developed a theology of "the one and the many,"[4] which he expanded to all areas of theology, but specifically to the person of Christ as the "corporate person," further developing it in the theology of the Eucharist.[5] For the Orthodox Church, the Eucharist is of central importance;[6] thus, the-one-and-the-many concept for Zizioulas is the basis for his theology of eucharistic-ecclesiology.[7] However, behind this theology, Zizioulas has also developed an ontology of person as being-in-communion.[8]

In chapter 4, Zizioulas's Dictum was matched against other contemporary trinitarian theological thought. The focus was on Zizioulas's emphasis on "mode of existence" for trinitarian personhood. Zizioulas's trinitarian ontology is rooted in the Cappadocian Fathers and their revelatory use of *hypostasis* to explain the persons of the Trinity.[9] Furthermore, the *monarchia* of the Father as the cause (*aitia*) of the Trinity is

---

Christ's event on the cross as a transaction (i.e., Christ's death to justify humans which brings life) (Käsemann, *Romans*, 215–16, 218), he stresses the work of the Holy Spirit, "Only the Spirit gives freedom from the powers of sin and death" (Käsemann, *Romans*, 218). For a discussion on the problems and benefits in recovering the topic of original sin, see Anderson, "*Necessarium Adae Peccatum*," 22–44.

3. Zizioulas, "Holy Trinity," 47, 51–52. Schaff, *Creeds of Christendom*, 27–29.

4. Zizioulas, *Being*, 136–39, 145–49; Zizioulas, *Communion*, 107, 145–46; Zizioulas, *Eucharist*, 54–58, 67; Zizioulas, *Eucharistic Communion*, 12–19; Zizioulas, *Lectures*, 50–54; cf. Gunton, *One, Three, Many*, 188–96; Dunn, *Neither Jew Nor Greek*, 816–19.

5. Zizioulas, *Being*, 130; Zizioulas, *Communion*, 105; Zizioulas, *One and Many*, 51, 68, 78, 142, 143, 146, 152, 244.

6. Steenberg, "Eucharist," 185. McGuckin says the Eucharist is "the mystical drama" of salvation and is received in a joyful spirit of celebration (McGuckin, *Orthodox*, 288–96).

7. Zizioulas, *Being*, 20–22, 24, 143–69, 215–17, 247; Zizioulas, *Eucharist*, 14, 17, 115, 117, 118–19; Zizioulas, *One and Many*, 16, 38, 61–74, 146, 176, 179, 198, 199, 208, 219, 228, 232, 242, 280, 311–20.

8. Zizioulas, *Being*, 15, 16, 19, 20–22, 24–25, 53–59.

9. Zizioulas, *Being*, 36–41; Zizioulas, *Communion*, 157–58; Zizioulas, "Holy Trinity," 47; Zizioulas, *Lectures*, 50–51.

the core for Zizioulas's mode of existence as it highlights the person of God over the substance of God.[10] Zizioulas uses the church fathers to rediscover trinitarian theology for contemporary theological needs such as eucharistic-ecclesiology, Ecumenical Vision, and Ecological Concern. The second half of chapter 4 under the subtitle "Trinitarian Pneumatology" was dedicated to the fact that there remains a deficiency in Zizioulas's presentation of pneumatology and anthropology. The point of issue with Zizioulas's underdeveloped pneumatology is found in his belief that an economy of the Holy Spirit threatens the unity of God.[11] There needs to be clearer pneumatology because the person of the Holy Spirit is equal in divinity and dignity with the Father and the Son.[12] Furthermore, in the absence of Jesus Christ, who ascended, a human being's contact with God is through the Holy Spirit.[13] A complete trinitarian perspective would conclude that if personhood is found in relation with another, as developed by Zizioulas's Dictum, being-as-communion, then Christian personhood resides in a new set of relationships; as a new creation (*kaine ktisis*), or redeemed and reconciled in Christ.[14] The person becoming a new creation with a new set of relationships is the fulfillment to love God and love others made possible by the presence of the Holy Spirit.[15]

In part 2 of this thesis, "Trinitarian Pneumatological Personhood," we aim to use Zizioulas's persons-in-relation concept as a springboard for Christian anthropology while also offering a three-fold correction to establish that a Christian person is constituted through trinitarian pneumatology, which the Holy Spirit initiates. Zizioulas's theology of the Trinity, personhood, and Holy Spirit are critiqued and further developed

10. Zizioulas, *Being*, 17, 41, 44–45, n. 40; Zizioulas, *Communion*, 131–34; 143–44; Zizioulas, "Holy Trinity," 51, 52; Zizioulas, *Lectures*, 59; Wilks, "Ontology," 81.

11. Zizioulas, *Lectures*, 81; Zizioulas, *One and Many*, 77.

12. See "The Constantinopolitan Creed of 381," in Schaff, *Creeds of Christendom*, 29; Basil, *Spirit*, 16.37–38; Gregory of Nazianzus, *Orations*, "On the Holy Spirit," 10, 12.

13. Farrow points out that in the absence of Jesus Christ, the Holy Spirit comes to human beings, but rather than present himself to human beings, the Holy Spirit presents Jesus Christ (Farrow, *Ascension*, 177, 257, 266). For Zizioulas, the Holy Spirit comes to human beings by way of constituting the Christ event in the Eucharist and "sustaining" the community through *koinōnia* (Zizioulas, *Being*, 111, 165).

14. 2 Cor 5:17; Gal 6:15; also Rom 6:4; Eph 4:22–24. Barnett, *2 Corinthians*, 113; Kinlaw, *Jesus*, 139.

15. Wesley, "Scriptural Christianity," 1.4–7; Wesley, "Bondage and Adoption," 3.7; Wesley, "Marks," 219–20.

through personal-relational exemplifications. The three critical examples developed in part 2 are "particularity" in chapter 5, "presence" in chapter 6, and "participation" in chapter 7. These theological components are derived from Zizioulas's theology and will reflect a reworking of Wesleyan theology. If, as Zizioulas presents, the core of being is persons-in-communion, then why not begin Christian anthropology with the particular person at the place where the presence of a relational Triune God[16] meets that person? The presence of a personal God engaging a particular human being may happen during the sacrament. However, in an evangelical conversion, it happens before baptism or Eucharist leading the person toward eventually participating in the sacraments, or in the case of infant baptism, where the presence of God is initiated, yet may fully come later.[17]

The purpose of part 2 is to correct Zizioulas's limited pneumatology while building on his trinitarian ontology and persons-in-communion as starting points from a Wesleyan theological perspective. The pneumatological corrections along with the anthropological implications enhance Wesleyan theology. The result is that the Christian person is each particular person who has encountered the presence of God and continues to live in that presence by participating in the life of the Trinity initiated and sustained by the Holy Spirit.

In chapter 5, "Particularity in God and in Human Being," we will argue that Zizioulas's emphasis on the relational aspect of persons leads to a loss of particularity of person both in the Trinity, especially with the person of the Holy Spirit, and also with humans in the Church. The topic of particularity is important to theology while still maintaining a balance with community. Chapter 6, "Personal Presence: A Shadow of Things to Come," deals with the irony that there is no personal, relational contact in Zizioulas's theology between God and humans to constitute human personhood. If persons are defined by relationship, then there must be

16. For the historical-philosophical-theological development of a personal-relational Triune God, see chapter 1, "Trinitarian Personhood: East and West."

17. Oswalt, "Wesley and the Old Testament," 290–91. Ulrich Zwingli argues that the Holy Spirit prepares the person for the sacrament and not the sacrament as a means to receive the Holy Spirit. Zwingli further argues that if the sacrament prepared the person for the Holy Spirit then one would know "where, whence and whither the Spirit is borne" (cf. John 3:8). "If the presence and efficacy of grace are bound to the sacraments, they work whithersoever they are carried; and where they are not used, everything becomes feeble." Zwingli, On Providence, 46–47. On the topic of "prevenient grace" (i.e., grace that goes before) and Wesley's ordo salutis, see Collins, Wesley, 73–82, 169–72.

a theological understanding of the human Christian person based on a personal relationship with God. Finally, chapter 7, "Participation and Christian Anthropology," explores the Christian person's ongoing relationship with God. However, if the Christian person is such by a new relationship with God, then sin is the cause of a non-Christian person. Furthermore, sin is the barrier of relationships; thus, sin keeps one from being (i.e., having the character of God) and doing (i.e., the mission of God) the things of God.

Chapter 5

Particularity in God and in Human Being[1]

> "A theology giving central place to particularity is
> precisely what the modern age needs."
>
> —COLIN E. GUNTON[2]

INTRODUCTION

THIS CHAPTER CHALLENGES ZIZIOULAS's limited value on the economic Trinity, extreme monarchial view of the Father, corporate view of Christology as found in his eucharistic-ecclesiology, and soteriological under-pinnings while building on his concept of persons-in-relation. The purpose is to show a significant and equal place for particularity in

---

1. "Particular" and "particularity" is used throughout this chapter in a philosophical description as "A manner of class as opposed to the property which defines the class" (Benjamin, "Particular," 226), and determined by the context is synonymous with unique, different, and distinct (along with their cognates). Every attempt is being made *not* to use the word "individual," except where necessary, or at least to use it sparingly for the same reason Zizioulas avoids the word as it has the connotation of "autonomy" and "independent." Zizioulas, *Being*, 27, 28–29, 106, 109, 113, 172; Zizioulas, "Capacity and Incapacity," 405–10, 437, 440; Zizioulas, *Communion*, 99–100. Also, Gunton opposes Descartes's emphasis on the intellect which makes the person an individual and relationships secondary and "problematic" (Gunton, *Trinitarian Theology*, 84–87). Gunton's solution is *hypostasis* as particular persons-in-relation (e.g., Jesus Christ) (Gunton, *Trinitarian Theology*, 98–99).

2. Gunton, *One, Three, Many*, 181.

theology alongside studies of a corporate, community, and unity applied to God and humans.[3] The thought here is that since humans were created in the image and after the likeness of God (Gen 1:26), and particularity and unity within the Trinity has been established in the creeds,[4] therefore then a corrective to Zizioulas's emphasis on community and unity should be balanced with a theology of particularity, but not to the fault of autonomous individuality.

PARTICULARITY

Zizioulas grounds his theological Dictum in what he terms "the historical revolution" of the fourth century, when, for the sake of trinitarian theology, the Cappadocians identified the particular person with the term *hypostasis*.[5] This historical theological shift on *hypostasis* freed the definition and idea of person from substance. In other words, the idea of person no longer had to be described in a manner to "how" persons are alike in a uniformly collective whole, but rather categorically, persons could be described as to their particularity and difference, one from another. Zizioulas states that for the first time in history, the Cappadocian Fathers separated the essence of God (*ousia*) from the persons of God (*hypostasis*).[6] Thus, Zizioulas concludes that God is simultaneous "One" and "Many."[7] The problem with Zizioulas's presentation of the Cappadocian revolution is his stress on the monarchy of the Father (as originator or source) who causes everything, including "God to exist as Trinity."[8]

3. Wesleyan theology has a pietistic slant (i.e., the particular human heart *wholely* united with God) as found in the Wesleyan *ordo salutis*, but always with a goal toward unity in love with others. See Wesley, "Catholic Spirit," 492–504. For personal pietism in Wesleyan theology, see Leclerc, *Discovering*, 174, 278–79. For historical-theological studies in the pietistic vein of the modern United Methodist Church, see O'Malley and Vickers, *Methodist and Pietist*. For a discussion on Wesley's *ordo salutis*, see Collins, *Wesley*, 307–12.

4. See the Nicene and Constantinopolitan Creeds in Schaff, *Creeds of Christendom*, 27–29.

5. Zizioulas, *Being*, 36–41; Zizioulas, *Communion*, 157–58; Zizioulas, "Holy Trinity," 47; Zizioulas, *Lectures*, 50–51; Zizioulas, *One and Many*, 28–29.

6. Zizioulas, *Being*, 35–41, 83–89; Zizioulas, "Capacity and Incapacity," 409–10; Zizioulas, *Communion*, 185–86; Zizioulas, *Lectures*, 50–51.

7. Zizioulas, *Being*, 141, 145–49; Zizioulas, *Lectures*, 50–54. See also, Gunton, *One, Three, Many*, 210–31.

8. Zizioulas, *Lectures*, 53. Also, Zizioulas, *Being*, 17, 40–41, 44; Zizioulas,

Specifically, Zizioulas interprets the Cappadocian trinitarian teaching as the person of the Father, who is a relational being, in contrast to impersonal substance or divine nature, and as a result is the "'cause' of the Holy Trinity" revealed through the trinitarian order (*taxis*) of Father, Son, and Holy Spirit.[9] In this theology, the Son and Holy Spirit are subordinate to the Father; therefore, the particular can become lost in the One.[10] Furthermore, the ecclesial outcome is one where the particular Christian believer becomes absorbed into the homogenous whole as the church is gathered around the Eucharist table.[11] Zizioulas states that "particularity is not ontologically absolute."[12] The conclusion is that the personal particularity and uniqueness, in Zizioulas's ecclesiology, is at the least blurred if not eventually lost in the unity.[13] Awad highlights this point well when he comments that "Zizioulas reduces 'unity' to an absolutely singular, ontic 'oneness' by reducing the source of divinity to one, single *hypostasis* (i.e., the Father). He [Zizioulas] over-stresses the ontic reduction to an extent that could lead to the conclusion that the Son and the Spirit are substantially of a *different* nature from the Father."[14]

Finally, and most importantly, we have established that while the Cappadocians freed persons (*hypostasis*) from substance (*ousia*), thus making person an absolute category, a person is not autonomous as in the existential idea of person as individual; instead, person has unique,

---

Communion, 137; Zizioulas, "Holy Trinity," 52, 54–55; Zizioulas, *One and Many*, xv, 10–14, 22–24, 39, 41–45; LaCugna, *God*, 245. Cf. Holmes, *Quest*, 13; McCall, *Which Trinity?*, 193–95; Wilks, "Ontology," 78–79.

9. Zizioulas, *Communion*, 137–38. In *Lectures*, Zizioulas says, "He [the Father] is the source of their [the Son and the Spirit] being and thus of the existence of the Trinity" (Zizioulas, *Lectures*, 79). Also, Zizioulas, *Lectures*, 61; Zizioulas, *One and Many*, 10–12; Grenz, *Rediscovering*, 142–44; Awad, "Between," 187–90, 193; Papanikolaou, "Divine Energies," 368.

10. Torrance, *Persons*, 289–93. See also, Wilks, "Ontology," 78–79, 82; McCall, *Which Trinity?*, 198–99. Awad, "Personhood," 8.

11. Gunton, *One, Three, Many*, 180–81, 184, 187; Grenz, *Rediscovering*, 144–45. Also see Wendebourg, "Cappadocian Fathers," 194–98.

12. Zizioulas, *Communion*, 102.

13. Zizioulas, *Being*, 145–49; Zizioulas, *Communion*, 286–89; Zizioulas, *Eucharist*, 112–17; Zizioulas, *One and Many*, 264–68.

14. Awad, "Personhood," 8.

particularity,[15] and yet finds their completeness as persons-in-relation with another or being-as-communion.[16]

The issue is that while God has created human beings in his image and after his likeness, which reflects persons-in-relation, he has also bestowed freedom upon human beings. However, human freedom is qualified by *givenness*, in that, unlike God, who has absolute freedom, human beings are allowed to operate freely by what they have been *given* in the created world (i.e., time and space as boundaries).[17] Rather than operate one's freedom in a manner similar to God in an *ekstatic* way toward another for the other's good, humans tend to focus on the self and, in doing so, the other is either feared or manipulated for personal gain and to build-up the self.[18] As a result, this reversal of freedom toward the self develops individuality in the person and a false sense of autonomy.[19] The person is, then, an incomplete person operating in self-love.[20] In Zizioulas's terms, humans are held by this self-love and need to be freed in order to love others (i.e., "*ekstasis* of personhood").[21] What must change to overturn self-love and bring about completeness or wholeness in persons who will operate in an *ekstatic* way of self-giving love is salvation from sin and selfishness.[22] Salvation is given by the Father's will and through

15. McConville shows the contrast between individual and particular with the hermeneutical approaches of either "spiritualizing" meaning internalizing the text which leads to individuality, or "spiritual sense" of a text meaning which apply to the larger aspects of life (McConville, *Being Human*, 87–91).

16. Zizioulas, *Communion*, 99–112, 168–69. See Gunton, *One, Three, Many*, 214–19.

17. Zizioulas, "Creation (vol. 13)," 2; Zizioulas, *Being*, 19; Zizioulas, *Eucharist Communion*, 167.

18. LaCugna, *God*, 289. Zizioulas, *Being*, 106–7; Zizioulas, *Communion*, 52–53. Cf. *Dasein* and the "they" in Heidegger, *Being and Time*, 1.1.4§27.

19. Zizioulas, "Capacity and Incapacity," 406.

20. Zizioulas, *Communion*, 43–55, 84.

21. Zizioulas, "Capacity and Incapacity," 425–29, 432–33, 434–37; Zizioulas, *Being*, 44–46, 50, 113; Zizioulas, *Lectures*, 105–15.

22. Zizioulas, "Capacity and Incapacity," 407–9, 433. This is what Zizioulas terms "de-individualization" that must occur in Christology, see Zizioulas, *Being*, 107–9. Also see Gunton, *One, Three, Many*, 217n5. Further, Gunton says, "What we receive from and give to others is constitutive: not self-fulfilment but relation to the other as other is the key to human being, universally" (Gunton, *One, Three, Many*, 227). The secular existentialist philosopher, Sartre says, "Man is all the time outside of himself: it is in projecting and losing himself beyond himself that he makes man to exist; and, on the other hand, it is by pursuing transcendent aims that he himself is able to exist" (Sartre, *Existentialism and Humanism*, 66–67).

the person of Jesus Christ and is communicated by the Holy Spirit.[23] Receiving this salvation and growing in grace completes the person and makes them precisely a Christian person who has entered into a new set of relationships.[24] As a result of a new divine-human relationship, a characteristic of God found in the persons of the Trinity of mutual self-giving love is made available to the Christian person.[25] This characteristic that the original humans initially had was destroyed in their self-fulfilling act of sin, resulting in a marred image of God in humans, separating human from human and human from God.[26] Therefore, the relational fulfillment of God with human beings serves as a Christian anthropology constituted by the person of the Holy Spirit.[27] That is to say, pneumatologically constituted personhood of communion is established within the Trinity and serves as God's design for his image-bearers.[28] While Zizioulas would agree on the constitutional ability of the Holy Spirit, he would not go so far as to apply it directly to anthropology. Zizioulas says that the Holy Spirit con-stitutes the Church, while Christ in-stitutes the Church.[29] The

---

23. From the perspective of "pneumatologically constituted Christology," see Zizioulas, Being, 110–14. For a functional perspective of the Holy Spirit, see Käsemann, Romans, 215–16, 218. For the perspective of "adoption," through the Holy Spirit, see Sanders, Deep, 162–71. For the perspective of the Spirit-anointed Christ as a paradigmatic expression to be emulated by all believers, see Burge, Anointed Community, xvi–xviii, 30, 41–45, 110, 147–49, 177–78, 197, 204, 221. For a perspective of the Holy Spirit as the secessionist teacher for the community, see Brown, Community, 138–44.

24. Sanders, Deep, 177–79.

25. Ware, Orthodox Way, 27–29.

26. Gen 3; Kinlaw, Jesus, 107–25; Kinlaw further states the marred image of God is a heart turned in upon itself in reference to Isa 53:6 and Martin Luther's "cor incurvatus ad se" in Kinlaw, We Live, 32. Jones, God the Spirit, 57–58. In Gregor, Philosophical Anthropology, "sin" is described as self-love and termed "incurvature" first found in Adam (Gregor, Philosophical Anthropology, 61). These points (sin, mutual-self-giving love, character of God, from a relational perspective) are further developed in chapter 7, "Participation and Christian Anthropology."

27. Farrow, Ascension and Ecclesia, 59–60; LaCugna, God, 296–300; Lossky, Mystical Theology, 156–73; McConville, Being Human, 48, 51–52, 59, 179–80; Schwarz, Human Being, 8, 9–10, 17–19, 26, 167–68, 175, 185, 190, 211. On the practical side, Schwarz shows that for humans to survive the environment given, humans must rely on God for survival and life (Schwarz, Human Being, 26).

28. Gen 1:26, 27. McConville, Being Human, 26–27; Gunton, One, Three, Many, 181–84.

29. Zizioulas, Being, 125, 130–40, 210–11, 212.

human person as a Christian person for Zizioulas is constituted through baptism and Eucharist, which are pneumatologically constituted.[30]

A more fulsome answer to the human person as person-in-relation demands a theological perspective on particulars. For instance, Scripture presents God's personal particularity as Father, Son, and Holy Spirit.[31] Furthermore, Genesis 1–2 showcases God's personal particularity by creating particular human beings in God's image and likeness.[32] Zizioulas certainly deals with particularity in God and human beings to a limited extent[33] as the (*monarchia*) Father, Son, and Holy Spirit are submerged into the Christocentric Eucharist of the-one-and-the-many, where Christ is met by the unified Church, which is a collection of people.[34] Without a fulsome understanding of the particular, God is reduced at least to modalism, if not mono-theism, and human beings lose meaning and purpose as they are melted into a homogenous whole.[35] The fear, of course, is going too far in the other direction resulting in tritheistic tendencies to explain God followed by an application leading in the direction of social-trinitarian concepts where human beings are viewed as individuals with little or no connection to other human beings, God, or creation.[36] This chapter will look at Zizioulas's limited use of the particular as applied to God and human beings to expand it by using Gunton's theology of the particular.[37] A Christian anthropology that is theologically trinitarian and a concept of personhood constituted by the Holy Spirit to re-create

30. Zizioulas, *Being*, 135–36, 137–38, 159–60, cf. 164–66.

31. See John 13:20; 14:16–17, 26; 15:26; 16:12–15. Torrance, *Doctrine*, 164–67. Furthermore, Torrance says, "The fact that God the Father and God the Holy Spirit are fully involved with God the Son in our redemption, means that the doctrine of the economic and ontological Holy Trinity is of the greatest evangelical relevance to us in our daily life of faith" (Torrance, *Doctrine*, 254). Also see Burge, *Anointed Community*, 36–38, 107, 138, 140–43, 200–202, 213, 215, 216; Keener, *Spirit Hermeneutics*, 158–59; Dunn, *Pneumatology*, 16–18.

32. McConville, *Being Human*, 12–29; Schwarz, *Human Being*, 27.

33. Zizioulas, *Communion*, 32–43, 59–62, 66–70, 73, 75, 76, 89.

34. Zizioulas, *Being*, 15, 67–122; Zizioulas, *Communion*, 131–34. Cf. Harrison, "Zizioulas," 298; Olson and Hall, *Trinity*, 114–15; Volf, *Likeness*, 100.

35. Gunton, *One, Three, Many*, 186–87, 197, 210, 213.

36. Zizioulas, *Being*, 15, 27; Zizioulas, "Holy Trinity," 48–49. Cf. Grenz, *Social God*, 267–336; Pannenberg, *Anthropology*, 74–79.

37. Awad, believes that Gunton's "unity-in-particularity" is a corrective to Zizioulas's being-as-communion for understanding the theology of the Trinity as well as the topic of personhood (Awad, "Personhood," 1–22).

the *imago Dei*[38] as persons-in-relation promotes particularity in God and in humans. Therefore, when an understanding of the complete person (i.e., personhood) as persons-in-relation who are oriented in self-giving love is set in place, as in the previous chapter,[39] particularity is then the next step to pressing closer into *a pneumatologically constituted personhood of communion as a specific Christian anthropology.*

PARTICULARITY IN GOD

As early as 130 CE, Christians referred to the complexity of divine agency through three persons while simultaneously being a unified agency toward human beings, as God's economy.[40] The term "economy," which describes God's activities as seen through the particular persons of the Trinity,[41] comes from the verb *oikonomeō* meaning "'to administer or oversee' a complex process or community"[42] and also, the idea of managing a household.[43] Later in the early Middle Age, economy was connected with "God's providential will."[44] In modern theological categories, *oikonomeō* is often used to describe the plan/administration/order of salvation.[45] However, on the one hand, Olson and Hall argue that there is a need for a proper understanding of the economy of God distinct from theology proper (*theologia*) in order to eliminate the idea of subordination which destroys trinitarianism.[46] This subordinational nuance can be illustrated by Jesus's human will, which is distinct from his divine will as displayed in the garden of Gethsemane where Jesus states, "My Father . . . not as I will, but as you will"[47] and also as Jesus teaches in the upper

---

38. Irenaeus, *Heresies*, 3.18.7; 3.21.10; 5.6.1; 5.21.1; Zizioulas, *Lectures*, 150; Farrow, *Ascension and Ecclesia*, 61–62.

39. Chapter 3, "Zizioulas and Contemporary Implications."

40. [Mathetes], *Diognetus*, 23, 28.

41. Grudem, *Systematic Theology*, 248–49. In LaCugna, *God*, specifically the work of the Son and the Holy Spirit (LaCugna, *God*, 2–3).

42. Oden, *God*, 273.

43. LaCugna, *God*, 2.

44. LaCugna, *God*, 2. Oden, *God*, 273–315. For early evidence of "economy" and "providence" in the Latin West, see Augustine, *City of God*, 5.11. For early evidence of "economy" and providence" in the Greek East, see John of Damascus, *Faith*, 2.29.

45. Michel, "οἰκονομία," 151–53.

46. Olson and Hall, *Trinity*, 36–37.

47. Matt 26:39.

room discourse, "the Father is greater than I,"[48] both of which indicate the Father is greater in a theological comparison.[49] However, when the economy of the incarnation (i.e., Jesus's humanity) is applied, we see that the Son's divine will is one (i.e., inseparable) with the Father's will while the Son's human will is subordinate and seeks to do (i.e., obedience) the will of the Father, which keeps the unity of the Trinity intact.[50]

However, LaCugna argues that *theologia* and *oikonomia* must be held together to understand the mystery of God and the mystery of salvation.[51] Furthermore, when *theologia* and *oikonomia* are held inseparably, then Jesus Christ expresses perfectly the Godself and way of being, which is relational, or in other words, "God for us is who God is as God."[52] The result of a theological study in the economy of God is that it allows us a glimpse into the particularity of God, who is uniquely Father, Son, and Holy Spirit, all the while acting as one.[53] The Trinity reveals an equality-with-headship.

For his part, Zizioulas has a critical and limited use for the economy of God. In response to Rahner's Rule, "*The 'economic' Trinity is the 'immanent' Trinity and the 'immanent' Trinity is the 'economic' Trinity,*"[54] Zizioulas said, the immanent Trinity is not exhausted in the economic Trinity.[55] Zizioulas's purpose for saying this is that he believes God's transcendence is in jeopardy.[56] If there is nothing else to know concerning the essence and character of God than what has been revealed in the activity of God toward creation, then Zizioulas reasons that God is fully known by his creation which eliminates God's transcendence. Therefore, Zizioulas has a unique understanding of the economy of God, which is

48. John 14:28.

49. Olson and Hall, *Trinity*, 37.

50. Olson and Hall, *Trinity*, 37. For a further study into Christ as the mediator "for-others" and the "scandal" and offense of the cross developed for a philosophical anthropology of the cross termed "the cruciform self," see Gregor, *Philosophical Anthropology*.

51. LaCugna, *God*, 4.

52. LaCugna, *God*, 304–5.

53. For a contemporary reading on the trinitarian economy see Sanders, *Deep*.

54. Rahner, *Trinity*, 22.

55. Zizioulas, *One and Many*, 9. While Zizioulas has moderately critiqued Rahner's Rule, Papanikolaou has pointed out that Zizioulas's definition of personhood founded in participation of the "how God exists" actually aligns with Rahner. See Papanikolaou, *Being*, 99–100.

56. Zizioulas, *One and Many*, 8–9.

tied into the being of God and helps explain his eucharistic-ecclesiology. Three questions need to be addressed: (1) How does Zizioulas understand the economy of God? (2) What purpose does Zizioulas's economy of God have toward human beings? and (3) In what way is Zizioulas's definition of the economy of God limiting to the being of God and the human being?

First, Zizioulas's entrance into the discussion on the economy of God is only through the filter of "how God is" (i.e., "the way in which God exists") and not "what God is" (i.e., God's nature).[57] By understanding the economy of God through "how God is," Zizioulas then develops a trinitarian ontology where the economic Trinity is not exhausted in the immanent Trinity, rather the economic Trinity is identified in Christ who is the "corporate personality."[58] The identification of Christ as the culmination of the trinitarian economy by being the corporate person (i.e., the-One-and-the-Many) further supports Zizioulas's argument for the *monarchia* of the Father, who in turn wills that the Son become history through the incarnation (leading to a eucharistic-ecclesiology), meanwhile the Holy Spirit is given no economy, but rather constitutes Christ's economy.[59] Zizioulas states, "There is no 'Economy of the Holy Spirit.' There is only the Economy of the Son."[60] But why does Zizioulas have an aversion to an economy of the Holy Spirit? Should not a thoroughly trinitarian theology and ontology offer a balanced approach of God through the economy of the three persons of the Trinity without the danger of going to the heretical extreme of tritheism? Since the way God is *for us* (economy of God) is experienced through the eucharistic-ecclesiology of Christ's body, which is constituted by the Holy Spirit through the-one-and-the-many, as presented by Zizioulas, the Holy Spirit, therefore, constitutes the Church as the "co-founder" with Christ.[61]

---

57. Zizioulas, *Communion*, 124–26, 129; Papanikolaou, *Being*, 6, 99.

58. Papanikolaou, *Being*, 101; Zizioulas, *Being*, 130. Zizioulas synonymously uses "corporate personality" and "corporate person" when speaking of Christ's activity in the Eucharist, see Zizioulas, *One and Many*, 51, 68, 78, 142, 143, 146, 152, 244.

59. Zizioulas, *One and Many*, 7, 32, 68, 77–80, 138, 141–42, 146, 244–45, 394; Zizioulas, *Being*, 111–12, 182, 211–12; Zizioulas, *Lectures*, 150–51. Cf. Kärkkäinen, *Pneumatology*, 109–10; Awad, "Personhood," 13.

60. Zizioulas, *One and Many*, 394. Compare with the apparent contradiction in Zizioulas, "there is a distinct 'economy of the Holy Spirit'" (Zizioulas, *Being*, 124–25).

61. Zizioulas, *Being*, 124–26, 131; Zizioulas, *One and Many*, 15–16; Kärkkäinen, *Pneumatology*, 110.

Here we can identify the pitfall for Zizioulas in his relational ontology of personhood. Zizioulas believes that an economy of the Holy Spirit separates the person of the Holy Spirit from the person of Christ, and since Christology in Zizioulas's theology is conditioned by pneumatology, Christ cannot be conceived in himself as though he were an individual.[62] Zizioulas further warns against an economy of the Holy Spirit: each person of the Trinity cannot be understood apart from the others.[63] The only economy of God is an economy of Christ where there is a corporate personality of one-and-many.[64] However, Zizioulas does believe there are distinctions of the persons of the Trinity but without division.[65] Zizioulas supports his two-fold view of the distinctions of trinitarian persons along with the economy of Christ through Basil's doxology. Basil changed the prepositions in the doxology from "through" and "in" to "and" and "with."[66] Before Basil, it read, "Glory to the Father, *through* the Son, *in* the Holy Spirit," but afterward it read, "Glory to the Father, *and* the Son, *with* the Holy Spirit."[67] Zizioulas's use of Basil's doxological shift, along with the idea that the Son *became* history through the incarnation while the Holy Spirit is *involved in* history, justifies in Zizioulas's thought the collapsing of the economic Trinity into the economy of Christ.[68] Without emphasizing the economic Trinity, Zizioulas's theology funnels soteriology through eucharistic-ecclesiology and further proves the perceived error of the *filioque* in Western theology.[69] All of this is important for Zizioulas because the Father's *monarchia* is protected, meaning the ontology of God as persons-in-relation is intact.[70] The pneumatologically

62. Zizioulas, *Being*, 110–11. Cf. Turcescu, "Misreadings," 528–29, 533–34, 536–37.

63. Zizioulas, *One and Many*, 77.

64. Zizioulas, *One and Many*, 16, 53, 80–81, 394; Zizioulas, *Eucharist*, 15–16; Zizioulas, *Being*, 111–12, 127, 130. See also, LaCugna, *God*, 292–96; Knight, "Introduction," 10; Turner, "Eschatology and Truth," 21; Volf, *Likeness*, 85–86.

65. Zizioulas, *Lectures*, 71–73; Zizioulas, *One and Many*, 9, 53.

66. Basil, *Spirit*, 1.3; 7.16; Zizioulas, *Communion*, 187–88; Zizioulas, *Lectures*, 73; Zizioulas, *One and Many*, 10n20; Papanikolaou, *Being*, 100.

67. Basil, *Spirit*, 1.3; emphasis mine. Zizioulas, *Communion*, 187–88; Zizioulas, *Lectures*, 73; Papanikolaou, *Being*, 100.

68. Zizioulas, *Being*, 107–9, 129–30; Zizioulas, *Communion*, 189–90; Zizioulas, *Lectures*, 71–72; Zizioulas, *One and Many*, 9, 34–36. Papanikolaou, *Being*, 100.

69. Zizioulas, *Being*, 21–22, 107–9, 129–33; Zizioulas, *Communion*, 187–90; Zizioulas, *Lectures*, 69–82; Zizioulas, *One and Many*, 32–40, 44–45, 59.

70. Zizioulas, *Communion*, 126–49; Zizioulas, *One and Many*, 89; Gunton, "Persons," 99–100.

constituted Christology for salvation is the source of eucharistic-ecclesi-ology because individualism is non-being and labeled as sin in Zizioulas's Dictum. Therefore persons-in-relation, as community gathered around the Eucharist, symbolizes the transformed Christian person.[71]

Moreover, the Holy Spirit blows where he wills, revealing freedom within God, setting the Son free from the bonds of history, and consti-tuting communion (*koinōnia*) and eschatology through the Eucharist.[72] Therefore, all activity in God *ad intra* is found in the Father, while God's activity *ad extra* is concentrated in Christ. Zizioulas's reduction of unity into an ontic oneness at least suggests subordination of the persons of the Trinity,[73] if not potentially leading to the conclusion that the Father is *essentially* different from the Son and Spirit.[74]

A notable corrective to Zizioulas's monarchial view of the Father is a more balanced approach that simultaneously understands the particu-larity of the Trinity. For instance, Harrison accuses Zizioulas of overly emphasizing the freedom and primacy of the Father while forgetting that the Son and the Spirit are equally "ontologically free."[75] Harrison presses the point forward by asking, "Now, since the Son and the Spirit do not constitute their own essence in the same way that the Father does, how, in Zizioulas's terms, are they absolutely free, which they must be since they are fully God?"[76] On one hand, Harrison's conclusion is acceptable by stating the Son, and the Spirit's "freedom consists in absolute love and self-offering to the Father and to each other" as divine freedom (i.e., eter-nally self-emptying, self-offering, self-giving, etc.),[77] on the other hand,

---

71. Zizioulas, *Being*, 101–5, 116–22. Zizioulas, *Eucharistic Communion*, 34. In *One and Many*, Zizioulas ties together baptism, confirmation, and Eucharist as insepa-rable sacraments that are forms of grace which encompass the soteriological mystery (Zizioulas, *One and Many*, 91–100). In "Capacity and Incapacity," Zizioulas defines sin as idolatry and idolatry is the loss of an *ekstatic* movement outside of the created world (i.e., individualism) (Zizioulas, "Capacity and Incapacity," 424–25). Also see Ziziou-las's concept of "*ecclesial hypostasis*" (Zizioulas, *Being*, 53–59). Turner, "Eschatology and Truth," 18.

72. Zizioulas, "Come Holy Spirit," 1–3; Zizioulas, *Lectures*, 108–9; Zizioulas, *Being*, 110–14; 120–21; 130–33; Zizioulas, "Capacity and Incapacity," 432–33, 434.

73. Wilks, "Ontology," 79.

74. Awad, "Personhood," 8.

75. Harrison, "Zizioulas," 279.

76. Harrison, "Zizioulas," 279.

77. Harrison, "Zizioulas," 279.

Harrison, and Zizioulas for that matter, fail to recognize the two-fold understanding of the monarchy of the Father.

Torrance carefully distinguishes the two-fold concept of the Father-hood of God yet admits the difficulty because "they [Father as *ousia* and Father as *hypostasis*] cannot be separated and always overlap, for God the Father is both *ousia* and *hypostasis*."[78] First, when the Father is thought of in an absolute way (*in se*, i.e., *ousia*), then the name Father is applied to God, or the Godhead and God the eternal Father in this sense is the monarchy, the *being* of God who *causes* the Son and the Spirit to proceed.[79] Second, when Father is understood relationally/relatively (*ad alios*, i.e., *hypostasis*), then the name Father is applied to the relation of the Father to the Son and the Holy Spirit. Thus the monarchy is synonymous to the Trinity and not limited to one person, "since each divine Person is the whole God."[80] Therefore, Torrance's two-fold understanding of the monarchy of the Father, which includes an economy of the Father, makes more sense than Zizioulas's monolithic presentation on the monarchy of the Father. Thus, while we find fault in Zizioulas's monarchial view of the Trinity, we likewise take issue with an egalitarian view of the Trinity as found in Boff.[81] Torrance has pointed out that the Father is viewed in two ways (*ousia* and *hypostasis*); therefore, there is a middle road under-standing of the trinitarian relationship between an extreme monarchy and extreme egalitarian views. This middle road is nuanced in *headship* or *order* within the Trinity, further demonstrated throughout the design of creation. This equality-with-order (or headship; or distinction-no-distinction)[82] design can be found analogously throughout Scripture. A few scriptural samples include husbands as the head (*kephalē*) of wife,[83]

---

78. Torrance, *Doctrine*, 141.

79. Torrance, *Doctrine*, 140–41. Also, Athansius, *Arians*, 3.1.1; 3.1.4–6; 4.1–3; Athanasius, *To Serapion*, 1.16, 20; Gregory of Nazianzus, *Orations*, "On the Son," 2; Gregory of Nazianzus, *Orations*, "On the Holy Spirit," 24; Gregory of Nazianzus, *Orations*, "On the Theophany," 8.

80. Torrance, *Doctrine*, 140–41. Also, Athanasius, *Arians*, 3.4–6; Gregory of Nazianzus, *Orations*, "On the Son," 2–21; 30.11; Irenaeus, *Heresies*, 6.1, 3.

81. Boff, *Trinity and Society*, 11, 151.

82. The Apostle Paul distinguishes between people groups (i.e., Jews and Gentiles, Rom 1:16) while also claiming no distinction of people groups who have faith in Christ (Rom 10:12–13).

83. Eph 5:23; cf. Gen 3:16; 1 Cor 11:3. The simile of husbands as head of wife is Christ is the head of the Church (Eph 5:22–32).

the Jew first (*prōton*) and also the Greek,[84] the firstborn son compared
to the other children,[85] Israel's king was to be "one from among your
brothers."[86] There is a designed order in each of these human illustrations;
however, the responsibility lies with the first or the head constraining
hard-and-fast monarchial and egalitarian views. Therefore we conclude
from the trinitarian formula of Father, Son, and Holy Spirit being three
hypostases (particularity) and one *ousia* (unity) that the three persons are
equal in *ousia* and dignity while operating (i.e., love and submission) in
a designed order and headship.[87] This trinitarian formula represents an
equality-with-headship.

Second, the purpose behind Zizioulas's presentation on the economy
of God is for "liturgical experience and worship"[88] as well as fostering an
acceptance of a pneumatological constitution of Christology and ecclesiology with the intention of an "ontological priority and ultimacy of the
person in existence."[89] As such, Zizioulas's persons-in-relation is the key
to understanding his motive behind the trinitarian economy actualized
in Christ as the corporate personality and the one-*for*-the-many.[90] Christ
is the source of the Church who unites all human beings to himself.[91]
Zizioulas's one-and-many economy is mirrored in the Trinity, where the
Father is the source of the Trinity, and later where the bishop is the source
of Church membership (i.e., congregation).[92] Therefore, Harrison's cri-

84. Rom 1:16; 2:9, 10; cf. "no distinction" in Rom 10:12; Gal 3:28; Col 3:11.

85. Num 18:15; Deut 21:15–17; compare to "firstfruits" in Exod 23:19; Lev 2:12;
23:10, 17; Num 18:12–13; Deut 26:2, 10; Neh 10:35.

86. Deut 17:15. Brueggemann, *Theology*, 600–602. In comparison, the ANE nations considered the king to be divine. See Routledge, *Theology*, 225–26.

87. Gregory of Nazianzus, *Orations*, "On the Holy Spirit," 3–7, 9–10, 12; Gregory
of Nazianzus, *Orations*, "On Baptism," 41; Gregory of Nazianzus, *Orations*, "On Pentecost," 9. Nazianzus does use the term "Monarchia" when describing the trinitarian
relationship saying, "When we look at the Godhead, or the First Cause, or the Monarchia, that which we conceive is One; but when we look at the Persons in Whom
timelessly and with equal glory have their Being from the First Cause—there are Three
Whom we worship" (Gregory of Nazianzus, *Orations*, "On the Holy Spirit," 14).

88. Zizioulas, *Communion*, 190.

89. Zizioulas, *Communion*, 205; Awad, "Personhood," 3–15; Papanikolaou, *Being*,
142–48.

90. Zizioulas, *Being*, 110–14, 145–49; Zizioulas, *Eucharistic Communion*, 13; Fox,
God as Communion, 79–80, 86, 203.

91. Zizioulas, *Eucharist*, 15, 16, 18, 54–58. "The Spirit makes the Church *be*"
(Zizioulas, *Being*, 132). Farrow, *Ascension and Ecclesia*, 42, 57, 60, 63, 66.

92. Harrison, "Zizioulas," 289. Cf. Zizioulas speaks of the priest and bishop as a

tique that Zizioulas's trinitarian model is collapsed into a Christological model is legitimate and that a trinitarian equality is needed as a corrective.[93] In addition, in Zizioulas's Christology, Farrow sees a Eutychian tendency (i.e., like Monophysitism believing Christ had one nature), affecting ecclesiology.[94] For Zizioulas, however, God's economy is found in Christ, who is the body of the Church and is experienced when the congregation participates in the Eucharist.[95] For this to occur, the Holy Spirit constitutes Christ and the Church by bringing about community thus causing it to be the "whole Church" by uniting all creation to Christ through the eucharistic event.[96]

Third, Zizioulas's definition of the economy of God is limiting in application to the being of God and the human being. While Zizioulas reminds us that what God is for us in the economic Trinity does not include all that God is in essence, thus indicating mystery and transcendence, he, however, collapses the persons of the Trinity into Christ and soteriology into the event of the Eucharist. In this singular event, *koinōnia* is experienced as the Holy Spirit constitutes it through the Eucharist at the point where the body of Christ (i.e., the Church) is gathered in one place as the-one-and-the-many included also is the presence of the Trinity through the pneumatologically constituted Christology making it Church.[97] More so, in this eucharistic event, the Church becomes literally the catholic (universal) Church; in Zizioulas's Dictum, this means the many (i.e., Father, Son, and Holy Spirit) become one in Christ, while the many participants become one church.[98] Zizioulas is correct in that to speak of one member of the Trinity is to speak of the other two members because of their

---

"mediator" in the sense of "corporate personality" in the idea of "representation by participation" as the ordained person stands in the place of Christ, who is bodily absent, yet spiritually present before the eucharistic community, offering and leading in the Eucharistic meal (Zizioulas, *Being*, 226–27, 230–31). Also see where Zizioulas labels the Bishop as the "'president' of the Eucharist" (Zizioulas, *Eucharist*, 62–68).

93. Harrison, "Zizioulas," 289. This is also the argument of Awad, "Between," 199.

94. Farrow, "Person and Nature," 121.

95. Zizioulas, *Being*, 60–61, 88–89, 111–12.

96. Zizioulas, "Informal Groups," 279; Zizioulas, *Being*, 150. Also, Fox, *God as Communion*, 199–201.

97. Zizioulas, *Being*, 110–14, 149–54; Zizioulas, *Communion*, 294–98; Zizioulas, *Eucharistic Communion*, 12–13.

98. Zizioulas, *Being*, 154–58; Zizioulas, *Eucharistic Communion*, 6–24, 46–47; Zizioulas, *One and Many*, 55; Zizioulas, *Lectures*, 108.

interrelatedness and interdependence.[99] When speaking of the persons of the Trinity and the economy of God, Zizioulas will allow a discussion on "distinct characteristics"[100] but avoids assigning "personal attributes" to the persons of the Trinity because assigning attributes to the economy, in his opinion, would lead to a necessity causing God to be bound by these attributes.[101] In contrast, Lossky describes the significance of the economy of the Trinity applied to the Church, and more specifically, the "two-fold divine economy" of Christ as the head of the body and the Holy Spirit who fills her with divinity.[102] The problem with Zizioulas's conclusion in opposing an economic approach to theology is that ultimately the divine makes contact with human beings through a united gathering (i.e., Church) where the Father, Son, and Holy Spirit are all in Christ (i.e., Eucharist), and every single believer is collected into the congregation by way of eucharistic participation.[103] On the surface, Zizioulas's eucharistic theology is aesthetically pleasing as expressed through the-one-and-the-many: the communion of the Father, Son, and Holy Spirit is extended through the one person, Jesus Christ; meanwhile, the many faithful human participants become one in this act.[104] However, in this theology, the uniqueness and distinctions from both participants, God, and humans, are lost.[105] In the eucharistic event, the Trinity is encased in Christ as the head of the Church, and the Church is a homogenous whole.[106] Thus, for all of Zizioulas's arguments against the approach of defining "being"

---

99. Zizioulas, *Being*, 41, 111–12; Zizioulas, *Lectures*, 53; Zizioulas, *One and Many*, 23, 29, 51, 55; Zizioulas, "Holy Trinity," 59–60; Pannenberg, "Divine Economy," 84–85.

100. Zizioulas, *Being*, 129. However, in Zizioulas's *Lectures*, he also denies the economy to "particular characteristics" for fear that it may logically determine to some extent the Trinity (Zizioulas, *Lectures*, 71).

101. Zizioulas, *Lectures*, 71.

102. Lossky, *Mystical Theology*, 156–57.

103. Zizioulas, *Being*, 149–54, 158–62; Zizioulas, *Lectures*, 115–19; Farrow, "Person and Nature," 119; Harrison, "Zizioulas," 279–81, 289; Grenz, *Rediscovering*, 132, 132, 138–39; Olson and Hall, *Trinity*, 114–15; Papanikolaou, *Being*, 100–101; Holmes, *Quest*, 14–15; Volf, *Likeness*, 99–100.

104. Zizioulas, *Being*, 15, 80–82, 94, 101, 112–13, 134–37, 149–52; Zizioulas, *Eucharist*, 107–28; Zizioulas, *One and Many*, 53–54.

105. Zizioulas, *Being*, 106–7; Olson and Hall, *Trinity*, 114–15; Awad, "Personhood," 9–10.

106. Zizioulas, *Being*, 21–22, 81–82; Zizioulas, *Lectures*, xv, xvii–xxi, 106, 123, 124, 126, 127, 133; Zizioulas, *One and Many*, 14–16, 67–73; Gunton, *One, Three, Many*, 180–83; Gunton, *Trinitarian Theology*, 56–58.

from a perspective of nature, substance, and essence, what appears, in the end, is a blurred vision of persons, both divine and human, in the moment of eucharistic participation.[107] The ecclesial homogeneity in Zizioulas's theology happens despite his attempts to speak at times of personal uniqueness as irreducible and unrepeatable persons.[108] The reason, therefore, Zizioulas's theology ends in collectivism can be found in his thesis where "relations" is the focus of persons-in-relation, and likewise, "communion" is the focus of being-in-communion. A further illustration can be given in Zizioulas's paradoxical statement concerning the-one-and-the-many applied to the Church, in which Zizioulas emphasizes the unified "one" or unity: "when *you become* ἐκκλησία" the local community becomes the "whole Church."[109] In this presentation, the particular and unique person is lost in the community.

Zizioulas's Dictum emphasizes the person of the Father (i.e., a particular person), not substance, who is the cause of the Trinity, and further freely causes (*aitia*) everything that exists.[110] Therefore, being cannot exist in-itself; being exists in relationship with another:[111] "True being comes only from the free person, from the person who loves freely—that is, who freely affirms his being, his identity, by means of an event of communion with other persons."[112] However, since Zizioulas limits the economy of God through the economy of Christ (the corporate personality) as the-one-and-the-many, God only comes into contact with humans (i.e., as God for us) through eucharistic-ecclesiology.[113] Whereas Zizioulas begins with the particular (i.e., the Father), he ends with the corporate and collegial body of Christ offered to the collective, collegial whole, called the Church, where particular and unique human beings are gathered for salvation.[114] Thus Zizioulas concludes, "The nature of the eucharistic

---

107. Zizioulas, *Being*, 27–40, 130–31, 134–38, 145–49, 149–54; Zizioulas, "Capacity and Incapacity," 403–7; Zizioulas, *Eucharistic Communion*, 14–24.

108. Zizioulas, *Communion*, 167, 213, 214. Turcescu, "Misreadings," 533.

109. Zizioulas, *Being*, 147–49. Cf. Loudovikos, "Christian Life," 128–30.

110. Zizioulas, *Being*, 17, 40–41; Zizioulas, *Communion*, 137; Zizioulas, "Holy Trinity," 52, 54–55; Zizioulas, *Lectures*, 53; Zizioulas, *One and Many*, xv, 10–14, 22–24, 39, 41–45; Awad, "Between," 188–90, 193; Grenz, *Rediscovering*, 141.

111. LaCugna, *God*, 246.

112. Zizioulas, *Being*, 18.

113. Zizioulas, *One and Many*, 53, 77, 394.

114. Zizioulas, *Being*, 135, 149–54. Bathrellos questions Zizioulas's emphasis of Eucharistic unity as based on the First Letter to the Corinthians (Bathrellos, "Church, Eucharist, Bishop," 143).

community was determined by its being 'eucharistic,' i.e., by the fact that it consisted in the communion of the Body of Christ in its totality and in its inclusiveness for *all*."[115] It is here in this all-inclusive eucharistic moment of communion, or the actual period of time from the liturgy to the consuming of the elements of bread and wine, where history is turned toward eschatology.[116] Zizioulas stresses unification in communion on three levels in the eucharistic event: the unity of the Trinity in Christ, the unity of people in the congregation, and the unity of Christ and the Church.[117] However, the extent of Zizioulas's point on unity in these three areas causes obscurity in particularity as applied to the economy of God, the personal identity of humans, and the Church.[118] Personal identity is being-as-communion through the Eucharist and *"by virtue of its eucharistic nature* a 'catholic Church.'"[119] Therefore, in Zizioulas's ecclesiology and theology, the universal and collective Church results from the Eucharist event.[120] For his part, Zizioulas recognizes potential problems with "unity in identity" that leads to collectivism, yet he leaves the topic hanging without addressing the issues.[121] Perhaps the most significant issues caused by Zizioulas's aversion to a trinitarian economy, along with the implications of his eucharistic-ecclesiology, are soteriological.

Some scholars have noted Zizioulas's underdeveloped soteriology. Volf criticizes Zizioulas's lack of "faith" in his soteriological writings instead of presuming *faith* upon the participation of the sacraments.[122] Volf reasons that *faith* is absent in Zizioulas's soteriology because it is a cognitive act that an individual must practice, and for Zizioulas's ecclesiology, an individual act cannot constitute a person or communion.[123] LaCugna

---

115. Zizioulas, *Being*, 154.

116. Zizioulas, *Being*, 114, 130–31, 138, 183–88; Zizioulas, *Eucharistic Communion*, 31–33; Zizioulas, *One and Many*, 87–88, 112, 143, 154–55, 310–13.

117. Zizioulas, "Capacity and Incapacity," 438; Zizioulas, *Eucharist*, 9–10, 14–24, 87–93; Zizioulas, *One and Many*, 68–73.

118. Awad, "Personhood," 8; Harrison, "Zizioulas," 279, 281, 285–87, 288–91, 298; Gunton, "Persons," 105–6; Volf, *Likeness*, 106, 114–15, 145, 181–82, 223–24.

119. Zizioulas, *Being*, 156. Also, for a more thorough description of Zizioulas's view on unity and the catholic church, see Zizioulas, *Eucharist*, 107–62.

120. Zizioulas, *Eucharistic Communion*, 12–19, 67–73, 100–103, 104–9, 159–60; Zizioulas, *Eucharist*, 107–28; Zizioulas, *One and Many*, 67–73, 99–100, 123.

121. Zizioulas, *Being*, 158n66.

122. Volf, *Likeness*, 95.

123. Volf, *Likeness*, 95. Cf. Zizioulas, *One and Many*, 75–90.

recognizes the importance of the economy of God for human salvation, calling it "the totality of God's life."[124] Furthermore, particularity by way of the economy of God is essential for particular people to enter into God's salvation in a manner that demonstrates truly and ontologically persons-in-relation. For instance, Gunton connects the redemption of creation with the image of God in human beings.[125] Thus, for salvation to occur and for human beings to be re-established in relation to God, the future of the whole creation depends on the action of a particular part.[126] Gunton continues by arguing, "we must affirm the traditional slogan, 'man is a microcosm', the one in whom the whole finds its meaning. A failure of at-one-ness here entails a failure of the whole project, which can therefore be achieved only by the reconciliation of those whose breach frustrates the destined outcome."[127] Furthermore, for Gunton, to be a created being means the Triune God has given creation (human and non-human) a direction and a dynamic.[128] Therefore, "Redemption thus means the redirection of the particular to its own end and not a re-creation."[129] In Gunton's soteriology, the redirection of particular humans is instituted by the sacrifice and resurrection of Jesus Christ (particular person) for the whole of humanity.[130] The Holy Spirit then enables particular people who become living sacrifices, who are reconciled to God, and who are able

124. LaCugna, *God*, 246.

125. Gunton, *Trinitarian Theology*, 185; Gunton, *Creator*, 56; Col 1:15.

126. Gunton, *Trinitarian Theology*, 185; Gunton, *Creator*, 56. Cf. Zizioulas, *Lectures*, 52–53.

127. Gunton, *Trinitarian Theology*, 186.

128. Gunton, *One, Three, Many*, 230. Cf. There is an allusion to Barth's "the covenant as the internal basis of creation" here in Gunton. However, for Barth the dynamic of creation is based on the doctrine of election where creation fulfills the covenant of grace in Jesus Christ (Mueller, *Barth*, 112).

129. Gunton, *One, Three, Many*, 230. See also, Gunton, *Trinitarian Theology*, 187. Gunton's substitution of "redirection" for "re-creation" does not go as far as the biblical reference where David prays to YHWH that he would grant him: "Create [*bārā'*] in me a clean heart" and in parallel "renew [*ḥădēš*] a right spirit within me" (Ps 51:11). For further biblical references on this concept of God recreating or giving a new heart and/or spirit, see Jer 24:7; Ezek 11:19; 36:26; and especially Eph 4:23, 24.

130. Gunton, *Trinitarian Theology*, 189–90. See also Torrance, *Mediation*, 56–59, 79–88.

to give God worship.[131] Thus, in its biblical sense, Gunton's soteriology requires an economy of God rather than an ontology.[132]

In contrast to Gunton's trinitarian economic approach to salvation,[133] Zizioulas's soteriology is primarily ontological, as demonstrated when he announces, "salvation is identified with the realization of personhood in man."[134] In Zizioulas's Dictum, to be a person is to be-in-relation with another, which means being and communion must coincide for a person to exist.[135] In that, as the Savior, Christ is ontologically a person and whose being is constituted by the Holy Spirit, so, Christology "removes the problem of truth from the realm of the individual and of the 'nature' to the level of the person."[136] Thus, Zizioulas's soteriology is an outgrowth of his Dictum as it means a conversion from individualism to personhood through the act of baptism.[137] In this stream of thought, existential truth is communion truth that is initiated through the new birth by baptism and participated in through the Eucharist.[138] As such, Zizioulas argues, "The application of Christ's existence to ours then amounts to nothing other than a realization of the community of the Church."[139] For Zizioulas, salvation comes about by realizing the eucharistic community rather than deliverance from sin and life turned in upon itself in selfishness.[140] Zizioulas's soteriology is aimed toward the one universal Church community as a priority in contrast to the many individual people, whom he views need salvation from individualistic isolation and can be freed to communion with others in the Eucharist.[141] For this reason, Gunton

---

131. Gunton, *Trinitarian Theology*, 190–91. Also, McIntyre, *Pneumatology*, 185–90.

132. Gunton, *Trinitarian Theology*, 197–200; Awad, "Personhood," 18.

133. Gunton, *Trinitarian Theology*, 179; Gunton, *Creator*, 205–6.

134. Zizioulas, *Being*, 50. See Awad, "Personhood," 3, 5, 13–14.

135. Zizioulas, *Being*, 106, 107; Zizioulas, "Capacity and Incapacity," 409–11, 435–36; Zizioulas, *Communion*, 13–14, 73, 240–41.

136. Zizioulas, *Being*, 108, 111; Zizioulas, *Communion*, 6, 244–45; Zizioulas, *One and Many*, 142–43.

137. Zizioulas, *Being*, 50–65, 113; Zizioulas, "Capacity and Incapacity," 437. See Papanikolaou, *Being*, 106, 117–20, 125–26, 134–35.

138. Zizioulas, *Being*, 113–14; Zizioulas, *One and Many*, 67–69; Papanikolaou, *Being*, 117–18.

139. Zizioulas, *Being*, 114.

140. Awad, "Personhood," 5. Cf. Kinlaw, *Jesus*, 98, 112–13, 115.

141. Zizioulas, *Being*, 50, 107–9, 111–13, 114–22; Zizioulas, *Communion*, 6–8, 244–45; Zizioulas, *One and Many*, 68, 78, 142–43; Awad, "Personhood," 5; Volf, *Likeness*, 181–82; Harrison, "Zizioulas," 274.

charges Eastern theologians, Zizioulas, among them, with a lack of dealing with the problem of human sin, and in turn, the human need for salvation.[142] Gunton then rhetorically asks, "Might we not ask for, and profit by, a more directly pneumatological construal of the nature of the particular person?"[143] In this question, Gunton prefaces the importance of particular persons-in-relation in God through the economic Trinity. The economic Trinity as particularity in God (i.e., persons-in-relation) also sheds light on anthropology as reflected through the *imago Dei* and toward the particularity in human beings.[144] More specifically, Holy Spirit speaks to the human spirit as to what it means to be a human being in relation to God our Creator.[145]

PARTICULARITY IN HUMAN BEING

We have noted that there is particularity within the Trinity (Father, Son, and Holy Spirit) and that there is particularity within human beings. We can add that the particular person of the Trinity, the Holy Spirit, works in particular people so that each may be united with God and with one another in the Christian community as a foreshadowing of the eschaton.[146] While Zizioulas's Dictum is rooted in Cappadocian didactic and

142. Gunton, "Persons, 104. Gunton's point on sin and salvation in Zizioulas's theology stems from a larger discrepancy between Eastern and Western theologians. See Nassif et al., *Three Views*, 122–24, 147, 150, 155–56, 159–60.

143. Gunton, "Persons," 107.

144. Volf, *Likeness*, 182, 185–86; LaCugna, *God*, 264–65; McConville, *Being Human*, 20, 25, 27; Middleton, *Liberating Image*, 49–60, 88–90; Jones, *God the Spirit*, 21–23.

145. Rom 8:16; 2 Cor 1:22; 5:5; Eph 1:13–14; 1 John 3:24. Gunton, *One, Three, Many*, 185; Wesley, "Journal," 23, 77, 90, 91, 92, 97, 106, 110, 117, 118, 127, 137, 140, 166, 168, 169, 187, 188, 195, 196, 197, 222, 227, 230, 236, 244, 257, 304, 328, 364, 380, 402, 433, 476, 488, 508, 526; Wesley, "Witness of the Spirit (Discourse 1)," 111–23; Wesley, "Witness of the Spirit (Discourse 2)," 123–34; Wesley, "Witness of our Own Spirit," 134–44; Fee, *Empowering*, 99–101.

146. Gunton, *One, Three, Many*, 180–84; Gunton, "Persons," 106–7; Farrow, *Ascension*, 59–66; Lossky, *Mystical Theology*, 160–65; Zizioulas, *Communion*, 243; Bonhoeffer, *Life Together*, 17–21; Fox, *God as Communion*, 199–203; Awad, "Between," 191–92, 197, 198; McConville, *Being Human*, 48. Käsemann, *Romans*, comments on Rom 8:5 and the use of *phroneō* ("to think," or "to set the mind"), that "the axiom of Pauline anthropology is presupposed. A person cannot live on his own. He is what he is because of his Lord and the power of his Lord, and he shows this in his acts. When all other differences and limitations are eschatologically relativized, commitment to flesh

apologetic writings for *hypostasis* to denote person in the Trinity, Zizioulas's soteriological application is not directed toward the human person
in particular, but rather, it is the Church aimed at in general: which is the
corporate collection of believers or persons-in-relation.[147] Papanikolaou
argues that weakness in Zizioulas's theology is a particular person's relationship with God.

> In his attempt to emphasize salvation as an event that is the
> simultaneous constitution of the one and the many, Zizioulas
> almost completely neglects that particular, ascetical struggle
> of a person in their particular relationship with God. It is as if
> Zizioulas is ignoring this dominant aspect of the Eastern tradi-
> tion for fear of insinuating that salvation is individualistic.[148]

If, as Zizioulas argues, the Cappadocian Fathers offered a new, clearer,
and workable understanding for persons of the Trinity as *hypostasis*, then
it could be argued that this pattern can also be understood and applied
to human personhood through the outcome of the *imago Dei*.[149] The economic Trinity is God reaching toward all humans, and whoever responds
with affirmation, through repentance, receives forgiveness of sins.[150]
Each particular person is not simply received into communion with God
and the Church through legal means,[151] but furthermore, truly becomes
a person by way of the *imago Dei* made possible by the Holy Spirit who
brings unity and peace between God and human being, and between
human and human.[152] This way of being is a trinitarian pneumatological personhood as a specific Christian anthropology. Unlike Zizioulas's

---

or Spirit and their possibilities and necessities marks a final and abiding distinction"
(Käsemann, *Romans*, 219).

147. Zizoulas, *Being*, 107–22.

148. Papanikolaou, *Being*, 125.

149. McConville, *Being Human*, 24–29; Gunton, *Trinitarian Theology*, 109–16;
Lossky, *Mystical Theology*, 100, 108–11, 114–16, 118–20, 122, 124–27; McIntyre,
Pneumatology, 180, 187, 191–93; Thiselton, *Holy Spirit*, 416–17.

150. Luke 1:77; 3:3; 24:45–47. Dunning, *Reflecting*, 48–53, 55–61; Kinlaw, *Jesus*,
107–25. The concept of salvation indicates a shift in humans from one state of being
to another state being. However, it is more popular for modern theologians writing
on the topic of salvation to deal with the state for which a person is saved *to* (e.g., life,
love, reconciliation, heaven, etc.), rather than the state for which a person is saved *from*
(e.g., death, sin, selfishness, hell, etc.). See chapter 7 under the subtitle, "The Problem
and Solution to Christian Anthropology."

151. Rom 2:12–19; 3:23–24; 5:1, 20–21; 6:14. See Oden, *Justification*, 53–59.

152. Rom 8:1–17; John 14:15–27. Sanders, *Deep*, 143, 144, 148, 150, 160, 163, 165,
170.

thought which begins with the monarchy of the Father who is the cause of the Trinity[153] and reaches toward humanity in the corporate person of Christ through the Eucharist so that the corporate gathering might be-as-communion,[154] here the three persons of the Trinity who are One in nature, yet having particular roles, offer to all humanity salvation, and communicate to people in their human particularity (i.e., uniqueness). Those people (i.e., particular, unique, distinct) who, in turn, respond positively to salvific grace by faith are drawn into the holy community (i.e., communion, relationship) with the Trinity in *perichoresis*.[155] These, who are saved, are further drawn into the corporate body of believers called the Church, yet without losing their distinctive particularity.[156] Since Zizioulas anchors his thought on the Cappadocians and other church fathers, there also should be historical evidence of the economic Trinity dealing with human particularity and the corporate body.

One of those church fathers for whom evidence of an economic trinitarian theology is developed is in the writings of Irenaeus. Since the purpose of the theological economy is to show diversity and unity in the activity of the particular trinitarian persons, the same theological method can be used in Christian anthropology to identify the particular person as an ecclesial person (i.e., diversity and unity). Irenaeus taught the significance of the human being is both flesh and spirit in that male and female are the "handiwork" of God who is termed as "perfect" when they receive the Holy Spirit.[157] Three points are significant here: (1) God engages particular (i.e., unique, distinct, different) persons, (2) God indwells particular persons, and (3) the particular persons are radically

153. Zizioulas, *Being*, 17, 40–41; Zizioulas, *Communion*, 137; Zizioulas, "Holy Trinity," 52, 54–55; Zizioulas, *Lectures*, 53, 61; Zizoulas, *One and Many*, xv, 10–14, 22–24, 39, 41–45; Awad, "Between," 187–90, 193; Holmes, *Quest*, 13; LaCugna, *God*, 245.

154. Zizioulas, *Eucharist*, 54. Also, Käsemann, *Romans*, 214–25, shows that particular Christians (i.e., "each individual person," "individual believers," "each Christian," "every member") are recognized by the Holy Spirit within them (Käsemann, *Romans*, 223). Cf. "like is known only by like" in Fee, *Empowering*, 99–101.

155. Gunton, *Trinitarian Theology*, 109–16, 141–43, 195–204; Sanders, *Deep*, 156–71, 177–81; Kinlaw, *Jesus*, 140, 146–49; LaCugna, *God*, 297–98.

156. Gunton, *One, Three, Many*, 214–19, 223, 225, 227, 229–31; LaCugna, *God*, 299–300; Torrance, *Faith*, 252–54.

157. Irenaeus, *Heresies*, 5.6.1. Also, Torrance, *Faith*, 91, 94; McConville, *Being Human*, 176. For an explanation on Irenaeus's use of "perfect" in his theology of creation, see Gunton, *Creator*, 55–56.

transformed from their former state of being. God certainly engages the corporate body of believers, but more specifically, Irenaeus points out that particular people within the Church are made perfect because the Spirit of God remains in them and operates through their lives in a manner, for example, of love toward their neighbor.[158] Second, God indwells particular people as Irenaeus refers to the Apostle Paul as distinguishing between spiritual people who "partake" of the Holy Spirit and are thus modeled after Jesus Christ.[159] Third, the communion of particular people with God through the indwelling of the Holy Spirit changes their personhood from imperfection to perfection according to the standards of God shown through their other relationships.[160]

The relational aspect of the persons of the Trinity is evident in Athanasius's writings. Athanasius qualifies the importance of a particular person to be unified with the Father through the Son can only happen through the Holy Spirit when the person repents and allows his/herself to be subjected to God.[161] When the Holy Spirit indwells the person, says Athanasius, "by the participation of the Spirit we are knit into the Godhead; so that our being in the Father is not ours, but is the Spirit's which is in us and abides in us."[162] While Athanasius's primary contribution to

---

158. Irenaeus, *Heresies*, 5.6.1. Gunton finds in Irenaeus's writings, God's "particularizing will" through Christology and pneumatology upon created particularity in human life (Gunton, *One, Three, Many*, 54). On this topic of Christian perfection as perfect love, compare the theology of John Wesley, e.g., Wesley, "Circumcision of the Heart," 202–12; Wesley, "Christian Perfection," 1–22; Wesley, "On Perfection," 411–23; Wesley, "Plain Account," 383–85, 442; Wesley, "Brief Thoughts," 446.

159. Irenaeus, *Heresies*, 5.6.1.

160. Irenaeus, *Heresies*, 5.6.1. Farrow emphasizes as a safeguarding factor in Irenaeus's recapitulation doctrine that Jesus as a particular divine-human person is the unifying Logos by descending and redeeming humans in their particularity (Farrow, *Ascension*, 51–58).

161. Athanasius, *Arians*, 3.25.25. The concept of God as Creator, for Athanasius is based on the relation between the Father, Son and Holy Spirit. The particular persons of Trinity are never without the other. However, God the Father as Creator is not the Fount of all creation in the same way that he is the Fount of the eternal Son, thus concluding that the Father is simply a "Maker and Shaper of being." "It is because God is inherently productive and creative in his very being as God, that he is Creator" (Torrance, *Faith*, 77, 79, 219). Furthermore, Torrance shows that in Athanasius and the Cappadocian Fathers, the Holy Spirit has come to humans as a relationship between God and human beings (Torrance, *Faith*, 229–31).

162. Athanasius, *Arians*, 3.25.24.

theology was in defense of the deity of Christ for a clear soteriology, this eventually led him to defend the divinity of the Holy Spirit as well.[163]

Like Athanasius, Basil also specifically wrote on the Holy Spirit from a trinitarian perspective. Basil notes that within the Trinity, three "particular" *hypostases* who are in continuous communion operating together in such a way that their work appears "commingled."[164] Therefore to receive the Holy Spirit is simultaneously to receive the Father and the Son.[165] Furthermore, Basil states that the "peculiarities" and "particular" modes of existence from the "distinct" persons of the Trinity are revealed through faith, and this same *hypostatic* pattern of distinctiveness can be applied to humans.[166] Moreover, the Holy Spirit indwells the particular person's soul (e.g., Paul, Daniel, etc.) and purifies them from evil.[167] The Holy Spirit indwells humans similar to the Aristotelian *Form* which is found in *Matter* making it the object it is, so too, the Holy Spirit indwells the Christian believer conforming and uniting them into the image of Jesus Christ.[168] For Basil, a Christian's sanctification and worship are made possible by the Holy Spirit, but the particular person must withdraw from the busyness of society to a "quiet" (*hesychia*)[169] place where this communion of the Holy Spirit with the self may take place.[170]

Hesychasm was further developed throughout Eastern Orthodoxy through the writings of those such as St. Symeon the Theologian, St. Gregory of Sinai, and St. Gregory of Palamas.[171] Palamas, for his part, is known as the theologian of *hesychasm* as he integrated mystical tradition

163. Burgess, *Holy Spirit*, 120. Cf. Athanasius, *Nicene Definition*, 3.14; Athanasius, *Arians*, 1.12.47–48, 50.

164. Basil, *Letter* 38.4. Hall, *Learning*, 112–17.

165. Basil, *Letter* 38.4. Also, Gunton, *One, Three, Many*, 182, 189–90.

166. Basil, *Letter* 38.3–4.

167. Basil, *Spirit*, 26.63. See Fedwick, *Basil*, 77–100.

168. Basil, *Spirit*, 26.61.

169. Later (fourth to sixth century), the Greek Orthodox Church formalized this idea of *hesychia* that became what is now known as *hesychasm* which has evolved from quiet, "non-iconic," prayer to an Invocation of Jesus's Name (fifth century) to "a psychosomatic technique, involving control of the breathing" (fourteenth century) (Diokleia, "Hesychasm," 241). "Neilos of Ankyra (d. ca. 430), 'It is impossible for muddy water to grow clear if it is constantly stirred up; it is impossible to become a monk without *hesychia*.' (Exhortation to Monks, PG 79:1236B)" (Diokleia, "Hesychasm," 241).

170. Fedwick, *Basil*, 31.

171. McGuckin, *Orthodox*, 353.

with Christian thought and linked it squarely on the Scriptures.[172] The Orthodox Church sanctioned Palamas's doctrine in 1351 and published it in the *Synodal Tome* and later in the *Synodikon of Orthodoxy* as one means of personal spirituality.[173] While Zizioulas admits that Palamas "was promoted as a standard-bearer of Orthodoxy and representative of the theology of self-purification," he does not believe Palamas's ecclesiology entirely subordinates the divine Eucharist to individual spirituality as is commonly portrayed with Palamas.[174] However, Palamas places the highest significance on particular persons keeping watch over Christ-followers' minds and hearts so that the "law of sin" is driven out by grace, so that one's mind and heart will be purified holy in love.[175] The intense prayer and quietness that Palamas discusses do not indicate "individual spirituality" as Zizioulas would term it since each particular person seeks his or her personhood in another (i.e., persons-in-relation, being-as-communion). In this case, Other is the eternal God who is Trinity, particularly the person of the Father, the person of the Son, and the person of the Holy Spirit. What is more, Palamas teaches that love will flow from one's life toward other people, whose whole being (i.e., personhood) is focused on God.[176]

In Hilary's writings, a focus on God implies personal experience of a relationship with God through the Holy Spirit. Hilary explains that faithful Christians are given the assurance of acceptance of God as they "enter the kingdom of heaven" by the Holy Spirit, which he calls "the Gift."[177] He further draws his audience into a personal experience with God through the Holy Spirit, "Let us therefore make use of this great benefit, and seek for personal experience of this most needful Gift."[178] Furthermore, Hil-

172. Meyendorff, *St. Gregory of Palamas*, 102.

173. Meyendorff, *St. Gregory of Palamas*, 99.

174. Zizioulas, *Lectures*, 124.

175. Palamas, *Triads*, 1.2.2; 1.2.8; 2.2.6; Meyendorff, *St. Gregory Palamas*, 74–75, 90.

176. Palamas, *Triads*, 1.2.8. Meyendorff, says, "The Christian mystic seeks a new life in Christ, an active life for his whole being and he knows that the grace of baptism and the eucharist have already given him that life; moreover he seeks it in the interior of his own being. That is why the hesychast movement of the fourteenth century never deteriorated into individualistic and subjective mysticism but led in fact to a revival of ecclesiastical sacramentalism" (Meyendorff, *St. Gregory Palamas*, 109).

177. Hilary, *Trinity*, 2.33. See Oden, *Spirit*, 49, Thiselton, *Holy Spirit*, 194–95.

178. Hilary, *Trinity*, 2.35. For the Holy Spirit as the personal agent of the Son in Hilary, see Oden, *Spirit*, 52, 57.

ary advocated individual and diverse spiritual gifts (*charismata*) of particular people by the person of the Holy Spirit for the good of the whole Christian community (the Church).[179] Interestingly, Burge says Hilary frequently "personalized" the evidence of the Holy Spirit in particular people's lives (i.e., St. Honoratus) as an "ideal" spirituality for building and unifying the Church.[180]

Spiritual experience for the Christian with the Holy Spirit is more pronounced in the teaching of Richard of St. Victor than most before him. Richard begins his study on the Trinity with the Western model of substance, which he qualifies as simple ("being which is from itself")[181] divine or supreme.[182] Richard further clarifies the division of substance into general, specific, and individual, echoing Boethius's teaching on substance.[183] However, he realizes the challenge to the human mind to comprehend the complexity of the Trinity in what he defined as the plurality of persons and the unity of divine substance. Therefore, Richard turns toward experience to understand the Trinity. This experience is inspired by the person of the Holy Spirit who comes into contact with humans.[184] He further describes "person" in a similar paradigm as Boethius, "person" is a rational substance, or the existence of a person (origin) is found in their personal property.[185] The personal property of the Father, Son, and Holy Spirit differentiates them from one another in their particularity.[186] The Father is differentiated from the Son and Holy Spirit in that his personal property is aseity,[187] while the Son and the Holy Spirit derive their being from the Father.[188] Zizioulas agrees with the aseity of the Father but only as it is applied ontologically and not economically.[189] Richard continues in his thought from the one divine substance to an economy of the Trinity,

179. Burgess, *Holy Spirit*, 171. Also, Thiselton, *Holy Spirit*, 195; Oden, *Spirit*, 61.

180. Burgess, *Holy Spirit*, 171. Also, Oden, *Spirit*, 303, 305.

181. Richard, *Trinity*, 1.11.

182. Richard, *Trinity*, 1.11–25.

183. Richard, *Trinity*, 2.12; cf. Evans makes reference to the influence of Boethius, *In Categorias Aristotelis* upon Richard (Evans, "Richard," 207).

184. Richard, *Trinity*, 4.2, 5. Also, Gunton, *One, Three, Many*, 190.

185. Richard, *Trinity*, 4.6, 12.

186. McCall, *Which Trinity?*, 99–100.

187. Richard, *Trinity*, 5.2–4.

188. Richard, *Trinity*, 5.5. McCall, *Which Trinity?*, 209.

189. Zizioulas, *Communion*, 137–40.

exploring the diversity of persons.[190] While Richard was motivated to show the distinctiveness and individuality of the particular persons in the Trinity, he operated from an understanding of unity as the necessity of love for another.[191]

While Zizioulas states clearly that ontological identity is not found in substance but in personal freedom to cross boundaries of the "self"[192] (e.g., selfishness, ego, prejudices, racism, and generally a fear of "the other,"[193] etc.) and live as persons-in-relation, free from boundaries,[194] Zizioulas's ontological identity applied to personal freedom implies crossing boundaries of the self and is a strength in his writings. This ontological freedom is applied both to God and humans converted from radical individualism to being-as-communion.[195] However, Zizioulas's goal and end result of an ontological freedom is a eucharistic community that becomes such by the Holy Spirit only in and through this eucharistic event.[196] The Eucharist is a "locus of truth" for Zizioulas as it frees the participants from divisions and individuality.[197] Zizioulas emphasizes the need to "de-individualize" the economy of the Trinity and modern existential philosophy,[198] so that unity of persons as a community becomes for Zizioulas the highest value.[199] Through the eucharistic event as presented by Zizioulas, theology becomes Christocentric (i.e., Christ is the One-and-Many),[200] and the congregation who are many become one through the corporate person of Christ.[201] It has further been interpreted

---

190. Richard, *Trinity*, 6.1, 3, 8–15. Cf. Zizioulas, *Communion*, 160–61.

191. Ury, *Trinitarian Personhood*, 184–200. Oden, *Spirit*, 26.

192. Zizioulas, "Capacity and Incapacity," 409; Zizioulas, *Lectures*, 105.

193. Zizioulas, "Capacity and Incapacity," 425–26, 427–28, 430; Harrison, "Zizioulas," 277; Grenz, *Rediscovering*, 139.

194. Zizioulas, "Capacity and Incapacity," 409, 410, 425; Zizioulas, *Lectures*, 108–10.

195. Zizioulas, *Being*, 107–13; Zizioulas, "Capacity and Incapacity," 409, 414, 428, 433, 434, 437.

196. Zizioulas, *Eucharist*, 10, 14–21; LaCugna, *God*, 264.

197. Zizioulas, *Being*, 114, 120–21.

198. Zizioulas, *Being*, 27, 107–14; Zizioulas, "Capacity and Incapacity," 441–42; Zizioulas, *Communion*, 99, 243–44; Fox, *God as Communion*, 43–44, 47.

199. Zizioulas, *Eucharist*, 17; Harrison, "Zizioulas," 274–75, 290; Papanikolaou, "Divine Energies," 365–67.

200. Zizioulas, *Being*, 130; Zizioulas, *Eucharist*, 53–58.

201. Zizoulas, *Eucharist*, 15–16; Zizoulas, *One and Many*, 145–46.

from Zizioulas's writings that institutional ecclesiology is more important than personal spiritual gifts imparted to people by the Holy Spirit.[202]

Gunton takes a different approach in the divine-human relationship, as opposed to Zizioulas, and the implications on modern society, in Gunton's opinion, which he sees as moving toward collectivism and ignoring particularity and distinctiveness.[203] Gunton argues that what is lost by a focus of collectivism is "the otherness-in-relation" that is preserved by focusing on the particular.[204] The Cappadocians "desynonymized" *ousia* from *hypostasis*, therefore, giving theology a clear definition of the particular person.[205] In addressing the modern problem of homogeneity, which robs people of their individuality and particularity, Gunton offers a pneumatological rather than a Christological solution as a balance and paradox of the-one-and-the-many, unlike Zizioulas's Christology. Rather, Gunton finds that within pneumatology, the Holy Spirit relationally crosses boundaries with the other, and secondly, the Holy Spirit preserves particularity which essentially formulates the distinctive persons in community.[206]

First, in Gunton's understanding of the Spirit crossing boundaries is that the "Spirit relates to one another beings and realms that are opposed or separate."[207] This boundary-crossing is God's way of coming into a relationship with the world and renewing it.[208] Furthermore, there is a relational and particularizing attribute in Gunton's pneumatology as he finds biblically that it is the particular Holy Spirit who draws particular human beings into a dynamic relationship with God.[209] Brown believes

---

202. Bathrellos, "Church, Eucharist, Bishop," 139–40.

203. Gunton, *One, Three, Many*, 47, 74.

204. Gunton, *One, Three, Many*, 49. Cf. "Personhood and Christian Existence" of Zizioulas's theology in Volf, *Likeness*, 181.

205. Gunton, *One, Three, Many*, 191. T. F. Torrance connects *hypostasis* with "name" (*onoma*) and "face" (*prosōpon*) to show theologically the economy of the "three distinctive hypostatic Realities or Persons" of the Trinity (Torrance, *Doctrine*, 156, 159–60).

206. Gunton, *One, Three, Many*, 181–83, 190. Cf. Zizioulas, *Being*, 130; Zizioulas, "Come Holy Spirit," 1–3; Farrow, *Ascension*, 60, 177, 257, 266, 271.

207. Gunton, *One, Three, Many*, 181. Cf. Zizioulas offers a pneumatologically constituted Christology where the Holy Spirit makes Christ the "universal being" who crosses all boundaries (e.g., spatial, time, geographical, racial, relational, etc.) in Zizioulas, *Lectures*, 108–11.

208. Gunton, *One, Three, Many*, 181.

209. Gunton, *One, Three, Many*, 163–64, 182.

that the Paraclete-Spirit crosses cultural boundaries and the boundary of time to bring the original message of Christ into each contemporary context (e.g., John 16:12–14).[210] Furthermore, the message is brought forth and "the personal presence of Jesus in the Christian" that is made possible by the Paraclete-Spirit.[211] For his part, Zizioulas also believes that the Holy Spirit crosses boundaries, but only in a manner that constitutes Christ in both his incarnation and his eschatological character.[212] Thus, Zizioulas explains that while the Son *becomes* history, the Spirit is *involved* in history through the conception of the Virgin Mary, as the forerunner at Christ's baptism, and existing "*beyond* history" ushering in the eschaton, all of this to say, the Spirit's task "is to liberate the Son and the economy from the bondage of history."[213] Therefore, Zizioulas concludes that pneumatology constitutes Christology by making Christ the corporate personality and the model of communion and eschatology, which are "fundamental elements of the Orthodox understanding of the [E]ucharist."[214] In quoting Irenaeus, "'Where the church is, there is the Spirit of God; and where the Spirit of God is, there is the church, and every kind of grace,'"[215] Farrow comments, "It is extraordinary how modern commentators have failed to appreciate the impressive pneumatological component in [Ireneaus's] theology."[216] Farrow continues, "The Spirit—not the sacraments—is 'that most limpid fountain which issues from the body of Christ.'"[217] Farrow appears to support Gunton's stress on the economy of the Holy Spirit for the *koinōnia* between God and humans made possible through salvation.[218]

---

210. Brown, *Churches*, 108; Brown, *John*, 2:716. Cf. Brown, *John*, 2:1135–44.

211. Brown, *John*, 2:1139.

212. Zizioulas, *Being*, 130.

213. Zizioulas, *Being*, 127–28, 130; Zizioulas, *Lectures*, 103, 106–7.

214. Zizioulas, *Being*, 131. Gunton, for his part, argues for a balance of communion/ecclesiology and eschatology dimensions in pneumatology: without the communion/ecclesiological dimension there becomes an over-realization of last things applied to the present, and without eschatology the Spirit becomes institutionalized within the Church (Gunton, *Trinitarian Theology*, 64).

215. See Irenaeus, *Heresies*, 3.24.1.

216. Farrow, *Ascension*, 69n107.

217. Farrow, *Ascension*, 69n107; Irenaeus, *Heresies*, 3.24.1.

218. Farrow, *Ascension*, 46–52, 59–66, 69–73, 84. Cf. Gunton, *One, Three, Many*, 181–82, 184–85, 187, 191; Gunton, *Trinitarian Theology*, 82.

Second, Gunton argues that the Holy Spirit preserves particularity which essentially formulates the distinctive persons in community.[219] In this, Gunton supports Basil, who preserved the particular distinctive roles of the persons of the Trinity in salvation. For example, Basil calls the Father the original cause, the Son he calls the creative cause, and the Holy Spirit the perfecting cause.[220] The Spirit's role is to perfect the human being into the imitation of Christ so that she and he may become holy.[221] However, while Basil speaks of the theological importance of baptism as the Christian covenant of salvation, he clarifies that it is not the sacrament or nature of water that provides grace which is received by repentance, rather what is significant is the baptism of fire which is "the presence of the Holy Spirit."[222] Thus, the Holy Spirit is the personal other who perfects human beings in a manner that brings salvation, sanctification, spiritual gifts to be used for others, assurance, and a relationship with God the Father through the atonement of the Son.[223] That is to say, human beings are offered a new particularity through the Holy Spirit because of the new particularity witnessed in Christ, whom himself was endowed by the Holy Spirit and engaged in a new relationship with the Father and humans.[224] Gunton saw this new particularity modeled in Christ as an example for Christ-followers when he states,

> According to this conception, the freedom of Christians derives from their institution into a new—particular—network of relationships: first with God through faith in Christ, and then with others in the community of the church. Just as the Spirit frees

219. Gunton, *One, Three, Many*, 181–83, 190.

220. Basil, *Spirit*, 16.38.

221. Basil, *Spirit*, 15.35.

222. Basil, *Spirit*, 15.35–36.

223. Irenaeus, *Heresies*, 3.24.1; 5.6.1–2; 5.8.1–2; 5.10.2; 5.11.1; Basil, *Spirit*, 16.38; Gunton, *One, Three, Many*, 189–81; Farrow, *Ascension*, 59–66; McIntyre, *Pneumatology*, 41, 57, 60–61, 63–68, 172–210; Thiselton, *Holy Spirit*, 70–75, 101–22; Turner, *Holy Spirit*, 147–49, 156–65, 336–47; Sanders, *Deep*, 137, 142, 143, 144, 147, 148, 150, 152, 159–60, 163, 165, 175, 194–99; Carter, *Holy Spirit*, 157–84; Owen, *Holy Spirit*, 1–5, 43–51, 83–93, 95–97, 100–101, 105–13; 136–54, 158–62. For more on the theme of Spirit-indwelled believers and expectation see "Participation in the Character of God" and "Participation in the Mission of God" in chapter 7, "Participation and Christian Anthropology."

224. Gunton, *One, Three, Many*, 183. Cf. For topics of indwelling and adoption of the Spirit, see Congar, *Holy Spirit*, 2.2.3.1; 2.2.3.3; 2.2.4.1; For gifts of the Spirit, see Irving, *Holy Spirit*, 2–3, 6–7, 8–18, 20–23, 25, 29–31, 36–49, 50–58, 60–68, 72–85. For the work of salvation and sanctification, see Owen, *Holy Spirit*, 43–51, 94–113.

Jesus to be himself, so it is with those who are "in Christ," that is, in the community of his people. The church is a community, not a collective: that is, a particular community into which particular people are initiated by the leading of the Spirit.[225]

Therefore, the particular person of the Trinity, the Holy Spirit, communicates to each particular Christian, thus opening up a new particular relationship.[226]

SUMMARY

In moving toward a Christian anthropology, trinitarian pneumatological personhood, we first began with particularity revealed in God and reflected in human beings through the *imago Dei*.[227] Zizioulas is correct in that the Cappadocians made a historic revolution to identify particular persons with the term *hypostasis* separated from substance (*ousia*).[228] Zizioulas also offers an important concept of persons as being-as-communion.[229] However, with these two concepts, Zizioulas uses *hypostasis* in a manner that focuses upon the Father as the cause of the Trinity, while the emphasis upon relation and communion causes the Spirit's personhood to be lost in constituting Christology and ecclesiology; meanwhile, particular humans are collectively assumed into the Church.[230] In fact, more balanced *hypostases* of the Trinity are found in Basil and Gunton, to name a few.[231] Furthermore, balanced *hypostases* of the Trinity lead to a more balanced approach to human particularity, which in turn must precede communion and will enrich an understanding of

225. Gunton, *One, Three, Many*, 183.

226. Gunton, *One, Three, Many*, 185. See Jones, *God the Spirit*, 35–46.

227. McConville, *Being Human*, 24–29; Zizioulas, "Capacity and Incapacity," 424; Schwarz, *Human Being*, 20–29; Middleton, *Liberating Image*, 24–29.

228. Zizioulas, *Being*, 36–41; Zizioulas, *Communion*, 157–58; Zizioulas, "Holy Spirit," 47; Zizioulas, *Lectures*, 50–51.

229. Zizioulas, *Being*, 18, 22.

230. Awad, "Personhood," 8; Volf, *Likeness*, 100; Harrison, "Zizioulas" 289.

231. Basil, *Spirit*, 16.37; 18.45; 18.46; 25.58; Basil, *Letter* 38.4; Gunton, *One, Three, Many*, 149–50, 153–54, 212–19, 225, 229–31; Gunton, "Persons," 103–7. See also Gregory of Nyssa, *Gods*, 334; Gregory of Nazianzus, *Orations*, "On the Holy Spirit," 5.3; 5.10; 5.26–27; 5.32; John of Damascus, *Faith*, 1.8; Volf, *Likeness*, 204, 208–13; McCall, *Which Trinity?*, 219–53; Sanders, "Trinitarian Theology," 21–41; Sanders, *Deep*, 67–88; Coppedge, *Triune*, 111–26.

being-as-communion.[232] To be a Christian-person is to be in relation with another (i.e., *perichoresis*).[233] The human problem is sin which hinders genuine relationship with God and other human beings.[234] For Zizioulas, sin is simply individualism which is cured through baptism into Christ, the corporate person, and the continual participation in Eucharist with the assembly.[235] However, a summation of the Scriptures indicates

> that each and every human being enters the world in a state of sin and acts sinfully against God, therefore sin is a two-fold problem and is a barrier of communion between human beings and God. The state of sin (i.e., inherited sin, original sin, depravity) is the condition of the heart which humans have inherited and is the marred image of God as a result of Adam and Eve's original sin of disobedience. The punishment for a contaminated soul is death, not just physically, but also an eternal spiritual death. Sin is also a willful transgression of a known law. The human being has an active free will to decide whether to obey or disobey.[236]

Therefore, for human beings to be a new creature by having a genuinely Christian personhood, the particular person, God the Father, must desire the act of reconciliation, and the particular person, God the Son, must redeem human beings by becoming human—dying and rising—to save humanity. The particular person, God the Spirit, must come to each particular person to convict, save, sanctify, and draw into communion.[237] This way of being a Christian person is a response to the Holy Trinity's salvific work as a new creature, or a complete person is initiated when the human being's life is connected within the Trinitarian life. This connection is made possible by the forgiveness of sins which brings about mutual

232. Gunton, *One, Three, Many*, 153, 180–81, 201, 203.

233. Zizioulas, *Being*, 16, 18, 46; Zizioulas, *Communion*, 9–10, 99–103, 106–12.

234. Gen 1:1–24; Rom 3:23; 5:9–11, 21. Lossky, *Mystical Theology*, 122–34; McConville, *Being Human*, 37–39; Schwarz, *Human Being*, 177–266, gives an historical and contemporary account on the hamartiology.

235. Zizioulas, *Being*, 50, 102–3, 109, 113, 116–18.

236. Adkins, "Article on Sin," 42, presented as a recommendation, voted, adopted, and published. Gen 3:1, 7, 11, 22; 11:6; Lev 26:14–45; Ps 14:1–3; 53:1–4; John 3:19–21; Rom 1:18; 2:8–9; 3:9, 23; 4:15; 5:10, 18; 6:23; 7:16–20, 24; Gal 3:19; Heb 2:2; 4:11; Rev 20:6, 14–15; 21:8.

237. Sanders, *Deep*, 113–53; Gunton, *One, Three, Many*, 158, 163, 205–9; 225n19; LaCugna, *God*, 41–44; Lossky, *Mystical Theology*, 58–62, 135, 138, 143–46, 149, 151–52, 156–58, 161–62, 166–67, 171–73; Torrance, *Doctrine*, 31; Torrance, *Faith*, 146–251; Olson and Hall, *Trinity*, 58, 72, 80, 98, 100, 105–6.

indwelling followed by a life to be lived where the particular Christian person can love his and her fellow human being, not for what is received in relationship, but rather, for what one can give in relationship.[238] The Holy Spirit causes particular people to be open to a new set of relationships, thus becoming more like Christ, which is the will of the Father.[239] Motivated by the Holy Spirit, these new relationships transform human beings into authentic Christian persons.[240] For Wesleyan theology, this is the "new birth" when the particular person experiences a "great change" in their soul as they are freed from sin.[241]

For there to be a relationship, there needs to be proximity (i.e., sociality) between two parties.[242] Chapter 6 speaks to the proximity of God with humans by the fact that God offers his personal presence to humans through the indwelling Holy Spirit. The indwelling presence of God within humans causes and identifies the human as genuinely a Christian person.

238. Gunton, *One, Three, Many*, 205–9; Phil 2:1–11; Kinlaw, *Mind*, 99–109. Cf. McConville, notices God's intention for relationship in the creation narrative (McConville, *Being Human*, 31–35). Also see Cross, *Presence*, 80–81, where Cross argues for the transforming power of the Holy Spirit in the life of believers to free them from the bondage of sin into a new creation which reflects the nature of Christ.

239. John 14:15–17, 26; 15:26; 16:12–14; Rom 8:9–17; 1 Cor 1:10–16; 12:4–11; Eph 2:11–22; 4:1–7; Phil 2:1–8; Col 3:1–17; Gunton, *One, Three, Many*, 183–84, 185, 187, 189, 190–92, 194, 196, 205–9.

240. Ezek 36:27; Joel 2:28; Rom 15:16; 1 Cor 3:16–17; 6:11; 2 Cor 3:18; 1 Thess 4:7–8; 2 Thess 2:13–14; Heb 10:14–17; 1 Pet 1:22–23; Gunton, *One, Three, Many*, 225, 227, 229; McIntyre, *Pneumatology*, 172–210; Owen, *Holy Spirit*, 136–42; Wesley, *Holy Spirit and Power*, 77, 85–86, 91, 93, 94, 123–37, 201–5, 217–19.

241. Wesley, "The New Birth," 193–94. See also, Collins, *Wesley*, 205–8.

242. Schwarz, *Human Being*, 55–60.

Chapter 6

Personal Presence

A Shadow of Things to Come[1]

> "In dealing with the Spirit, we are dealing with none
> other than the *personal presence* of God himself."
>
> —GORDON D. FEE[2]

INTRODUCTION

ZIZIOULAS HAS BUILT HIS ontological theology on reversing Greek philosophy by making the particular the cause of all things (rather than substance as the cause), as demonstrated in his extreme monarchial view of God. Zizioulas offers a helpful solution in that relationship must be offered into particularity to move personhood away from an isolated individualistic term for personhood and toward a definition and reality grounded in community.[3] Zizioulas's overture is found in the Chalcedonian definition of the Father-Son relationship and applied to humans

---

1. The phrase "a shadow of things to come" is an allusion, and a comparison, to the Levitical priesthood, the Torah, and religious practices which were a shadow of what was to come through Jesus Christ, the Messiah (Col 2:17; Heb 8:5; 10:1). Likewise, the presence of God through the Holy Spirit in the lives of believers while in the temporary world, is a shadow of the presence of God with his people eternally in the eschatological promise (Isa 4:4; Mal 3:2–3; Luke 3:16; John 17:24; Acts 2:1–4, 22–28, 33; Rev 21:3, 5, 22–27; 22:1–5).

2. Fee, *Empowering*, 6.

3. Zizioulas, *Communion*, 106–7.

through the Church by the sacraments of baptism and Eucharist.[4] The point of observation in this chapter is that while Zizioulas has correctly pointed out the need for relationship to be added to ontology to give being personhood,[5] connecting it with *hypostasis*,[6] he ultimately fails to apply it to human personhood in a relational way. Zizioulas's personhood remains within the Trinity as illustrated through his corporate Christology, but human personhood toward communion is experienced through baptism and Eucharist within the Church; a non-relational act.[7] Ironically, there is no personal, relational contact in Zizioulas's theology between God and humans to constitute human personhood. If relationship is the connection between being and personhood, as Zizioulas has suggested,[8] then where is the divine-human relationship to make the human person specifically a Christian person? The purpose of this chapter is to correct the divine-human relational deficiency in Zizoulas's theology by linking trinitarian personhood to human personhood, thus making the human person, specifically a Christian person whom the person of Holy Spirit constitutes. Thus, God's presence is with his people in a real, personal way.

In St. Mary's Episcopal Cathedral, Edinburgh, Scotland, hangs A. E. Borthwick's painting titled, "The Presence" (1910).[9] The painting depicts the darkened sanctuary inside St. Mary's Episcopal Cathedral as the congregants prepare for Holy Communion. The area around the high altar, where the elements of bread and wine have been prepared, is illumined with glorious light. However, as the observer's eye moves from the high altar perspective nearly in the center of the painting to the back left corner of the sanctuary, there is another illumined area where a penitent person remains kneeling in prayer, apparently alone and marginalized, except for the outline of the figure of Jesus Christ who stands behind the contrite person with an outstretched hand in the direction of this seeker. The irony and theology with which Borthwick captured were that the *presence* of Christ is not *in* the elements of bread and wine, but rather,

---

4. Zizioulas, *Being*, 145–54; Zizioulas, *Communion*, 109; Zizioulas, *Lectures*, 33–36, 45, 115–19, 150.

5. Zizioulas, *Communion*, 107.

6. Zizioulas, *Communion*, 111.

7. Zizoulas, *Being*, 114–22; Zizioulas, *One and Many*, 94–96.

8. Zizioulas, *Communion*, 107.

9. St. Mary's Episcopal Cathedral, "Inside the Cathedral." See the front cover of this book.

his *presence* is *with* the penitent person kneeling in prayer. The scene is reminiscent of the eschatological promise found in the Revelation, "'Behold, the dwelling place [tabernacle, *skēnē*] of God is with man. He will dwell [tabernacle, *skēnōsei*] with them, and they will be his people, and God himself will be with them as their God.'"[10] A fundamental and unique aspect of Christianity is the teaching that although bodily death ushers the soul into eternal life and the presence of God, in some way,[11] believers experience the presence of God in the temporal world while in the human body,[12] but not in the same manner, rather God's presence in the temporal world is a shadow of things to come.[13] The Church has included in her teachings the presence of God in this world;[14] however, at the same time, the Church is neither unified as to *how* God presents himself nor *why* God visits his people.

10. Rev 21:3.

11. It should be noted that the Catholic Church holds to a doctrine of purgatory which is an intermediate state after bodily death for those who died in grace. Those in purgatory can be freed from guilt and punishment through prayers and good works from those still living on earth. Purgatory prepares the dead for final judgment (Hayes, "purgatory," 675–76). For the doctrine of purgatory established at the Council of Trent, see Schroeder, *Canons and Decrees*, ses. 6, cn. 30; ses. 25. In contrast, Oden, for instance, writes of physical, spiritual, and eternal death, but gives no reference to an intermediate state between life on earth and heaven with God (*Spirit*, 372, 378–82). Middleton tackles some of the problem texts in Scripture which are used by those who profess the idea of an intermediate state after bodily death and concludes that "Authentic Christian hope does not depend on an intermediate state; nor do Christians need the Platonic notion of an immortal soul in order to guarantee personal continuity between present earthly existence and future resurrection life" (Middleton, *Heaven and Earth*, 236). The reason for this conclusion is that Middleton holds to a literal interpretation of the future based on the promise of the resurrection to a new heaven and a new earth (Middleton, *Heaven and Earth*, 227–37).

12. 1 Cor 3:16: "Do you not know that you are God's temple and that God's Spirit dwells in you?" See also 1 Cor 6:19; 2 Cor 6:16; Eph 2:21–22; cf. Lev 26:11–12; Ezek 37:26–27; Rev 21:3. See Sanders, *Deep*, 143.

13. John 3:16; 10:28; 14:16–17, 20, 23, 26; 15:26; 16:7, 13; 1 Cor 13:12. Congar, *Holy Spirit*, 2.2.3.1; Dunn, *Pneumatology*, 3–4, 10, 13, 14, 17–18; Fee, *Empowering*, 6–8; Grudem, *Systematic Theology*, 1163–64; Gunton, *Creator*, 9–10, 67, 176–78, 193–96, 200–206, 210, 223; Kinlaw and Oswalt, *Lectures*, 30–31, 36–37; Levison, *Filled*, 391–92; Macquarrie, *Christian Theology*, 149–50; McConville, *Being Human*, 24–29, 35–39; McKnight, *Open*, 56; Outler, "Focus on the Holy Spirit," 159–73; 161, 168; Pannenberg, *Anthropology*, 522–32. For an anthropological study of life after death, see Schwarz, *Human Being*, 357–76.

14. Here are examples of some recent studies on the topic of "presence": Anderson, *Presence*; Cross, *Presence*; Duvall and Hays, *Relational Presence*.

PRESENCE

Scripture and Presence

Biblical history testifies to the belief that God continued to visit Adam and Eve once the act of creation had taken place.[15] In turn, God proclaimed judgment on Adam and Eve for their transgression; they were driven out of the Garden Paradise and excommunicated from the presence of God.[16] Henceforth, throughout the Old Testament, the God of Israel occasionally visits people to pronounce his will, judgment, instruction, warning, or affirmation.[17] These divine communications vary in encounter: dreams, visions, theophanies, angels, and his Spirit.[18] The Spirit of God, in particular, rests on select people (e.g., prophets, messengers, kings) at specific times to deliver a specific message (e.g., prophecy, instruction, warning). However, an underlining eschatological motif that reinforces God's presence also runs throughout the Old Testament[19] is the notion of *Adventus*, God visiting his people through the coming of the Righteous One, or theologically called the messianic hope.[20] The presence of God in Old Testament eschatology is further developed through themes such

15. Gen 3:8. Gregory of Nyssa has used God's "walking in the garden in the cool of the day" as an analogy to demonstrate God's presence with the righteous person who lives and moves in steadfast faith with God in their life (Gregory of Nyssa, *Answer to Eunomius' Second Book*, 293). Duvall and Hays, *Relational Presence*, 1–2, 14–20.

16. Gen 3:14–19, 23–24. The verb in 3:23 is *šālaḥ* (to send or let go) used in the Piel, but is paralleled in 3:24 with the verb *gāraš* (to drive out or divorce) also used in the Piel emphasizing that Adam and Eve were "expelled." The verb *gāraš* is translated "divorce" in the Qal (Lev 21:7, 14; 22:13), but is used to mean "banish" when referring to nations in the Piel (Exod 23:28–30; 33:2; Num 22:11; Deut 33:27; Judg 2:3; 6:9). See Hamilton, *Genesis: 1–17*, 209–10.

17. E.g., Gen 12:1–3; Exod 19:1–31:18; Josh 1:1–9; Jer 6:1–30; Ezek 3:16–27. Gowan identifies worldly hope, God's sovereignty, corporate salvation, and comprehensive hope as the OT characteristics of eschatology (Gowan, *Eschatology*, 122–23).

18. E.g., Gen 28:10–22; Exod 3:1–6; Num 22:22–35; 1 Sam 16:13; Dan 7:1—8:27. VanGemeren, *Interpreting the Prophetic Word*, 25; Wenger, *God's Word Written*, 13–31.

19. Jenson, "Great Transformation," 33–34. For a theory of eschatology as earthly restoration, especially in the OT, see Middleton, *Heaven and Earth*, 77–128. For a philosophical perspective of eschatology and human history in the Scriptures, see O'Donovan, *Resurrection and Moral Order*, 53–75.

20. Isa 24:16; 53:11; cf. Acts 3:14; 7:52; 22:14. McCartney and Clayton, *Let the Reader Understand*, 51–54. Bock says, "[Jesus Christ] is seen as the fulfillment of promises God made in the Old Testament" (Bock, "Doctrine of the Future," 197). For a theory of *mešiah*/anointed one as not necessarily a particular person, but rather the office of kingship, see Gowan, *Eschatology*, 32–33.

as the Spirit offered to all rather than a select few,[21] God's law on the hearts of his people,[22] matrimony between God and his people,[23] God the Father's adoption of spiritual orphans in a familial theme,[24] and the *new* kingdom of God.[25] An illustration of the divine presence as the eschatological hope for Israel is given in Isaiah 32:9–20 that after Jerusalem is laid desolate, the Spirit will come upon the people, and the result will be fruitfulness, justice, righteousness, peace, and happiness. In referencing the Spirit's outpouring upon God's people in Isaiah 32:15, Oswalt says,

> If God's people were ever to share his character, an outcome devoutly to be hoped for, then it would have to come about through an infusion of God's Spirit into human beings. This development relates fundamentally to a crisis of Lordship. God cannot will where he does not rule. Thus, it is no accident that this statement occurs in this context of divine kingship. So long as human beings usurp ultimate rule of their lives, there is impotence, unrighteousness and dependence upon the very forces which would destroy us. It is only when we come to the end of ourselves and acknowledge God's right to rule our lives that we can experience the divine empowerment for righteousness.[26]

21. Isa 32:15; 44:3; Ezek 36:27; Joel 2:28; Fee, *Empowering*, 7, 27; Turner, *Power*, 349.

22. Ezek 11:19; 36:26; Jer 31:33–34; cf. Heb 8:10; Gowan, *Eschatology*, 69–73.

23. Isa 54:5; Jer 2:2–3; Hos 2:16, 19–20. For the nuptial metaphor in Scripture, see Kinlaw, *Jesus*, 57–64; VanGemeren, *Interpreting the Prophetic Word*, 114, 116, 117, 118.

24. Isa 56:5; Jer 31:9; cf. Deut 32:6; Ps 2:7; 2 Sam 7:14; Hos 11:1–2, 4, 8; VanGemeren, *Interpreting the Prophetic Word*, 114, 116; Coppedge, *Portraits*, 244–99. For the familial metaphor in Scripture, see Kinlaw, *Jesus*, 52–56.

25. Dan 2:44; 4:3, 34; 6:26; 7:14, 27; Mic 4:7. For an eschatological theology of the imminent kingdom of God and the present impact through futurity of Jesus's message, see Pannenberg, *Theology*, 51–55. For an eschatology of the kingdom of God through a trinitarian doctrine of human freedom, see Moltmann, *Trinity*, 202–12. Middleton does not believe that the eschatological hope is something new, but rather fixing or "restoring" what is already available (i.e., heaven and earth) (Middleton, *Heaven and Earth*, 163).

26. Oswalt, *Isaiah: 1–39*, 587–88. John Wesley translated Gerhard Tersteegen's poem, "God is Here!" (*Gott ist Gegenwaertig*); in the first stanza we read: "Lo, God is here! Let us adore, And own how dreadful is this place! Let all within us feel His power, And silent bow before His face; Who know His power, His grace who prove, Serve Him with awe, with reverence love." In the third stanza, lines 3 and 4 we read, "To Thee our will, soul, flesh, we give—O, take, O seal them for Thine own!" See Tersteegen, *Sermons and Hymns*, 26.

The eternal kingdom of God and its eternal king of righteousness serve as an Old Testament eschatological metaphor for the presence of God with his people who have access by their salvation.[27] Thus, Oswalt sees the presence of God as the apex of the Old Testament message for redemption:

> This is what redemption is about in the Old Testament. It is about God coming home—home to the dwelling place from which he had been driven out in the Fall. So it is that the climax of the book of Exodus is neither the Red Sea crossing nor the giving of the Sinai covenant, but rather the moment of the Glory's filling the tabernacle. That moment is what the whole program had been about—that God might dwell in the midst of his people. It was only the means to an end—the Glory in the sanctuary of the heart. That is what redemption is about.[28]

The New Testament opens up with the Triune God visiting his people in the same Old Testament manner of God speaking *to*,[29] and *through*,[30] one person, Zechariah, a priest while serving on duty at the Temple.[31]

---

27. Turner, *Power*, 133–37, 145; Middleton, *Heaven and Earth*, 166–68, 170; Deut 33:27; 2 Sam 7:13; 1 Kgs 9:5; 1 Chr 16:35–36; 17:14; 22:10; 28:7; Isa 9:6; 25:9; 33:22; 49:25; Jer 17:14; Ezek 36:29; 43:7, 9; Zech 8:7; 9:16; Dan 7:14, 18, 22, 27. Schleiermacher believes this kingdom happens in the present temporal world made possible by the Holy Spirit in the Church as expressed through Christian fellowship (Schleiermacher, *Christian Faith*, 660–62. For a study on Zion as the eschatological kingdom, see Gowan, *Eschatology*, 4–58.

28. Oswalt, "Wesley and the Old Testament," 287. Brueggemann argues that YHWH is an emancipator, an abundant giver, and a covenant-keeper which results in fidelity saying, "the quintessence of humanness is the practice of such fidelity that embraces neighborliness and that eventuates in a society of public justice. Thus, in the emancipatory-covenantal tradition of the Old Testament, human agents are in replication of the emancipatory, covenant-making God, charged with neighborly fidelity" (Brueggemann, *God*, 5). Brueggemann further argues that it is "interactive relationships" between God, self, and neighbor that makes the OT literature unique (Brueggemann, *God*, 21–22, 23, 28, 30, 32–33, 36–38). For Kaufmann, the presence, indwelling and relationship of YHWH into the life and history of Israel was only crystalized through the word of God: the book of Torah (Kaufmann, *Israel*, 157–66, 172, 208–11, 447–51).

29. Luke 1:13–23. Green points out the OT similarity of the *presence of God* in the form of "the angel of the Lord" also found in Luke 1:11. For more, see Green, *Luke*, 71–72.

30. Luke 1:62–66; Turner, *Power*, 147–48. Turner says, A Jewish reader would see the connection between the "Spirit of prophecy" and "filled with the Spirit" in both Zechariah's (1:67) and Elizabeth's (1:41) oracles (Turner, "Luke and the Spirit," 270).

31. Luke 1:5, 8–9; Green, *Luke*, 64, 68–71.

However, the presence of God is accelerated in the Gospels[32] through the Holy Spirit, and through other communicative means (media) like angels and natural phenomena (i.e., dreams, miraculous conception, birth, etc.), by visiting Joseph, Mary, shepherds, magi, Simeon, Anna, and later through the proclamation and ministry of John the Baptist.[33] All of these interactions support the climactic entrance of the presence of God the Son (Jesus Christ), who was the hidden presence,[34] made evident by God the Spirit.[35] At the conclusion of Jesus Christ's ministry on earth, he disclosed his impending absence, but that the presence of both he (Jesus Christ/Son of God) and God the Father would continue with the disciples and the following generations of believers through the presence of the Holy Spirit.[36] Farrow argues that in light of Jesus Christ's bodily ascension, the divinity of Jesus Christ is presented to the church by the Holy Spirit, presenting the "absent Jesus."[37] Farrow further points out that Jesus's ascension and the Pentecostal experience in Acts 2 is the "historical" fulfillment of Daniel 7 where the Son of Man/Ancient of Days' eternal dominion is established, and the presence of the eternal kingdom of God is with his people.[38] While Jesus ministered on earth, he proclaimed the presence of the kingdom of God in one aspect, yet the

32. Duvall and Hays, *Presence*, 167.

33. Matt 1:18–25; 2:1–12; 3:1–17; Luke 1:26–38; 2:8–15, 25–35, 36–38; 3:1–22. Turner, *Power*, 140–69. Cf. "the angel of the Lord" (e.g., Gen 16:7; 22:11; Exod 2; Num 22:22; 2 Sam 24:16, 17; Pss 34:7; 35:5–6; Isa 37:36; Zech 12:8) which is used at least fifty times in the OT as a divine messenger between God and humans (Wilson, *Psalms*, 569–70).

34. Ladd, *Presence*, 336.

35. Matt 1:20–23; 3:16–17; Mark 1:10–11; Luke 1:35; 3:21–22; John 1:32. For a view that Jesus's baptism in the Holy Spirit was a "unique messianic anointing," see Turner, *Power*, 175–80, 188–212. For a view of the baptism for which Jesus offers "the Holy Spirit and fire" (Luke 3:16) as a two-fold cleansing: (1) with the Holy Spirit upon the repentant person, and (2) with fire upon the unrepentant person, see Dunn, *Pneumatology*, 93–102; Rogers, *After the Spirit*, 98–134; Torrance, *Christ*, 56–59; Zizioulas, *Being*, 130; Zizioulas, *Communion*, 105; Zizioulas, *One and Many*, 51, 68, 78, 142, 143, 146, 152, 244.

36. John 14:16–17, 20, 23, 26; 15:26; 16:7, 13–15; Acts 1:4–5; Farrow, *Ascension*, 191–98, 220–29.

37. Farrow, *Ascension*, 257. Farrow's further point is that the Spirit unites the Church to the absent Jesus by the Word and the Sacrament. The result, Farrow states, is that, "'The Spirit's work is an infringement on our time, an eschatological re-ordering of our being to the fellowship of the Father and the Son, and to the new creation" (Farrow, *Ascension*, 257). Cf. Feingold, *Eucharist*, 6–7, 40–44, 63–65, 233–319.

38. Farrow, *Ascension*, 22–26.

kingdom of God was/is still expected to come, leaving the Church in the tension of what has arrived and that there is more to come.[39] Ultimately, the Gospels and the New Testament concludes with a promise that Jesus Christ will return, and judgment will take the place of the living, and the dead, and those who have been faithful will enter into an eternal presence *with* God, while those who are judged as unfaithful and unbelieving enter into an eternal absence *from* God.[40] However, this rich biblical history begs the most obvious questions, namely, until Christ's return, how is God's presence through the Holy Spirit realized?

Theological Tradition and Presence

Through traditional Roman Catholic theology, Western Christianity has taught that the Holy Spirit is encountered through the sacraments of baptism, Eucharist, and confirmation as elements of water, oil, bread, and wine "are transformed to mediate God's presence and grace."[41] While the sacraments are believed to impart grace as a sign of sanctification in Catholic theology and practice, the Eucharist is separated as the life of the Church being both human and divine.[42] Furthermore, in the Eucharist practice, both the Church and particular believers have communion with the Father by the death and resurrection of the Son through the Holy Spirit.[43] "The Eucharist makes possible this most intimate union through

39. Matt 4:17; Mark 1:15; Ladd, *Presence*, 114–21, 331–39.

40. Matt 25:31–46; Mark 13:24–27; Luke 21:25–28; John 14:1–4, 25–31; Rev 20:11—22:13. Origen's eschatology begins with Gen 1:26–28 and humans created in the image and likeness of God, but since God is perfect, human perfection is reserved for the consummation where there is the fulfillment that God is "all in all" (1 Cor 15:28) and the soul will be transformed into the likeness of God and remain with God for eternity. Origen's theology of the end times hints of universalism as "all rational souls have been restored to a condition [perfection]" and "remain an enemy [of God] no longer" (Origen, *First Principles*, 328). See Origen, *First Principles*, 321–32.

41. Fatula, "Holy Spirit," 374. The Council of Trent (1545–63) acknowledged seven sacraments: baptism, confirmation, Eucharist, penance, extreme unction, order, and matrimony through which justification and further grace is applied (Schroeder, *Canons and Decrees*, ses. 7, cn. 1). In the articles of Vatican II (1962–65), the role of the Holy Spirit is distinct in the initiation rite of adults which include the sacraments of baptism, confirmation, and Eucharist; see Vatican II, *Documents*, "Constitution on the Sacred Liturgy," ch. 1, par. 6, 7, 10. Also, Fatula, "Holy Spirit," 375.

42. Hellwig, "Sacrament," 731; Vatican II, *Documents*, "Constitution on the Sacred Liturgy," par. 2.

43. Fatula, "Holy Spirit," 374–75; Power, "Sacrament of Eucharist," 736–37; Feingold, *Eucharist*, 6–7.

Holy Communion."[44] As Feinberg puts it so pithily, the most intimate union is that the participant is not only given more sanctifying grace and charity but is indwelled by the Trinity.[45] At the theological core in the Catholic practice of the Eucharist is a cause-and-effect understanding. However, there are some nuances within Catholic theology of the presence of God in the sacrament of the Eucharist.

Aquinas argues, for instance, that God is the first (i.e., primary or uncreated) cause, *a priori*, and is known through his effects, *a posteriori*.[46] Furthermore, God, who is uncreated, first cause, creates many secondary causes described as "instrumental causes."[47] Using Aristotelian philosophy, Aquinas reasons that the primary cause cannot be the sign of its own effect, but rather, the instrumental cause is the sign as the instrument has no power of its own, but what is given to it by the primary cause.[48] Therefore, sacraments are not merely signs, making the sacraments completely comprehensible; likewise, sacraments are not merely causes, making the sacraments governable, but rather, sacraments are viewed as simultaneously being signs and causes. Thus, God, who is the primary cause, effects grace into the life of people through the instrument being the minister (and Christ) as officiant of the Eucharist (i.e., words/elements and form/matter) to offer the sign of grace through the substances of bread and wine.[49] The grace of God and the sacraments of the Church are intimately bound together in Aquinas's theology; humans are affected upon by the primary cause as the congregants participate in the acts of the sacraments, that is to say, "we have it on the authority of many saints that the sacraments of the New Law not only signify, but also cause grace."[50] The grace of God is manifested in and through the presence of God.

Studying in Paris at the same time as Aquinas was the Franciscan, Bonaventure, who is called the "Second Founder of the Franciscan Order."[51] While Bonaventure is known for his mystical writings on the spiritual life and pastoral concerns as a Franciscan, he was also a Scholastic

---

44. Feingold, *Eucharist*, 8.

45. Feingold, *Eucharist*, 8.

46. Aquinas, *Summa Theologiae*, I.2.1–2.

47. Venard, "Sacraments," 274.

48. Aquinas, *Summa Theologiae*, III.62.1.

49. Venard, "Sacraments," 271, 272–74, 276–77, 278; Aquinas, *Summa Theologiae*, III.77.1.

50. Aquinas, *Summa Theologiae*, III.62.1; Venard, "Sacraments, 272, 278.

51. Bonaventure, *Eucharist*, 2. Dreyer, "Bonaventure," 99.

theologian and professor at the University of Paris.[52] In his spiritual writings, Bonaventure expresses a theology of holiness of heart, God the Father's love and grace, the inseparability of Creator and creation, the Son of God as the Eternal Truth, and the Holy Spirit as the Gift.[53] However, in contrast to Bonaventure's creative, pastoral, and pragmatic writings on the mystical life, he also wrote speculative and theological commentaries and books. One such commentary is on Peter Lombard's *Sentences*, especially dealing with the topic of the Eucharist and the presence of God. In it, Bonaventure uses a philosophical methodology that resembles Aquinas's thesis-antithesis method found in *Summa Theologiae*. Bonaventure accepts a "realist spiritualism" approach to the Eucharist which affirms the "real presence of the body of Christ; what remains is to recognize that God may be doing several things at once in the Eucharist, joining us not only to his human nature to enable a natural causality, but also uniting us in faith into the mystical body."[54] In his work *Holiness of Life*, Bonaventure offers the practices of a contemplated life through self-knowledge, humility, poverty, silence, prayer, remembrance of Christ's passion, love for God, and perseverance, saying, "The altar of God is your heart."[55] In his commentary on the Eucharist, Bonaventure says, "Christ is on the altar" meaning the elements of bread and wine truly become the body and blood of Jesus Christ and so the very presence of Christ appears through the consecration[56] of the priest in the elements and is consumed by the participant.

On the one hand, in Bonaventure's mystical writings, for a believer to truly experience the presence of God, the believer must participate in external exercises (i.e., meditation, prayer, and contemplation) that cleanses one of sin and elevates one in spiritual wisdom which will, in turn, cause the heart to *love the Spouse* (Jesus Christ) and *desire his presence*.[57] On the other hand, in Bonaventure's speculative theological writings, the real

---

52. Dreyer, "Bonaventure," 99.

53. Bonaventure, *Journey*, 5–58.

54. Bonaventure, *Eucharist*, 5.

55. Bonaventure, *Holiness*, 29.

56. Bonaventure uses the word "confect" ("*conficere*") which means *consecrate* but in a more technical manner in that the priest is co-acting in changing the elements of bread and wine into the body and blood of Jesus Christ through liturgy and prayer, thus completing the sufficiency of the sacrament (Bonaventure, *Eucharist*, 47, dist. 13, art. 1).

57. Bonaventure, *Triple Way*, ch. 1, c. 16. Bonaventure does not mention the practice of participating in the sacraments in his mystical writings.

presence of the Triune God is experienced by participation in the Eucharist, where there is a warning that if one is negligent in participating, then the penalty is excommunication.[58] Either way, through exterior exercises or participation in the Eucharist, Bonaventure ultimately offered a cause-and-effect approach to experiencing the presence of God.

Turning now from Western Christianity to Eastern Christianity, traditional Greek Orthodox theology has taught that the Holy Spirit is encountered through the sacraments of baptism and Holy Eucharist (especially at/during the Epiclesis), and also through prayers.[59] While the Orthodox teach of experiencing the presence of the Holy Spirit through different mystical means, the Eucharist is considered the "chief of the church's mysteries" by which believers may be unified with the Trinity and with each other through the Holy Spirit.[60] Thus, verbal descriptions of the activity of the Holy Spirit are inferior to a life that is lived out in relation to the Holy Spirit in Orthodox theology.[61] Furthermore, St. Seraphim of Sarov taught that the acquisition of the Holy Spirit is the goal of the Christian life toward godliness.[62] The Orthodox Church has maintained this basic view of the presence of the Holy Spirit through the Eucharist, but rather than an Aristotelean cause-and-effect philosophy, Orthodox theology suggests an incorporation of believers into the life of Christ.

One of the Three Holy Hierarchs of the Orthodox Church,[63] John Chrysostom, said, God "Himself is present,"[64] through the Holy Spirit who operates through the sacraments of baptism, chrismation, and Eucharist, and yet has far-reaching effects in the life of believers.[65] Chryso-

58. Bonaventure, *Eucharist*, dist. 10, art. 1, q. 1; dist. 12, art. 2, q. 1.

59. Trostyanskiy, "Holy Spirit," 249. McGuckin compares these means by which one may receive the presence of the Holy Spirit and the supremacy of the Eucharist this way: "If baptism and chrismation are the mystical synopses of the whole pattern of the Lord's economy of salvation, by means of which his church is brought in to the shared experience of his saving death and resurrection, and in to the Pentecostal gift of his most Holy Spirit, then the Eucharist is the mystical drama of that salvation given to us, as a renewable feast, in a great spirit of joy" (McGuckin, *Orthodox*, 288).

60. Steenberg, "Eucharist," 185.

61. Ware, *Orthodox Way*, 91.

62. Seraphim, *Acquisition*, 55.

63. The other two Holy Hierarchs of the Orthodox Church are Sts. Basil and Gregory the Theologian.

64. Chrysostom, *St. Matthew*, 50.3.

65. Chrysostom, *St. Matthew*, 5.1; 10.2; 11.5–6; 12.1; Chrysostom, *Corinthians*, 1 Cor 12.14; 27.7.

stom is concerned with the effects of the Holy Spirit in transforming people from a life of sin to a life of holiness.[66] He further emphasizes the necessity of holiness by believers participating in Christ's life through Holy Communion, which unifies the body of believers with each other and with Christ.[67] This unifying presence of God through the Holy Spirit is demonstrated in a prayer of invocation in the Eucharistic Liturgy assigned to Chrysostom: "Grant that we may find grace in Thy sight, that our sacrifice may become acceptable to Thee, and that the Good Spirit of Thy grace may rest upon us, and upon these gifts spread before Thee, and upon all Thy people."[68] The prayer for God's presence and *koinōnia* intensifies as followed by beaconing the congregation:

> Let us pray on behalf of the precious gifts (i.e., the bread and wine) which have been provided that the merciful God who has received them upon His holy spiritual altar beyond the heavens may in return send down upon us the divine grace and the fellowship of the Holy Ghost.[69]

While the Holy Spirit comes upon the particular person at baptism,[70] at the sacrament of Holy Communion, God communicates to the participants through the Holy Spirit[71] and further distinguishes the Church from the world.[72] The Holy Spirit then unites the many into one body so that it is the Church and the body of Christ.[73] Furthermore, the Holy Spirit indwells believers at baptism and cleanses them from sin. However, more than a forensic cause-and-effect work, the redeemed recipient is to live a holy life by which the Holy Spirit continues to communicate, convict, and comfort, thus changing the recipient's disposition (*kainon*

---

66. Chrysostom, *Catechumens*, 2.1–2; Chrysostom, *St. John*, 25.1–3; 26.1–3; 27.1–3; 31.1; 33.2. Also, Burgess, *Holy Spirit*, 123–24.

67. Chrysostom, *St. John*, 25.2–3; 46.3–4.

68. Chrysostom, *Priesthood*, bk. 3.4.

69. Chrysostom, *Priesthood*, bk. 3.4.

70. Chrysostom, *St. John*, 78.3; Chrysostom, *Corinthians*, 30.2.

71. Chrysostom, *Corinthians*, 24.3. Chrysostom maintains that while the Holy Spirit is present and ministering to the participants during Holy Communion, the whole Trinity is involved because they in themselves are a community and they in turn create community at the rite (Chrysostom, *St. John*, 78.3).

72. Chrysostom understands the "world" in contrast to the Church to be people who do not have the grace of the Holy Spirit in their life and who are led by their own rational mind over against faith in Christ. Chrysostom, *Timothy*, hom. 5, 10.

73. Chrysostom, *Corinthians*, 24.4.

anthropon)[74] through a new set of relationships with the persons of the Holy Trinity.[75]

Cyril of Alexandria's contribution to theology is the one nature (*physis*) of Jesus Christ being fully divine and fully human while remaining one person (*hypostatic union*) against Nestorius's teaching that Jesus Christ had two natures (*physeis*), divine and human, which he taught operated in *conjunction* (Gr.: *synapheia*; Lat.: *conjunctio*) within Jesus Christ, yet who remained as two persons (*prosopa*).[76] Cyril's work is ultimately significant for understanding the presence of God through the incarnation. Essentially, Cyril was asking, "'How can you [Nestorius] say that Jesus Christ is consubstantial (*homoousios*) with God and with humans if you say that he was completely human?'"[77] In this case, God has not indeed visited his people, and further, Christians would, in turn, be worshiping a human.[78] Furthermore, Cyril warns that the Word of

74. The apostle Paul contrasts *new man* [*human*] (*kainon anthropon*) from *old man* [*human*] (*troteran anthropon*) to express the new disposition of redeemed persons which includes morality, behaviors, thinking etc. Chrysostom expounds upon this in *Homilies on Ephesians*, hom. 13, by contrasting the "righteous life" to the "unrighteous life." On the use of the terminology "disposition," see Jeremias, "ἄνθρωπος," 365.

75. Rom 6:4-6; 12:1-2; Eph 4:22-24; Chrysostom, *Corinthians*, 18.3-6; Chrysostom, *Romans*, hom. 11; Chrysostom, *Ephesians*, hom. 13; Chrysostom, *St. John*, 78.3.

76. Cyril of Alexandria, "Twelve Chapters," 282-93; González, *Story*, 1:253-55; Olson, *Story*, 209-20. There remains concern among some theologians that Cyril's attacks on Nestorius were over-the-top, crude and exaggerated (González, *Early Christian Literature*, 360). Furthermore, Nestorius, himself reveals in his writing, *The Bazaar of Heraclides*, written near the end of his life, that he was given no due process by which to defend himself, and that Cyril acted as judge and "'the whole tribunal'" (González, *Early Christian Literature*, 362). On the other side, McGuckin who has written extensively on Cyril of Alexandria and the Christological controversy by in most part defends Cyril and points out that Nestorius had the seat of power being the archbishop of Constantinople, was further primarily dismissive early on of Cyril's concerns, and finally that Nestorius was condemned a heretic and exiled by the Council of Ephesus 431. In scholarly fashion, McGuckin records Nestorius's defense and further accusations that Cyril may have influenced Emperor Theodosius with gold, who had originally supported Nestorius and in the end judged against him. See McGuckin, *Cyril*, 20-22, 53-107; Cyril of Alexandria, *Unity of Christ*, 16-31.

77. Olson, *Story*, 215. Cyril's arguments to Nestorius are based on tradition with reference to the Constantinopolitan Creed on Jesus Christ's consubstantiality with God along with scriptural support. Cyril further shows that the Christian doctrine of salvation and resurrection collapses under a Christology that does not hold to the *hypostatic union* of the two natures being in one person (Cyril of Alexandria, "Second Letter," 262-65; Cyril of Alexandria, "Third Letter," 266-75; Cyril of Alexandria, *Unity of Christ*, 60).

78. Cyril of Alexandria, "Second Letter," par. 6.

God does not indwell the human Jesus Christ in the same manner that God indwells Christians. Jesus Christ *is* the Word of God and God who dwelled among humans in a bodily form in Christ; "for [Jesus Christ] was naturally united to, but not changed into, flesh, in that kind of indwelling which the soul of man can be said to have with its own body."[79] While there is a profound difference in comparing the incarnate Jesus Christ, God as man, to the promise of God indwelling humans through the Holy Spirit (i.e., "You know him [Spirit of truth], for he dwells with you and will be in you")[80] the former is analogous to the latter:

> Cyril understands that the incarnation of God as man is not a static event but rather the pattern and archetype of a process. He points to the seamless union of God and man in the single divine person of Jesus, truly God and man at one and the same time, founded on the single subjectivity of Christ, as not merely a sacrament of the presence of God among us, but a sacrament of how our own human lives are destined to be drawn into his divine life, and transformed in a similar manner. In short, for Cyril the manner of the incarnation is analogous to the manner of the sanctification and transformation of Christ's disciples.[81]

For Cyril, human salvation leading to union with God ("deification by grace") is a result of the incarnation as there is a "metaphysical transformation" of humans through the "paradigm of salvation" demonstrated in "[t]he physical interchange that occurs when the believer communicates with his Lord in the eucharistic mysteries [and] is no less than a metamorphosis—healing and salvation are given."[82] The hypostatic union of Christ being one person while simultaneously being both divine and human is analogous to the intimately close relationship a believer has in unity with Christ through the Eucharist ("mystical blessing").[83] In other places, Cyril speaks strongly on the indwelling of the Holy Spirit as a necessity of the Christian life through "faith" for "refashioning us into [Christ's] image" without reference to the sacraments.[84]

Later, the Protestant Reformation in the West conceived distinct and diverse theological perspectives on various topics. Included in the

---

79. Cyril of Alexandria, "Third Letter," par. 4; John 1:14; Col 2:9.

80. John 14:17.

81. McGuckin, "Introduction," 35.

82. McGuckin, *Cyril*, 187–88.

83. Cyril of Alexandria, *John*, 2:214.

84. Cyril of Alexandria, *John*, 1:311.

differing opinions on numerous theological categories were developments made in the Eucharist and the presence of Christ, resulting in a real union between the believer and the Triune God.[85] Prior to the Protestant Reformation, Catholic theology widely accepted Aquinas's metaphysical theology, saying that the substance (the hidden form) of the Eucharist changed during the blessing of the Eucharist while the accidents (the outward form) remained the same.[86] This sacramental theology became known as transubstantiation; thus, the bread becomes the real presence/ body of Christ, and the wine becomes the real presence/blood of Christ.[87] Therefore, when communicants consume the bread and wine, they consume the real presence of Christ and are thus changed or sanctified holy.[88]

In contrast, the Swiss Reformer, Zwingli, argued that Christ's human body was destroyed in death, and Christ in the resurrected body is present in heaven; thus, the real presence of Christ is in heaven, and his divinity can only spiritually be everywhere.[89] Therefore, the true presence of Christ is a spiritual presence that can be known at the Eucharist through "the contemplation of faith."[90] The communicant is encouraged and stirred to change, solely by faith, through the Holy Spirit working in place of Christ.[91] Theologically, Luther's teaching on the Eucharist (or in Luther's terms: the Lord's Supper, Holy Communion, or Sacrament of the Altar)[92] and presence (not including God's presence through the Word)[93] is situated between that of Aquinas and Zwingli as he taught the real presence of Christ hidden *in*, *with* and *under* the bread and wine, rather than becoming Christ's body and blood (Aquinas) or simply being a spiritual ascent (Zwingli).[94] Like Aquinas, Luther argued that the communicant partakes in the true body and blood of Christ by the power of

---

85. On this last point of the Magisterial Reformers and their contribution of union between the believer and God through the person of the Holy Spirit, see Kärkkäinen, *Pneumatology*, 74.

86. Aquinas, *Summa Theologiae*, III.75.1, 4–6; Feingold, *Eucharist*, 268–73.

87. Aquinas, *Summa Theologiae*, III.75.1, 4; Feingold, *Eucharist*, 259–91.

88. Feingold, *Eucharist*, 20–25; Venard, "Sacraments," 270–74.

89. Zwingli, *On Providence*, 49–56.

90. Zwingli, *On Providence*, 49, 254.

91. Zwingli, *On Providence*, 248, 252, 254–56, 257–58.

92. Olson, *Story*, 392; Luther, *Small Catechism*, 28–29.

93. Luther, *Table Talk*, 3–37; Bainton, *Here I Stand*, 173–74; Olson, *Story*, 380, 385–87.

94. Luther, *Small Catechism*, 28, 323, 326, 329–30.

Christ's Word, but unlike Aquinas, Luther did not believe the substance of bread and wine changes. In participation by faith, Luther taught the communicant receives forgiveness of sin for salvation only made possible by Christ suffering for humans ("theology of the cross").[95] However, Luther did teach of the personal presence of the Holy Spirit in the life of the believer by calling, enlightening, sanctifying, and keeping one "in the true faith" as described in his Catechism.[96] Finally, Calvin's view of the Eucharist and presence could be placed between Luther and Zwingli as Calvin rejected metaphysical categories (i.e., substance and accidents), retained language of the real presence of Christ through signs/symbols in the Eucharist while rejecting the bread and wine as simply a representation of Christ.[97] Calvin further taught that the presence of the Holy Spirit descends upon the communicant to quicken the soul by the external symbols of bread and wine.[98] Therefore, the difference in Calvin's eucharistic theology is the union of the communicant with Christ made possible by the personal presence of the Holy Spirit, who is the real Administrator of the sacrament(s).[99] Compared to the Protestant Reformers, the Holy Spirit's presence and the activity in the Eucharist event have a different focus and purpose in Zizioulas's theology.

Zizioulas and Presence

Theologically, the presence of God with humanity, for Zizioulas, is understood through the hypostatic union of Christ.[100] The connection of God's presence through the hypostatic union toward personhood has three

95. Luther, *Small Catechism*, 331–37; Luther, *Table Talk*, 228; Olson, *Story*, 380–84.

96. Luther, *Small Catechism*, 17–18.

97. Calvin, *Institutes*, 4.17.1, 3–5, 10–12, 14, 19.

98. Calvin, *Institutes*, 4.17.24.

99. Calvin, *Institutes*, 4.17.33; Kärkkäinen, *Pneumatology*, 74–75. Speaking of the Eucharist and the work of the Holy Spirit, Calvin says, "that the Spirit truly unites things separated by space" and "there exerting an efficacy of the Spirit by which he fulfills what he promises" (Calvin, *Institutes*, 4.17.10). Calvin further says, "The sacraments duly perform their office only when accompanied by the Spirit, the internal Master, whose energy alone penetrates the heart, stirs up the affections, and procures access for the sacraments into our souls." Also, "that in our hearts it is the work of the Holy Spirit to commence, maintain, cherish, and establish faith, then it follows, both that the sacraments do not avail one iota without the energy of the Holy Spirit; and that yet in hearts previously taught by that preceptor, there is nothing to prevent the sacraments from strengthening and increasing faith" (Calvin, *Institutes*, 4.14.9).

100. Zizioulas, *Being*, 55–59; Zizioulas, "Capacity and Incapacity," 437.

interlocking parts. First, the nature of a particular being is described in its relationship to another being.[101] Therefore, the being of God is not the (one) substance of God, but rather, the particular persons, Father, Son, and Holy Spirit, are themselves particular persons-in-relationship to/with one another who (three persons) and which (relationships) make (the One) God exist.[102] Second, relation (*schesis*) is constitutive of a particular being as found in the filial relationship of the Trinity: "Christ's particular being is the filial relationship between the Father and the Son in the Holy Spirit in the Trinity, and in this sense, Christ's person can be called 'divine person.'"[103] Thus, the filial relationship between the Father and the Son serves as the ideal model of what it means to be a particular person.[104] Third, for humans to receive personhood, it can only occur through a divine-to-human (*hypostatic*) relationship through Christ, who is fully divine and human and is expressed as salvation (from the self, i.e., de-individualization).[105] For Zizioulas, the Eucharist is the means and the place where this transformation occurs and is made possible by Christ's corporate personality, the-one-and-the-many.[106] However, while Zizioulas holds to a traditional Orthodox view[107] of Christ's identification through the elements of bread and wine, "this is my body, this is my blood,"[108] Zizioulas's attention is squarely on the recipients: "for you" and "for many."[109] The presence of God with humans is experienced through

101. Zizioulas, "Capacity and Incapacity," 436; Zizioulas, *Being*, 105–7.

102. Zizioulas, *Being*, 40–41.

103. Zizioulas, "Capacity and Incapacity," 436.

104. Zizioulas, "Capacity and Incapacity," 437; Zizioulas, *Being*, 107–9; Zizioulas, *Lectures*, 33, 101.

105. Zizioulas, "Capacity and Incapacity," 437; Zizioulas, *Being*, 105–22; Zizioulas, *Communion*, 6, 244–45; Zizioulas, *One and Many*, 142, 143.

106. Zizioulas, *Being*, 130–31; Zizioulas, *Communion*, 106–10; Zizioulas, *Eucharist*, 15–18, 53–58.

107. The Orthodox Church believes that the "real presence" of Christ is present both *in* and *with* the Eucharist, making it the Mystical Meal, although the Orthodox view is very close to the Roman Catholic view (i.e., transubstantiation), the Orthodox Church denies the Catholic's scientific explanation through Aristotelian categories of substance and accidents. However, the Orthodox term *metousiosis/metastoicheiosis* ("change of elements") is comparable to transubstantiation. Participation in Eucharist is understood as a reception of salvation and deification (Steenberg, "Eucharist," 185–87).

108. Matt 26:26, 28; Mark 14:22, 24; Luke 22:19; 1 Cor 11:24.

109. Matt 26:28; Mark 14:24; Luke 22:19; 1 Cor 11:24; Zizioulas, *Eucharistic Communion*, 12–14.

the Eucharist because the corporate person of Christ (Father, Son, and Holy Spirit) is consumed by particular people making them one church through communion, which is for Zizioulas the eschatological vision. The Holy Spirit, who constitutes Christ and causes the church to *be*, that is, to exist, inevitably means that, according to Zizioulas, the particular person cannot know God or experience God's presence outside of the communion-with-others, or community, which is the Church gathered around the eucharistic table.[110] The human person only comes to know the presence of Christ through the community in participation of the sacraments, and chief of these is the Eucharist.[111] Finally, for Zizioulas, at this point of presence of Christ to/with the community, the Holy Spirit actualizes for the church both the historical event of Christ's sacrifice and the eschatological hope of eternal presence.[112]

Our question has been: Until Christ's return, how is God's presence through the Holy Spirit realized? Scripturally, God planned to be present in the lives of humans as depicted in the Garden of Eden.[113] Adam and Eve's rebellion against God severed the divine-human relationship.[114] Even so, there appears to be a teleological answer to the real presence of God's faithful followers gathered eternally around him.[115] The real

110. Zizioulas, *Being*, 126–38, 165, 169; Zizioulas, *Eucharistic Communion*, 12–14, 20–22; Zizioulas, *Lectures*, 115–19, 124, 126, 132, 135–36, 139–40, 148–64. Cf. "there is no salvation out[side] of the Church" (Cyprian, "Epistles," 72.21).

111. Zizioulas, *Eucharistic Communion*, 20–22.

112. Zizioulas, *Being*, 130–31; Zizioulas, *One and Many*, 87–88, 110, 132–33, 138, 147–50. "The Church is the eschatological community" (Zizioulas, *One and Many*, 152, 154). The Holy Spirit does not work outside of Christ, but rather, the Holy Spirit is "a divine Person who makes Christ inclusive, that is, eschatological" (Zizioulas, *One and Many*, 394).

113. In Gen 3:8, Adam and Eve heard the sound of the LORD God (YHWH ʾᵉlōhîm) "walking in the garden in the cool of the day." Kinlaw says the implications are first, the LORD "came for companionship and fellowship with His creatures" and second, that there were other evenings which the LORD had walked in fellowship with Adam and Eve "in unbroken fellowship" before they sinned, but not afterward (Kinlaw and Oswalt, *Lectures*, 130–31).

114. Gen 3; Calvin, *Genesis*, 46, 50. See Hamilton, *Genesis: 1–17*, 209–10, wherein Gen 3:23, twenty-four parallel verbs are used to describe the action God took against Adam and Eve ("the man") when he "sent away" or "expelled" (šālaḥ in the Piel, v. 23) and "drove out" or "divorced" (gāraš in the Qal v. 24, cf. Lev 21:7, 14; 22:13) Adam and Eve out of the Garden and away from God's presence.

115. Isa 4:4–6; Mal 3:2–5; Matt 24:30–31; 25:31–46; Luke 3:16; John 17:24–26; Acts 2:1–4, 22–28, 33; Rev 21:3, 5, 22–27; 22:1–5; Toussaint, "Doctrine of Future and Hope," 53–69; Laing and Laing, "Doctrine of Future, God, and Prophecy," 77–101. For

presence of God was initiated by the incarnation of Jesus Christ, the Son of God.[116] Then upon his ascension and absence, the Holy Spirit was provided to faithful followers, indicating that they would always have God's presence and not be orphaned.[117] However, formalized theological trends throughout Church history have grappled in large part with the *Person and Work* of the Holy Spirit: Who is the Holy Spirit and what does he do,[118] and less with the *Personal-Relational* aspect of the Holy Spirit: Why has the Holy Spirit been sent and what are the expected results?[119]

an opposing view of linear teleological eschatology, see McGuckin, "Revelation and Orthodox Eschatology," 113–34, esp. 128–30).

116. Irenaeus, *Heresies*, 5.15.4; 5.16.1–3; Athanasius, *Incarnation*, §§1, 4, 8–9, 15–17; Gregory of Nazianzus, *Orations*, "On Holy Lights," 39.16.

117. John 14:16–18, 25–26; Acts 1:7–11; 2:1–4. Farrow, *Ascension*, 25–26, 36–38.

118. E.g., Irenaeus, *Heresies*, 3.17.1–4; 3.24.1; 5.6.1; 5.8.1–2; Basil, *Spirit*, chs. 1–8, 10–18, 20–30; Augustine, *Trinity*, 6.5.7; Williams, "God Who Sows," 611–27; Burgess, "Rupert of Deutz," 38–40; Burgess, "Hildegard of Bingen," 98–103; Torrey, *Person and Work*.

119. E.g., Basil, *Spirit*, chs. 9, 19; Gregory the Great, *Forty Gospel Homilies*, 236–47; John of the Cross, "Flame of Love," 638–715; Simons, *Writings of Menno Simons*, 97, 301, 506, 818, 681, 924, 965, 990, 1044. See McEwan, "Continual Enjoyment," 49–72. However, since the 1980s scholarship from Pentecostal theologians have contributed to the burgeoning interest and development in pneumatology. A sample of those significant contributers include: Stronstad, *Charismatic Theology of St. Luke*; Menzies, *Empowered for Witness*, traces Lukan pneumatology back into earlier Jewish literature which presents the Holy Spirit as prophetic inspiration over against a modern rendering of soteriology. Macchia, *Baptized*, approaches pneumatology from the perspective of the Holy Spirit as a person and attempts to expand Pentecostal theology on Spirit baptism to include Paul's soteriology toward a global theology. The thesis of Cross, *Presence* is the necessity of God's "direct" presence through the Holy Spirit in power, governance and authority. In Yong, *Holy Spirit?*, the Holy Spirit is the fulfillment of the promise to restore the kingdom of God, which Yong understands to mean "our being open to receiving the Spirit's empowerment so that we also might be agents who hasten the kingdom, which is in some respects already present, even if it is in other respects still to come" (Yong, *Holy Spirit?*, 11). Atkinson, *Baptism*, first, summarizes the historical-theological debate initiated by Dunn's *Baptism in the Holy Spirit* which questioned the traditional Pentecostal meaning of spirit baptism as a separate experience from "conversion-initiation." Second, Atkinson provides Pentecostal response and engagement to Dunn's work by using the works of Roger Stronstad, Max Turner, Howard Ervin, David Petts, James Shelton, and Robert Menzies. Third, Atkinson argues that Dunn has made a two-fold error: (1) Dunn fails to differentiate the pneumatology of Luke from Paul, and (2) Dunn has misunderstood Pentecostalism as there is both a soteriological and Pentecostal aspects to Spirit reception (103–7). Atkinson, *Trinity*, borrows Yong's "pneumatological imagination" analogically as a means by which one experiences God charismatically, christologically, and critically (Atkinson, *Trinity*, 14) through the Spirit to conceptualize the Trinity (i.e., personally and impersonally)

The former is theological in its quest, while the latter is anthropological, dealing with the effects of such a divine-human relationship. Here again, is the irony of Zizioulas's Dictum where he argues for an ontology based on relationships; the means of attaining such an ontology of being-as-communion is through an external act of Eucharist.[120] The Holy Spirit does not relate to the human person by indwelling, but rather the Holy Spirit constitutes the community making it the Church through partici-pation of the Eucharist—the body and blood of Christ as the one for the many.[121] An emphasis of Zizioulas, and many throughout Church his-tory, concerning God's personal presence is understood through the li-turgical, sacramental ceremony. As important, beautiful, and meaningful this sacrament with its liturgies are, the interpretation of God's presence depends on the Church and communicant's doctrinal perspective of this particular sacrament (i.e., real presence, sign, symbol, faith-act, memo-rial, etc.).[122] Sanders points out the inadequacies of sacramental soteriol-ogy and confusion for congregants to understand and choose the right church which emphasizes the proper sacrament.[123] Inevitably, "a refer-ence to the saving life of Christ" is left out, and Sanders comments that the search to identify the proper soteriology with the proper sacrament

---

(Atkinson, *Trinity*, 33). On a personal-relational aspect of the Holy Spirit, Atkinson says, "if the Spirit can relate personally with the Trinity . . . then it will be more likely than not that the Spirit will at least in rare ways relate personally to . . . Christians" (At-kinson, *Trinity*, 60). Studebaker's, *Pentecost*, approach is "the liminal, constitutional, and eschatological work of the Spirit in the biblical drama of redemption points to the Spirit's identity in the Trinity. The implication is that the Spirit consummates the Trini-tarian God and as such plays a role in the identity formation of the Son and the Father" (Studebaker, *Pentecost*, 3). Studebaker's work has elements of constructive Pentecostal trinitarianism, ecumenical goals, and modern ecological implications. Snavely, *Life*, is focused on Christians living "life in the Spirit" (i.e., "constitutive ingredient") which is the ability to live life as Jesus did (i.e., Spirit-Christology) in relation with the Trinity as the "cruciform life."

120. Zizioulas, *Being*, 149–54; Zizioulas, *Eucharist*, 16–17; Zizioulas, *One and Many*, 67–73.

121. Zizioulas, *Being*, 130, 136–38, 145–69, 215–17, 247; Zizioulas, *Communion*, 105, 107, 145–46; Zizioulas, *Eucharist*, 14, 17, 54–58, 67, 115, 117, 118–19; Zizioulas, *Eucharistic Communion*, 12–19.

122. Zizioulas weakly defends Gregory Palamas as holding the Eucharist equal with personal spirituality, even though Zizioulas offers no evidence and a majority of theologians recognize that Palamas held a high view of personal spirituality in rela-tionship with the Trinity, writing extensively on the topic with very little reference to the Eucharist. See Zizioulas, *Lectures*, 124.

123. Sanders, *Deep*, 180.

among congregants is "the classic case of the sacramental tail wagging the soteriological dog."[124] The sacraments are holy and instituted by Christ, but is this the only way Christ's presence is known by his followers (i.e., realized), and furthermore, what are the effects of God's presence on the constitution of the human being? In other words, why does God desire to be present with humans, and what changes in the person who lives in the presence of God before bodily death? Such are the issues that Zizioulas initiates in his trinitarian and ecclesiological ontology, for which his concluding answer is being-as-communion.[125] However, Zizioulas's conclusions leave the Christian-person lost in a homogenous gathering at the eucharistic table and relatively only changed by their openness to others (*ekstasis*).[126] All of these questions concerning Zizioulas's eucharistic-ecclesiology cause one to consider that *if the sacrament of Eucharist is the sign and symbol of God's grace, then is it not the person that the sacrament represents greater (Christ)?* More specifically, *Is the sacrament greater than the person of the Holy Spirit (sent by the Father, through the Son)?*[127] *Is there anything the sacrament does that the Holy Spirit cannot do better?*[128]

PRESENCE AND CHRISTIAN ANTHROPOLOGY

The personal presence of God comes today to humans through the Holy Spirit, and this encounter transforms human life.[129] There is an intimate conversation between Moses and God revealed in Exodus 33:12–23

124. Sanders, *Deep*, 180.

125. Zizioulas, *Being*, 18–19, 21–23, 27, 88, 106, 107, 114–15, 138; Zizioulas, *Communion*, 99–103.

126. Zizioulas, *Being*, 39, 44, 88; Gunton, *One, Three, Many*, 180–81, 184, 187; Grenz, *Rediscovering*, 144–45; Wendebourg, "From Cappadocian Fathers to Gregory Palamas," 194–98.

127. John 13:20; 14:16, 20, 23, 26; 15:26; 16:7, 12–15; see also Rogers, *After the Spirit*, 31. 2 Cor 3:8–9: "Will not the ministry of the Spirit have even more glory? For if there was glory in the ministry of condemnation, the ministry of righteousness must far exceed it in glory."

128. Speaking on the sacrament of baptism, Dunn says, "it is not what baptism does to a man, nor something which God is supposed to do to a man through baptism, but what man does with baptism and how he uses it, which is decisive for salvation" (Dunn, *Baptism*, 219). See also Cross's argument for a direct encounter with God through media and the focus on the personal presence of God and not on the media itself (Cross, *Presence*, 16–19, 102–3, 106, 108).

129. Cross, *Presence*, 7, 8, 10, 15, 57, 63, 81, 120–23, 128, 136, 137, 154, 175.

concerning the commission for Moses from God to lead the Israelites from Mount Sinai to the Promised Land. First of all, this conversation is personal as God's personal name, YHWH, is used, and in turn, YHWH knows Moses by his personal name.[130] Secondly, the conversation becomes more intense after YHWH offers his "presence" to Moses, and Moses's response ironically is that he can neither lead nor follow through in the commission without the "presence" (lit. *pânîm*, "face") of YHWH going with him and the nation.[131] This admission is followed by Moses asking to see the glory of YHWH, but while being denied to see YHWH's face, Moses is permitted to view his back.[132] Thirdly, the purpose for Moses's intercession, asking for the presence of YHWH on the part of the Israelite people, precisely is that *they will effectually become* a distinct people,[133] thus fulfilling YHWH's will and covenant purpose.[134] In parallel, Je-

130. Exod 33:12, 17. The personal aspect of this conversation is also given through the directional verb, "bring up" (this people). Here YHWH is not sending the people away or toward something or someone, rather YHWH says, "bring up" (*hǎ' ǎl*, hiphil imperative) in the sense that he is drawing the people to himself.

131. Exod 33:15. The success or failure of the entire "exodus enterprise" rested upon the greatness of Israel's God to personally see them through their journey, see Stuart, *Exodus*, 702–3. Hamilton says the phrase "My face will go with you" is a Hebrew idiom meaning "I will personally go with you" (cf. Deut 4:37) (Hamilton, *Exodus*, 565). Duvall and Hays, *Presence*, 13–14, 35–38.

132. Exod 33:18–23. Ratzinger, shows that the idiom "face to face" by which conversation between YHWH and Moses is described is not literal but rather an idiom for "personal conversation" (Ratzinger, *Jesus of Nazareth*, 4–5). The idiom is explained through Exod 33:11 where the face-to-face conversation is described in a simile, "as a man speaks to his friend." This supports the apparent contradiction when YHWH later tells Moses, "'you cannot see my face, for man shall not see me and live'" (Exod 33:20). Also, in Levison, *Filled*, God's presence is equated with those who live before God's face; thus, death is God turning his face away (Levison, *Filled*, 26).

133. The rhetorical question from Moses reads, "Is it not in your going with us, so that we are distinct, I and your people, from every other people on the face of the earth?" (v. 16). The effectual result of being a distinguished people rests on the presence of God (lit., *to walk* [*bᵉlĕkᵉtᵉkā*] *with us*) and is grammatically found in the use of "If not" (*hᵃlô'*) and "so that we are distinct" (*vᵉnip̄lênû* a niphal perfect, first person common plural). Thus Israel's distinctiveness is contingent upon the presence of God. Stuart says, "The lesson is clearly put by Moses: it was God's presence with his people, and all that that implied, that made his people special—they did not have within themselves any particular intrinsic characteristics to 'distinguish' them. God's distinction was what they received derivatively but did not possess innately" (Stuart, *Exodus*, 703). Also, Garrett, *Exodus*, 647–48. In Levison, *Filled*, there is a depth of meaning ("lavishness") in the OT of "to fill" (*ml'*) that connotes "completion, full-filling, fruition, wholeness, fullness" (Levison, *Filled*, 55–58).

134. Cf. Exod 19:5–6. See also Lev 20:26; Deut 7:6; 14:2, 21; 26:18, 19; 28:9; Ps 135:4; Isa 62:12; Mal 3:17; Tit 2:14; 1 Pet 2:5, 9; Rev 1:6; 5:10; 20:6.

sus[135] had an intimate conversation with his disciples concerning the commission for them to fulfill by taking the gospel of repentance and forgiveness of sins into all nations.[136] First, the significance of Christ's personal presence is heightened as salvation is effective only through Jesus Christ and through his name.[137] Secondly, the pronouncement of the gospel of salvation in Jesus's name by a messenger for the reception of forgiveness for sins and salvation is only effective through the personal presence of the Holy Spirit.[138] The disciples were directly given their commission from Jesus, but they were to wait to execute this commission until the Holy Spirit arrived to empower them.[139] Thirdly, the distinguishing characteristic of the Christian person from all other religious people is a living, personal relationship with God through the Holy Spirit made possible by Jesus Christ.[140] In New Testament and post-New Testament

135. Ratzinger builds a thesis of Jesus as the second-Moses in a hermeneutical approach to the Gospels based on the promise and fulfillment that God would provide another Moses-type ("a prophet like me," Deut 18:15; cf. 34:10) one who conversed with God face-to-face (Exod 33:11). However, the second-Moses, or new-Moses, is greater than the first as he *is* the face of God and leads his flock out of sin and into the eternal promise land (Ratzinger, *Jesus of Nazareth*, 3–6).

136. Luke 24:47. Green says, "'Repentance' will be a key term describing the appropriate response to the offer of salvation in Acts, and connotes the (re)alignment of one's life—that is, dispositions and behaviors—towards God's purpose. Forgiveness has been throughout the Gospel and will continue to be in Acts central to the content and experience of salvation" (Green, *Luke*, 858). For an argument on reading Luke-Acts from a theological perspective over a historical-critical approach, see Spencer, "Preparing the Way," 104–24; Turner, *Power*, 346–47.

137. Luke 24:44–49. In Peter's Pentecost Sermon (Acts 2:14–41), he begins with a quote from Joel 2:28–32 and ties together YHWH (*kyrios*) with Jesus Christ as the name by which one is saved (Schnabel, *Acts*, 140). Salvation, healing and baptism in the "name of Jesus" is thematic in Acts 2:21, 22–41; 3:6, 16; 4:10, 12, 30; 8:12, 16; 9:14, 15, 27, 29; 10:43; 15:26; 16:18; 19:5, 13, 17; 21:13; 22:16; 26:9. See also, Lord (*kyrios*) meaning YHWH and Jesus Christ, Isa 45:23 in Phil 2:10–11; Rom 14:11; also, Ps 34:8 in 1 Pet 2:3; also, Isa 8:13 in 1 Pet 3:15; Bock, *Acts*, 118.

138. Specifically in Acts 1:2, 8; 2:14–41; 6:5; 8:14–17; 9:17; 10:38, 44–48; 11:15–18, 22–24; 13:2, 4, 9; 15:8–9; 16:6–7; 19:2, 6, 21. See Bruce, *Acts*, 30–31, 36, 50–51, 67, 68, 69–71, 168–69, 213–14, 216–17, 245–46, 290, 306, 363, 364, 371. Also, Turner, "Luke and the Spirit," 283–87.

139. Luke 24:48–49; Acts 1:8. Green says, "It is the Holy Spirit who will empower them for their role as witnesses" (Green, *Luke*, 859). Turner, *Power*, 341–42, 346–47.

140. Ezek 11:19–20; 36:26–28; 37:14; Joel 2:28–32; Matt 3:11–12; 28:19; Luke 3:16–17; 11:13; 12:12; 24:48–49; John 13:20; 14:16–17, 26; 15:26; 16:7, 13; Acts 1:4–8; 2:1–4, 14–41; Rom 5:5; 8:1–17; 14:17; 1 Cor 2:12–16; 6:19; 12:3; 2 Cor 6:3–10; Gal 5:16–25; Eph 1:13–14; 1 Thess 1:5; 4:8; 2 Tim 1:14; Tit 3:5–7; Heb 2:4; 6:4–6; 10:15–18;

theology, the presence of God as the Holy Spirit indwelling the human person is essential because indwelling is designed and modeled from the essence of the trinitarian God, persons-in-relation (mutual indwelling),[141] who makes the human person specifically a Christian person.[142] Nothing is added to the essence of the human person, instead, they have been forgiven of sin and proceed in a transformation[143] that leads to an ever-growing relationship with God and others.[144] The persons of the Trinity and the personal relationship between God and humans is more significant than the sacraments they represent.

---

1 Pet 1:12; 2 Pet 1:21; 1 John 5:6–9; Jude 20. Dunn understands the gift of the Holy Spirit to be typical of conversion and living the Christian life (Dunn, *Pneumatology*, 3, 10–21, 25–28, 39–41, 43–61, 62–80, 222–42). Irenaeus, *Heresies*, 5.6.1; 5.8.2; 5.10.2; Gregory of Nazianzus, *Orations*, "On the Holy Spirit," 5.26–27; Bobrinskoy, "'Pneumatic Christology,'" 55, 65. Cross, *Presence*, 17–18, 63; Fee, *Empowering*, 827–29. Sanders, *Deep*, 160, 163–65, 175; Turner, *Power*, 358–60.

141. Sanders, *Deep*, 89–98, 126, 136–37, 143, 148, 150. In turn, Sanders shows that the dominant description in the NT is that the Holy Spirit *indwells* believers and believers are *in* Christ. Only a few instances is it described that Christ is in humans, but where it does, Sanders points out that "the work of the Spirit is mentioned" (Sanders, *Deep*, 175). Duvall and Hays, *Presence*, 303–5.

142. Athanasius, *To Serapion*, §§24, 35–37; Basil, *Letter 38*, 137–41; Basil, *Spirit*, 19.50; 26.61–64; Bobrinskoy, "'Pneumatic Christology,'" 49–65; Congar, *Holy Spirit*, 2.2.1; 2.2.3; Farrow, *Ascension*, 59–60, 64; Fee, *Empowering*, 5–9, 827–45; Gregory of Nazianzus, *Orations*, "On the Holy Spirit," 5.26–27; 5.32; Gunton, *One, Three, Many*, 185; McCall, *Which Trinity?*, 67; Moltmann, *Trinity*, 220; Palamas, *Triads*, 1.2.1; 3.1.27–28; 3.1.34; Sanders, *Deep*, 159–60; Symeon, *Discourses*, 15.3; 15.5; 19.4; 23.2; 23.5–8; Ware, *Orthodox Way*, 90–102. Levison, *Filled*, 238–41, in contrast to Fee, *Empowering*, 332–35, does not recognize the reference to "Holy Spirit" in the apostle Paul's writing as the person of the Holy Spirit, but rather *a holy spirit* in the sense of a "locus of virtue." Duvall and Hays, *Presence*, 301–3.

143. Gregory of Nazianzus argues that a believer is changed like Zacchaeus (Luke 19:1–9, was "lost" and became "saved") because the Holy Spirit comes to convert and indwells them, drawing that one toward heaven. Gregory of Nazianzus, *Orations*, "On Holy Baptism," 40.31.

144. Zizioulas, *Communion*, 213; Green, *Luke*, 858; Kinlaw, *Jesus*, 70, 78–101; LaCugna, *God*, 292–300; see also Pannenberg's work on "exocentricity" of the human person whose existence is found outside of themselves and in another, in *Anthropology*, 37, 63–67, 76, 80–83, 95, 97, 105–7, 159–60, 164, 185, 187, 194, 200, 210, 226, 237, 266–69, 338, 384, 397, 408, 412–13, 415, 475, 480, 486, 490–92, 516–19, 524–26, 529–32. For Sanders, trinitarian theology is soteriologically-centric where the economy of salvation is the economy of the Trinity (Sanders, *Deep*, 98–101, 111–12, 115, 118, 126, 132–37, 142–43, 144, 147, 148, 150, 191–94). For a debate on the timing of the Holy Spirit indwelling the Christian person, see Dunn, *Baptized*; also in Turner, *Power*, 38–85.

The personal presence of God as the person (*hypostasis*) of the Holy Spirit indwelling the human person can be understood more fully through trinitarian theology.[145] An economy of the Holy Spirit is a trinitarian economy just as an economy of Christ is trinitarian or an economy the Father is trinitarian, where each one finds their existence in the others.[146] Gregory of Nazianzus says,

> No sooner do I conceive of the One than I am illumined by the Splendour of Three; no sooner do I distinguish Them than I am carried back to the One. When I think of any One of the Three I think of Him as the Whole, and my eyes are filled, and the greater part of what I am thinking of escapes me. I cannot grasp the greatness of That One so as to attribute a greater greatness to the Rest. When I contemplate the Three together, I see but one torch, and cannot divide or measure out the Undivided Light.[147]

Likewise, Basil speaks about the particularity of the three persons of the Trinity and declares that each trinitarian person cannot be conceived without the others because they are inseparable and have their eternal communion in one another. Furthermore, the believer who has been consecrated and indwelled by the Holy Spirit finds his/her own life/existence "commingled" into the community of the trinitarian persons equating a holy community.[148] This trinitarian concept of person is also a theological reflection on anthropology.[149]

Trinitarian theology presents a concept of person who is free in reliance and relation upon another.[150] Some, like Pannenberg, for instance,

145. Duvall and Hays, *Presence*, 303–5.

146. Zizioulas, *Being*, 124–25, 129–30; Zizioulas, *One and Many*, 16, 53, 80–81, 394; Zizioulas, *Eucharist*, 15–16; Gunton, *One, Three, Many*, 188–91; LaCugna, *God*, 246.

147. Gregory of Nazianzus, *Orations*, "On Holy Baptism," 40.41.

148. Basil, *Letter 38*, 138–39; Basil, *Spirit*, 9.23; 18.47; 19.50; 22.53; 26.61–63.

149. Pannenberg calls for theologians not to simply come into "contact" with what he calls "nontheological anthropology," but rather, anthropology needs to be "critically appropriated" meaning: "The aim is to lay theological claim to the human phenomena described in the anthropological disciplines" (Pannenberg, *Anthropology*, 19).

150. This concept is contrasted to the thought that persons (as individuals from a nature perspective) live in fear of one another, thus living closed, defensive lives where others are a threat and are often subjected for individual gain. See Zizioulas, *Being*, 68–70, 103–5; Zizioulas, "Capacity and Incapacity," 405–8; Zizioulas, *Communion*, 13–14, 19–20, 39–47, 51–55, 73, 91–92, 99–101, 102, 106–8; Gunton, "Persons and Particularity," 99, 100, 101; Macmurray, *Self*, 84–92, 106–13, 116–18.

have taken this concept of relational, dependent, person and further developed it beyond theological categories. Thus, Pannenberg's work in the area of human history attempts to use elements from all of the sciences (i.e., anthropology, biology, historiography, philosophy, psychology sociology, etc.) as "partial aspects" in building an understanding of human beings.[151] Primarily, Pannenberg's focus is on philosophical anthropology and the work of Herder (humans are perfectible, but only from outside forces including God, the world, culture, education, etc.), Scheler (humans are spiritual, apart from biological and humans can be "open to the world" which meant open to God), Plessner (humans have their center not only within themselves but also outside of themselves making humans exocentric and self-reflecting) and Gehlen (humans are "active beings" constructing their own environment making them open to the world).[152] For Pannenberg, a human person, or the spirit of a person (e.g., Scheler), can freely transcend their personal human boundaries (i.e., disposition, including culture) and can be present with someone or something other than themselves *as other* (i.e., different, distinct).[153] The human person has the capacity to recognize, acknowledge, and even live with the other *as other*, which is self-transcendence, making the human person open to the world in a manner of exocentricity.[154] Finally, Pannenberg is interested in the history of culture, communities, and the individuals who live together, finding their existence, identification, and fulfillment in the shared world.[155] The human relationship with God leads to a unified world; as Pannenberg argues that "Human exocentricity compels men and women to find outside themselves a center that will give unity and identity to their lives."[156] Pannenberg believes religion is the best example

151. Pannenberg, *Anthropology*, 22–23, 485–87.

152. Pannenberg, *Anthropology*, 35–40, 45–47, 52–55; Onah, *Self-Transcendence*, 12–19, 21–22, 29–31, 98–99.

153. Pannenberg, *Anthropology*, 41–42, 61–62, 76, 85–86. See Zizioulas's thesis that ontologically "being other" and "being free" are two aspects of the same reality (Zizioulas, *Communion*, 13–98).

154. Pannenberg, *Anthropology*, 62–64, 76, 85; Onah, *Self-Transcendence*, 21, 43n72, 62, 63. Cf. Zizioulas, "Capacity and Incapacity," 408–10, 414, 417, 420, 425–26, 432–33, 434–39, 442, 446; Gunton, *One, Three, Many*, 182–83, 190–91, 194.

155. Pannenberg, *Anthropology*, 397–98, 476–80, 485–87. Cf. Zizioulas, *Being*, 154–69; Zizioulas, *Eucharistic Communion*, 46–47, 79–81, 123–31; Zizioulas, *One and Many*, 49–60, 379–87, 388–401; Boff, *Trinity and Society*, 11–13, 107–8, 118–20; Grenz, *Social God*, 304–36; Volf, *Likeness*, 259–82; Moltmann, *Trinity*, 212–22.

156. Pannenberg, *Anthropology*, 480; also, 312, 490. Onah explains, "The German

where individuals can live exocentrically as the very purpose of religion is the "unity of the world."[157] In other words, the "divine source" being the Trinity (persons-in-relation) function in religion, giving religion its meaning, including the sacraments.[158] Therefore, there is nothing that the sacrament can do, that the Holy Spirit cannot do better.

Zizioulas mirrors Pannenberg's thoughts in identifying the key concepts in personhood as communion, freedom, and love, making the person other-oriented ("*ek-stasis* of being").[159] However, for Zizioulas, only the Trinity contains these characteristics, saying,

> Only God can claim to be a personal being in the genuine sense I have just indicated: he is the only being that is in an ultimate sense "itself," i.e., *particular*, but whose particularity

word *Exzentrizität* may be translated as 'eccentricity' or as 'exocentricity.' Etymologically it is derived from the Latin '*eccentros*' which is in turn derived from the Greek '*ek-kentros*' or '*exo-kentros*,' an adjective used in Mathematics to describe circles, etc., not having a common center or whose axles are out of the center. In astronomy, the same adjective is used to describe the position of an orbit deviating from a circular motion. In common English usage, the adjective eccentric describes an unconventional or odd behavior. In modern philosophical anthropology, exocentric or eccentric describes the position of the center in relation to the human being. The center is outside of the human being" (Onah, *Self-Transcendence*, 43n72).

157. Pannenberg, *Anthropology*, 473; also 224–42, 473–84. Fiddes seeks a more balanced approach to person and the world than does Pannenberg. Fiddes offers four pastoral concerns or balances which includes: Tournier's "gap" theory, a balance between "person" and "personage"; using Pannenberg's anthropology, a balance between the "self" and "openness to the world" (ecstatic, self-transcending); using Carr's "relationship" and "relatedness," a balance between "the individual" and "the community"; and finally, a balance between unity and diversity (Fiddes, *Participating*, 19–28).

158. Pannenberg, *Anthropology*, 473–74; Schleiermacher, *Christian Faith*, 5–6; 29–31. While Pannenberg and Schleiermacher seem to agree that religion is the *unity of reality*, Schleiermacher is very clear that the sacrament of Holy Communion is the "indissoluble bond" and "entrance into the living fellowship" with Christ and other believers, and therefore the "fellowship should periodically be nourished" or practiced, or participated in by believers, calling it the "climax of public worship" (Schleiermacher, *Christian Faith*, 638–43). The point here is not to demean the sacraments from their holy and unique status, but rather to elevate the persons of the Trinity and the relationship offered to humans by which the sacraments represent as a sign and symbol of that grace as one of the means by which humans participate in that relationship.

159. Zizioulas, "Capacity and Incapacity," 408, 410. In Zizioulas's descriptions of *ek-stasis*, or *ekstatic*, he means the transcendent-self, catholic person, person as hypostatic, communion, relational (*schesis*), etc. (Zizioulas, "Capacity & Incapacity," 408–10; Zizioulas, *Being*, 44, 52–59, 62–65, 86–88, 91–92, 94, 104, 106–7, 134; Zizioulas, *Communion*, 112, 212–15). Zizioulas uses the term *ekstasis* in the same manner that Pannenberg uses "exocentric" or "exocentricity."

> is established in full ontological freedom, i.e., not by virtue of
> its boundaries (he is "incomprehensible," "indivisible" etc.), but
> by its ekstasis of communion (he is eternally Trinity and love)
> which makes it unique and indispensable. When we say, there-
> fore, that God *is*, we do not refer to a being as being but to the
> Father—a term which denotes being in the sense of hypostasis,
> i.e. of Person.[160]

Humans, for Zizioulas, can create to a certain extent but cannot be
eternally present, like God, as human persons deal with the "tragedy"
of death which brings about absence.[161] Therefore, the only chance for
humans to exist is through the human capacity of faith in *another*, which
is "ekstatic personhood," making the human being a person-in-relationship because the opposite is individuality as the autonomous-self leading to non-being.[162] The only way a human being understands and lives
(*ekstaticly*, cf. *exocentricity*) as a human person and in relationship with
others in communion is through baptism and Eucharist.[163] As a means
of understanding the place and significance of the sacraments and the
presence of God through the Holy Spirit, the question could be asked, *Is
there anything the sacrament does that the Holy Spirit cannot do better?*[164]

   While the Christian faith affirms the presence of the Holy Spirit in
the formalized events of the sacraments of baptism and Eucharist, the
Christian Scriptures and theology reveal that God is personal and desires

160. Zizioulas, "Capacity and Incapacity," 410.

161. Zizioulas, "Capacity and Incapacity," 411–12, 414.

162. Zizioulas, "Capacity and Incapacity," 406, 421–23, 426; Zizioulas, *Being*, 18, 109, 111, 112, 113; Zizioulas, *Communion*, 244–45.

163. Zizioulas, "Capacity and Incapacity," 423n1, 434–38. Also, Zizioulas, *Being*, 15–16, 22, 80, 145–69; Zizioulas, *Communion*, 9–10, 106–12; Zizioulas, *Eucharist*, 16; Zizioulas, *Eucharistic Communion*, 20–24; Zizioulas, *One and Many*, 336–38, 404–5.

164. Aquinas's teaching on signs and causes (Venard, "Sacraments," 271, 272–74, 276–77, 278; Aquinas, *Summa Theologiae*, III.62.1; III.77.1) and the Greek Orthodox Church's practice of "The Epiclesis" (the priest's prayer for the decent of the Holy Spirit upon the Eucharistic gifts; McGuckin, *Orthodox*, 297) brings up issues of cause/effect, words/elements and form/matter. Our point here is the freedom of the Holy Spirit who "blows where it wishes" (John 3:8) and the presence of the Holy Spirit upon hu-mans is not limited to the sacraments. In Cross, *Presence*, 15–24, there are two ways God through the Holy Spirit encounters humans: Primary and Secondary. Primary encounters are *direct* encounters where the Holy Spirit connects with the human spirit. Secondary encounters happen when through media (physical, tangible sign) the Holy Spirit can encounter the human in an *indirect* way. Therefore, we can rhetorically ask, "Which is better, a Primary, direct encounter with the person of the Holy Spirit, or a Secondary, indirect encounter with a sign/medium of the Holy Spirit?"

a personal relationship with humans.[165] In addition, if personhood is understood as exocentric, persons-in-communion/relation, then there are two levels of relationships: the temporal-material and the eternal-non-material as human-with-human relationship and divine-with-human relationship.[166] While the former is essential for living life within the bounds of time and space, the latter is ultimate life in an inclusive understanding of a transcendent life both inside and outside of time and space illustrated in an eschatological hope.[167] The divine-human relationship occurs and is maintained by the indwelling of the Holy Spirit as the personal presence of God in the life of the believer, making them a Christian person.[168] Thus, there is nothing the sacrament can do that the Holy Spirit cannot do better.

165. Ezek 11:19–20; 36:26–27; 37:14; John 13:20; 14:15–17, 20, 23, 25–26; 15:26; 16:12–13; Fee, *Empowering*, 17–19, 21–28, 556–70, 722, 827–31; Gunton, *Father, Son, & Holy Spirit*, 195–200; Oden, *Spirit*, 54–58, 72, 74; Pinnock, *Flame*, 24, 30, 37–42, 149–55, 157–59.

166. See McConville, where double embodiment of humans is the totality of the individual and the potential of the human as the image and likeness of God, in God's world (McConville, *Being Human*, 59, 64–67). In McConville also see the divine-human relationship as the "spiritual sense" (McConville, *Being Human*, 87–91). Pannenberg's term is "The openness of persons to their divine destiny" which is also connected to community (Pannenberg, *Anthropology*, 224–42). Farrow, *Ascension*, 36–38; Gunton, *Father, Son, & Holy Spirit*, 196–97.

167. For the importance of *Dasein* and time, see Heidegger, *Being and Time*, 2.3.65, 309–16; 2.6.78–80, 385–99. See "self-transcendence" in Pannenberg, *Anthropology*, 60–63, 76, 85–86, 94, 108, 112, 260–61, 524–27; Farrow, *Ascension*, 50, 59–51, 177, 240, 242–43, 257, 262–63, 266, 269, 271. Cf. Zizioulas, *Eucharistic Communion*, 130–31.

168. Dunn, *Baptism*, 4, 17–18, 20–22, 23–25, 32–37, 40–43, 47, 51–54, 68, 77–78, 82, 89, 91–92, 94–95, 96, 102, 112, 115, 137–38, 147, 149, 151, 156, 159, 160, 170–72, 174, 181–82, 191–94, 199–200, 204, 211, 213–14, 223, 224–29; Farrow, *Ascension*, 5–6, 59–60, 177, 240, 267, 271; Fee, *Empowering*, 31, 542–54; Pinnock, *Flame*, 162; Sanders, *Deep*, 177–81; Turner, *Power*, 404–6. Wesley shows that the teaching on receiving the Holy Spirit at sanctification is *not* scriptural, but rather a believer receives the Holy Spirit at the moment of new birth. Wesleyan theology of the Holy Spirit and soteriology could be stated this way: At justification a believer receives all of the Holy Spirit (not partial), but at sanctification, the Holy Spirit receives all of the believer through the act of complete surrendering the *self* to God. This is *openness to another* or living in an *exocentric* manner. Furthermore, in Wesley's theology it could be stated there is a *mutual exocentric relationship* where the will of the Father is for human salvation, the Son's *kenosis* is for human salvation, and the Holy Spirit indwells the human believer, so that the believer finds his and her life in the Triune God. Wesley, "Mr. Joseph Benson," 415–16; Wesley, "Scriptural Christianity," 37–52; Wesley, "Witness of the Spirit (Discourse 1)," 114–15, 120; Wesley, "Witness of the Spirit (Discourse 2)," 126–28,

SUMMARY

Zizioulas has identified the connection between particularity and community for a being to have personhood is relationship.[169] Applied to human personhood, Zizioulas argues that a person is transformed into a Christian person through the sacraments and established relationally in the Church.[170] This chapter has shown that the relationship among the particular persons of the Trinity serves as a perfect design for (holy) community. This design is God's will for humans. God makes this (holy) community or persons-in-relationship possible by the indwelling of the Holy Spirit within the human person transforming them into a Christian person.

Scriptures reveal, and theology affirms, that God revealed as Father, Son, and Holy Spirit, is motivated by love in desiring (exocentric) a personal relationship with humans.[171] However, human sin comes in the form of selfishness (egocentric), which inhibits such a relationship.[172] In the act of gracious-love, God the Father presented God the Son to the world in the form of humanity, yet fully God, who was the personal presence of the Triune God.[173] Upon the Son's crucifixion, resurrection and ascension, believers were neither orphaned nor powerless, but rather the personal presence of God through the Advent of the Holy Spirit has maintained the personal-relationship between God and humans who believe, giving "personhood in human existence."[174] This personhood is made possible through reconciliation with God, whose desire is a close

---

130, 132; Wesley, "Holy Spirit," 509–12, 514–17. Leclerc calls the false teaching that Wesleyans fully receive the Holy Spirit not until one is entirely sanctified, "folk theology" (Leclerc, *Discovering*, 180).

169. Zizioulas, *Communion*, 106–8.

170. Zizioulas, *Being*, 110–22; Zizioulas, *Eucharist*, 16–19; Zizioulas, *Eucharistic Communion*, 20–22.

171. Exod 20:6; 34:6–7; Ps 51:1; John 3:16; Rom 5:8; Zizioulas, *Being*, 21–22, 27, 49, 105–7; Zizioulas, "Capacity and Incapacity," 408–10; Zizioulas, *Communion*, 106–12; Pannenberg, *Anthropology*, 37. Duvall and Hays, *Presence*, 1–2, 325–28.

172. Phil 2:3–4; Pannenberg, *Anthropology*, 224–26, 529; Schwarz, *Human Being*, 160, 163–65, 170–75, 215–16, 241, 254.

173. Phil 2:5–6; Rom 8:3–4; Zizioulas, *Being*, 46, 49–50, 92, 93–98, 130–31; Zizioulas, "Holy Trinity," 55–58; Farrow, *Ascension*, 59–60; Irenaeus, *Heresies*, 3.18.6–7.

174. Luke 24:49; John 14:16, 18, 26; Acts 1:8; Rom 8:13–17; Zizioulas, "Holy Trinity," 56; Zizioulas, *Being*, 110–14; Pannenberg, *Anthropology*, 298; LaCugna, *God*, 292–300.

relationship with humans.[175] The divine-human relationship is so intimate that the Scriptures speak of the Holy Spirit indwelling believers, which is necessary to be a Christian person.[176]

Throughout Church history, it has been taught that the Holy Spirit encounters the believer through the sacraments of the Church.[177] However, there are differing doctrinal opinions about what the Holy Spirit is doing in the sacramental event and how the Holy Spirit is experienced?[178] Therefore, while Christ *instituted* the sacraments as a means of grace, the personal presence of God—the Holy Spirit—with humans is more significant and meaningful as it is this presence *with*, *in*, and *into* the believer that *constitutes* the Christian person.[179] What follows is Christian anthropology based on this divine-human relationship where the character of the human person is transformed into the character of God, and they too find their identity in another: first in God, and second in other humans.[180] In Wesleyan theology, this new set of relationships is founded on an inward change where sin has been forgiven, and the Holy Spirit resides in "perfect love."[181]

175. Isa 32:15; 44:3; Ezek 36:27; Joel 2:28. Sanders, *Deep*, 113–30, 137; Fee, *Empowering*, 864–65, 868–69; McKnight, *Open*, 38, 141; Rogers, *After the Spirit*, 119; Yarnell, *Holy Spirit*, 20–22, 91.

176. Acts 11:14–17; 19:1–7; Rom 8:9; 1 Cor 6:19; Gal 4:6; 1 Thess 4:8; Cross, *Presence*, 10–11; Fee, *Empowering*, 5–9, 135–37, 270, 294; 722, 843–45, 846, 854–55, 864, 872; McKnight, *Open*, 19, 56, 63–64; Sanders, *Deep*, 140–53, 160–66; Yarnell, *Holy Spirit*, 99, 105; For Levison, being filled with the Spirit is not that one is filled with the third person of the Trinity, but rather one is filled with the gospel values, see *Filled*, 55–57, 80. Duvall and Hays, *Presence*, 333–34.

177. *The Teaching of the Twelve Apostles*, chs. 7, 9; Fatula, "Holy Spirit," 374–75; Vatican II, *Documents*, ch. 1, par. 6, 7, 10; Trostyanskiy, "Holy Spirit," 249; Steenberg, "Eucharist," 185.

178. Feingold, *Eucharist*, 28–29, 491, 514–16. Zizioulas, *Being*, 130, 136–38, 145–69, 215–17, 247; Zizioulas, *Communion*, 105, 107, 145–46; Zizioulas, *Eucharist*, 14, 17, 54–58, 67, 115, 117, 118–19; Zizioulas, *Eucharistic Communion*, 12–19. Luther, *Small Catechism*, art. 3, 17–18. Calvin, *Institutes*, 4.17.24, 33.

179. Notice that the Scriptures do not speak of the Holy Spirit's presence in, with and under the elements of Holy Communion, as Luther adhered (Luther, *Small Catechism*, 28, 323, 326, 329–330), rather the Holy Spirit's presence is *in* and *into* human lives: Rom 8:9 (*oikei en humin*); 1 Cor 6:19 (*en humin*); Gal 4:6 (*eis tas kardias*); 1 Thess 4:8 (*eis humas*).

180. Zizioulas, *Being*, 84–85; Rom 8:5–11; 12:2; Phil 2:2–11; Irenaeus, *Heresies*, 5.6.1–2; 5.8.1–2; McConville, *Being Human*, 7–10, 14, 20, 24–29; Pannenberg, *Anthropology*, 490, 516, 524–25, 531; Volf, *Likeness*, 182–83, 185, 186.

181. Wesley, "Plain Account," 371–72, 374–79, 387, 388–89, 393, 394–95, 397, 416, 417, 418–19. Wesley, "Witness of the Spirit (Discourse 1)," 115–17, 118–19, 120.

For there to be a relationship, there needs to be mutuality. The Holy Scriptures reveal mutuality among the Father, Son, and Holy Spirit as mutual self-giving love.[182] Therefore, how shall the Christian person join in a relationship with God? What is the response from the Christian person in relationship with God?

Chapter 7 examines the initiation, life, and mission of the Christian person in relationship with God by participation in the life of the Trinity through the Holy Spirit as the human response. As demonstrated in Moses's encounter with God on Mount Sinai[183] and paralleled with the disciples' encounter with Jesus before his ascension,[184] the commission given to the Christian person is preceded by the presence of God in the Christian person's life. Therefore, a new set of relationships, constituted by the Holy Spirit, makes the Christian person. The Christian person does not have a passive relationship with God through the Holy Spirit but rather a dynamic relationship.[185] The Christian person participates in a relationship with the Holy Trinity made possible by the will of the Father, the *kenōsis* of the Son, and the presence of the Holy Spirit. In Wesleyan theology, an active relationship includes participating in the means of grace.[186] Chapter 7 will show that the significant barrier of sin must be dealt with first to understand broken relationships. Second, a redeemed and reconciled Christian person can actively participate in a relationship with God. Third, the burgeoning relationship with God can transform the Christian person so that they participate in the holy-love character of God. Finally, the result of the presence of God in the Christian person's life is that they can participate in the mission of God for the world.

---

182. E.g., John 13:20; 14:16–17, 26; 15:26; 16:12–15; 17:1–5, 8, 21–23.

183. Exod 33:12–23.

184. Matt 28:16–20; Luke 24:45–53; Acts 1:4–11.

185. Collins, *Wesley*, 249–70; Henderson, *Wesley's*, 128–39; Taylor, *Formulation*, 223–28. An active participation in the Christian life is somewhat skewed by the word "works" for which Wesleyans are commonly accused of a "works-righteousness." These are activities by the Christian person in response to God's grace first given through the Holy Spirit (Lindström, *Wesley and Sanctification*, 205–15).

186. Wesley, "Journal," Nov. 1, 1739; Dec. 31, 1739; June 24, 1740; Wesley, "Means of Grace," 185–201; Wesley, "Working Out," 510–11; Wesley, "Minutes of Several Conversations 1744–1789," 322–24.

Chapter 7

Participation and Christian Anthropology

> "Then the Spirit of the LORD will rush upon you, and you will
> prophesy with them and be turned into *another man*."
>
> —SAMUEL, THE PROPHET[1]

INTRODUCTION

OUR QUESTION HAS BEEN, "Does Zizioulas's trinitarian personhood successfully accomplish an anthropological definition?" Zizioulas's Dictum (i.e., mode of existence) "being as communion," or what we have been calling "persons-in-relation," serves as a foundational starting point for understanding personhood and the Trinity. However, Zizioulas's development of the mode of existence through the monarchy of the Father, corporate Christology, and eucharistic-ecclesiology lacks an anthropological definition, mainly when applied to the Christian person. The critical deficiencies in Zizioulas's Dictum include, first, a lack of particularity to balance his goal for community. Second, Zizioulas misplaces relationship for human personhood by placing it solely within the ecclesial community as a post-Christian reality without a relational initiation through

---

1. 1 Sam 10:6. *Emphasis mine* on the term "another man" which is a literal translation of *'ish ' aher*. Cf. 1 Sam 10:10–12; 11:6; 16:13–15. See Brueggemann, *Samuel*, 75, who explains the phrase as "a new creature empowered for God's special purpose." Also, Hertzberg sees the emphasis on the verb "and be turned" (*vᵉnĕhᵉpăkᵉtă*) literally meaning to "over-throw" which is also directed at Sodom and Gomorrah (Gen 19:25; Hertzberg, *Samuel*, 85).

the personal presence of the Holy Spirit. Third, Zizioulas's theology on human participation in relationship with the Trinity is inherently tied to the sacraments within the ecclesial community and speaks of nothing toward a transformation within the human person that makes them a Christian person in relationship with God. Therefore, our working hypothesis has been that a Christian person is constituted through trinitarian pneumatology, which the Holy Spirit initiates. We believe that this conclusion is a corrective to Zizioulas's trinitarian personhood by going back to his starting point of persons-in-relation. The result of this contribution is that the Christian person is each particular person who has encountered the presence of God and continues to live in that presence by participating in the life of the Trinity initiated and sustained by the Holy Spirit.

This thesis understands the mystery of the Holy Trinity to be described as three persons of one essence. We do not believe there are three volitions as Holmes accused Zizioulas, but three persons operating with one will.[2] The uniqueness of the persons in their roles reveals a depth of richness in the dynamic holy community for which they are one in their *perichoresis*. Furthermore, the roles viewed through the names indicate unequal roles, although all three persons participate in every activity. Gunton describes this as person with relational particularity or "otherness—between the persons"[3] while maintaining the *perichoresis* for which Awad ascribes to Gunton's description of the Trinity as "unity-in-particularity."[4] Similarly, along those lines, Atkinson describes this observation of differing levels in the roles of the persons as limited reciprocation or "inequality among the persons of the Trinity" while maintaining the *perichoresis*.[5] However, like Gunton, we would ascribe to the unity of God in relations; additionally, we find a paradox of the qualities of those persons to be essentially unifying.[6]

In like manner, we see the particular persons of the Trinity operating in *perichoresis* as mutual self-giving love and equality-with-headship.

2. Holmes, *Quest*, 14.

3. Gunton, *Trinitarian Theology*, 133.

4. Awad, "Personhood," 1, 8, 16, 19.

5. Atkinson, *Trinity*, 150–51. Also, Wilks comes close to this interpretation of the Cappadocian Fathers being the *hypostases* are ontologically equal, but functionally unequal (Wilks, "Ontology," 72).

6. This is unlike Wilks's view of absolute equality of different *hypostases* thus holding to the *ousia* as the unity of the Trinity (Wilks, "Ontology," 72, 82).

Harrison is correct when she says that the essence of the Trinity is ontologically dependent upon the persons of the Trinity.[7] However, when
she argues for more emphasis on the equality of the persons of the Trinity through mutual-self-giving to affirm "full personhood," she does not
describe what is being (mutually) given or shared to all three persons.[8]
Likewise, many constructive pneumatological trinitarians hold to a trinitarian view of oneness like Augustine, where the Spirit is the bond of love
holding the Trinity in tack.[9] In contrast, we hold that the love of God
is like the volition of God where all three persons share in (perfect) love
and express themselves through love. Therefore divine (perfect) love is
self-giving. That means that all three persons express (perfect) love in
their reciprocal relationship toward one another and outwardly in the
soteriological activity toward humans.[10] This view of the Trinity allows
for equality-with-headship, unlike Volf, who attempts to rectify the constitutional and relational qualities of the Trinity by offering "a polycentric
and symmetrical reciprocity of the many," which correlates well with his
ideas for Free Church ecclesiology and congregationalist church structure.[11] That is to say that, while Volf opposes Zizioulas's monarchial view
of the Father in the Trinity, he, like Zizioulas, emphasizes communion
when applying trinitarian theology to ecclesiology to the point that both
Volf and Zizioulas demonstrate a loss of particularity for homogeneity in the church gathering community, that Volf calls the "trinitarian
fellowship."[12]

The purpose of this chapter is to demonstrate three general but
foundational outcomes as a result of trinitarian pneumatology that constitutes the Christian person. These outcomes are seen as participation
in relationship with God, participation in the character of God, and participation in the mission of God. Beginning with the particular persons-
in-relation of the Holy Trinity, the particular persons (Father, Son, Holy

---

7. Harrison, "Zizioulas," 279.

8. Harrison, "Zizioulas," 289–90.

9. Yong, *Spirit-Word-Community*, 62–71; Macchia, *Baptized*, 116–17, 119;
Studebaker, *Pentecost*, 98, 111, 113–17; Snavely, *Life*, 48. Cf. Atkinson states that this
view (Augustinian's bond of love) is not scriptural and the Spirit is not the love between the persons of the Trinity but "the means of expressing the love" that the Father
has for the Son ("an impersonal function of the Spirit") (Atkinson, *Trinity*, 54).

10. 1 John 4:7–21.

11. Volf, *Likeness*, 216–18, 234–39.

12. Volf, *Likeness*, 18, 78–79, 186–89.

Spirit) give and share in mutual will and love (and freedom). From this abundant will, love, and freedom, humans are created in the same image of God. Therefore, this chapter will show that upon a particular human becoming a Christian person through an encounter with the Holy Spirit, their personhood is sustained and further developed through a relationship first with God and then with their world. As shown in chapter 6, God desires to be present with humans. God's presence indwells human lives through the Holy Spirit, making each believer a Christian person. Chapter 6 also showed that mission or commission is an outcome of the personal presence of God. It follows that in this chapter, we revisit the barrier of sin from a trinitarian pneumatological perspective where the personal presence of the Holy Spirit constitutes a Christian person. Second, earthen vessels will serve as a biblical analogy for human beings' post-fall and whose disposition is a marred image of God. We will show that trinitarian pneumatological personhood goes further soteriologically than a forensic justification where there can be interpreted distance between the Justifier and the justified. Third, from an object-subject dialectic, God has a standard of expectation for those whom he relates. That standard is a new character of holy-love through a growing divine-human relationship for the Christian person. However, this character is only nourished through a new set of relationships with God and other humans. Fourth, the results of a new character within the Christian person through a relationship with God are various missions and works that introduce and help sustain a trinitarian pneumatological relationship between God and humans, and humans and humans.

Also, in this chapter, to reach the implications of a trinitarian pneumatological personhood, a Wesleyan theological dialectic will be more prevalent in three ways. First, Wesleyan theological topics on sin and rebirth as recreation will be used to correct Zizioulas's topics of "non-being/non-personal" (i.e., individual, archaeological being) and eucharistic-ecclesiology. Second, Wesleyan theological distinctive on the topics of the Christian life (i.e., holy life), entire sanctification, and holy-love will be reworked through the terms participation, relationship, and character. Third, the Wesleyan expectations of discipleship and evangelism will be blended into mission. Furthermore, the Wesleyan emphasis on the holy life anthropologically understood as the Christian person will be further developed using Zizioulas's persons-as-relation paradigm. From this perspective, we will reconstruct Wesleyan thought, suggesting that the holy life of a Christian person is the personal, relational presence of God in the particular person who in turn (reciprocally) participates in the life of Christ relationally, characteristically, and missionally. However, the Christian person's growth expands throughout the whole Wesleyan *ordo salutis*. There is a *perichoretical* aspect to the indwelling of the Holy Spirit as the indwelling of the Trinity to love God and love others in mutual self-giving love (holy-love).

THE PROBLEM AND SOLUTION TO CHRISTIAN ANTHROPOLOGY

"Sin," says House, "is humanity's chief impediment to glorifying God and enjoying him forever."[13] Carson states, more specifically, the significance on the topic of sin is "There can be no agreement as to what salvation *is* unless there is agreement as to that from which salvation rescues us. The problem and the solution hang together: the one explicates the other."[14] In light of these theological insights, Zizioulas's theology has almost no mention of sin, although he speaks of salvation.[15] For Zizioulas, salvation transforms from a fallen nature (archaeological being) to an eschatological personhood. Therefore, if there is such a thing as sin within Zizioulas's theology, it is explained in philosophical terms as a condition or mode of (non)existence of non-being, non-personal, individual, selfish, autonomous, non-existent, Adam-like, and certainly, an archaic-being. The opposite is true of a saved person, or ecclesial-human in Zizioulas's terms, the Christian is a ("true") being, personal, de-individualized, self-giving, relational, existent, Christ-like, and eschatological.[16] To answer the deficiency of sin in Zizioulas's theology, we need to engage the problem of sin in humans.

An encounter with God through the Holy Spirit transforms the human being so that we become, and are becoming, more Christ-like.[17] When the Holy Spirit encounters humans, we are invited to participate[18]

---

13. House, "Sin," 39.

14. Carson, "Sin's Contemporary Significance," 22.

15. Zizioulas, *Being*, 50.

16. Zizioulas, *Being*, 50, 102–3, 109, 113–16, 132; Zizioulas, "Capacity and Incapacity," 407–33, 424–25; Zizioulas, *Communion*, 213, 214; Zizioulas, *Eucharistic Communion*, 34, 143, 145, 174; Zizioulas, *One and Many*, 91–100.

17. Cross, *Presence*, 15, 17, 18; Jones, *God the Spirit*, 78–83; Carter, *Holy Spirit*, 314–16; Pinnock, *Flame*, 173–77; McFarland, *Why Do You Believe?*, 131.

18. "Participation" used here and throughout is the term for *koinōnia*, which is

in a relationship with God made possible through Jesus Christ and in the Holy Spirit.[19] In this new reconciled relationship, "The old has passed away; behold, the new has come."[20]

What has brought us to this point where human participation in the life of the Trinity is essential to Christian anthropology is first demonstrated in Zizioulas's ontological approach to the doctrine of the Trinity founded on the "Cappadocian revolution" as persons-in-relation or being-as-communion which can bring meaning to being a Christian person.[21] The being of God cannot be reduced solely to divine substance, but rather the being of God is persons, and persons exist in a personal relationship.[22] From this starting point, we can deduce that the Father, the Son, and the Holy Spirit are mutually[23] giving (i.e., participating) in love to one another before the creation of the world.[24] This eternal,

---

the abstract form of *koinōnos* (e.g., "fellow," "participant") and *koinōneō* (e.g., "to share with someone in something he/she has done," "to take part" "to have a share with someone in something which he/she did not have," "to give part," or "to impart"), meaning an especially close bond in "participation," "fellowship," "sharing," or "impartation" expressed in a two-sided relationship. See Hauck, "κοινωνία," 797–98.

19. Basil, *Spirit*, 9.23; Zizioulas, *Being*, 94; Cross, *Presence*, 102–3, 119–21; Pinnock, *Flame*, 151, 152–55; Yarnell, *Holy Spirit*, 103, 104, 105. Torrey, *Holy Spirit*, 50–51, 66–68, 73. Dunn mentions the biblical texts where the Holy Spirit convicts people of sin which leads to conversion, but he stresses the gift of the Holy Spirit comes "*in* conversion" (Dunn, *Baptism*, 94–95).

20. 2 Cor 5:17; Barnett, *2 Corinthians*, 113–14; Owen, *Holy Spirit*, 49–50.

21. Farrow, "Person and Nature," 119; Zizioulas, *Being*, 15–16, 36–41; Zizioulas, *Communion*, 157–58; Zizioulas, "Holy Trinity," 47; Zizioulas, *Lectures*, 50–51.

22. Zizioulas, *Being*, 15, 16, 18, 40–41; Zizioulas, "Capacity and Incapacity," 410–12, 414–18, 419–20; Zizioulas, "Holy Trinity," 47–48, 50–58; Coppedge, *Triune*, 168–81; Cross, *Presence*, 37, 44–47; Kinlaw, *Jesus*, 19–37, 41–46, 68–70; Moltmann, *Trinity*, 4–5, 17–20, 32–33; Volf, *Likeness*, 181–89, 204–13. Richard of St. Victor says, "a person proceeds from a person" (Richard of St. Victor, *Trinity*, 5.6, 7). Leithart says, "Relations constitute each Person as the Person he is, and so mutual relations constitute the Trinity as Trinity" (Leithart, "No Son, No Father," 120).

23. The significance and use of "mutuality" is found in Gunton who says that the persons of the Trinity "mutually constitute one another" (Gunton, *One, Three, Many*, 191).

24. Ps 102:25–27; Heb 13:8; Rev 1:4, 8; cf. 1 John 4:8–9 ("God is love"). Augustine, *Trinity*, 6.5.7; 9.1.1—9.10.15; Coppenger, "Community of Mission," 61–62; Rahner, *Trinity*, 22; Zizioulas, *Being*, 16, 18; Zizioulas, "Capacity and Incapacity," 410, 414, 426, 428–29, 433–34, 436–37; Fox, *God as Communion*, 50–51, 137–42; Gunton, *Creator*, 9, 26, 176; Reeves, *Delighting*, 19–38, 40–47, 94–96. For *perichoresis*, see John of Damascus, *Faith*, 4.28; Torrance, *Doctrine*, 102–4, 210, 244–46; Torrance, *Faith*, 234; cf. LaCugna, argues that *perichoresis* is not an intradivine relationship of the persons

mutual, self-giving love can be described as communication and com-munion between the persons of God;[25] thus, the Trinity, *ad intra*, is in a state of (holy) community and act in (holy) communion.[26] What is more, trinitarian activity, *ad extra*, is demonstrated as holy, selfless, love toward others, through creation in general and toward an other in particular.[27]

Second, the Holy Trinity created a universe, and within that uni-verse, a specific world has been designed for which a man and a woman were created in the image and likeness of God (e.g., good, holy, and incorrupt).[28] The original man and woman were given what nothing else created were given, by grace,[29] Adam and Eve were given God's intimate "breath of life" (Heb.: *nišᵉmāṯ ḥăyyîm*; Gk.: *pnoēn zōēs*), which appears to be either the Spirit of God or at least an analogy for the Spirit of God.[30] However, the "breath of life" used in Gen 2:7 shows intimacy

of the Trinity, but rather *perichoresis* reflects a divine-human relationship/dance (LaCugna, *God*, 274). Also, Cross, in similar fashion as LaCugna, illustrates the Trin-ity's *perichoresis* by the phrase "making room for the other" (Cross, *Presence*, 50–54).

25. Gunton, *One, Three, Many*, 223.

26. John of Damascus, *Faith*, 3.4. Fiddes says, "there is no other God than one who is open to others in outward-going love, and the God who *makes* communion in the world must already *be* communion" (Fiddes, *Participating*, 6). Zizioulas says, "God's being is communion in itself" (Zizioulas, *Being*, 94). Also, Zizioulas, *Being*, 15–18, 21, 44, 81–82, 83, 94, 101–5, 110–14, 211–14, 226; Zizioulas, *Lectures*, 115–16; Coppedge, *Triune*, 127–48; Cross, *Presence*, 45, 47–50; Gunton, "Relation and Rela-tivity," 97; Kinlaw, *Jesus*, 32–34, 38–41, 43–45, 73, 83, 93; Moltmann, *Trinity*, 57–60; Reeves, *Delighting*, 94–98, 102–4. For an article on the topic of non-hierarchical mu-tuality within the Trinity written against Bruce Ware and Wayne Grudem's view that the Son is "eternally subordinate," see Leithart, "No Son, No Father," 109–22. In fact the entire book, *Trinity without Hierarchy: Reclaiming Nicene Orthodoxy in Evangelical Theology*, edited by Bird and Harrower, is a polemical collection of sixteen contribu-tors from the disciplines of biblical studies, historical theology, and systematic theol-ogy in response to Ware and Grudem's view that the Son is "eternally subordinate" to the Father.

27. Basil, *Spirit*, 18.47; Zizioulas, *Being*, 106, 134–35; Zizioulas, "Capacity and Incapacity," 408, 410, 435, 446; Zizioulas, *Eucharistic Communion*, 12–24; Ziziou-las, *Lectures*, 116–17; Coppedge, *Triune*, 149–65; Gunton, "Relation and Relativity," 97–100, 103–9; Kinlaw, *Jesus*, 28–32, 43–46; 64–70, 97–102, 129, 133–35; Marshall, *Dance*, 9–12, 13, 45–48, 74–77, 158–60.

28. Gen 1. Athanasius, *Incarnation*, 3.3; Augustine, *Trinity*, 1.7.14; 7.6.12; 12.6.6; Gunton, *Creator*, 18–20, 166–71, 193–96, 208, 210; Irenaeus, *Heresies*, 4.6.6; 4.20.2–4; 5.6.1; 5.18.1–3; Leclerc, *Discovering*, 58; Richard, *Trinity*, 5.6, 7; 6.1, 23; Middleton, *Liberating Image*, 55–60; Torrance, *Doctrine*, 212–14, 216–18, 240–41.

29. Lossky, *Mystical Theology*, 117–18.

30. Gen 2:7; cf. Gen 1:30; 7:15, 22. Irenaeus uses Isa 42:5 and 57:16 to show that

from a personal God for humans above all other creations illustrated by

the breath of life is created, temporal, and common among other living creatures in contrast to the Holy Spirit who is "peculiar to God" and later in the NT is the source of adoption for believers into the family of God (Irenaeus, *Heresies*, 5.12.2). Levison speaks of "a holy spirit" which is breathed into the original humans and throughout his work the Scriptures, Jewish literature, and other ancient literature are held as equally inclusive to show that "a" holy spirit is given to offer life and virtue (Levison, *Filled*, 15, 17–18, 22–23, 26, 28, 102, 142–51, 202–7, 220–21, 237, 247, 267, 309–16, 369–70, 386–88, 424). Cross does not equate the breath of God with the Holy Spirit in 2:7, but only says that the creation of humans by the hands and breath of God is unique to anything else created (Cross, *Presence*, 65). Marshall opposes interpreting the breath of God as the Spirit of God; instead, she differentiates them by saying, "The Spirit of God evokes the spirits of all that are created, enabling them to participate in the perichoretic movement of God with creation, the dance of the universe" (Marshall, *Dance*, 25). In opposition, Sanders says "spirit" means "breath" and "the word 'breathing' has been applied to the relation of origin of the Spirit" (Sanders, *Deep*, 97). Philo interpreted the "breath of God" as the divine rational Spirit given to humans supplying them with spiritual-ethical wisdom. Philo's interpretation was more *dunamis* (power) and less personal (Turner, *Power*, 124–25). Augustine shows that he understands the LXX use of *pnoēn* (wind, breath) rather than *pneuma* (wind, breath, spirit), yet clearly states that humans were given life by the Holy Spirit or "the uncreated Creator Spirit" (Augustine, *City of God*, 13.24). Thompson sees the resurrected Jesus blowing his breath upon the disciples (John 20:22–23) as a parallel to Gen 2:7 comparing creation with new creation (Thompson, "Breath of Life," 71). This in fact is Dunn's point against Pentecostal theology that says the Holy Spirit comes to the believer sometime after conversion. However, on the critique of Pentecostal theology, Atkinson clarifies the theological point of baptism in the Spirit and points out Dunn's error (in Atkinson's view) as the difference between Luke's use of the term and Paul's use of the term concluding that certainly Pentecostals believe that Christians are indwelled with the Spirit at initiation (Atkinson, *Baptism*, 92, 103–8, 120–22). Dunn finds in the LXX the use of *enephusēsen* ("breathe upon") in Gen 2:7; Ezek 37:9; Wis 15:11 to describe the creation of humans. John uses the same word in his Gospel to signify the new creation in humans (John 20:22). Furthermore, Dunn argues the unique and transitional period of time between the resurrection and Pentecost was included conversion for the disciples (e.g., Johannine theology and saving belief includes receiving the Spirit) and they initially received the Holy Spirit (*Baptism*, 179–82). Similarly, Köstenberger recognizes the use of *enephusēsen* in Gen 2:7 and John 20:22, saying that "God breathes his Spirit into Adam, which constitutes him as a 'living being.'" However, in the parallel comparison with John 20:22, Köstenberger does not say that the Holy Spirit is given or that particular people are constituted as new creations, but rather, "Jesus constitutes them as the new messianic community, in anticipation of the outpouring of the Spirit subsequent to his ascension" (Köstenberger, *John's Gospel and Letters*, 400). Congar, clearly associates the breath of God with the Spirit of God (Congar, *Holy Spirit*, 1.1). Reeves states that the Spirit's breathing out life "is always the Spirit's work" and not only in the beginning at creation, but the Spirit also revitalizes, refreshes, gives fruit, beauty, etc. (Reeves, *Delighting*, 51). Yarnell, associates the Spirit of God with the *being* of the Holy Spirit and the breath of God with the *activity* of God, therefore, the breath of God is the Holy Spirit (Yarnell, *Holy Spirit*, 8, 12, 52, 70). Pinnock, who attributes all the shift in the scriptural text to God's personal name.[31] In Genesis 1, the transcendent Creator (as an attribute) is named God (*'ĕlōhîm*) as the universe and world are created, and in Genesis 2, the immanent Creator (as an attribute) is named YHWH (added to *ᵉlōhîm*) as Adam and Eve are created.[32] The "breath of life" into the dust-formed man caused Adam to become a "living person" (*ḥayyā nĕpĕš*).[33] Furthermore, the image and the likeness of God upon humans are multifaceted in meaning,[34] and one of those meanings is that the human being is not autonomous but rather was created to be in relationship with another.[35] The existential freedom

of creation to the Spirit following Gen 1:2 also ties together the breath of life with the person of the Holy Spirit as explained by Jesus, "'It is the spirit that gives life'" (John 6:63) (Pinnock, *Flame*, 50, 52, 73). Hamilton shows that the more popular word *rûăḥ* (nearly four hundred times in the OT) used to describe God, man, animals, and false gods is *not* used in Gen 2:7, but rather the word *nᵉšāmâ* (twenty-five times in the OT) is used and is a word reserved only for YHWH and humans (except for an indirect use in Gen 7:22), thus, "it is man [i.e., humans], and man [i.e., humans] alone, who is the recipient of the divine breath" (Hamilton, *Genesis: 1–17*, 159).

31. For the theological significance for the name of God, see Brunner, *Christian Doctrine*, 117–27. Fiddes shows that the OT does not have an "extended personality" of God, but rather God is present through personifications and "breath of God" or "breath of life" are personifications used to indicate the Holy Spirit (Fiddes, *Participating*, 254–59).

32. Duvall and Hayes, *Presence*, 15. Duvall and Hayes do not equate the "breath of God" with the person of the Holy Spirit, but rather stop short by saying God's activity reveals God's "spatial presence" (Duvall and Hayes, *Presence*, 15) and "God's relational presence" (Duvall and Hayes, *Presence*, 331). See also Davidson, "Creation Theme," 184.

33. Wolff, *Anthropology*, 22. Wolff shows seven OT uses for the term *nĕpĕš*, including: throat, neck, desire, soul, life, person, and pronouns (Wolff, *Anthropology*, 10–25).

34. Brueggemann, *Theology*, 452–53; Green, *Body, Soul, Human Life*, 62; Grenz, *Social God*, 141–82; Gunton, *Creator*, 196–98; Jewett, *Man as Male and Female*, 23–40. Lossky, *Mystical Theology*, 115–16; McConville, *Being Human*, 11–29, 35–45, 190; Oswalt, *Myths*, 69–70; Schwarz, *Human Being*, 22, 23, 28, 343. Taylor, *Formulation*, 31–33. Calvin states that Adam "possessed the fullness of the Spirit" in reference to Gen 1:27, but does not mention this point in reference to Gen 2:7 (Calvin, *Genesis*, 16).

35. Collins writes, "In its most general sense, the *imago Dei* must be understood in a *relational* way as the very emblem of holy love. 'God is love,' Wesley observes, 'accordingly man at his creation was full of love, which was the sole principle of all his tempers, thoughts, words, and actions.' In other words, both the mind and will of Adam and Eve, as well as their desires, were all properly oriented to God as their highest end. Being in proper *relation* to the Most High, they rightly enjoyed the fruits of serenity, grace, and innocence" (Collins, *Wesley*, 51–52). Routledge says the phrase "image and likeness of God" implies that human beings: "share spiritual characteristics

of the Trinity constitutes self-giving love (*ekstasis*) and persons (*hyposta-sis*) of the Trinity reflected in the creation of humans.[36] The original hu-mans were free to live and act among the *givens* of their environment.[37] The beauty of this personal-relational creation model (i.e., *imago Dei*) was that humans were invited to participate in the holy community and holy communion with the Holy Trinity.[38] Furthermore, these human be-ings were giving love to one another through mutual self-giving love (as

---

with God," "are made for relationship with God," "are given authority to rule on behalf of God," and "made to reflect the glory of God" (Routledge, *Theology*, 140–41). Cross, *Presence*, 69, 71; Farrow, *Ascension*, 59–60; Green, *Body, Soul, Human Life*, 62–65; Grenz, *Social God*, 173–77, 183–85, 268; Käsemann, *Romans*, 218–19; Leclerc, *Dis-covering*, 158; Kinlaw, *Jesus*, 101; Oswalt, *Myths*, 70; Wolff, *Anthropology*, 159–61. For Zizioulas, the image of God (or sometimes "image of the Trinity") in human beings is freedom, and freedom leads toward an *ecstatic* existence which is demonstrated in self-giving love and found in community where the church-community reflects the Trinitarian-community. See Zizioulas, *Being*, 15, 44–46, 50; Zizioulas, "Capacity and Incapacity," 424–26, 428–29, 446; Zizioulas, *Communion*, 39; Zizioulas, *One and Many*, 33, 34, 36–37, 53, 71, 79–80.

36. Zizioulas, *Being*, 15–16, 87–88; Zizioulas, "Capacity and Incapacity," 408–9; Zizioulas, *One and Many*, 404; Grenz, *Rediscovering*, 138–39, 142; Anatolios, "Person-hood," 147–64; Rosenthal, *One God or Three?*, 25.

37. Zizioulas, *Eucharist Communion*, 167, 168–69.

38. Anderson, *Presence*, 69–70, 189, 192–202. Duvall and Hays, *Presence*, 1, 17–19, 325, 326, 331. Johnson connects the OT human person (*nĕpĕš*) containing all of the complexities (i.e., "psychological whole") with household (*bāyĭt*) in which both indicate a center of power. Therefore, since humans were created in the image and likeness of God, humans model God who shows Godself as both a corporate Spirit (*rûăḥ*, i.e., God is Spirit) and as a particular Holy Spirit (*rûăḥ*) as one member (per-sonality) of the household or court of God, indicating The-one-and-the-many within the Godhead (Johnson, *One and the Many*, 1–2, 4, 7, 16). Brueggemann states, "to me the central concern of Israel regarding humanity: namely, that the human person is *a person in relation to Yahweh*, who lives in an intense mutuality with Yahweh" (Bruegge-mann, *Theology*, 453). Plantinga calls God "a radiant and hospitable community, of three persons" (Plantinga, *Not the Way*, 12). Kruger says, "Why this is so, why God is this way, why the Father, Son and Spirit set the fullness of their love and lavish grace upon us and determined such a glorious destiny of us, can only be answered by peer-ing into the mutual love the Father and Son and Spirit" (Kruger, *Jesus*, 19). See also Coppedge, *Portraits*, 153–54; Duvall and Hays, *Presence*, 17, 189; LaCugna, *God*, 249; Lossky, *Mystical Theology*, 121–26. One suggestion for the end of Gen 2 with the men-tion that Adam and Eve were shamelessly naked is to show that there was no barrier between them. Thus, the contrast is found in Gen 3:9–11 where Adam and Eve hide themselves from YHWH-Elohim as there became a barrier between themselves and YHWH-Elohim as a result of their sin (Hamilton, *Genesis: 1–17*, 181, 193). See also, Shults's presentation of Barth's "I-Thou" relationality in connection with the *imago Dei* (Shults, *Anthropology*, 124–31, 217–20).

opposed to self-love, illustrated as *cor incurvatus ad se)*[39] as they were designed and created.[40] That is to say, their concern and love were modeled after their Creator: other-oriented, rather than defensive (or fearful) of others.[41] Therefore, in the created earthly environment, there was a holy community by which each person was mutually giving in selfless love to the other.[42] This holy community and communion were demonstrated by humans living and thriving in an existence of mutual self-giving love with God and with each other as abundant life.[43]

Third, the freedom given to the original humans on that fateful day of original sin was exercised in a manner opposite of mutual self-giving love.[44] In and of itself, Adam's transgression was freedom toward individual self-love and the lie that humans can live independent from God.[45] Another way of saying it is that Adam and Eve willfully chose

39. Luther, *Romans*, 245, 291, 313, 345, 346, 513. Also, Gregor, *Philosophical Anthropology*, 61.

40. Wolff, *Anthropology*, 169, 171–72. Kinlaw presents an overview of the biblical nuptial metaphor to show the "deep personal intimacy" that God desires with humans (Kinlaw, *Jesus*, 57–64, 67–68). Also, Anderson, *Presence*, 141–77; Zizioulas, "Capacity and Incapacity," 407–9, 433; Gunton, *One, Three, Many*, 217n5; Kruger, *Jesus*, 23–24.

41. Zizioulas, *Being*, 43, 51; Zizioulas, *Communion*, 1–2, 4–5, 9, 18, 26, 55, 86; Zizioulas, *One and Many*, 22, 32–33, 182. Also, Buber, *I and Thou*, 64, 69–70; Pannenberg, *Anthropology*, 85, 87–88, 95, 119, 244, 258–65; Shults, *Anthropology*, 82–83.

42. Duvall and Hays, *Presence*, 15–19; Dyrnes, *Themes*, 81–83; Eichrodt, *Man*, 35–36; Gunton, *One, Three, Many*, 225, 227.

43. John 10:10; Anderson, *Presence*, 69–70; Zizioulas, *Being*, 44; Dyrnes, *Themes*, 83–84; Gunton, *One, Three, Many*, 217, 230; John of Damascus, *Faith*, 2.11; Dunning, *Reflecting*, 77–84, 85–95. Irenaeus, *Heresies*, 4.20.3–4; McKnight, *Open*, 56. Working backward from the NT to the OT as a theological answer to what is being renewed in Col 3:10, Webster answers that the renewed image of the self's creator is that fellowship (*koinōnia*) that constitutes sanctification through an obedient life (Webster, *Holiness*, 85). Cf. Macmurray, *Self*, 174, 220.

44. Original sin understood theologically as "personal will" rather than "impersonal law" is more in line with the direction of love (outward or inward) and freedom found in humans created in the image and likeness of God. See Eichrodt, *Man*, 24–26; Oden, *God*, 284.

45. Zizioulas, *Being*, 43–44; Dyrnes, *Themes*, 101. Taylor calls Adam and Eve's sin, "self-separation" (Taylor, *Formulation*, 52, 53–54). Adam and Eve's sin which resulted in broken fellowship with God began turning them back to *nothing* from which they had come (Athanasius, *Incarnation*, 4.2–6). For a discussion on sin as the misuse of freewill, see Mascall, *Via Media*, 42, 45–46, 82. Green intersects natural science (esp. neurobiology) and the Scriptures to conclude that freewill or choice is not necessarily abstract but rather is somewhat determined by human character, disposition, social culture, relationships, and contextual-self-reflexive contemplation (Green, *Body, Soul*,

individuality over community with God, whether or not they fully understood the extent of their actions.[46] For Zizioulas, individualism is irrational as it is a state of non-being. To be, or to be a person, is to be in relation-with-another (i.e., personhood). Therefore, sin is ultimately individualism because it claims autonomy that a person cannot have and exist. Zizioulas desires to de-individualize the church and people by offering a theology of Christ who is pneumatalogically constituted.[47] The selfish act of self-indulgence, self-love, and self-desire severed this holy community into two communities.[48] Humans could no longer participate in the holy community between God and humans as they did before and, in effect, were ex-communicated from God and their paradise setting.[49] Secondly, the human community from that point on would be

Human Life, 72–105).

46. McConville, Being Human, 64–67.

47. Zizioulas, Being, 109, 111, 112, 113; Zizioulas, Communion, 6, 244–45; Zizioulas, One and Many, 142, 143.

48. Kruger, Jesus, 25. Grudem argues against what he calls a non-biblical definition of sin as "selfishness." However, he makes one exception as he notes an out-of-print book (Strong, Systematic Theology), which was widely circulated in its day, used the definition of "selfishness" for sin in a specific way that renders it theologically biblical as "a fundamental and positive choice of preference of self instead of God, as the object of affection and the supreme end of being" (Strong, Systematic Theology, 572). Grudem, Systematic Theology, 491.

49. Routledge says, "In the OT, physical death also has a spiritual dimension: it brings relationship with God to an end. Similarly life is more than mere existence: it is also about continuing to enjoy the blessings of God's presence (Deut. 30:15–16, 19–20). The real threat and real punishment here is expulsion from the garden, and with it exclusion from the blessings of being in God's presence" (Routledge, Theology, 152). Basil, Spirit, 15.35; Duvall and Hays, Presence, 19–20. The OT shows both a theological and anthropological significance in connecting people with their place, land, and environment along with memory which serves as self-understanding (McConville, Being Human, 97–105, 110–11). Therefore, excommunication, exile, or expulsion (e.g., from the Garden Paradise, from the presence of a king [Absalom from David, 2 Sam 14:24], from Jerusalem) is a curse of death, or separation from blessing. For an explanation on the significance of God's people exiled from God's Land, see Hertzberg, Judaism, 208–17. Also dealt with in Hertzberg is that although there is a separation between the people and the land, God's presence (Shekhinah) is enslaved with his people (ref., Deut 30:3; 1 Sam 2:27; 2 Sam 7:23; Ps 91:15; Isa 43:14; 63:10; Jer 49:38, Hertzberg, Judaism, 210). Thus, God always leaves a way of redemption/restoration for his people (Hertzberg, Judaism, 221–28). On excommunication, exile, expulsion, etc., see Brueggemann, Jeremiah, 14, 17, 488–90; VanGemeren, Interpreting the Prophetic Word, 57, 183, 314, 383; Dunn, "Excommunication," 364–65. For a discussion on šālaḥ (expelled) and gāraš (drive out, or divorce), see Hamilton, Genesis: 1–17, 209. Kruger says, "The Fall of Adam constitutes a staggering communication

wrecked (evil, unholy, corrupted) by personal: agendas, passions, desires, and gain.[50] This degree of corruption, and more, fill the human void where the Holy Spirit as the (spiritual) life of the person once lived because sin *misguides* love causing humans to become egocentric.[51] God's image in humans was marred, and the secular became the identity of life where the sacred and holy once reigned.[52] The result of sin[53] is death, rot, disease, pain, destruction, and absence from the presence of God,[54] and without rescue, could lapse into non-being.[55]

Fourth, something constitutive of human beings was lost[56] or dead due to Adam and Eve exercising their will to please themselves, thus breaking God's law and sinning (*parabasis*).[57] Human history reveals

problem for God. For now there is a great ugly ditch between who God actually is and who Adam *believes* God is" (Kruger, *Jesus*, 27).

50. Eph 5:3–6; Col 3:5–8; Grudem, *Systematic Theology*, 493; Hauerwas, "Sinsick," 7–15; Kinlaw, *Jesus*, 143; Plantinga, *Not the Way*, 39–51.

51. Augustine, *City of God*, 14.7; Pannenberg, *Anthropology*, 81–82, 85–86, 106, 109, 146, 201, 293–94, 297–98, 407–8, 528–29; Shults, *Anthropology*, 87, 89, 90–91; Zizioulas, *One and Many*, 186, 402–6, 410. Wesley says, "but he who had been made in the image of God, afterwards became mortal, when the more powerful Spirit was separated from him" (Wesley, "Holy Spirit," 513).

52. Athanasius argues that what humans lost at the fall was their knowledge of God, Athanasius, *Incarnation*, §11; Taylor, *Formulation*, 33–39, 83; Kinlaw, *Jesus*, 112–13, 117–20; Purkiser, *Exploring*, 209–10. Wesley claims that the natural image of God was marred in humans (Collins shows that Wesley held to a threefold understanding of the *imago Dei* in humans: natural, political, and moral image) adversely affecting human understanding, will, and liberty (Collins, *Wesley*, 51–64).

53. For a biblical overview of terms (Hebrew and Greek) for "sin," see Taylor, *Formulation*, 62–65. For a list of terms (English) identified as "sinful" in the NT, see Taylor, *Formulation*, 66–68.

54. Rom 5:12; 6:23; 8:18–23; Kinlaw, *Jesus*, 117–19; Kruger, *Jesus*, 21–22; Taylor, *Formulation*, 47–48, 54–61, 89–91; Wiley and Culbertson, *Christian Theology*, 171–73, 179. Cf. Eichrodt, *Man*, 36.

55. Athanasius, *Incarnation*, §§4–5 (i.e., "non-existence"); Zizioulas, "Capacity and Incapacity," 422–24.

56. Calvin's list of what was lost in humans after the original sin include: liberty, righteousness, goodness, glory, divine communication, free will, the blessed life (i.e., faith, love to God and others, righteousness, holiness), intellect, and knowledge of spiritual things (Calvin, *Institutes*, 2.2.1, 12, 22). For Arminius "original righteousness" and "primeval holiness" were lost (Stanglin and McCall, *Arminius*, 147). For Lutherans "goodness" was lost (Volz, "Human Participation," 85–86).

57. Rom 5:14 ("like the sin [*parabasis*] of Adam"). The term *parabasis* for sin "denotes 'sin in its relation to law'" rather than the typically used *hamartia* (esp. Rom 5:12–14) which is used more generically as "shortcomings" or "faults" (Taylor,

the striving for self-fulfillment in the human void.[58] However, despite human individuality and hunger to rule the self which is the original temptation and sin that leads to death, it is the Father's will that no one would be destroyed or live outside his presence.[59] Therefore, in mutual self-giving love, the Father sent the Son to reveal the Father's love.[60] The Son in mutual self-giving love was obedient to the Father[61] and became a servant to humans and died to (destroy) sin so that upon belief, repentance, and forgiveness of sins, the human being can be justified and created anew in the image and likeness of God.[62] God the Father raised Jesus Christ back to life in mutual self-giving love through the indwelling Holy Spirit.[63] In mutual self-giving love, the Father sends the Holy

---

Formulation, 62–63). Thus, where there is a law there is the will of the lawgiver and a will of the law-receiver (e.g., Heb 2:2) (Schneider, "παραβαίνω," 739–40). Purkiser et al., *God, Man, & Salvation*, 281–84. For scriptural references for either being spiritually dead while being physically alive, or physically dead and spiritually alive, see e.g., John 5:24; 6:50; 8:51–52; Eph 2:1, 5; Col 2:13; 1 John 3:14.

58. Gunton, *One, Three, Many*, 64–65. Gen 6:11; Pss 10:3; 78:30–31; Prov 7:18; 14:14; 18:1; 31:4; Isa 2:7–8; Ezek 7:19; 27:25; Gal 5:16, 24; Eph 2:3; Phil 2:21; Col 3:5; 1 Tim 6:9; 2 Tim 3:1–5; 4:3; 2 Pet 4–22. Self-fulfillment in history is specifically found in humanistic ideals (e.g., secular humanism, materialism) and existential philosophy in the modern era. See Noebel, *Understanding the Times*, 59–64, 101–6, 137–44, 179–86, 225–30, 259–64, 297–302, 331–36, 369–74, 405–10; Blackham, *Six Existentialist Thinkers*; Kierkegaard, *Training*, 53–62; Schaeffer, *Escape*, 10, 18, 26–28, 31, 37, 42–45, 48, 80–82; Wood, *God and History*, 126–33, 155–62, 205–15. For the spread of humanism in Europe, see Grimm, *Reformation*, 52–72.

59. Ps 67:2; Ezek 18:23, 32; 33:11; 1 Tim 2:4, 6; 4:10; Titus 2:11; 2 Pet 3:9. The Ezekiel passages in particular emphasizes personal-individual accountability to repent for sins. Chisholm addresses scholarly debate as to how this is reconciled with so many OT texts that deal with corporate sin and repentance. He concludes that both individual and corporate responsibility must be held in balance (Chisholm, *Prophets*, 254–55, 276).

60. John 3:16–17; Rom 5:8; Eph 2:4–5; 2 Thess 2:16; 1 John 3:1; 4:9, 10, 14; Ware, *Father, Son, & Holy Spirit*, 53–55, 77–78, 105. While Ware shows the trinitarian love *ad extra* for salvation, his primary emphasis is *ad intra* and the eternal submission of the Son to the Father (Ware, *Father, Son, & Holy Spirit*, 72–87). Sanders, *Deep*, 91–92, 94, 126–27; Torrance, *Doctrine*, 244–46.

61. Phil 2:5–8. See Kinlaw, *Mind*, 99–101.

62. For Christ dying to sin, see Rom 4:25; 8:3; 2 Cor 5:21; Gal 3:13; Oden, *Justification Reader*, 60–62. For new creation/creatures in Christ, see Rom 6:4; 2 Cor 5:17. Athanasius, *Incarnation*, 44.1–7; Fee, *Empowering*, 533; Gunton, *Creator*, 169, 170–71.

63. Fee interprets Rom 8:11 as "If the Spirit of him [God the Father] who raised Jesus from the dead dwells in you, he [God the Father] who raised Christ Jesus from the dead will also give life to your mortal bodies through his Spirit who dwells in you" (ESV). Fee shows that the Holy Spirit is not the agent of resurrection, but rather the

Spirit through the Son so that human beings can become new creatures
(or a new creation) and live again in holy communion with God and
other humans.[64] Therefore, the Holy Spirit, whose personhood is only
understood through the trinitarian-relationship,[65] likewise constitutes
Christian anthropology by indwelling the Christian person[66] making
that person a complete person while drawing the human person to participate in a relationship with God[67] and with others as humans were
originally designed to live in holy community.[68] The holy community

Father is the agent of resurrection and will do so to those who have been indwelled by
the Holy Spirit. Therefore, the Holy Spirit becomes the guarantor of Christian hope (2
Cor 5:5). Fee declares that this interpretation "demonstrates the thoroughly Trinitarian presupposition of Paul's way of talking about 'salvation in Christ'" (Fee, *Empowering*, 554). See also Fee, *Empowering*, 552–54, 808–11.

64. Harrison, "Zizioulas," 287; Cross, *Presence*, 8, 10, 11, 17; new humanity and
new communion: 86–92. Wiley and Culbertson show that the Holy Spirit was present
and operative in the life of Adam, making him holy and having "communion" with
God, but after his sin, the Holy Spirit departed, and Adam was unholy and excommunicated from the presence of God (Wiley and Culbertson, *Christian Theology*,
159, 165, 173). On this point of "away from the presence of God" see the correlation
of the cherubim guarding the eastern side of the Garden and the generational move
eastward (away from) in Duvall and Hays, *Presence*, 19–20. Eichrodt, *Man*, 75–76;
Shults, *Anthropology*, 241. Green states, "The renewal of the human being in the divine
image is profoundly personal, and embraces the human person in his or her totality.
This means that (trans)formation is fully embodied within a nest of relationships, a
community" (Green, *Body, Soul, Human Life*, 69). The "new creation" and "holy community" that we are talking about here is Christ's restoration made possible by his first
coming recognized through a dualistic eschatology of "fulfillment without consummation," or "this age and the age to come," or "the almost but not yet" (Ladd, *Presence*,
114–21, 195–217). This restored community-of-relations is temporal in this world and
is a shadow of things to come (chapter 6, "Personal Presence: A Shadow of Things to
Come").

65. Basil writes against the Pneumatomachians, who claimed the Holy Spirit was
created, "the Holy Spirit is inseparable and wholly incapable of being parted from the
Father and the Son" in *Spirit*, 16.37. Cross, *Presence*, 120; Gunton, *One, Three, Many*,
205; Shults, *Anthropology*, 92–93; Torrance, *Doctrine*, 147–55.

66. Basil, *Spirit*, 22.53; 26.63; Irenaeus, *Heresies*, 4.20.6; Cross, *Presence*, 18, 121;
Fee, *Empowering*, 134–37, 526–28, 545–48, 552–54, 809; Kinlaw, *Jesus*, 121; Yarnell,
points out two "mutual indwelling[s]" in Romans 8; 1) "the Spirit with Christ and
God," i.e., "God with God"; 2) "God in believers" through the Holy Spirit (Yarnell, *Holy
Spirit*, 105–6, 113, 119).

67. 1 Cor 2:12–16; 6:17–20; 2 Cor 1:22; Cross, *Presence*, 11, 57, 60–63; Dyrness,
Themes, 207–8; Marshall, *Dance*, 6–9, 31, 39–45. See McIntyre, *Pneumatology*, 172–83.
For an emphasis on spirit-christology and the implications to human participation in
the life of God, see Lampe, "Holy Spirit," 111–30.

68. Eph 4:1–16; Cross, *Presence*, 50–52; Duvall and Hays, *Presence*, 335–36. See

is founded on Jesus Christ and is united by the Holy Spirit who indwells particular Christian people whose gathering make-up the one Church.[69] God's saving act for divine-human reconciliation,[70] which requires a positive human response to Christ's self-sacrifice, brings about a change in humans as persons-in-relationships and wholeness within human beings.[71] Since the notion of persons-in-relation is vital for Christian anthropology, and humans, given the gospel invitation, are invited into the life-giving relationship with the Trinity (*perichoresis*)[72] through the Holy Spirit, the question remains: in what ways do humans participate in this relationship of communion with the Trinity?[73]

In the same way that the activity of the Trinity, *ad extra*, reveals the interrelationship of the Trinity, *ad intra*; likewise, as Jesus taught, the externally visible behavior of a human person reveals the inner-life of the person.[74] Therefore, human activity of participation in the life of God becomes a response to an *encounter* with God, who is personal-relational and transforms the human person.[75] The transformed believer participates in relationship with God, the character of God, and in the mission

McConville's OT concept of "double embodiment" as the individual person in particular totality, and the individual person embodied in society (McConville, *Being Human*, 47–59). Shults, *Anthropology*, 89; McIntyre, *Pneumatology*, 183–85.

69. Congar, *Holy Spirit*, 2.1.1; 2.1.2.

70. Purkiser et al., *God, Man, & Salvation*, 403–5; 2 Cor 5:14–21.

71. Zizioulas says, "Consequently salvation is identified with the realization of personhood in man" (Zizoulas, *Being*, 50; cf. 211–12). Cross, *Presence*, 102–3; Jones, *God the Spirit*, 43; Harrison, "Zizioulas," 285; Hughes, "Beholding the Beholder," 131, 132. Kinlaw, *Jesus*, 97; LaCugna, *God*, 265; Leclerc, *Discovering*, 156–59; Levison, *Filled*, 55–58. Farrow demonstrates in Irenaeus an anthropology of becoming through communion with Christ through the Holy Spirit (Farrow, *Ascension*, 51, 59).

72. John 13:20; 14:16–17, 26; 15:16; 16:12–15; 17:21; Cross, *Presence*, 37, 103; LaCugna, *God*, 274; Marshall, *Dance*, 6–14; Volf, *Likeness*, 208–13. Marshall asks, "Can we expand the image [of *perichoresis*] so that there is room for humanity—even for the whole of creation—to join in this dance within God's own life?" While we agree with Marshall's construction of *perichoresis* and the Holy Spirit as the contact for humans to join in the life of the Trinity, we do not agree with her further construction that *perichoresis* and the Holy Spirit is the connection for "all of creation," thus placing human beings on the same plane as all creation, since humans are unique in "all creation" and were given dominion over the created material world (Gen 1:28). See Marshall, "Participating," 145.

73. McEwan, "Continual Enjoyment," 60; Käsemann, *Romans*, 218–19; Zizioulas, *Being*, 94; cf. Harrison, "Zizioulas," 282, 283.

74. Matt 12:34; 15:18; 23:27–28. France, *Matthew*, 586–87, 875.

75. Cross, *Presence*, 119–21, 190–91, 205–8.

of God. These three illustrations of participation serve as essential examples of a transformed life.

PARTICIPATION IN RELATIONSHIP WITH GOD

The first illustration of a transformed life is human participation in relationship with God. An ontologically transformed person into a Christian person results from a relationship with God through an encounter with the Holy Spirit.[76] The problem is that the marred image of God after the original sin left humans excommunicated from the presence of God, resulting in a spiritual void of incompleteness in every human being.[77] Zizioulas connects the transformed life and participation with God through the event of the Eucharist.[78] Furthermore, some biblical scholars like Brown and O'Day have opened up sacramental interpretations in Johannine literature, which may prove enriching at one point but may miss the intended meaning at another point.[79] Illustrated in this way, while there might be an allusion to eucharistic symbolism in the story of the wedding at Cana of Galilee, the reality is that Jesus's glory (John 2:11) is that he is the Christ who has come to transform (save) lives.[80] This transformation signifies less to functional activity and more to relational being-ness. For instance, John records Jesus's first sign signifying his glory as the Son of God taking place at a wedding banquet in Cana of Galilee.[81] The drama unfolds as Mary, Jesus's mother, notifies Jesus that the wine has run out (v. 3). John signals to his audience the more profound significance of the story with Jesus's words, "My hour has not come" (v. 4), and Mary's command to the servants, "Do whatever he tells you" (v. 5). In the Johannine genre, with the grammatical use of double

76. Wesley, "Way," 77–80, 86; Wesley, "Marks," 212–23; Wesley, "Witness of the Spirit (Discourse 1)," 111–23; Wesley, "Holy Spirit," 508–12, 514–20.

77. Basil, *Spirit*, 15.35; Brueggemann, *Jeremiah*, 14, 17, 488–90; Duvall and Hays, *Presence*, 19–20; Hertzberg, *Judaism*, 208–17; Kruger, *Jesus*, 27; McConville, *Being Human*, 97–105, 110–11; VanGemeran, *Interpreting the Prophetic Word*, 57, 183, 314, 383.

78. Zizioulas, *Being*, 20–21; 143–69, 215–17, 247; Zizioulas, *Eucharist*, 14, 17, 115, 117, 118–19; Zizioulas, *One and Many*, 16, 38, 61–74, 146, 176, 179, 198, 199, 208, 219, 228, 232, 242, 280, 311–20.

79. Brown, *John*, 1:109–10; O'Day, *John*, 87.

80. Morris, *John*, 160, 162–64. Beasley-Murray interprets the manifestation of Jesus's glory as the coming of the kingdom of God (Beasley-Murray, *John*, 35–36).

81. John 2:1–11. Brown, *Introduction*, 56, 298–300, 305.

entendre, irony, signs, and symbols, the reader recognizes the detailed mention of six stone water jars for the Jewish purification rites are significant for interpreting the deeper intended meaning of this miracle story, beyond the fact that they are not intended to be used as wine vats.[82] The obedient servants pour water into the stone jars and draw out wine (v. 8). However, the climax of the drama rests on the butler's (*architriklinos*, or head waiter) words, "Everyone serves the good wine first, and when people have drunk freely, then the poor wine. But you have kept the good wine until now" (v. 10), to the groom (*numphios*, or bridegroom), who seemingly remains unaware of the heightened drama and is never recorded as speaking.[83]

First, the Jewish purification jars made of carved/chiseled stone rather than clay pottery probably indicate ceremonial vessels for washing hands and feet.[84] While much has been made of the number six accounting for the number of vessels,[85] the sheer quantity of six vessels holding twenty to thirty gallons should not be overlooked. The fact that there is an astounding 120–80 gallons of water turned into wine at the end of the wedding banquet draws the reader into one of the themes of John's Gospel that being, what Jesus has to offer is extravagant, superior, or in (super)abundance to what the old covenant or the material world has to offer.[86] Second, this theme and interpretation are carried further by what the butler says and what the groom does not say (vv. 9–10). The words from the butler indicate an inverted socio-cultural practice by

82. For an exhaustive work on the layers of linguistic and literary devises in the grammar of John's Gospel, see Köstenberger, *John's Gospel and Letters*, 127–67. For an emphasis on the figurative language of this text, see Bultmann, *John*, 117–21.

83. The parenthetical statement in v. 9 shows that only the obedient servants knew what had happened concerning the water becoming wine. For a discussion on Johannine use of parenthetical statements as a literary device, see Köstenberger, *John's Gospel and Letters*, 135–41.

84. Burge, *John*, 92; O'Day, *John*, 537.

85. Barrett sees the number of six for the stone water jars as symbolic of imperfection (i.e., incompleteness) in the Jewish dispensation as seven being perfect, then six is minus one. Barrett also connects this event taking place on the sixth day in Johannine literature (Barrett, *John*, 160). For an engagement into six jars representing the six days of creation, see Bultmann, *John*, 120–21n2. Brown believes that symbolism for six jars and the content representing the blood of Christ is a stretch (Brown, *John*, 1:100).

86. Brown, *John*, 1:105; O'Day, *John*, 537–38, 539–40. Cf. John 3:15–16; 4:10; 6:13, 27, 33; 8:12; 11:25, 42–44; 13:34–35; 14:2, 25–26. Notice that the vessels are filled to the brim (v. 7, *heōs anō*) literally, "as far as they would go," further indicating abundance.

offering the "good wine" at the end of the wedding feast. However, the groom, who is assumed to have been unaware of the drama, and further has the most to lose in a socio-culture of honor-and-shame, has more than likely served his "good wine" first, signaling that what Jesus serves is far superior to the groom's best wine, and further pointing to Jesus as the superior-groom.[87] It is further applicable that the stone purification jars have not changed, but that the content of those vessels has changed as a miracle and a sign of Jesus's glory as of the Son of God who has come to transform lives (i.e., purify us from within) both now in the temporal world and for eternity for those who will believe.[88]

The point we are making here is that the metaphoric use of vessel (Heb.: *kăd*, *kᵉlî*, *ḥĕrĕś* or *nēḇĕl*; Gr.: *skeûos*) with its composition of a void for the human condition throughout Scripture is to communicate usefulness in doing or being what it (vessel/human) was created to do or be through the indwelling of the Holy Spirit.[89] Theologically, for a person to become one whom God designed, a transformation needs to take place,[90] and Scriptures indicate the saving, sanctifying transformation takes place at the interior of the person (i.e., heart, mind, soul, will),[91] even while, the

---

87. For socio-cultural milieu on honor-and-shame, see Gundry, *New Testament*, 36–37. Burge, *John*, 92; O'Day, *John*, 538, 540. Cf. John 3:29.

88. Brown, *John*, 1:104–5; Burge, *John*, 99, 102–3; O'Day, *John*, 540. For Bruce, Jesus's miracle is one of turning the old creation into a new creation (Bruce, *Gospel & Epistles*, 72). Bultmann believes this story in John 2:1–11 is myth taken from Dionysus and edited with Jesus as the hero (Bultmann, *John*, 118–19; cf. Barrett, *John*, 157).

89. Ps 31:12; Eccl 12:6–7; Isa [29:16]; 45:9; Jer 18:1–11; 19:10–11; Lam 4:2; Hos 8:8; Rom 9:20–24; 2 Cor 4:7; 2 Tim 2:20–21; 1 Pet 3:7. See Williams, *Paul's Metaphors*, 22, 168–69. For the plan and purpose of the indwelled Holy Spirit, see Ps 51:10; Isa 11:2; 32:15; Jer 31:33; Ezek 11:19–20; 36:26–27; 37:14; 39:29; Zech 12:10; Joel 2:28–29; John 7:37–39; 14:16–17, 25–26; 15:26; 16:7, 13; 20:22; Acts 2:3–4, 33, 38–39; Collins, *Wesley*, 121–31, 198; Cross, *Presence*, 118–23; Fee, *Empowering*, 6, 7, 8, 843–45; Leclerc, *Discovering*, 147–52; Yarnell, *Holy Spirit*, 91, 99, 103–4, 105.

90. E.g., Matt 5:6, 10, 20; 6:33; 25:46; Mark 1:15, 17; 2:5, 14, 17; 3:35; 5:19, 34, 36; 8:21, 34; 9:23; 10:52; 11:22–25; Luke 3:3; 7:50; 8:48; 19:10; 23:42–43; 24:47; John 3:3, 5, 7; Acts 2:38. Calvin, *Institutes*, 2.6.1; Oden, *Justification*, 36–37.

91. Green shows that soteriology in Luke-Acts is "embodied conversion" (Green, *Body, Soul, and Human Life*, 106–39). Taylor says, "The human spirit is the locus of this [new] birth" in reference to John 3:1–8 (Taylor, *Formulation*, 135). For further soteriological interior effects on the human being (i.e., will, consciousness, spirit, thinking/mind, life, heart) see the concomitants of the new birth in Taylor, *Formulation*, 135–51. Also, Oden, *Justification*, 154–59. Cf. McConville warns that a strictly inward spiritual focus of religion leads to individualistic tendencies (McConville, *Being Human*, 88–89).

physical body/vessel is dying.[92] This saving and sanctifying transformation cannot be earned through right behaviors, benevolent acts, or religious activities,[93] but rather salvation and sanctification result from God's gracious self-giving love through an encounter with people.[94] God has revealed his self-giving love through Jesus Christ and the presence of the Holy Spirit in the lives of believers.[95] The Holy Spirit, then, is God's gift of participation for believers in the life of the Trinity.[96] Barnett explains the dynamic of the Spirit's indwelling from 2 Cor 4:7, "But we have this treasure in jars of clay, to show that the surpassing power belongs to God and not to us," when he says,

> The earthen jar in which this treasure is contained, the human body, is subject to decay and vulnerable to disease and injury. It is in ultimate terms, powerless.

92. Rom 8:10. This does not mean that God is not concerned about the human body. In fact, the human body is important as the Son of God puts on a human body (Matt 1:18—2:1a; Luke 1:30–33; 2:7). In Jesus's ministry, he healed people's physical afflictions (e.g., Matt 12:9–14; Mark 10:46–52; Luke 8:40–56; John 11:38–44). Finally, the Scriptures speak of the resurrected, glorified, body of Jesus (Luke 24:36–43; John 20:26–27) and of believers (1 Cor 15:12–57). For a discussion on the resurrected body, see Green, *Body, Soul, and Human Life*, 166–80.

93. Stanglin and McCall, *Arminius*, 151–57. A counterpoint could be made from the pericope in the Synoptic Gospels which is known as the Rich Young Man (Matt 19:16–30; Mark 10:17–21; Luke 18:18–30) who asks what he "must do to inherit eternal life?" While Jesus responds with selling possessions and giving the money to the poor and becoming one of his followers as a means to inherit eternal life, the lesson which follows in the Synoptic Gospels reveal the deeper truth of self-denial, or "where your treasure is, there our heart will be also" (Matt 6:21), thus *being* precedes *doing*.

94. Oden, *Justification*, 81–106. For a clear picture of soteriology from a trinitarian theological perspective over against a Western, legalistic, satisfaction theory of atonement, see Kruger, *Jesus*, 19, 20, 37–40, 41–57. For a synergistic approach to soteriology through the lenses of Lutheranism and the Orthodox Church, see McDaniel, "Salvation," 67–83; Jones, *God the Spirit*, 82; Leclerc, *Discovering*, 179.

95. Cross, *Presence*, 52, 82–86, 207, 213–16; Fee, *Empowering*, 13, 383, 384, 489, 493, 495–98, 499–501, 502, 507, 515–19, 525–30, 535–48, 563–67, 843–45; Levison, *Filled*, 307–8; Yarnell, *Holy Spirit*, 91, 99, 103–4, 105, 112–13. Käsemann states, "God's will is learned only through the Spirit" (Käsemann, *Romans*, 216). Volf says, "Thus the identification of Christ and church stands for *the particular kind of personal communion* between Christ and Christians, a communion perhaps best described as 'personal interiority'; Christ dwells in every Christian and is internal to that person as person. . . . Christian juxtaposition of Christ and Christians is actually first constituted through the Holy Spirit" (Volf, *Likeness*, 143).

96. Shults, *Anthropology*, 77–78, 84; Yarnell, *Holy Spirit*, 103.

This is not accidental, but deliberate, *to show that this all-surpassing power is from God* (verse 7). The power to lift man [humans] out of his [their] powerlessness in the face of suffering, decay and death does not come from within himself [themselves]; it comes from God. Man [Humans] is [are] like a jar of clay in order that the *all-surpassing power* might be from God, and not ourselves.[97]

It is the Holy Spirit's work to encounter people at the spiritual level where the Holy Spirit indwells believers, renewing the holy image and likeness that was marred and the relationship that had been severed.[98] Therefore, a Christian person is identified as one who has the presence of the Holy Spirit in their life.[99] The indwelling of the Holy Spirit in/with the Christian person opens up a new set of relationships with God and with other people.[100] Furthermore, an interior change affects the exterior activity, or put another way, an inward transformation by God (holy communion with the Trinity) affects outward behaviors toward others (community).[101] The inward change is not a change in substance (cf. water and wine), but rather a change in character and direction because of divine-human relationship (cf. purification in quality of the person).[102]

PARTICIPATION IN THE CHARACTER OF GOD

The second illustration of a transformed life after the Christian person is brought into a relationship with God is human participation in the

97. Barnett, *2 Corinthians*, 87.

98. Bobrinskoy, "'Pneumatic Christology,'" 55, 56–57, 67; Kruger, *Jesus*, 33–34; Tozer, *The Divine*, 121–28.

99. Behr, "Trinitarian Being," 171; Cross, *Presence*, 118–19, 123, 128; Dunn, *Baptism*, 93, 94–95, 149; Farrow, *Ascension*, 59–60; Fee, *Empowering*, 564; Irenaeus, *Heresies*, 4.20.6; Käsemann, *Romans*, 218–19, 222, 223; Pannenberg, *Anthropology*, 298; Wesley, "Farther Appeal," 49; Yarnell, *Holy Spirit*, 99; Rom 8:9, 15–16; 2 Cor 1:21–22; Eph 1:13–14; 1 John 3:24; 4:13.

100. Shults, *Anthropology*, 58–60. The inward transformation is accomplished by the Holy Spirit who gives new life but only after killing sin: "The Spirit negates the ego-controlled sinful nature of the 'flesh' that is bound by sin. Only after dying to sin and to self is the Christian freed to new life" (Shults, *Anthropology*, 89).

101. Collins, *Wesley*, 226–28; Green, *Body, Soul, and Human Life*, 109–13; Leclerc, *Discovering*, 230–35; McEwan, "Continual Enjoyment," 64–71.

102. Jones, *God the Spirit*, 79; Leclerc, *Discovering*, 186–91; McEwan, "Continual Enjoyment," 57, 59–64. Zizioulas, *Being*, 39–42, 44, 46, 49–50, 88, 106, 108–9; Zizioulas, *Communion*, 6, 244–45, 247–49, 302–3.

character of God. After a Christian person is initiated into a relationship with God through the Holy Spirit, biblical Wesleyan theology, in particular, calls for the Christian person to grow in grace and love becoming holy and loving as God while remaining in a fallen world.[103] This statement is pregnant with difficulty as character is typically associated with essence, and there is a fundamental difference between the essence of divinity and the essence of humanity. However, Aristotelian philosophy does not place "character" as the genus or essence of a being, but rather (virtue of) character is the mean, or moderate condition (actions and feelings), between virtues and vices.[104] For instance, good (i.e., self-control, temperance) is the mean of pleasure and pain. However, the question could be raised whether a virtuous character (i.e., ethic, morality) is correctly and universally found in the moderate course of action?[105] Furthermore, the (theological) pitfall[106] with this definition of character is twofold: first, a human can act *other* than his/her nature. For instance, a human can flap her arms up and down while making a chirping sound, but that act does not make her a bird; it is, instead, theatrics. The second pitfall to this definition of character is that the act does not *change* the human's essence. No matter if one dresses like a king and calls out certain commands while being a common laborer at the local factory, he will doubtfully become a king, no matter how much he, himself, believes it. Jesus says this much when addressing a false view of religious cleanliness (i.e., holiness) that was more connected with following traditions, as the Pharisees taught than proper cleanliness (holiness) from the heart: "For out of the heart come evil thoughts, murder, adultery, sexual immorality, theft, false witness, slander. These are what defile a person. But to

---

103. Wesley, "On Perfection," 411–24; Wesley, "Plain Account," 366–446; Wesley, "Circumcision of the Heart," 202–11; Wesley, "Christian Perfection," 1–22. Taylor, *Formulation*, 157–66, 167–69, 187–212.

104. Aristotle, *Nicomachean Ethics*, 2.3; 2.5; 2.6; 2.9; Aristotle, *Eudemian Ethics*, 2.2. In the twentieth century, psychologists moved away from character studies for studies in personality, however, there has been a resurgence in character study by those in scientific psychology. It is within this resurgence of psychology that we get a definition of character as "'characteristics that are descriptive of actions, cognitions, emotions, and motivations that are considered to be relevant to right and wrong according to a relevant moral standard.'" See Fleeson et al., "Personality Science," 42.

105. Geisler, *Christian Ethics*, 19.

106. Aristotle does not see these points as pitfalls, but rather puzzles, yet he states, "So it is correct to say that a person comes to be just from doing just actions, and temperate from doing temperate ones" (Aristotle, *Nicomachean Ethics*, 2.4).

eat with unwashed hands does not defile anyone."[107] Therefore, while in Aristotelian philosophy, character is an obedient soul operating between what one wants to do and what one should do, the person's character is separated from the person's being, and furthermore, the person's actions supersede the being of the person.[108]

While human beings can boast of great things (Jas 3:5), it would indeed be a rare human being who does not understand they are mortal and are not omnipresent, omniscient, or omnipotent as found in the divine character/attributes.[109] Furthermore, God's character is self-disclosed through the revelation of Scripture and the life and ministry of Jesus Christ.[110] What is even more remarkable is that God reveals his character as holy and says, "You shall be holy, for I am holy,"[111] and reveals his character as love ("God is love"),[112] commanding that followers must love as God loves.[113] If the character of God is revealed as holy and love (among other attributes), and divinity and humanity are separated by attributes, how can God command humans to be something humans are not by character? Oden helps answer this question by explaining that God's actions are consistent with his attributes/character, which indicate that attributes are distinguishable from actions:

107. Matt 15:19–20. Mahony, "Theology of Sin," 197–98; Thorsen, *Quadrilateral*, 91, 152, 224.

108. Aristotle, *Eudemian Ethics*, 2.1–2; Aristotle, *Nicomachean Ethics*, 2.1; 2.3; 2.6. In evangelical-theological terms, Aristotelian philosophy of virtuous character (or virtuous pagan) could be understood in the paradox of "sinning-saints." See Sweeten, *Sinning Saints*, 68–83. Similarly in political terms, the prince does not need to be virtuous, but only act virtuous, in Machiavelli, *Prince*, ch. 18.

109. Grudem, *Systematic Theology*, 156–57.

110. Oden, *God*, 35.

111. Lev 11:44; 1 Pet 1:16; cf. Exod 19:6; Matt 5:48. Routledge draws on Wright's OT ethical triangle (Theological Angle: God; Social Angle: Israel; and The Economic Angle: The Land) as the practical implication unfolded in God's command: "be holy, for I am holy" (Routledge, *Theology*, 239–40).

112. 1 John 4:8b, 16; cf. Deut 7:9; 1 Kings 8:23; 2 Chr 6:14; Pss 36:7; 69:13; 98:3; 109:21; Joel 2:13; Jonah 4:2; Mic 7:18; Zeph 3:17; 2 Cor 13:11; Gal 2:20; 1 John 3:1; 4:7. Brunner, *Christian Doctrine*, 183–99; Coppedge, *Portraits*, 244–51.

113. John 13:34. Notice the promise of a new covenant in Jer 31:31–40, especially with reference to God's law written upon the heart, an intimate personal relationship between God and his people, and love for neighbor (vv. 33–34). Waltke argues that the new covenant is found in the Sabbath theology where Jesus Christ fulfills the Sabbath requirements in the NT which becomes a sanctified heart. See Waltke and Yu, *Theology*, 424–25. Cf. Lev 19:18; Deut. 6:5; Matt 5:44; 19:19; 22:37–40; Gal 5:14.

Accordingly, knowing is not a divine attribute, but that mode of knowing which knows all is a quality attributable only to God. Merely having will is not an attribute of God, for creatures have wills, but having a will that is perfect in *holy love* and able to perform all that it desires is an attribute of God. Having life is not an attribute of God, because all living things have life, but having life in such an incomparable way that all things live through that life is an attribute of God.[114]

In addition, Grudem differentiates between God's "communicable attributes" and "incommunicable attributes."[115] For instance, eternal, omnipresent, omniscient, and omnipotent are examples of incommunicable attributes. In contrast, examples of God's communicable attributes are holy, love, knowledge, mercy, and justice, for which Grudem qualifies as not totally communicated to humans, but yet are attributes that are *partially shared* with humans.[116] For instance, one attribute of God's character is freedom.[117] Humans are also free to act but are subject to limitations from outside of the self, like the *givens* of earth, culture, government, and the limitations from within the self, like mental, physical, educational, etc.[118] Therefore, unlike Aristotelian philosophy, theology associates character with attributes and nature. Humans can share/participate in some attributes of God to each one's particular capacity, but only in the *ekstasis* of the person, meaning, God initiates this participation to happen (i.e., grace), while humans respond (i.e., to grace).[119]

God, then, who is holy, commands humans to be holy. Likewise, God, who is loving, commands humans to love.[120] If a human person acts

---

114. Oden, *God*, 36; emphasis mine.

115. Grudem, *Systematic Theology*, 156–225.

116. Grudem, *Systematic Theology*, 156–57.

117. Zizioulas, *Being*, 18, 40, 41.

118. Zizioulas, *Communion*, 9–10; Zizioulas, *Eucharistic Communion*, 168–71; Gregory of Nyssa, *On Virginity*, ch. 12.

119. Zizioulas, "Capacity and Incapacity," 407–8. More specifically, it is the capacity of Jesus Christ to take sin and sinners into himself for the purpose of saving humans from sin, death and the devil, and further to make humans holy and loving (Kinlaw, *Jesus*, 132–35). Cf. John 3:16. See also "monergistic" versus "synergistic" views of soteriology throughout church history in Olson, *Story*, 255–56, 263–64, 267–67, 282, 287, 346, 365, 372, 439, 455, 457, 465, 502–3, 512, 515, 535, 595, 612, 624, 635.

120. E.g., Lev 11:44; 1 Pet 1:16; 1 John 4:8b, 16. In reference to 1 John 4:8, Marshall says, "A person cannot come into a real relationship with a loving God without being transformed into a loving person" (Marshall, *Epistles of John*, 212).

holy and acts loving without having a holy and loving character, then it could be said that they are actors who are operating theatrics and hypocrisy or at least modeling Aristotle's virtuous pagan.[121] For humans to live out these characteristics in their life, they must have these characteristics. Thus, a change must take place within the human person.[122] The change that can occur within a person is the grace of God to save them from sin. God's saving grace is made possible through Jesus Christ and delivered by the Holy Spirit, who indwells the person, making the person a Christian person.[123] There is a change in disposition and attitude for the Christian person by a new relationship with God.[124] While the person will not take on God's total character, human participation in the new relationship with God will affect the Christian's characteristic attitudes changing them to imitate God as demonstrated in Jesus Christ.[125] Therefore, human participation with God includes an act of *imitatio Dei* or *imitatio Christi* in the New Testament[126] as a means of living a sanctified life between God's mercy and judgment, or God's holiness and love. Thus, the Christian's actions in holy-love flow from their transformed being by loving God and choosing to imitate God's character of holy-love.[127] Therefore, "character" in reference to God will mean "attributes," but "character" for human beings will mean "'characteristics that are descriptive of actions, cognitions, emotions, and motivations that are considered to be relevant to right and

121. *"Hypocritēs"* was the Greek term for actors, those who role-play in the theatre (Ferguson, *Backgrounds*, 90). Knobel, "Wisdom," 351–67.

122. Plantinga, *Not the Way*, 96–112; Kinlaw, *Jesus*, 138–40.

123. Dunn, *Pneumatology*, 3, 10–21, 25–28, 39–41, 43–61, 62–80, 222–42. Irenaeus, *Heresies*, 5.6.1; 5.8.2; 5.10.2; Gregory of Nazianzus, *Orations*, "On the Holy Spirit," 5.26–27; Bobrinskoy, "'Pneumatic Christology,'" 55, 65. Cross, *Presence*, 17–18, 63; Fee, *Empowering*, 827–29. Sanders, *Deep*, 160, 163–65, 175; Turner, *Power*, 358–60.

124. Leclerc, *Discovering*, 159; Kinlaw, *Jesus*, 137–53; Taylor, *Formulation*, 187–212.

125. Leclerc, *Discovering*, 260–62; Cairns, *Image*, 60.

126. 1 Cor 4:16, 17; 11:1; Eph 5:1; 1 Thess 1:6; 2:14; Heb 6:12. Davids, *Peter*, 17–18. Zizioulas denies *imitatio Christi* on the grounds that it is not ontologically significant for anthropology (Zizioulas, *Communion*, 244).

127. Brueggemann, *Theology*, 427–29; Collins, *Wesley*, 19–48, 124–27; Gunton, *One, Three, Many*, 196, 203, 205–7; Kinlaw, *Jesus*, 46, 88, 138–40; Sanders, *Deep*, 144, 150, 160, 170. Cf. For Zizioulas, it is the Church (the collective assembly) who becomes holy by God's character for the salvation of the world (Zizioulas, *One and Many*, 72, 88, 229, 314, 348, 369). For Purkiser, the Christ-like person is so in personality which is a result of "the *metamorphosis*, the complete transformation of character, includes the translation of the inner conformity into outward personality, and in this respect is a gradual process" (Purkiser et al., *God, Man & Salvation*, 512).

wrong according to a relevant moral standard.'"[128] The moral standard we will use is God's moral standard, as revealed in Scripture.[129]

The holy-love character of God for which humans are intended to share through relationship is best demonstrated by the theology of covenant (*bᵉrît*).[130]

> The specific role of a covenant is to give permanency to a *relationship* with the aim of securing lasting benefits hence covenants in the ANE [i.e., Ancient Near East] and in the Bible often feature an oath or they use the father-son *relation* as a metaphor (e.g., Exod 4:22; 2 Sam 7:14), or they employ "forever" language to stress the perpetuity of the bond forged (e.g., Ezek 37:24–28). Covenants are needed in a world where people often fail to keep their promises or to live up to their obligations. The biblical covenants reassure God's people that God will fulfill his promises, and they remind them of what they are obligated to do as people in *relationship* with God.[131]

God demonstrates his character of holy-love by binding himself to human beings relationally and legally.[132] The relational-legal covenant

---

128. Fleeson et al., "Personality Science," 42.

129. The biblical understanding of Christians obtaining the characteristics of God is found in the fruit of the Spirit (Gal 5:22–23). See Burnett, *Shadow of Aldersgate*, 149–50.

130. Arnold and Beyer, *Old Testament*, 94; Brueggemann, *Theology*, 198–201; Dyrness, *Themes*, 27–28; Kaufmann, *Israel*, 298. For an article on the Covenant Code in Exodus 20:22—23:33, see Hamilton, *Exodus*, 358–61. See Stuart for the topics of Covenant People (Stuart, *Exodus*, 37–38), "Excursus: The Exodus-Leviticus Covenant" (Stuart, *Exodus*, 439–40), and "Excursus: The Paradigmatic Nature of Biblical Law" (Stuart, *Exodus* 442–45). Routledge, *Theology*, 160–64. Kessler reveals that archeologists have identified four types of covenants from Ancient Near East materials: bilateral parity covenants, bilateral suzerainty treaties, loyalty oaths, and promissory covenants (Kessler, *Old Testament*, 178–81). Speaking specifically of the divine-human covenant at Mount Sinai, Kessler claims that a majority of OT scholars today support the type of covenant where both parties enter into it willingly like those found in the bilateral suzerainty covenant based on the form of the treaty/covenant (Kessler, *Old Testament*, 181–83).

131. Goswell, "Two Testaments," 691; emphasis mine. Kessler says, "The concept of relationship is a fruitful starting point for studying the theology of the OT" (Kessler, *Old Testament*, 69). He further says that the OT texts "served a relational purpose" and is "part of the warp and woof of all these texts" (Kessler, *Old Testament*, 69–70). Lastly, Kessler says the OT texts "expressed the conviction that Israel stood in a true relationship with Yahweh, who was also a 'personal' being" (Kessler, *Old Testament*, 70).

132. Brueggemann, *Theology*, 417–18. Routledge, *Theology*, 169; Waltke and Yu, *Theology*, 353, 357–59, 435–38. See the OT connection of ḥĕsĕd and bᵉrît in Kinlaw and Oswalt, *Lectures*, 177–78.

comes to the forefront in Malachi's YHWH oracle to those God is bound to by a covenant, "I have loved you" (1:2), but to those, God is not bound by covenant, he says, "Esau I have hated" (1:3).[133] Thus, the covenant became the symbol of God's desire and commitment to bring (all) people into a relationship with him and where all could enjoy the self-giving love and presence of God.[134] Oswalt argues that the covenant reveals God's *holy* character in three ways: "grace," "ethical righteousness," and "faithfulness."[135] First, the covenant reveals that God's character is holy-grace.[136] In light of the corruption of human beings, God did not destroy humans but rather committed himself to humans by binding himself to the human.[137] Second, the covenant reveals God's character is holy-ethical, treating "persons in ways that are first of all consistent with their needs, and only secondarily with his."[138] God demonstrated his holy-ethical character by delivering his people from the bondage of Egypt, teaching them God's holy character, and in turn transforming their character to imitate God's character.[139] Third, the covenant reveals

133. Goswell, "Two Testaments," 688; VanGemeren, *Interpreting the Prophetic Word*, 205–6.

134. Oswalt, *Holy*, 22.

135. Oswalt, *Holy*, 17–44. In a similar presentation on the character of YHWH using adjectives, especially: merciful, gracious, steadfast love, true/truth, forgives, and pardon (esp. Exod 34:6–7), see Brueggemann, *Theology*, 215–18. For an expanded study of God's character specifically through God's action (verbs) (Brueggemann, *Theology*, 145–212), and nouns (Brueggemann, *Theology* 229–66). Later, Brueggemann ties together YHWH's character with human persons' character through what he calls "covenantal humanness" (Brueggemann, *Theology* 450–91). For more on God's character in Exod 34:1–9, see House, "Sin," 41–45. Routledge sees God's desire that Israel be holy in functional terms as Israel is "elected" to the service of being set apart as a kingdom of priests and a holy nation for the purpose of being an intermediary to the nations (Routledge, *Theology*, 172–73; cf. 239). See also Torrance, *Christ*, 17–23.

136. Waltke shows that covenant theology established in Genesis and then reflected in the subsequent covenants (i.e., Noahic, Abrahamic, Mosaic, and Davidic) presumes God's holy-sovereignty and asserts "unassisted human faithfulness is an impossibility" (Waltke and Yu, *Theology*, 255). Humans are entirely dependent upon God and God's grace is necessary in the covenant relationship (Waltke and Yu, *Theology*, 204–5, 248, 255, 259–60, 285, 363).

137. Oswalt, *Holy*, 22–27; Routledge, *Theology*, 173–74; Waltke and Yu, *Theology*, 285, 287–90.

138. Oswalt, *Holy*, 27. Brueggemann, *Theology*, 173–74.

139. Oswalt, *Holy*, 27–34. A NT fulfillment of this point is found in Paul's writing, "but God shows his love for us in that while we were still sinners, Christ died for us" (Rom 5:8). Garrett, *Exodus*, 139–43; Stuart, *Exodus*, 38.

that God's character is holy-faithful[140] as witnessed in God's righteous anger with the children of Israel, who immediately broke the covenant at Mount Sinai by worshipping an image of a golden calf. God's faithfulness is seen in the fact that he did not annihilate the covenant-breakers but listened to Moses's plea for forgiveness.[141] It is interesting that prior to the golden calf breach of covenant (Exod 32), when God "spoke" (*dbr*) the Ten Commandments to Moses (Exod 20), God's character of holy-love was displayed in the second commandment prohibiting idolatry.[142] God juxtaposed discipline for sin with blessing for obedience:

> "You shall not make . . . a carved image . . . for I the LORD your God am a jealous God, visiting the iniquity of the fathers on the children to the third and the fourth generation of those who hate me, but showing steadfast love [*ḥěsěd*] to thousands of those who love me and keep my commands."[143]

The "steadfast love" (*ḥěsěd* meaning loyal, faithful, kind, gracious love) for which God blesses those who lovingly obey him is often accompanied with the word "truth" (*ʾěmět*) which reveals God's character in holy-faithfulness.[144] There is a great gulf in light of God's revealed character and the human condition, yet God desires to share his characteristics with humans.[145]

In response to the command, "You shall be holy, for I am holy," we find ourselves echoing Mary's words upon her hearing the angelic announcement that she would be indwelled by the Holy Spirit and give

---

140. Cf. For Abraham's faith in God's promises/faithfulness, see Waltke and Yu, *Theology*, 333–37. Also, God's faithfulness to the covenant, Waltke and Yu, *Theology*, 363.

141. Hamilton, *Exodus*, 556, 558–59; Stuart, *Exodus*, 659–60, 672.

142. Waltke and Yu, *Theology*, 417–18; Stuart, *Exodus*, 454. Exod 20:1.

143. Exod 20:4–6; Janzen, *Exodus*, 147. It is further interesting to note the OT abstention from an image of God created by human hands as a functional symbol of worship compared to the NT's message that Jesus Christ is the (personal) image of God (Col 1:15); see Fretheim, *Exodus*, 227.

144. Waltke says that God's use of *ḥěsěd* shows God's "covenant faithfulness" (Waltke and Yu, *Theology*, 418). Routledge, *Theology*, 195–201. Oswalt identifies twenty of the thirty-three times *ḥěsěd* and *ʾěmět* occur together deal with God's character (Oswalt, *Holy*, 37n7). See also Kinlaw and Oswalt, *Lectures*, 173–77.

145. Luke 16:26. Cross, *Presence*, 96; McConville, *Being Human*, 24, 44, 190–91; Oswalt, *Holy*, 33; Waltke and Yu, *Theology*, 407.

birth to the Son of God, "But how can this happen?"[146] In light of the human condition and inability to keep the human side of the covenant, God bound himself even more closely to humans through the incarnation of the Son of God, the perfect God-man.[147] The purpose of the incarnation was to save and sanctify humans, recreating in the human being the image and likeness of God, and by being transformed, humans might share in the characteristics of God.[148] Would it be consistent with God's character, then, to demand something of humans, whom God dearly loves, for which humans could not attain?[149] The key is found in the gift of the Holy Spirit.

By faith, those who will believe in Jesus Christ as Lord and Savior are given the Holy Spirit as the breath of new life and the sign of a new covenant.[150] The Holy Spirit's work beginning at prevenient grace convicting a person of sin and bringing them to the point of justification (the freedom from the guilt of sin),[151] continues through sanctification (the freedom from the power of sin), which is the development of God's holy-love character within the Christian person.[152] Shults demonstrates the contingency of the Holy Spirit in comparison to what it means to be a whole Christian person.[153]

146. Luke 1:34 NLT. Kinlaw reflects that the typical human response to the scriptural commands to be holy is to question scriptural terminology (Kinlaw, *Mind*, 80).

147. Torrance, *Doctrine*, 13–18, 144; Torrance, *Christ*, 8–10, 27–29, 30–31, 32–34; Zizioulas, *Being*, 96–98.

148. Athanasius, *Incarnation*, §§13–14; Irenaeus, *Heresies*, 5.6.1; 5.8.1; 5.16.1–3; 5.20–21.1. Kinlaw says that the only proper response to God's ḥĕsĕd is for humans to respond in kind which is not only directed toward God, but is demonstrated by showing ḥĕsĕd to others (Zizioulas, *Lectures*, 169, 181).

149. Wesley, "Plain Account," 369, 390, 443–46; Dayton, *Entire Sanctification*, 12; Merritt, *Christian's Manual*, 11, 15.

150. Acts 15:8–9. Irenaeus, *Heresies*, 5.1.1; 5.6.1; 5.8.1; 5.10–12.1; Reeves, *Delighting*, 87–88, 90–93. Also see Turner's summary of the impact of Dunn's work on the gift of the Holy Spirit as the new covenant (Turner, *Power*, 48–53). See also McKnight, "Covenant and Spirit," 41–54.

151. Collins, *Wesley*, 73–82; Jones, *God the Spirit*, 61–63. Calvin also speaks of the grace of God that is given at "the very commencement of conversion in the will" (Calvin, *Institutes*, 2.3.6), but this grace is only applied to those who have been elected and predestined to salvation (Calvin, *Institutes*, 3.21.1).

152. Leclerc, *Discovering*, 174, 176, 178, 182–84, 260.

153. McConville, *Being Human*, 56. Cf. Kärkkäinen, *Pneumatology*, 150–54; African pneumatology resembles the NT church where in contrast to Western pneumatology which is limited to individual spiritual salvation, African pneumatology in

A person only begins to fulfill her or his destiny to become a copy of Christ the prototype when she or he receives the Spirit. Through participation in the church as the body of Christ, and by the work of the Spirit, human beings are fashioned after the image and likeness of God.[154]

The Holy Spirit is the union and communion for the Christian person with the Holy Trinity and with the earthly community, which is the Church, for the world, thus fulfilling what was marred and missing in human beings after the original sin.[155]

PARTICIPATION IN THE MISSION OF GOD[156]

The third illustration of a transformed life is human participation in the mission of God. A Christian person must have a living, ongoing relationship with God through the Holy Spirit, where the Christian person is growing in grace by taking on the character of God for the Christian person to be motivated to do the mission of God. The Holy Spirit initiates the relationship for humans with the triune God, and building on that encounter (i.e., conversion-initiation),[157] a deeper, more intimate

---

salvation is inclusive, understanding the whole person: "salvation implies deliverance, healing, and wholeness, including the wholeness and reconciliation of communities" (Kärkkäinen, *Pneumatology*, 152).

154. Shults, *Anthropology*, 222.

155. Fiddes, *Participating*, 259–62; Cross, *Presence*, 205–6; Morgan, "Sin," 156–57. Shults further states, "The essence of human creatureliness is disclosed by its end—being formed by the Spirit into the image of Jesus Christ. The *imago Dei* as the goal of personal and communal being, the telos of humanity, was revealed in the resurrection of the incarnate Word and the outpouring of the Spirit at Pentecost. Humans are created 'in' the image and 'after' the likeness of God because their very being as persons is oriented toward sharing in the wisdom of the One whose Spirit raised Christ from the dead (Rom. 8:11)" (Shults, *Anthropology*, 241).

156. "Mission" is used here in the singular in the same manner that Wright explains by the metaphor of "science" where there can be many different branches of science and different types of scientific activities. Therefore this term is used theologically. See Wright, *Mission*, 25–26. This subsection on "Participation in the Mission of God" is a further development of presence and mission found in chapter 6 under the subheading, "Presence and Anthropology" as illustrated in God's presence and the mission with Moses and Israel (Exod 33:12–23; Luke 24:44–49).

157. Dunn, *Baptism*, 94–95; Turner, *Holy Spirit*, 45–46. Cf. those who believe the Holy Spirit comes later to the believer (e.g., baptism of the Holy Spirit) in acts of charismata, see Anderson, *Pentecostalism*, 189–95; Cartledge, *Encountering*, 88–100; Logan, "Controversial Aspects," 34, 37; Ward, "Pentecostal Theology," 195. For a more

relationship is formed where the Holy Spirit purifies the human heart[158] transforming the character of the person (without losing particularity of personality) into the character of God's likeness.[159] Spirit-filled people connect in *koinōnia* to worship God, thus becoming the church: "Since ecumenical consensus holds that the presence of the Spirit of Christ makes a church a church."[160] As this transformation is happening, the person, and persons within the church, become mobilized for the mission of God.[161] One of Migliore's seven theses for missionary theology reads: "*The missionary activity of the church is a participation in the mission of the Spirit of the triune God. The work of the Holy Spirit is marked by the renewal of persons and the creation of a new community of the remarkably diverse.*"[162] The Holy Spirit constitutes the Christian person by opening up the *koinōnia-vertical*[163] and then constitutes the Christian community by opening up the *koinōnia-horizontal*[164] with the goal that

---

subtle explanation between the two poles of whether the Holy Spirit is received at conversion or at a later event, see Pinnock, *Flame*, 162–72. For a historical and theological comprehension of this debate by showing the Pentecostal opinion of Dunn's errors and the traditional Pentecostals, see Atkinson, *Baptism*.

158. For heart cleansing analogies, see Acts 15:8–9: "And God, who knows the heart, bore witness to them, by giving them the Holy Spirit just as he did to us, and he made no distinction between us and them, having cleansed their hearts by faith." Also, Ps 51:10; Heb 10:22; 1 Pet 1:22. Mahony, "Theology of Sin," 197–98.

159. Congar, *Holy Spirit*, 2.1.1; Gunton, *One, Three, Many*, 217–18; Kinlaw, *Jesus*, 139, 145, 149, 150, 152–53; Kinlaw, *Mind*, 91–93, 104–7; Oswalt, *Holy*, 17–44; Owen, *Holy Spirit*, 219–23, 225–27; Shults, *Anthropology*, 222.

160. Volf, *Likeness*, 130. Also, Congar, *Holy Spirit*, 2.1.1; 2.1.2; Cross, *Presence*, 15–19; Irenaeus, *Heresies*, 3.24.1; Kärkkäinen, *Pneumatology*, 49, 94–95, 105; Lossky, *Mystical Theology*, 159, 162, 166–68. In contrast, Zizioulas says that the Church as a community is not established by the Holy Spirit, but rather by Christ, the God-man, through the Divine Eucharist (Zizioulas, *Eucharist*, 15–17). Bathrellos points out Zizioulas's ecclesiological approach that the Church is (the whole) Christ himself in an ontological understanding as opposed to a pneumatocentric ecclesiology (Bathrellos, "Church, Eucharist, Bishop," 134). For "communion ecclesiology," see Behr, "Trinitarian Being," 166–67.

161. Carter, *Holy Spirit*, 223–45; Pinnock, *Flame*, 215–16, 218–23.

162. Migliore, "Missionary," 21.

163. *Koinōnia-vertical* describes the relationship a Christian person can have with God through the Holy Spirit, namely the Father (1 John 1:3), the Son (1 Cor 1:9; 10:16; Phil 3:10; 1 John 1:3, 6), and the Holy Spirit (2 Cor 13:13 [Gr.]; 2 Cor 13:14 [Eng.]; Phil 2:1. Also, participation in the work (i.e., gospel) of God see Phil 1:5.

164. *Koinōnia-horizontal* describes the Christian relationships with each other (the many) made possible by the one Holy Spirit (Acts 2:42; Rom 15:26; 2 Cor 6:14; 8:4; 9:13; Gal 2:9; Heb 13:16; 1 John 1:3).

Christian persons within the church will become unified one-with-God and one-with-each other,[165] by *koinōnia-circuitous*[166] in and for the world. Therefore the Holy Spirit makes the mission of the Church a personal reality[167] empowering the Church, and the persons therein, to have the character of Christ because of a new set of relationships and participate in fulfilling the mission of Christ within the Church and outside the Church in the world.[168]

The mission of Christ is made possible by the Holy Spirit and motivated by the sending-Father, meaning; the mission can only be understood in trinitarian terms.[169] A trinitarian mission crimps together Luke's two-volume work.[170] The Father is the faithful, sovereign sender of the Son and the Holy Spirit.[171] The Holy Spirit constitutes Jesus Christ[172] as

165. John 17:11, 23.

166. *Koinōnia-circuitous* describes the reciprocal, mutual-self-giving love, and "open *perichoresis*" (Marshall, *Dance*, 6–9; Marshall, "Participating," 144–48) overflowing through the mission of church which is embodied by the presence of the Holy Spirit, who in turn is transforming people into a new, holy community in the image and likeness of God (John 15:26–27; 17:18, 21; 2 Cor 13:13 [Gr.]; 2 Cor 13:14 [Eng.]; 1 John 1:3). In other words, this is the trinitarian-pneumatological-personhood. On perichoretical movement and space, see Fiddes, *Participating*, 72–73: "The *actions* of love of two human lovers, or of members of a Christian congregation, can interpenetrate and occupy the same social space simultaneously in a way that the personal *subjects* cannot, even though they can put themselves 'in each other's place' through empathy and imagination. . . . The patterns of a dance overlap and intersect in perichoresis where the human dancers can only circle *round* each other."

167. Migliore, "Missionary," 14, 18 21, 22; Zizioulas, *One and Many*, 187; Volf, *Likeness*, 143.

168. Cross, *Presence*, 107–9, 224–25; Pinnock, *Flame*, 116–19, 141–47; Wright, *Mission*, 29–30. Fiddes says, "action can only be ascribed to an agent who *has* relationship" (Fiddes, *Participating*, 83). The Holy Spirit acts upon the church because of the eternal trinitarian relationship of Father, Son, and Holy Spirit. The church can only effectively act in Christ's mission for the world because of the church's relationship with the Trinity through the indwelling presence of the Holy Spirit and because of Christ's *kenosis* (Phil 2:7).

169. Newbigin, *Gospel*, 118–19; Migliore, "Missionary," 17–18; Cross, *Presence*, 205–7; Sexton, "Confessing," 182–84.

170. Green argues for a unified narrative reading of Luke-Acts (Green, *Luke*, 6–10). Cf. Bock points out the difference in genre of Luke's Gospel as narrative in contrast to the Acts of the Apostles which is a "historical monograph" (Bock, *Acts*, 2–3). However, Bock recognizes the Spirit as the link between the Gospel and the Acts (Bock, *Acts*, 7).

171. Luke 24:49; Acts 1:7; 2:23, 27, 30, 32, 36, 39. Sexton, "Confessing," 182. Bock states that the real core of the book of Acts is God's sovereign work over the mission (Bock, *Acts*, 7, 33); Fiddes, *Participating*, 51.

172. Zizioulas, *Being*, 132, 139; Zizioulas, "Capacity and Incapacity," 438; Zizioulas,

seen in the immaculate conception, baptism, and resurrection of Jesus Christ, who is the resurrected Son of God, the fulfillment of prophecy, whose name alone brings about forgiveness for sins, and is the messenger of this good news.[173] The Holy Spirit is the promise and gift of the Father who communicates, initiates, and empowers believers.[174] The Father, Son, and Holy Spirit work together in the mission "that repentance and forgiveness of sins should be proclaimed in his [Jesus Christ's] name to all nations, beginning from Jerusalem."[175] The Holy Spirit indwells particular people who make up the church, the holy community, to edify one another (*ad intra*) and to do the activity (*ad extra*) of the triune God: to teach-preach and love-selflessly.[176] The trinitarian mission of Christ reveals the equality-with-headship formula.

Luke has given the church a clear picture that the presence of the Holy Spirit precedes the missional work of God.[177] Cross shows that when the Holy Spirit enables and mobilizes believers and the church for mission, it is two-fold as Christian persons are unified in commonality, and then the church is to turn its focus upon the world.[178] At the point and place where the Holy Spirit is sanctifying the human heart,[179] self-

---

Communion, 131–32; Zizioulas, *Eucharistic Communion*, 105; Knight, "Introduction," 10; Turner, "Eschatology and Truth," 21, 26–27.

173. Luke 1:35; 24:25–26, 44, 46–47; Mark 1:10; Acts 1:3, 4b–5, 7–8; 2:22–36, 38; Rom 8:11. See the Gospel of Luke's Christology in Culpepper, *Luke*, 13–19. See also Marshall, *Acts*, 56–57, 59, 74–81.

174. Luke 24:49; Acts 1:8; 2:4, 17–21, 33, 38–39; Green, *Luke*, 22–23, 858; Thiselton, *Holy Spirit*, 49–51. Turner, "Luke and the Spirit," 279. Bock, *Acts*, 36–37.

175. Luke 24:47; Green, *Luke*, 856–59.

176. Cross, *Presence*, 107–9, 224–25; Migliore, "Missionary," 14; Newbigin, *Gospel*, 117–18; Luke 24:47; Acts 2:38–39, 42–47.

177. Luke 24:49; Acts 1:4, 8. Kinlaw, *Mind*, 91–93; Moltmann, *Trinity*, 122–23; Turner, *Power*, 343–44.

178. Cross, *Presence*, 205–6, 208–10, 224–29; Fiddes, *Participating*, 85, 86.

179. Wesleyan *ordo salutis* includes "initial sanctification" which occurs at the moment of salvation followed by "progressive sanctification" until there comes a moment of "entire sanctification" in which the Holy Spirit breaks the bonds of the sin nature (as opposed to the acts of sin dealt with at the new birth) and gives the gift of *agapē* (holy-love) for God and others, followed again by "progressive sanctification" which continues the spiritual growth in grace until death/glorification. See Leclerc, *Discovering*, 174–79, 182–84; Collins, *Wesley*, 297, 300–303, 310–12. Cf. Knight, "Spirit and Persons," 184.

giving love (*agapē*) is demonstrated through the edification within the church and mission outside of the church.[180]

First, participation in the mission of God deals with the quality of the interior of a person (i.e., heart, mind, soul, will)[181] and the collective persons in holy community.[182] For edification to occur among the persons of the holy community, there must be holy communion (i.e., self-giving love) which begins with Christian persons being open to one another (*ekstasis*) for instruction to grow in grace and holy-love.[183] The Holy Spirit unifies redeemed people despite their particular personality differences allowing people within the Church to be different without division.[184] Next, Christian persons edify and keep one another accountable to God through both personal and corporate disciplines so that the whole community is moving toward the holy-love character of God as an act of faithful response for what God has mercifully done through Christ.[185] Some of those personal and corporate disciplines in faith include but are not limited to worship, Scripture reading, prayer, sacraments (Protestant evangelical, e.g., baptism, Holy Communion), discipleship, testimonies, confession, serving, fasting, and tithing income.[186] Wesleyan theology refers to these practices (and others) as "means of grace," indicating they

180. Cross, *Presence*, 207, 208, 227; Migliore, "Missionary," 18. It is our opinion here that *missio Dei* flows from ecclesiology as it originates as the Trinity's *ekstatic-love* (mutual-self-giving-love) *to* and *through* Christian people and the Church for the world. Coppenger comes very close to this concept but stops short by entertaining the concept of "God-the-community" with mutual-self-giving-glory (similar to Gregory of Nyssa, *Spirit*, 324), rather than mutual-self-giving-love. The reason that Coppenger stops short of God-the-community with glorification rather than love is because he begins his missiology with God as sovereign (royal language), rather than a personal God as Father (relational language). Coppenger carries this theme throughout his article in Coppenger, "Community of Mission," 61–62.

181. Green, *Body, Soul, Human Life*, 106–39; Taylor, *Formulation*, 135. Cf. McConville, *Being Human*, 88–89.

182. Moltmann, *Trinity*, 220; Pinnock, *Flame*, 231. It is important to note that the early church also relied on the Holy Spirit to keep unity and oneness among the church members against false prophets. See Ignatius, *Ephesians*, ch. 9.

183. Zizioulas, *Being*, 112; Zizioulas, "Capacity and Incapacity," 407–9; Zizioulas, *Communion*, 9–10; Fiddes, *Participating*, 38; Pannenberg, *Anthropology*, 37, 63–69, 298.

184. Volf, *Likeness*, 182–85, 186; Gunton, *One, Three, Many*, 213; LaCugna, *God*, 403; Zizioulas, *Communion*, 244–47; Zizioulas, *One and Many*, 53–55, 84, 333–48.

185. Acts 2:42, 46; 4:32; 12:12; 14:27; 1 Cor 14:26; Gal 6:10; Eph 5:19–21; Heb 10:23–25; Grenz, *Social God*, 320–22; Webster, *Holiness*, 53–54, 57–64, 84–86.

186. Wesley, "Minutes of Several Conversations 1744–1789," 322–23.

are not "ends" toward grace, and there is nothing intrinsic in the practices themselves.[187] These edifying practices within the holy community are responses of love (or cooperation with grace) and cannot be separated from the Spirit of God.[188] The means of grace are practices that can enable one's heart to be freed from the self and opened to more of God's grace to grow deeper qualitatively in relationship with the triune God.[189]

Second, participation in the mission of God engages the quantity of needs that are exterior or outside of the holy community in the secular community and the world at large.[190] The Holy Spirit equips, enables, and empowers the church to do the work of Jesus Christ in the world.[191] Since the relationship with God constitutes the Christian person made possible by the indwelling of the Holy Spirit, because of the self-sacrifice of Jesus Christ, motivated by the holy-love and will of God the Father, the mission of the church is also a self-giving love act in her worship of the Triune God and motivation to draw people into the life of the Trinity for purpose and wholeness.[192] Newbigin says that "the Church is not the source of witness; rather, it is the locus of witness."[193] That is to say, that mission of the church as the holy community, indwelled by the Holy

187. Collins, *Wesley*, 257–59; Leclerc, *Discovering*, 260–61.

188. Burtner and Chiles, *Wesley's Theology*, 231–32; Collins, *Wesley*, 258–59; Leclerc, *Discovering*, 261–70. Cf. Pannenberg, *Anthropology*, 298.

189. The idea of a human person being freed from the self to grow further in relationship with the Triune God fits within Zizioulas's concept of *ekstasis* as an understanding of personhood. See Zizioulas, "Capacity and Incapacity," 408–9, 419, 445; Zizioulas, *Communion*, 212–13; also, Moltmann, *Trinity*, 202–3, 213–18.

190. Cross, *Presence*, 224–26. Cross distills the church's missional activities down to witness and serve (Cross, *Presence*, 229–37). Also see "works of grace" as an outflow of a sanctified heart for needs in secular society in Collins, *Wesley*, 267–70. LaCugna, *God*, 401–3; Pratt, "Heart of Mission," 48–50. Zizioulas accuses Western Protestant churches of secularization because of its close relationship with society and mission (Zizioulas, *Lectures*, 120–21). Zizioulas further critiques the Western Protestant churches of individualism through the emphasis on preaching and mission (Zizioulas, *Lectures*, 121).

191. Dunn says that "Luke presents Pentecost as the beginning of world mission" (Dunn, *Pneumatology*, 214). Sexton, "Confessing," 182–83, 185.

192. Coppenger, "Community," 57; Newbigin says, "Mission is an acted out doxology" (Newbigin, *Gospel*, 127). "Wholeness" here means the result of one who has heard the witness of Jesus Christ (which may include physical needs being met), received forgiveness of sins and welcomed into the holy community (Rom 10:14–17). Thus, a new set of relationships have been entered into through *koinōnia-vertical* and *koinōnia-horizontal* making the reconciled person a Christian person.

193. Newbigin, *Gospel*, 120; Pinnock, *Flame*, 219; Sexton, "Confessing" 183.

Spirit, is to live the reality of a reconciled people in relationship with God.[194] This Spirit-indwelled community, Newbigin believes, will cause the world to ask the questions that the gospel can answer.[195] If we take Rahner's axiom, "*The 'economic' Trinity is the 'immanent' Trinity and the 'immanent' Trinity is the 'economic' Trinity*," and further apply it to the church and mission, we conclude that the church is to engage the world hypostatically as the personification of Christ, filled by the Holy Spirit, by the will of the Father for the salvation of the world.[196] However, Migliore reminds us that while the church lives and works in the world, it should not be confused or transformed by the world.[197] The church is to transform the world.[198] Migliore points out that influences of the world like individualism, secularism, oppressive practices, and a loss of "a compelling theological vision" have damaged the church's mission in the world.[199] The church does not do missions but rather "is a missionary community because God is a missionary God."[200] God is missionary because God is *ekstatic* in personhood and activity.[201] Therefore the Christian person and the church participate in the relational mission, which is the self-giving love of the triune God who invites all to come and be saved and enter into the holy community.[202]

194. Newbigin, *Gospel*, 119; Wright, *Mission*, 96–113.

195. Newbigin, *Gospel*, 119; Ashford, "Gospel and Culture," 109–10, 118–27; Wright, *Mission*, 186–90.

196. Rahner, *Trinity*, 22, 24–30. Whitfield explains that "the *foundation* of God's mission is built on the attributes of God" and that "the relational nature of the triune God [is] the *pattern* of God's mission" (Whitfield, "Triune God," 23, 25). Zizioulas, *Being*, 97–98, 107, 140, 145–49, 179; Zizioulas, *Eucharistic Communion*, 7, 124, 128; Zizioulas, *Lectures*, 123, 132, 148. Mark 16:15; John 3:17; 16:28; 17:18.

197. Migliore, "Missionary," 24; John 15:19; 17:14, 16. Cf. Carter and Carter, "Gospel and Lifestyle," 128–43.

198. Newbigin, *Gospel*, 128–29, 133, 141. Matt 24:14; 28:19–20; Mark 16:15–18; Luke 24:46–49; John 13:34–35; 17:14–18; Acts 1:8–9; 2 Cor 5:18–20.

199. Migliore, "Missionary," 15–16. Carter and Carter, "Gospel and Lifestyle," 129.

200. Migliore, "Missionary," 17. In a similar, but less impactful way, Whitfield says, "Mission exists because God exists" (Whitfield, "Triune God," 17).

201. Cross, *Presence*, 224–29; Pinnock, *Flame*, 38; LaCugna, *God*, 351–52, 355–56.

202. Migliore, "Missionary," 18; Wright, *Mission*, 210–11. Ezek 18:23, 32; 1 Tim 2:4; 4:10. Zizioulas, *One and Many*, 187.

SUMMARY

Christian anthropology is viewed here as a Christian person constituted through trinitarian pneumatology initiated by the Holy Spirit. The
Christian person is each particular person who has encountered the
presence of God and continues to live in God's presence by participating
in the life of the Trinity initiated and sustained by the Holy Spirit. As
explained herein chapter 7, the Holy Spirit who eternally lives and dwells
in relationship with the Father and the Son is the agent of conversion by
bringing Christ's salvation to the human person who is delivered from
spiritual death to spiritual life in abundance.[203] The Holy Spirit draws the
new believer into a new relationship by this new birth with the whole
Trinity made possible by the holy-love will of the Father and the *kenōsis*
and resurrection of the Son.[204] Through repentance and faith in Christ,
a human person's sin is forgiven, and the Holy Spirit indwells the human heart drawing the Christian into a deeper relationship of truth.[205]
The Holy Spirit constitutes the Christian person as adopted into the
family of God and a follower of Jesus Christ.[206] Humans were made for
community, but the result of sin is disunity from one another and excommunication from God.[207] However, along with the "new humanity"
comes a "new community": the church.[208] As the relationship grows, the
Christian person continues to change within as their human character
becomes transformed into the character of Christ (i.e., holy-love) and
taking on the mission of Christ.[209] The Christian person's particularity is
not lost but instead redeemed and sanctified for God's purposes.[210] Ul-

203. Collins correctly captures Wesleyan theology when he refers to the Holy
Spirit as a sovereign agent of human restoration, saying, "the Holy Spirit must play
a leading, superintending role in the process of repentance: convicting, illuminating,
and teaching—even actively wooing the sinful soul" (Collins, *Wesley*, 122–23). Turner,
"Spirit and Salvation," 103–16.

204. Congar, *Holy Spirit*, 2.1.1; Sanders, *Deep*, 140–53.

205. Acts 2:38–39; Turner, *Power*, 346–47, 433–38.

206. Rom 8:14–15; Behr, "Trinitarian Being," 171; Cross, *Presence*, 118–19, 123,
128; Dunn, *Baptism*, 93, 94–95, 149; Farrow, *Ascension*, 59–60; Fee, *Empowering*, 564;
Irenaeus, *Heresies*, 4.20.6; Käsemann, *Romans*, 218–19, 222, 223; Pannenberg, *Anthropology*, 298; Wesley, "Farther Appeal," 49; Yarnell, *Holy Spirit*, 99.

207. Duvall and Hays, *Presence*, 1, 17–19, 325, 326, 331; Routledge, *Theology*, 152.

208. Coppenger, "Community," 61–62, 65–66, 74–75; Cross, *Presence*, 86–92.

209. Kinlaw, *Mind*, 99–109; Shults, *Anthropology*, 222.

210. Purkiser, *Exploring*, 349–51. Wesley understands Christian perfection to

timately, God's plan for the world is accomplished through the church's mission, empowered by the Holy Spirit, redeemed by the Son, and willed by the Father.[211] This trinitarian pneumatological participation in the life of humans maintains a Wesleyan theological distinctive.

While Wesleyan theology includes the doctrines of the Trinity, pneumatology, hamartiology, soteriology, and humanity, a fresh theological expression through trinitarian pneumatological personhood may help express the Wesleyan distinctive. Zizioulas's Dictum of persons-in-relation based on a reading of the Cappadocian Fathers gives a fresh perspective and a starting point for understanding the Triune God and humans.

---

include both an inward and outward expression. The inward perfection includes personality or character with all of one's passions and desires which is a result of obedience to God. See Lindström, *Wesley and Sanctification*, 158–59.

211. Zizioulas, *Being*, 182–83, 184–85, 189; Newbigin, *Gospel*, 118–19; Pinnock, *Flame*, 141–47; Whitfield, "Triune God," 27–28. Cf. Coleman, "Agents of Mission," 36–47.

Conclusion

OUR WORKING RESEARCH QUESTION has been, "Does Zizioulas's trinitarian personhood successfully accomplish an anthropological definition?" We have answered "no" and offered this hypothesis: "A Christian person is constituted through trinitarian pneumatology which the Holy Spirit initiates." Therefore our contribution to this research is that the Christian person is each particular person who has encountered the presence of God and continues to live in that presence by participating in the life of the Trinity initiated and sustained by the Holy Spirit.

John Zizioulas's theology has brought to light the need to study personhood alongside theology in a manner that implies a divine-human relationship. The Triune God is three relational persons (*hypostases*) while simultaneously united in communion (*koinōnia*). However, Zizioulas fails to offer balanced *hypostases* of Trinitarian persons because he opposes an economy of persons.[1] In Zizioulas's theology, the Trinity is under the Father's *monarchy*; the Holy Spirit constitutes the Son making him one-and-many, thus instituting the church through the Eucharist.[2] The many become absorbed into the one from two directions in Zizioulas's theological application of ecclesiology or eucharistic personality. The whole Trinity becomes encapsulated in Christ at the Eucharist, while the human participants become the one church, saved from their individuality.[3] In all, the particular is lost in the unified whole. If personhood is found in relation with another, as developed by Zizioulas's Dictum, being-as-communion, then Christian personhood resides in a new set of relationships; as a new creation (*kaine ktisis*), or redeemed and reconciled

---

1. Zizioulas, *Lectures*, 81; Zizioulas, *One and Many*, 77.

2. Zizioulas, *One and Many*, 10–14. See Zizioulas, *Being*, 44–45n40.

3. Zizioulas, *Being*, 110–14; Zizioulas, *Communion*, 6, 244–45.

in Christ.[4] Furthermore, a balanced *hypostasis* of the Trinity leads to a more balanced approach to human particularity, which in turn must precede communion enriching an understanding of being-as-communion.[5] The result is that to be a Christian person is to be in relation to another (i.e., *perichoresis*).[6] The divine-human relationship is so intimate that the Scriptures speak of the Holy Spirit indwelling believers, which is necessary to be a Christian person.[7]

Zizioulas's work has spurred further research and writing in the areas of the Trinity, ecclesiology, and personhood.[8] Zizioulas, himself, has called for more work to be done in anthropology from a trinitarian perspective.[9] Personhood as anthropology in Zizioulas's theology is found in Christ, the human *par excellence*, whose "mode of existence" is *ekstatic*, or persons-in-relation/being-as-communion.[10] Humans can enter into this meaningful existence, not through a relationship, but through participation in the Eucharist in Zizioulas's theology.[11]

While grateful for Zizioulas's trinitarian-personhood and the *ekstatic* mode of existence found in Christ through the incarnation and atonement for the world's salvation, a *fulfillment* of persons-in-relation must come by *means* of persons-in-relation. Upon Jesus's ascension into heaven, God the Father sent the Holy Spirit (initiated through Jesus Christ) as the personal presence of the Father and the Son until the Son,

---

4. 2 Cor 5:17; Gal 6:15; also Rom 6:4; Eph 4:22–24; Barnett, *2 Corinthians*, 113; Kinlaw, *Jesus*, 139.

5. Gunton, *One, Three, Many*, 153, 180–81, 201, 203.

6. Zizioulas, *Being*, 16, 18, 46; Zizioulas, *Communion*, 9–10, 99–103, 106–12.

7. Acts 11:14–17; 19:1–7; Rom 8:9; 1 Cor 6:19; Gal 4:6; 1 Thess 4:8; Cross, *Presence*, 10–11; Fee, *Empowering*, 5–9, 135–37, 270, 294, 722, 843–45, 846, 854–55, 864, 872; McKnight, *Open*, 19, 56, 63–64; Sanders, *Deep*, 140–53, 160–66; Yarnell, *Holy Spirit*, 99, 105. For Levison, being filled with the Spirit is not that one is filled with the third person of the Trinity, but rather one is filled with the gospel values (Levison, *Filled*, 55–57, 80). Duvall and Hays, *Presence*, 333–34.

8. E.g., Awad, "Between"; Awad, "Personhood;" Ciraulo, "Sacraments and Personhood," 993–1004; Degenkolb, "Participatory Personhood"; De Halleux, "Personnalisme"; Fox, *God as Communion*; Grenz, *Rediscovering*; Harrison, "Zizioulas"; Papanikolaou, *Being with God*; Torrance, *Persons*; Turcescu, "Misreadings"; Ury, *Trinitarian Personhood*; Volf, *Likeness*; Wilks, "Ontology."

9. Zizioulas, *One and Many*, 6, 30–31, 383. Cf. Zizioulas, *Communion*, 243–45.

10. Zizioulas, *Communion*, 245.

11. Zizioulas, *Being*, 143–69; Zizioulas, *Communion*, 296–98; Zizioulas, *Eucharist*, 45–58; Zizioulas, *Eucharistic Communion*, 12–23, 123–31; Zizioulas, *Lectures*, 117–19; Zizioulas, *One and Many*, 49–60.

Jesus Christ, returns.[12] The whole Trinity is present with the Holy Spirit as the economy of trinitarian persons cannot be conceived in themselves but are interdependent. Therefore, a Christian person is constituted by the Holy Spirit made possible by the incarnation, crucifixion, resurrection, and ascension of the Son and the Father's will. When a person is convicted of sin, repents, and places their faith and belief in Jesus Christ, that new Christian comes into a living relationship with God, through Jesus Christ, by the Holy Spirit. The point of connection in the divine-human relationship is the person of the Holy Spirit.

Those not theologically evangelical will undoubtedly disagree with these conclusions, arguing that the Christian person receives the Holy Spirit through the sacramental act. Non-evangelicals who seek a more corporate soteriology may find this theology individualistic, although strides have been made to move away from an overt individualism in preference for particularity and uniqueness of persons. Constructive Pentecostalism, especially those who have articulated a pneumatologically oriented trinitarianism, may point to similarities of thought which are unintentional on our part. Others will desire to see more emphasis on the experience and results of the pneumatological encounter.

Finally, trinitarian pneumatological personhood applies to a theological perspective in anthropology, soteriology, ecclesiology, and Christian counseling. Further research in trinitarian pneumatological personhood applied to anthropology could deal with the unborn, mentally challenged, the person in a comatose state, and the dying in an unresponsive state. Further research in soteriology could be developed where interviews may be conducted to analyze (evangelical) pre and post-conversion experiences, characteristics, and behaviors. Trinitarian pneumatological personhood can help Wesleyan theology understand more clearly and articulate its doctrines of ecclesiology, including the sacraments and ministry of an ordained pastor, and entire sanctification. Our opinion is that a trinitarian pneumatological personhood approach to theology can enhance a Wesleyan articulation of theology and engage current modern issues. Practically, trinitarian pneumatological personhood can be applied in the field of Christian counseling. These are a few of the areas where further research in trinitarian pneumatological personhood can be developed.

---

12. Luke 24:44–53; Acts 1:1–11.

Bibliography

Adkins, Ronald L., II. "Article on Sin." *The East Central Conference of the Evangelical Church: Journal* (2018) 42.

Albertz, Rainer. *A History of Israelite Religion in the Old Testament Period.* Vol 1, *From the Beginning to the End of the Monarchy.* Louisville: Westminster John Knox, 1994.

Allison, Gregg R., and Andreas J. Köstenberger. *The Holy Spirit.* The Theology for the People of God. Nashville: B&H Academic, 2020.

Ambrose. *On the Holy Spirit.* In vol. 10 of *Nicene and Post-Nicene Fathers, Second Series*, edited by Philip Schaff and Henry Wace, translated by H. De Romestin, 91–158. Peabody, MA: Hendrickson, 2004.

Anatolios, Khaled. "Personhood, Communion, and the Trinity in Some Patristic Texts." In *The Holy Trinity in the Life of the Church*, edited by Khaled Anatolios, 147–64. Holy Cross Studies in Patristic Theology and History. Grand Rapids: Baker Academic, 2014.

Anderson, Allan. *An Introduction to Pentecostalism.* Cambridge: Cambridge University Press, 2004.

Anderson, Gary A. "*Necessarium Adae Peccatum:* The Problem of Original Sin." In *Sin, Death, and the Devil*, edited by Carl E. Braaten and Robert W. Jenson, 22–44. Grand Rapids: Eerdmans, 2000.

Anderson, Tim L. *Into His Presence: A Theology of Intimacy with God.* Grand Rapids: Kregel Academic, 2019.

Angell, Norman. *The Great Illusion: A Study of the Relation of Military Power to National Advantage.* 4th ed. 1913. Reprint, San Francisco: Bottom of the Hill, 2012.

Aquinas, Thomas. *Compendium Theologiae.* Translated by Cyril Vollert. London: Herder, 1947.

———. *The Faith of the Church: Trinity.* http://www.malankaraworld.com/library/Faith/Trinity/Trinity_thomas-aquinas-part-7.htm.

———. *Summa Theologiae.* https://www.newadvent.org/summa/.

Aristotle. *The Eudemian Ethics.* Translated by Anthony Kenny. Oxford World's Classics. Oxford: Oxford University Press, 2011.

———. *History of Animals: Books I–III.* Edited by G. P. Goold. Translated by A. L. Peck. Loeb Classical Library 437. 1965. Reprint, Cambridge: Harvard University Press, 1993.

————. *Metaphysics: Books I–IX*. Edited by G. P. Goold. Translated by Hugh Tredennick. Loeb Classical Library 271. 1933. Reprint, Cambridge: Harvard University Press, 1996.

————. *Nicomachean Ethics*. Translated by C. D. C. Reeves. Indianapolis: Hackett, 2014.

————. *On Length and Shortness of Life*. Edited by G. P. Goold. Translated by W. S. Hett. Loeb Classical Library 288. 1936. Reprint, Cambridge: Harvard University Press, 1995.

————. *On the Soul*. Edited by G. P. Goold. Translated by W. S. Hett. Loeb Classical Library 288. 1936. Reprint, Cambridge: Harvard University Press, 1995.

————. *Selections*. Translated by Terence Irwin and Gail Fine. Indianapolis: Hackett, 1995.

Arnold, Bill T., and Bryan E. Beyer. *Encountering the Old Testament: A Christian Survey*. Edited by Eugene H. Merrill. Encountering Biblical Series. Grand Rapids: Baker, 1999.

Ashford, Bruce Riley. "The Gospel and Culture." In *Theology and Practice of Mission: God, the Church, and the Nations*, edited by Bruce Riley Ashford, 109–27. Nashville: B&H Academic, 2011.

Athanasius. *Against the Heathen (Contra Gentes)*. In vol. 4 of *Nicene and Post-Nicene Fathers, Second Series*, edited by Philip Schaff and Henry Wace, translated by Archibald Robertson, 1–30. Peabody, MA: Hendrickson, 2004.

————. *Four Discourses against the Arians*. In vol. 4 of *Nicene and Post-Nicene Fathers, Second Series*, edited by Philip Schaff and Henry Wace, translated by Archibald Robertson, 431–47. Peabody, MA: Hendrickson, 2004.

————. *De Synodis, Councils of Ariminium, and Seleucia*. In vol. 4 of *Nicene and Post-Nicene Fathers, Second Series*, edited by Philip Schaff and Henry Wace, translated by Archibald Robertson, 448–80. Peabody, MA: Hendrickson, 2004.

————. *Defence of the Nicene Definition*. In vol. 4 of *Nicene and Post-Nicene Fathers, Second Series*, edited by Philip Schaff and Henry Wace, translated by Cardinal Newman, 149–72. Peabody, MA: Hendrickson, 2004.

————. *Historica et Dogmatica*. In vol. 26 of *Patrologiae Cursus Completus*, translated by J. P. Migne, 1–1450. Turnholti: Typographi Brepols Editores Pontificii, n.d.

————. "Letter LIX, to Epictetus." In vol. 4 of *Nicene and Post-Nicene Fathers, Second Series*, edited by Philip Schaff and Henry Wace, translated by Cardinal Newman, 570–74. Peabody, MA: Hendrickson, 2004.

————. *The Letters of Saint Athanasius Concerning the Holy Spirit*. Translated by C. R. B. Shapland. London: Epworth, 1951.

————. *On the Incarnation*. In vol. 4 of *Nicene and Post-Nicene Fathers, Second Series*, edited by Philip Schaff and Henry Wace, translated by Archibald Robertson, 31–67. Peabody, MA: Hendrickson, 2004.

————. *To Serapion on the Holy Spirit*. Middletown, DE: U.S.A., 2018.

Athenagoras. *A Plea for the Christians*. In vol. 2 of *Ante-Nicene Fathers*, edited by Alexander Roberts and James Donaldson, translated by B. P. Pratten, 129–48. Peabody, MA: Hendrickson, 2004.

Atkinson, William P. *Baptism in the Spirit: Luke-Acts and the Dunn Debate*. Eugene, OR: Pickwick, 2011.

————. *Trinity after Pentecost*. Eugene, OR: Pickwick, 2013.

Augustine. *The City of God.* In vol. 2 of *Nicene and Post-Nicene Fathers, First Series,* edited by Philip Schaff, translated by Marcus Dods, 1–511. Peabody, MA: Hendrickson, 2004.

———. *The Confessions of St. Augustine.* In vol. 1 of *Nicene and Post-Nicene Fathers, First Series,* edited by Philip Schaff, translated by J. G. Pilkington, 45–207. Peabody, MA: Hendrickson, 2004.

———. *Gospel according to John.* In vol. 7 of *Nicene and Post-Nicene Fathers, First Series,* edited by Philip Schaff, translated by John Gibb and James Innes, 7–452. Peabody, MA: Hendrickson, 2004.

———. *On the Trinity.* In vol. 3 of *Nicene and Post-Nicene Fathers, First Series,* edited by Philip Schaff, translated by Arthur West Haddan, 1–228. Peabody, MA: Hendrickson, 2004.

———. *Sermons on Selected Lessons of the New Testament.* In vol. 6 of *Nicene and Post-Nicene Fathers, First Series,* edited by Philip Schaff, translated by R. G. MacMullen, 237–545. Peabody, MA: Hendrickson, 2004.

———. *Soliloquies.* In vol. 7 of *Nicene and Post-Nicene Fathers, First Series,* edited by Philip Schaff, translated by H. Browne, 537–60. Peabody, MA: Hendrickson, 2004.

———. *Treatise on Faith and the Creed.* In vol. 3 of *Nicene and Post-Nicene Fathers, First Series,* edited by Philip Schaff, translated by S. D. F. Salmond, 321–33. Peabody, MA: Hendrickson, 2004.

Awad, Najeeb G. "Between Subordination and Koinonia: Toward a New Reading of the Cappadocian Theology." *Modern Theology* 23 (2007) 181–204.

———. "Personhood as Particularity: John Zizioulas, Colin Gunton, and the Trinitarian Theology of Personhood." *Journal of Reformed Theology* 4 (2010) 1–22.

Bainton, Roland H. *Here I Stand: A Life of Martin Luther.* New York: Mentor, 1956.

Balentine, Samuel E. *The Hidden God: The Hiding of the Face of God in the Old Testament.* Oxford: Oxford University Press, 1983.

Barnes, Timothy David. *Tertullian: A Historical and Literary Study.* Oxford: Oxford University Press, 1971.

Barnett, Paul. *The Message of 2 Corinthians: Power in Weakness.* The Bible Speaks Today. Downers Grove, IL: InterVarsity, 1988.

Barrett, C. K. *The Gospel according to St. John: An Introduction with Commentary and Notes on the Greek Text.* New York: Macmillan, 1956.

Barth, Christoph. *God with Us: A Theological Introduction to the Old Testament.* Edited by Geoffrey W. Bromiley. Grand Rapids: Eerdmans, 1991.

Barth, Karl. *Church Dogmatics.* Edited by G. W. Bromiley and T. F. Torrance. 31 vols. Study ed. London: T. & T. Clark, 2010.

Basil. *The Hexaemeron.* In vol. 8 of *Nicene and Post-Nicene Fathers, Second Series,* edited by Philip Schaff and Henry Wace, translated by Blomfield Jackson, 51–108. Peabody, MA: Hendrickson, 2004.

———. *Letters.* In vol. 8 of *Nicene and Post-Nicene Fathers, Second Series,* edited by Philip Schaff and Henry Wace, translated by Blomfield Jackson, 109–327. Peabody, MA: Hendrickson, 2004.

———. *On the Spirit.* In vol. 8 of *Nicene and Post-Nicene Fathers, Second Series,* edited by Philip Schaff and Henry Wace, translated by Blomfield Jackson, 1–50. Peabody, MA: Hendrickson, 2004.

Bathrellos, Demetrios. "Church, Eucharist, Bishop: The Early Church in the Ecclesiology of John Zizioulas." In *The Theology of John Zizioulas: Personhood and the Church*, edited by Douglas Knight, 133–46. Burlington, VT: Ashgate, 2007.

Beasley-Murray, George R. *John*. 2nd ed. Word Biblical Commentary 36. Nashville: Nelson, 1999.

Beauregard, Mario, and Denyse O'Leary. *The Spiritual Brain: A Neuroscientist's Case for the Existence of the Soul*. New York: Harper One, 2007.

Behr, John. *The Nicene Faith*. Vol. 1, *True God of True God*. The Formation of Christian Theology 2. Crestwood, NY: St. Vladimir's, 2004.

———. *The Nicene Faith*. Vol. 2, *One of the Holy Trinity*. The Formation of Christian Theology 2. Crestwood, NY: St. Vladimir's, 2004.

———. "The Trinitarian Being of the Church." In *The Holy Trinity in the Life of the Church*, edited by Khaled Anatolios, 165–82. Holy Cross Studies in Patristic Theology and History. Grand Rapids: Baker Academic, 2014.

Benjamin, A. Cornelius. "Particular." In *Dictionary of Philosophy*, edited by Dagobert D. Runes, 226. Totowa, NJ: Littlefield, Adams, 1977.

Bird, Michael F., and Scott Harrower, eds. *Trinity without Hierarchy: Reclaiming Nicene Orthodoxy in Evangelical Theology*. Grand Rapids: Kregel Academic, 2019.

Blackham, H. J. *Six Existentialist Thinkers*. New York: Harper & Brothers, 1959.

Bloesch, Donald G. *The Holy Spirit: Works & Gifts*. Christian Foundations Series. Downers Grove, IL: InterVarsity, 2000.

Bobrinskoy, Boris. "The Indwelling of the Spirit in Christ: 'Pneumatic Christology' in the Cappadocian Fathers." *St. Vladimir's Theological Quarterly* 28 (1984) 49–65.

Bock, Darrell L. *Acts*. Baker Exegetical Commentary on the New Testament. Grand Rapids: Baker Academic, 2007.

———. "The Doctrine of the Future in the Synoptic Gospels." In *Eschatology: Biblical, Historical, and Practical Approaches*, edited by D. Jefferey Bingham and Glenn R. Kreider, 197–210. Grand Rapids: Kregel Academic, 2016.

Boethius. *Theological Tractates: The Consolation of Philosophy*. Translated by H. F. Stewart et al. Loeb Classical Library 74. Cambridge: Harvard University Press, 1973.

Boff, Leonardo. *Trinity and Society*. Translated by Paul Burns. 1988. Reprint, Eugene, OR: Wipf & Stock, 2005.

Bonaventure. *Holiness of Life*. In *Saint Bonaventure: Collection*, translated by Laurence Costello, 5–42. Lexington, KY: Aeterna, 2019.

———. *The Journey of the Mind to God*. In *The Works of Bonaventure*, translated by José de Vinck, 1–58. Paterson, NJ: St. Anthony Guild, 2016.

———. *On the Eucharist (Commentary on the Sentences, Book IV, dist. 8–13)*. Translated by Junius Johnson. Dallas Medieval Texts and Translations 23. Bristol, CT: Peeters, 2017.

———. *The Triple Way or Love Enkindled*. In *The Works of Bonaventure*, translated by José de Vinck, 59–94. Paterson, NJ: St. Anthony Guild, 2016.

Bonhoeffer, Dietrich. *Life Together*. Translated by John W. Doberstein. New York: Harper & Brothers, 1954.

Bratsiotis, Panagiotis I. "The Fundamental Principles and Main Characteristics of the Orthodox Church." In vol. 1 of *The Orthodox Ethos: Studies in Orthodoxy*, edited by A. J. Philippou, 23–31. Oxford: Holywell, 1964.

Brown, Alan. "On the Criticism of *Being as Communion* in Anglophone Orthodox Theology." In *Theology of John Zizioulas*, edited by Douglas Knight, 35–78. Burlington, VT: Ashgate, 2007.

Brown, John Pairman. *Ancient Israel and Ancient Greece: Religion, Politics, and Culture.* Minneapolis: Fortress, 2003.

Brown, Raymond E. *The Churches the Apostles Left Behind.* New York: Paulist, 1984.

———. *The Community of the Beloved Disciple: The Life, Loves, and Hates of an Individual Church in the New Testament Times.* New York: Paulist, 1979.

———. *The Gospel according to John.* 2 vols. Anchor Yale Bible 29–29A. New Haven: Yale University Press, 2008.

———. *An Introduction to the Gospel of John.* Edited by Francis J. Moloney. The Anchor Bible Reference Library. New York: Doubleday, 2003.

Brown, William. "Gender and Power Dynamics in Enūma Eliš and the Priestly Creation Account: A Comparative Analysis." *Intermountain West Journal of Religious Studies* 7 (2016) 1–45.

Bruce, F. F. *The Book of the Acts.* Rev. ed. The New International Commentary on the New Testament. Grand Rapids: Eerdmans, 1988.

———. *The Gospel and Epistles of John: Introduction, Exposition, and Notes.* Grand Rapids: Eerdmans, 1983.

Brueggemann, Walter. *A Commentary on Jeremiah: Exile and Homecoming.* Grand Rapids: Eerdmans, 1998.

———. *First and Second Samuel.* Interpretation, a Bible Commentary for Teaching and Preaching. Louisville: Knox, 1990.

———. *God, Neighbor, Empire: The Excess of Divine Fidelity and the Command of Common God.* Waco, TX: Baylor University Press, 2016.

———. *Theology of the Old Testament: Testimony, Dispute, Advocacy.* Minneapolis: Fortress, 1997.

Brunner, Emil. *The Christian Doctrine of God.* Vol. 1. Translated by Olive Wyon. Philadelphia: Westminster, 1949.

Buber, Martin. *I and Thou.* Translated by Ronald Gregor Smith. New York: Scribner's Sons, 1957.

Bullard, Roger Aubrey. *The Hypostasis of the Archons.* Translated by Roger Aubrey Bullard. Berlin: de Gruyter, 1970.

Bultmann, Rudolf. *The Gospel of John: A Commentary.* Edited by R. W. N. Hoare and J. K. Riches. Translated by G. R. Beasley-Murray. Philadelphia: Westminster, 1971.

Burge, Gary M. *The Anointed Community: The Holy Spirit in the Johannine Tradition.* Grand Rapids: Eerdmans, 1987.

———. *John.* The NIV Application Commentary. Grand Rapids: Zondervan, 2000.

Burgess, Stanley M., ed. *Christian Peoples of the Spirit: A Documentary History of Pentecostal Spirituality from the Early Church to the Present.* New York: New York University Press, 2011.

———. "Hildegard of Bingen." In *Christian Peoples of the Spirit: A Documentary History of Pentecostal Spirituality from the Early Church to the Present,* edited by Stanley M. Burgess, 98–103. New York: New York University Press, 2011.

———. *The Holy Spirit: Ancient Christian Traditions.* Peabody, MA: Hendrickson, 2002.

———. *The Holy Spirit: Medieval Roman Catholic and Reformation Traditions (Sixth–Sixteenth Centuries).* Peabody, MA: Hendrickson, 2006.

———. "Rupert of Deutz." In *The Holy Spirit: Medieval Roman Catholic and Reformation Traditions (Sixth–Sixteenth Centuries)*, 36–40. Peabody, MA: Hendrickson, 2006.

Burnett, Daniel L. *In the Shadow of Aldersgate: An Introduction to the Heritage and Faith of the Wesleyan Tradition*. Eugene, OR: Cascade, 2006.

Burtner Robert W., and Robert E. Chiles, eds. *A Compend of Wesley's Theology*. New York: Abingdon, 1954.

Cairns, David. *The Image of God in Man*. London: Fontana Library Theology & Philosophy, 1973.

Calvin, John. *John Calvin's Commentary on Genesis: Chapters 1–50*. Translated by Thomas Tymme. Lexington, KY: Legacy, 2018.

———. *Institutes of the Christian Religion*. Translated by Henry Beveridge. Peabody, MA: Hendrickson, 2008.

Carson, D. A. "Sin's Contemporary Significance." In *Fallen: A Theology of Sin*, edited by Christopher W. Morgan and Robert A. Peterson, 21–38. Wheaton, IL: Crossway, 2013.

Carter, Alan, and Katherine Carter. "The Gospel and Lifestyle." In *Theology and Practice of Mission: God, the Church, and the Nations*, edited by Bruce Riley Ashford, 128–44. Nashville: B&H Academic, 2011.

Carter, Charles Webb. *The Person and Ministry of the Holy Spirit: A Wesleyan Perspective*. Grand Rapids: Baker, 1974.

Cartledge, Mark J. *Encountering the Spirit: The Charismatic Tradition*. Traditions of Christian Spirituality Series. Maryknoll, NY: Orbis, 2006.

Cattoi, Thomas. "The Relevance of Gregory of Nyssa's *Ad Ablabium* for Catholic-Orthodox Ecumenical Dialogue of the Trinity and the Church." In *The Holy Trinity in the Life of the Church*, edited by Khaled Anatolios, 183–98. Grand Rapids: Baker Academic, 2014.

Chadwick, Henry. *East and West: The Making of a Rift in the Church: From Apostolic Times until the Council of Florence*. Oxford: Oxford University Press, 2009.

Chisholm, Robert B., Jr. *Handbook on the Prophets: Isaiah, Jeremiah, Lamentations, Ezekiel, Daniel, Minor Prophets*. Grand Rapids: Baker Academic, 2002.

Chrysostom, John. *The Epistle to the Romans*. In vol. 11 of *Nicene and Post-Nicene Fathers, First Series*, edited by Philip Schaff, translated by J. B. Morris and W. H. Simcox, 335–566. Peabody, MA: Hendrickson, 2004.

———. *Homilies on the Epistles of Paul to the Corinthians*. In vol. 12 of *Nicene and Post-Nicene Fathers, First Series*, edited by Philip Schaff, translated by Talbot W. Chambers, 1–420. Peabody, MA: Hendrickson, 2004.

———. *Homilies on the Gospel of St. John*. In vol. 14 of *Nicene and Post-Nicene Fathers, First Series*, edited by Philip Schaff, translated by Charles Marriott, 335–566. Peabody, MA: Hendrickson, 2004.

———. *Homilies on Gospel of St. Matthew*. In vol. 10 of *Nicene and Post-Nicene Fathers, First Series*, edited by Philip Schaff, translated by George Prevost Baronet, 1–534. Peabody, MA: Hendrickson, 2004.

———. *Homilies on Timothy*. In vol. 13 of *Nicene and Post-Nicene Fathers, First Series*, edited and translated by Philip Schaff, 407–518. Peabody, MA: Hendrickson, 2004.

———. *Instructions to Catechumens*. In vol. 9 of *Nicene and Post-Nicene Fathers, First Series*, edited by Philip Schaff, translated by W. R. W. Stephens, 159–71. Peabody, MA: Hendrickson, 2004.

Cicero. *De Amicitia*. Edited by G. P. Goold. Translated by William Armistead Falconer. Loeb Classical Library 20. Cambridge: Harvard University Press, 1996.

———. *De Oratore: Books I–II*. Edited by G. P. Goold. Translated by William E. W. Sutton and H. Rackham. Loeb Classical Library 3. Cambridge: Harvard University Press, 1996.

Ciraulo, Jonathan Martin. "Sacraments and Personhood: John Zizioulas's Impasse and a Way Forward." *The Heythrop Journal* 53 (2012) 993–1004.

Clark, Stephen R. L. *Aristotle's Man: Speculations upon Aristotelian Anthropology*. Oxford: Clarendon, 1975.

Clegg, Jerry S. *The Structure of Plato's Philosophy*. Lewisburg, PA: Bucknell University Press, 1977.

Clement of Rome. *The First Epistle to the Corinthians*. In vol. 1 of *Ante-Nicene Fathers*, edited by Alexander Roberts et al., 5–21. Peabody, MA: Hendrickson, 2004.

Cockerill, Gareth Lee. *The Epistle to the Hebrews*. The New International Commentary on the New Testament. Grand Rapids: Eerdmans, 2012.

Cohen, Abraham. *Everyman's Talmud: The Major Teachings of the Rabbinic Sages*. 1949. Reprint, New York: Schocken, 1995.

Cohen, S. Marc, and C. D. C. Reeve. "Aristotle's Metaphysics." In *The Stanford Encyclopedia of Philosophy*, edited by Edward N. Zalta. https://plato.stanford.edu/archives/win2021/entries/aristotle-metaphysics/.

Coleman, Doug. "The Agents of Mission: Humanity." In *Theology and Practice of Mission: God, the Church, and the Nations*, edited by Bruce Riley Ashford, 36–47. Nashville: B&H Academic, 2011.

Collins, Kenneth J. *The Theology of John Wesley: Holy Love and the Shape of Grace*. Nashville: Abingdon, 2007.

Collins, Paul. "Authority and Ecumenism." In *The Theology of John Zizioulas: Personhood and the Church*, edited by Douglas H. Knight, 147–58. Burlington, VT: Ashgate, 2007.

Congar, Yves. *I Believe in the Holy Spirit*. Translated by David Smith. Milestones in Catholic Theology. New York: Crossroad, 2016.

Coppedge, Allan. *The God Who Is Triune: Revisioning the Christian Doctrine of God*. Downers Grove, IL: IVP Academic, 2007.

———. *Portraits of God: A Biblical Theology of Holiness*. Downers Grove, IL: InterVarsity, 2001.

Coppenger, Jedidiah. "The Community of Mission: The Church." In *Theology and Practice of Mission: God, the Church, and the Nations*, edited by Bruce Riley Ashford, 60–75. Nashville: B&H Academic, 2011.

Cottrell, Jack. *The Holy Spirit: A Biblical Study*. Joplin, MO: College, 2006.

Cross, F. L., and E. A. Livingstone, eds. "Marcellus." In *ODCC* 1033.

Cross, Terry L. *The People of God's Presence: An Introduction to Ecclesiology*. Grand Rapids: Baker Academic, 2019.

Crouzel, Henri. *Origen: The Life and Thought of the First Great Theologian*. Translated by A. S. Worrall. San Francisco: Harper & Row, 1989.

Culpepper, R. Alan. *The Gospel of Luke: Introduction, Commentary, and Reflection*. In vol. 9 of *The New Interpreter's Bible*, edited by Leander E. Keck, 1–490. Nashville: Abingdon, 1995.

Cyprian of Carthage. *The Epistles of Cyprian*. In vol. 5 of *Ante-Nicene Fathers*, edited by Alexander Roberts and James Donaldson, translated by Ernest Wallis, 275–420. Peabody, MA: Hendrickson, 2004.

Cyril of Alexandria. *Commentary on John*. Edited by Joel C. Elowsky. Translated by David R. Maxwell. 2 vols. Ancient Christian Texts 1–2. Downers Grove, IL: InterVarsity, 2013–15.

———. "Explanation of the Twelve Chapters." In *Saint Cyril of Alexandria and the Christological Controversy: Its History, Theology, and Texts*, translated by John McGuckin, 282–93. Crestwood, NY: St. Vladimir's Seminary Press, 2004.

———. *On the Unity of Christ*. Translated by John Anthony McGuckin. Popular Patristics Series 13. Crestwood, NY: St. Vladimir's Seminary Press, 1995.

———. "The Second Letter of Cyril to Nestorius." In *Saint Cyril of Alexandria and the Christological Controversy: Its History, Theology, and Texts*, translated by John McGuckin, 262–65. Crestwood, NY: St. Vladimir's Seminary Press, 2004.

———. "The Third Letter of Cyril to Nestorius." In *Saint Cyril of Alexandria and the Christological Controversy: Its History, Theology, and Texts*, translated by John McGuckin, 266–75. Crestwood, NY: St. Vladimir's Seminary Press, 2004.

Cyril of Jerusalem. *Catechetical Lectures*. In vol. 7 of *Nicene and Post-Nicene Fathers, Second Series*, edited by Philip Schaff and Henry Wace, translated by Edwin Hamilton Gifford, 1–202. Peabody, MA: Hendrickson, 2004.

Daly, Robert J. "Eucharist and Trinity in the Liturgies of the Early Church." In *The Holy Trinity in the Life of the Church*, edited by Khaled Anatolios, 15–38. Holy Cross Studies in Patristic Theology and History Series. Grand Rapids: Baker Academic, 2014.

Davids, Peter H. *The First Epistle of Peter*. The New International Commentary on the New Testament. Grand Rapids: Eerdmans, 1990.

Davidson, Richard M. "The Creation Theme in Psalm 104." In *The Genesis Creation Account and Its Reverberations in the Old Testament*, edited by Gerald A. Klingbeil, 149–88. Berrien Springs, MI: Andrews University Press, 2015.

———. "The Genesis Account of Origins." In *The Genesis Creation Account and Its Reverberations in the Old Testament*, edited by Gerald A. Klingbeil, 59–130. Berrien Springs, MI: Andrews University Press, 2015.

Dayton, Wilber T. *Entire Sanctification: The Divine Purification and Perfection of Man*. Salem, OH: Schmul, 2000.

deClaissé-Walford, Nancy, et al. *The Book of Psalms*. The New International Commentary on the Old Testament. Grand Rapids: Eerdmans, 2014.

Degenkolb, Ramon R. "Participatory Personhood: An Evangelical Essay on Christian Anthropology." PhD diss., Trinity International University, 2010.

De Halleux, André. "Personnalisme ou essentialisme trinitaire chez les Pères cappadociens? Une mauvaise controverse (Première partie)." *Revue théologique de Louvain* 17 (1986) 129–55. https://www.persee.fr/doc/thlou_0080-2654_1986_num_17_2_2174.

———. "Personnalisme ou essentialisme trinitaire chez les Pères cappadociens? Une mauvaise controverse (suite)." *Revue théologique de Louvain* 17 (1986) 265–92. https://www.persee.fr/doc/thlou_0080-2654_1986_num_17_3_2191.

Demand, Nancy H. *The Mediterranean Context of Early Greek History*. Chichester: Wiley-Blackwell, 2011.

De Mijolla-Mellor, Sophie. "Character Formation." https://www.encyclopedia.com/psychology/dictionaries-thesauruses-pictures-and-press-releases/character-formation.

Descartes, René. *Descartes' Philosophical Writings*. Edited by Norman Kemp Smith. New York: Modern Library, 1958.

Didache. In *50 Foundational Documents for Christian Teachers & Ministers*, edited by Robert F. Lay, 11–14. Marion, IN: Indiana Wesleyan, 2004.

Dietrich, Veit. *Table Talks*. Edited and Translated by Theodore G. Tappert. Luther's Works 54. Philadelphia: Fortress, 1967.

Diokleia, Metropolitan Kallistos. "Hesychasm." In *CEOC* 241–46.

Dix, Dom Gregory. *The Shape of the Liturgy*. London: Westminster Dacre, 1945.

Dostoyevsky, Fyodor. *The Devils (The Possessed)*. Translated by David Magarshack. London: Penguin, 1971.

Douglass, Scot. *Theology of the Gap: Cappadocian Language Theory and the Trinitarian Controversy*. American University Studies Series 7. Theology and Religion Series 235. New York: Lang, 2007.

Doukhan, Jacques B. "'When Death Was Not Yet': The Testimony of Biblical Creation." In *The Genesis Creation Account and Its Reverberations in the Old Testament*, edited by Gerald A. Klingbeil, 329–42. Berrien Springs, MI: Andrews University Press, 2015.

Dreyer, Elizabeth. "Bonaventure, St." In *TMCE* 99–100.

Dunn, James D. G. *Baptism in the Holy Spirit: A Re-Examination of the New Testament Teaching on the Gift of the Spirit in Relation to Pentecostalism Today*. 2nd ed. London: SCM, 2010.

———. *The Christ and the Spirit*. Vol. 2, *Pneumatology*. Grand Rapids: Eerdmans, 1998.

———. "Excommunication." In *NIDB* 2:364–65.

———. *Neither Jew nor Greek: A Contested Identity*. Christianity in the Making 3. Grand Rapids: Eerdmans, 2015.

———. *Unity and Diversity in the New Testament: An Inquiry into the Character of Earliest Christianity*. 3rd ed. London: SCM, 2006.

Dunham, Scott A. *The Trinity and Creation in Augustine: An Ecological Analysis*. New York: State University of New York Press, 2004.

Dunning, H. Ray. *Reflecting the Divine Image: Christian Ethics in Wesleyan Perspective*. Downers Grove, IL: InterVarsity, 1998.

Duvall, J. Scott, and J. Daniel Hays. *God's Relational Presence: The Cohesive Center of Biblical Theology*. Grand Rapids: Baker Academic, 2019.

Dyrnes, William. *Themes in Old Testament Theology*. Downers Grove, IL: InterVarsity, 1979.

Eichrodt, Walther. *Man in the Old Testament*. Studies in Biblical Theology 4. London: SCM, 1961.

———. *The Theology of the Old Testament*. Vol. 1. Translated by J. A Baker. The Old Testament Library. Philadelphia: Westminster, 1961.

Epiphanius of Cyprus. *Ancoratus*. Translated by Young Richard Kim. The Fathers of the Church 128. Washington DC: Catholic University of America Press, 2014.

Evans, Christopher P. "Richard of St. Victor: On the Trinity: Introduction and Translation." In *Trinity and Creation: A Selection of Works of Hugh, Richard, and Adam of St. Victor*, edited by Boyd Taylor Coolman and Dale M. Coulter, 197–208.

Victorine Texts in Translation: Exegesis, Theology and Spirituality from the Abbey of St. Victor 1. Hyde Park, NY: New City, 2011.

Everitt, Anthony. *Cicero: The Life and Times of Rome's Greatest Politician*. New York: Random House, 2001.

Farrow, Douglas. *Ascension and Ecclesia: On the Significance of the Doctrine of the Ascension for Ecclesiology and Christian Cosmology*. Grand Rapids: Eerdmans, 1999.

———. "Person and Nature: The Necessity-Freedom Dialectic in John Zizioulas." In *Theology of John Zizioulas*, edited by Douglas Knight, 109–24. Burlington, VT: Ashgate, 2007.

Fatula, Mary Ann. "Holy Spirit." In *TMCE* 370–76.

Fedwick, Paul Jonathan. *The Church and the Charisma of Leadership in Basil of Caesarea*. Eugene, OR: Wipf & Stock, 1979.

Fee, Gordon D. *God's Empowering Presence: The Holy Spirit in the Letters of Paul*. Grand Rapids: Baker Academic, 2011.

Feingold, Lawrence. *The Eucharist: Mystery of Presence, Sacrifice, and Communion*. Steubenville, OH: Emmaus Academic, 2018.

Ferguson, Everett. *Backgrounds of Early Christianity*. 2nd ed. Grand Rapids: Eerdmans, 1993.

Fiddes, Paul S. *Participating in God: A Pastoral Doctrine of the Trinity*. Louisville: Westminster John Knox, 2000.

———. "Relational Trinity: Radical Perspective." In *Two Views on the Doctrine of the Trinity*, edited by Jason S. Sexton, 159–85, 204–6. Counterpoints Bible & Theology. Grand Rapids: Zondervan, 2014.

Fitzgerald, John T. "The Passions and Moral Progress: An Introduction." In *Passions and Moral Progress in Greco-Roman Thought*, edited by John T. Fitzgerald, 1–26. London: Routledge, 2008.

Flanagan, James W. "Chiefs in Israel." In *Community, Identity, and Ideology: Social Science Approaches to the Hebrew Bible*, edited by Charles E. Carter and Carol L. Meyers, 311–34. Winona Lake, IN: Eisbrauns, 1996.

Flechere, John William de la. "The Portrait of St. Paul, or The True Model for Christians and Pastors." Translated by John Gilpin. The Works of the Reverend John Fletcher 3. Salem, OH: Schmul, 1974.

Fleeson, William, et al. "Personality Science and the Foundations of Character." In *Character: New Directions from Philosophy, Psychology, and Theology*, edited by Christian B. Miller et al., 41–71. New York: Oxford University Press, 2015.

Florovsky, Georges. *Bible, Church, Tradition: An Eastern Orthodox View*. Collective Works of Georges Florovsky 1. Belmont, MA: Nordland, 1972.

———. "The Legacy and the Task of Orthodox Theology." *Anglican Theological Review* 31 (1949) 65–71.

Fox, Patricia A. *God as Communion: John Zizioulas, Elizabeth Johnson, and the Retrieval of the Symbol of the Triune God*. Collegeville, MN: Liturgical, 2001.

France, R. T. *The Gospel of Matthew*. The New International Commentary on the New Testament. Grand Rapids: Eerdmans, 2007.

Frank, Daniel H. "What Is Jewish Philosophy?" In *History of Jewish Philosophy*, edited by Daniel H. Frank and Oliver Leaman, 1–10. Routledge History and World Philosophies 2. New York: Routledge, 1997.

Fretheim, Terence E. *Exodus*. Interpretation, a Bible Commentary for Teaching and Preaching. Louisville: John Knox, 1991.

Friedländer, Paul. *Plato*. Vol. 3. Translated by Hans Meyerhoff. Bollingen Series 59. Princeton: Princeton University Press, 1969.

Garrett, Duane A. *A Commentary on Exodus*. Grand Rapids: Kregel Academic, 2014.

Geisler, Norman L. *Christian Ethics*. Grand Rapids: Baker, 1989.

González, Justo L. *A History of Early Christian Literature*. Louisville: Westminster John Knox, 2019.

—————. *The Story of Christianity*. Vol. 1, *The Early Church to the Dawn of the Reformation*. San Francisco: Harper & Row, 1984.

—————. *The Story of Christianity*. Vol. 2, *The Reformation to the Present Day*. San Francisco: Harper & Row, 1985.

Goswell, Gregory. "The Two Testaments as Covenant Documents." *Journal of the Evangelical Theological Society* 62 (2019) 677–92.

Gowan, Donald E. *Eschatology in the Old Testament*. 2nd ed. New York: T. & T. Clark International, 2006.

Greathouse, William H. "The Book of Zechariah." In vol. 5 of *Beacon Bible Commentary*, edited by A. F. Harper et al., 337–406. Kansas City: Beacon Hill, 1966.

Green, Arthur. *Seek My Face: A Jewish Mystical Theology*. Woodstock, VT: Jewish Lights, 2012.

Green, Joel B. *Body, Soul, and Human Life: The Nature of Humanity in the Bible*. Grand Rapids: Baker Academic, 2008.

—————. *The Gospel of Luke*. The New International Commentary on the New Testament. Grand Rapids: Eerdmans, 1997.

Gregor, Brian. *A Philosophical Anthropology of the Cross: The Cruciform Self*. Bloomington: Indiana University Press, 2013.

Gregory, Andrew. *Ancient Greek Cosmogony*. London: Bloomsbury Academic, 2012.

Gregory the Great. *Forty Gospel Homilies: Gregory the Great*. Translated by Dom David Hurst. Christian Studies Series 123. Kalamazoo, MI: Cistercian, 1990.

Gregory of Nazianzus. *Orations*. In vol. 7 of *Nicene and Post-Nicene Fathers, Second Series*, edited by Philip Schaff and Henry Wace, translated by Charles Gordon Browne and James Edward Swallow, 203–436. Peabody, MA: Hendrickson, 2004.

Gregory of Nyssa. *Against Eunomius*. In vol. 5 of *Nicene and Post-Nicene Fathers, Second Series*, edited by Philip Schaff and Henry Wace, translated by William Moore and Henry Austin Wilson, 33–249. Peabody, MA: Hendrickson, 2004.

—————. *Answer to Eunomius' Second Book*. In vol. 5 of *Nicene and Post-Nicene Fathers, Second Series*, edited by Philip Schaff and Henry Wace, translated by William Moore and Henry Austin Wilson, 250–314. Peabody, MA: Hendrickson, 2004.

—————. *Ex Communibus Notionibus*. In vol. 45 of *Patrologiae Cursus Completus*, translated by J. P. Migne, 175–86. London: Forgotten, 2015.

—————. *On the Faith*. In vol. 5 of *Nicene and Post-Nicene Fathers, Second Series*, edited by Philip Schaff and Henry Wace, translated by William Moore and Henry Austin Wilson, 337–39. Peabody, MA: Hendrickson, 2004.

—————. *On the Holy Spirit against Macedonius*. In vol. 5 of *Nicene and Post-Nicene Fathers, Second Series*, edited by Philip Schaff and Henry Wace, translated by William Moore and Henry Austin Wilson, 315–25. Peabody, MA: Hendrickson, 2004.

———. *On the Holy Trinity.* In vol. 5 of *Nicene and Post-Nicene Fathers, Second Series,* edited by Philip Schaff and Henry Wace, translated by William Moore and Henry Austin Wilson, 326–30. Peabody, MA: Hendrickson, 2004.

———. *On the Making of Man.* In vol. 5 of *Nicene and Post-Nicene Fathers, Second Series,* edited by Philip Schaff and Henry Wace, translated by William Moore and Henry Austin Wilson, 387–427. Peabody, MA: Hendrickson, 2004.

———. *On "Not Three Gods."* In vol. 5 of *Nicene and Post-Nicene Fathers, Second Series,* edited by Philip Schaff and Henry Wace, translated by William Moore and Henry Austin Wilson, 331–36. Peabody, MA: Hendrickson, 2004.

———. *On Virginity.* In vol. 5 of *Nicene and Post-Nicene Fathers, Second Series,* edited by Philip Schaff and Henry Wace, translated by William Moore and Henry Austin Wilson, 343–71. Peabody, MA: Hendrickson, 2004.

Grenz, Stanley J. *Rediscovering the Triune God: The Trinity in Contemporary Theology.* Minneapolis: Fortress, 2004.

———. *The Social God and the Relational Self: A Trinitarian Theology of the Imago Dei.* The Matrix of Christian Theology Series. Louisville: Westminster John Knox, 2001.

Grenz, Stanley J., and Roger E. Olson. *20th Century Theology: God & the World in a Transitional Age.* Downers Grove, IL: InterVarsity, 1992.

Grimm, Harold J. *The Reformation Era, 1500–1650.* 2nd ed. New York: Macmillan, 1973.

Groppe, Elizabeth Teresa. *Yves Congar's Theology of the Holy Spirit.* New York: Oxford University Press, 2004.

Grudem, Wayne. *Systematic Theology: An Introduction to Biblical Doctrine.* Grand Rapids: Zondervan, 2000.

Gundry, Robert H. *A Survey of the New Testament.* 4th ed. Grand Rapids: Zondervan, 2003.

Gunton, Colin E. *Father, Son, and Holy Spirit: Toward a Fully Trinitarian Theology.* New York: T. & T. Clark, 2003.

———. *The One, the Three, and the Many: God, Creation, and the Culture of Modernity.* The Bampton Lectures 1992. Cambridge: Cambridge University Press, 2004.

———. "Persons and Particularity." In *The Theology of John Zizioulas: Personhood and the Church,* edited by Douglas Knight, 97–108. Burlington, VT: Ashgate, 2007.

———. *The Promise of Trinitarian Theology.* 2nd ed. New York: T. & T. Clark, 2006.

———. "Relation and Relativity: The Trinity and the Created World." In *Trinitarian Theology Today: Essays on Divine Being and Act,* edited by Christoph Schwöbel, 92–112. Edinburgh: T. & T. Clark, 1995.

———. *The Triune Creator: A Historical and Systematic Study.* Edinburgh Studies in Constructive Theology Series. Grand Rapids: Eerdmans, 1998.

Hall, Christopher A. *Learning Theology with the Church Fathers.* Downers Grove, IL: InterVarsity, 2002.

Hamilton, Victor P. *The Book of Genesis: Chapters 1–17.* The New International Commentary on the Old Testament. Grand Rapids: Eerdmans, 1990.

———. *The Book of Genesis: Chapters 18–50.* The New International Commentary on the Old Testament. Grand Rapids: Eerdmans, 1995.

———. *Exodus: An Exegetical Commentary.* Grand Rapids: Baker Academic, 2011.

Harrison, Nonna Verna. "Zizioulas on Communion and Otherness." *St. Vladimir's Theological Quarterly* 42 (1998) 273–300.

Hasel, Gerhard F., and Michael G. Hasel. "The Unique Cosmology of Genesis 1 against Ancient Near Eastern and Egyptian Parallels." In *The Genesis Creation Account and Its Reverberations in the Old Testament*, edited by Gerald A. Klingbeil, 9–30. Berrien Springs, MI: Andrews University Press, 2015.

Hauck, Friedrich. "κοινός, κοινωνός, κοινωνέω, κοινωνία, συγκοινωνός, συγκοινωνέω, κοινωνικός, κοινόω." In *TDNT* 3:789–809.

Hauerwas, Stanley. "Sinsick." In *Sin, Death, & the Devil*, edited by Carl E. Braaten and Robert W. Jenson, 7–21. Grand Rapids: Eerdmans, 2000.

Hayes, Zachary. "Purgatory." In *TMCE* 675–76.

Hefele, Charles Joseph. *A History of Christian Councils, from the Original Documents, to the Close of the Council of Nicaea A.D. 325*. Translated by William R. Clark. 2nd ed. Edinburgh: T. & T. Clark, 1894.

Heidegger, Martin. *Being and Time*. Edited by Dennis J. Schmidt. Translated by Joan Stambaugh. SUNY Series in Contemporary Continental Philosophy. Albany: State University of New York Press, 2010.

Hellwig, Monika K. "Sacrament." In *TMCE* 731–33.

Henderson, D. Michael. *John Wesley's Class Meeting: A Model for Making Disciples*. Nappanee, IN: Evangel, 1997.

Hertzberg, Arthur. *Judaism*. New York: Braziller, 1962.

———, ed. *Judaism: The Key Spiritual Writings of the Jewish Tradition*. Rev. ed. New York: Simon & Schuster, 1991.

Hertzberg, Hans Wilhelm. *I & II Samuel: A Commentary*. Translated by J. S. Bowden. 2nd ed. The Old Testament Library. Philadelphia: Westminster, 1964.

Hilary of Poitiers. *On the Trinity*. In vol. 9 of *Nicene and Post-Nicene Fathers, Second Series*, edited by Philip Schaff and Henry Wace, translated by E. W. Watson and L. Pullan, 40–234. Peabody, MA: Hendrickson, 2004.

Hill, Jonathan. *The History of Christian Thought*. Downers Grove, IL: InterVarsity, 2003.

Hill, William Bancroft. *The Apostolic Age: A Study of the Early Church and Its Achievements*. New York: Revell, 1922.

Hippolytus. *The Refutation of All Heresies*. In vol. 5 of *Ante-Nicene Fathers*, edited by Alexander Roberts and James Donaldson, 9–162. Peabody, MA: Hendrickson, 2004.

Holmes, Stephen R. "Classical Trinity: Evangelical Perspective." In *Two Views on the Doctrine of the Trinity*, edited by Jason S. Sexton, 25–48. Counterpoints Bible & Theology. Grand Rapids: Zondervan, 2014.

———. *The Quest for the Trinity: The Doctrine of God in Scripture, History, and Modernity*. Downers Grove, IL: InterVarsity, 2012.

Horne, Brian L. "Art: A Trinitarian Imperative?" In *Trinitarian Theology Today*, edited by Christoph Schwöbel, 80–91. Edinburgh: T. & T. Clark, 1995.

House, Paul R. "Sin in the Law." In *Fallen: A Theology of Sin*, edited by Christopher W. Morgan and Robert A. Peterson, 39–64. Wheaton, IL: Crossway, 2013.

Hugh of St. Victor. *On the Three Days*. In *Trinity and Creation: A Selection of Works of Hugh, Richard, and Adam of St. Victor*, edited by Boyd Taylor Coolman and Dale M. Coulter, translated by Hugh Feiss, 49–102. Victorine Texts in Translation: Exegesis, Theology and Spirituality from the Abbey of St. Victor 1. Hyde Park, NY: New City, 2011.

Hughes, Amy Brown. "Beholding the Beholder: Precision and Mystery in Gregory of Nyssa's *Ad Ablabium*." In *Trinity without Hierarchy: Reclaiming Nicene Orthodoxy in Evangelical Theology*, edited by Michael F. Bird and Scott Harrower, 123–40. Grand Rapids: Kregel Academic, 2019.

Huxley, Aldous. *The Doors of Perception & Heaven and Hell*. New York: Harper Perennial Modern Classics, 2009.

Ignatius of Antioch. *Epistle to the Ephesians*. In vol. 1 of *Ante-Nicene Fathers*, edited by Alexander Roberts et al., 45–58. Peabody, MA: Hendrickson, 2004.

———. *Epistle to the Magnesians*. In vol. 1 of *Ante-Nicene Fathers*, edited by Alexander Roberts et al., 59–65. Peabody, MA: Hendrickson, 2004.

Irenaeus. *Against Heresies*. In vol. 1 of *Ante-Nicene Fathers*, edited by Alexander Roberts et al., 309–567. Peabody, MA: Hendrickson, 2004.

Irving, Edward. *Edward Irving's Holy Spirit Writings*. Edited by David W. Dorries. North Charleston, SC: CreateSpace, 2011.

Jackson, Blomfield. *Prolegomena: Sketch of the Life and Work of Saint Basil*. In vol. 8 of *Nicene and Post-Nicene Fathers, Second Series*, edited by Philip Schaff and Henry Wace, translated by Edwin Hamilton Gifford, xiii–lxxvii. Peabody, MA: Hendrickson, 2004.

Jacobs, Louis. *A Concise Companion to the Jewish Religion*. Oxford: Oxford University Press, 1999.

Janzen, J. Gerald. *Exodus*. Westminster Bible Companion. Louisville: Westminster John Knox, 1997.

Jeeves, Malcolm. *Mind Fields: Reflections on the Science of Mind and Brain*. Grand Rapids: Baker, 1993.

Jenni, Ernst, and Claus Westermann, eds. *Theological Lexicon of the Old Testament*. Vol. 2. Translated by Mark E. Biddle. Peabody, MA: Hendrickson, 1997.

Jenson, Robert W. "The Great Transformation." In *The Last Things: Biblical and Theological Perspectives on Eschatology*, edited by Carl E. Braaten and Robert W. Jenson, 33–42. Grand Rapids: Eerdmans, 2002.

Jeremias, Joachim. "ἄνθρωπος, ἀνθρώπινος." In *TDNT* 1:364–67.

Jewett, Paul K. *Man as Male and Female: A Study in Sexual Relationships from a Theological Point of View*. Grand Rapids: Eerdmans, 1983.

Jewett, Robert. "The Question of the 'Apportioned Spirit' in Paul's Letters: Romans as a Case Study." In *The Holy Spirit and Christian Origins: Essays in Honor of James D. G. Dunn*, edited by Graham N. Stanton et al., 193–206. Grand Rapids: Eerdmans, 2004.

John of the Cross. "The Living Flame of Love." In *The Collected Works of St. John of the Cross*, translated by Kieran Kavanaugh and Otilio Rodriguez, 633–715. Washington, DC: ICS, 2017.

John of Damascus. *Exposition of the Orthodox Faith*. In vol. 9 of *Nicene and Post-Nicene Fathers, Second Series*, edited by Philip Schaff and Henry Wace, translated by S. D. F. Salmond, 1–101. Peabody, MA: Hendrickson, 2004.

Johnson, Aubrey R. *The One and the Many in the Israelite Conception of God*. Cardiff: University of Wales Press, 1961.

Johnson, Elizabeth A. *She Who Is: The Mystery of God in Feminist Theological Discourse*. 10th ed. New York: Crossroad, 2002.

———. *Women, Earth, and Creator Spirit*. The Madeleva Lecture in Spirituality 1993. New York: Paulist, 1993.

Johnson, Lawrence J. *Worship in the Early Church: An Anthology of Historical Sources*. Vol. 2. Collegeville, MN: Liturgical, 2009.

Jones, Beth Felker. *God the Spirit: Introducing Pneumatology in Wesleyan and Ecumenical Perspective.* Wesleyan Doctrine Series 5. Eugene, OR: Cascade, 2014.

Jüngel, Eberhard. *The Doctrine of the Trinity: God's Being Is in Becoming.* Translated by Horton Harris. Grand Rapids: Eerdmans, 1976.

Jungkuntz, Theodore R. *Confirmation and the Charismata.* Eugene, OR: Wipf & Stock, 1997.

Justin Martyr. *Dialogue with Trypho, a Jew.* In vol. 1 of *Ante-Nicene Fathers,* edited by Alexander Roberts and James Donaldson, 194–270. Peabody, MA: Hendrickson, 2004.

———. *The First Apology of Justin.* In vol. 1 of *Ante-Nicene Fathers,* edited by Alexander Roberts and James Donaldson, 159–87. Peabody, MA: Hendrickson, 2004.

———. *The Second Apology of Justin.* In vol. 1 of *Ante-Nicene Fathers,* edited by Alexander Roberts and James Donaldson, 188–93. Peabody, MA: Hendrickson, 2004.

Kant, Immanuel. *Critique of Pure Reason.* Translated by Marcus Weigelt. New York: Penguin Classics, 2007.

Kärkkäinen, Veli-Matti. *The Holy Spirit: A Guide to Christian Theology.* Louisville: Westminster John Knox, 2012.

———. *Pneumatology: The Holy Spirit in Ecumenical, International, and Contextual Perspective.* 2nd ed. Grand Rapids: Baker Academic, 2018.

———. *The Trinity: Global Perspective.* Louisville: Westminster John Knox, 2007.

Käsemann, Ernst. *Commentary on Romans.* Edited and Translated by Geoffrey W. Bromiley. Grand Rapids: Eerdmans, 1980.

Kaufmann, Yehezkel. *The Religion of Israel: From Its Beginnings to the Babylonian Exile.* Translated by Moshe Greenberg. Chicago: University of Chicago Press, 1960.

Keener, Craig S. *Spirit Hermeneutics: Reading Scripture in Light of Pentecost.* Grand Rapids: Eerdmans, 2016.

Kessler, John. *Old Testament Theology: Divine Call and Human Response.* Waco, TX: Baylor University Press, 2013.

Kihlstrom, John F., and Reid Hastie. "Mental Representations of Persons and Personality." In *Handbook of Personality Psychology,* edited by Robert Hogan et al., 711–35. San Diego: Academic, 1997.

Kierkegaard, Søren. *Training in Christianity and the Edifying Discourse Which 'Accompanied' It.* Translated by Walter Lowrie. Princeton: Princeton University Press, 1952.

Kimbrough, S. T., Jr., ed. *Orthodox and Wesleyan Spirituality.* Crestwood, NY: St. Vladimir's Seminary Press, 2002.

Kinlaw, Dennis F. *Let's Start With Jesus: A New Way of Doing Theology.* Grand Rapids: Zondervan, 2005.

———. *The Mind of Christ.* Nappanee, IN: Asbury, 1998.

———. *We Live as Christ: The Christian Message in a New Century.* Edited by John N. Oswalt. Clinton, TN: Partnership, 2001.

Kinlaw, Dennis F., with John N. Oswalt. *Lectures in Old Testament Theology.* Anderson, IN: Asbury, 2010.

Knight, Douglas H. "Introduction." In *The Theology of John Zizioulas: Personhood and the Church,* edited by Douglas H. Knight, 1–14. Burlington, VT: Ashgate, 2007.

————. "John Zizioulas's Lectures in Christian Dogmatics—Editor's Introduction." *Resources for Christian Theology*, February 25, 2008. http://www. resourcesforchristiantheology.org/category/john-zizioulas/.

————. "The Spirit and Persons in the Liturgy." In *The Theology of John Zizioulas: Personhood and the Church*, edited by Douglas H. Knight, 183–96. Burlington, VT: Ashgate, 2007.

————, ed. *The Theology of John Zizioulas: Personhood and the Church*. Burlington, VT: Ashgate, 2007.

————. "Zizioulas on Eschatology." *Resources for Christian Theology*, June 10, 2008. http://www.resourcesforchristiantheology.org/category/john-zizioulas/.

Knobel, Angela. "A Different Kind of Wisdom." In *Character: New Directions from Philosophy, Psychology, and Theology*, edited by Christian B. Miller et al., 351–67. New York: Oxford University Press, 2015.

Köstenberger, Andreas J. *A Theology of John's Gospel and Letters*. Biblical Theology of the New Testament. Grand Rapids: Zondervan, 2009.

Köster, Helmut. "ὑπόστασις." In *TDNT* 8:572–89.

Kruger, C. Baxter. *Jesus and the Undoing of Adam*. Jackson, MS: Perichoresis, 2003.

LaCugna, Catherine Mowry. *God for Us: The Trinity and Christian Life*. San Francisco: HarperSanFrancisco, 1991.

Ladd, George Eldon. *The Presence of the Future: The Eschatology of Biblical Realism*. Grand Rapids: Eerdmans, 1974.

Laing, John D., and Stefana Dan Laing. "The Doctrine of the Future, the Doctrine of God, and Predictive Prophecy." In *Eschatology: Biblical, Historical, and Practical Approaches: A Volume in Honor of Craig A. Blaising*, edited by D. Jeffrey Bingham and Glenn R. Kreider, 77–101. Grand Rapids: Kregel Academic, 2016.

Lampe, G. W. H. "The Holy Spirit and the Person of Christ." In *Christ, Faith, and History: Cambridge Studies in Christology*, edited by S. W. Sykes and J. P. Clayton, 111–30. Cambridge: Cambridge University Press, 1972.

Langford, Thomas A. *Practical Divinity*. Vol. 1, *Theology in the Wesleyan Tradition*. Nashville: Abingdon, 1983.

Leach, E. Frank. *The Hebrew Concept of Corporate Personality*. New York: Vantage, 1975.

Leclerc, Diane. *Discovering Christian Holiness: The Heart of Wesleyan-Holiness Theology*. Kansas City: Beacon Hill, 2010.

Leithart, Peter J. *Athanasius*. Foundations of Theological Exegesis and Christian Spirituality. Grand Rapids: Baker Academic, 2011.

————. "No Son, No Father: Athanasius and the Mutuality of Divine Personhood." In *Trinity without Hierarchy: Reclaiming Nicene Orthodoxy in Evangelical Theology*, edited by Michael F. Bird and Scott Harrower, 109–22. Grand Rapids: Kregel Academic, 2019.

Leo the Great. "Letter XXVIII: The Tome." In vol. 12 of *Nicene and Post-Nicene Fathers, Second Series*, edited by Philip Schaff and Henry Wace, translated by Charles Lett Feltoe, 38–43. Peabody, MA: Hendrickson, 2004.

Levison, John R. *Filled with the Spirit*. Grand Rapids: Eerdmans, 2009.

Lindström, Harald. *Wesley and Sanctification: A Study in the Doctrine of Salvation*. Nappanee, IN: Asbury, 1980.

Logan, James C. "Controversial Aspects of the Movement." In *The Charismatic Movement*, edited by Michael P. Hamilton, 33–48. Grand Rapids: Eerdmans, 1975.

Lohse, Eduard. "πρόσωπον, εὐπροσωπέω, προσωπολημψία, προσωπολήμπτης, προσωπολημπτεω, ἀπροσωπολήμπτης." In *TDNT* 6:768–80.

Lonergan, Bernard. *The Way to Nicaea: The Dialectical Development of Trinitarian Theology*. Translated by Conn O'Donovan. Philadelphia: Westminster, 1976.

Lossky, Vladimir. *The Mystical Theology of the Eastern Church*. Crestwood, NY: St. Vladimir's Seminary Press, 1976.

———. "Tradition and Traditions." In *Eastern Orthodox Theology: A Contemporary Reader*, edited by Daniel B. Clendenin, 125–46. Grand Rapids: Baker, 1995.

Loudovikos, Nicholas. "Christian Life and Institutional Church." In *The Theology of John Zizioulas: Personhood and the Church*, edited by Douglas Knight, 125–32. Burlington, VT: Ashgate, 2007.

Louth, Andrew. "Man and Cosmos in St. Maximus the Confessor." In *Toward an Ecology of Transfiguration: Orthodox Christian Perspectives on Environment, Nature, and Creation*, edited by John Chryssavgis and Bruce Foltz, 59–72. New York: Fordham University Press, 2013.

Luther, Martin. *An Instruction to Penitents concerning the Forbidden Books of Dr. M. Luther*. Edited by Helmut T. Lehmann. Translated by James Atkinson. Luther's Works 44. Philadelphia: Fortress, 1966.

———. *Lectures on Romans: Glosses and Scholia*. Edited by Hilton C. Oswald. Translated by Walter G. Tillmanns and Jacob A. O. Preus. Luther's Works 25. Saint Louis: Concordia, 1972.

———. *Luther's Small Catechism with Explanation*. St. Louis: Concordia, 2017.

———. *Table Talk*. Translated by William Hazlitt. Orlando: Bridge-Logos, 2004.

Macchia, Frank D. *Baptized in the Spirit: A Global Pentecostal Theology*. Grand Rapids: Zondervan, 2006.

Machiavelli, Niccolò. *The Prince*. Translated by W. K. Marriott. New York: Everyman's Library, 1992.

Mackinnon, D. M. "'Substance' in Christology—A Cross-Bench View." In *Christ, Faith, and History: Cambridge Studies in Christology*, edited by S. W. Sykes and J. P. Clayton, 279–300. Cambridge: Cambridge University Press, 1972.

Macmurray, John. *Persons in Relation*. Amherst, NY: Humanity, 1999.

———. *The Self as Agent*. Gifford Lectures 1953. Amherst, NY: Humanity, 1999.

Macquarrie, John. *Principles of Christian Theology*. 2nd ed. New York: Scribner's Sons, 1977.

Maddox, Randy L. "John Wesley and Eastern Orthodoxy: Influences, Convergences, and Differences." *Asbury Theological Journal* 45 (1990) 29–53.

Mahony, John W. "A Theology of Sin for Today." In *Fallen: A Theology of Sin*, edited by Christopher W. Morgan and Robert A. Peterson, 187–218. Wheaton, IL: Crossway, 2013.

Marshall, I. Howard. *The Acts of the Apostles: An Introduction and Commentary*. Tyndale New Testament Commentaries. Grand Rapids: Eerdmans, 1986.

———. *The Epistles of John*. The New International Commentary on the New Testament. Grand Rapids: Eerdmans, 1978.

Marshall, Molly T. *Joining the Dance: A Theology of the Spirit*. Valley Forge, PA: Judson, 2003.

———. "Participating in the Life of God: A Trinitarian Pneumatology." *Perspectives in Religious Studies* 30 (2003) 139–50.

Martens, Peter. "Holy Spirit." In *The Westminster Handbook to Origen*, edited by John Anthony McGuckin, 125–28. The Westminster Handbooks to Christian Theology. Louisville: Westminster John Knox, 2004.

Mascall, E. L. *Via Media: An Essay in Theological Synthesis*. New York: Longmans, Green, 1956.

[Mathetes]. *The Epistle of Mathetes to Diognetus*. In vol. 1 of *Ante-Nicene Fathers*, edited by Alexander Roberts et al., 23–30. Peabody, MA: Hendrickson, 2004.

Maximus the Confessor. *Commentary on the Our Father*. In *Selected Writings*, translated by George C. Berthold, 99–125. New York: Paulist, 1985.

———. *The Four Hundred Chapters on Love*. In *Selected Writings*, translated by George C. Berthold, 33–98. New York: Paulist, 1985.

———. *On Difficulties in the Church Fathers: The Ambigua*. Vol. 2. Dumbarton Oaks Medieval Library. Cambridge: Harvard University Press, 2014.

May, Gerhard. *Creatio Ex Nihilo: The Doctrine of 'Creation Out of Nothing' in Early Christian Thought*. Translated by A. S. Worrall. New York: T. & T. Clark, 2004.

McCall, Thomas H. "Relational Trinity: Creedal Perspective." In *Two Views on the Doctrine of the Trinity*, edited by Jason S. Sexton, 113–37, 156–58. Counterpoints Bible & Theology. Grand Rapids: Zondervan, 2014.

———. *Which Trinity? Whose Monotheism? Philosophical and Systematic Theologians on the Metaphysics of Trinitarian Theology*. Grand Rapids: Eerdmans, 2010.

McCartney, Dan, and Charles Clayton. *Let the Reader Understand: A Guide to Interpreting and Applying the Bible*. Eugene, OR: Wipf & Stock, 2000.

McConnell, Timothy P. *Illumination in Basil of Caesarea's Doctrine of the Holy Spirit*. Minneapolis: Fortress, 2014.

McConville, J. Gordon. *Being Human in God's World: An Old Testament Theology of Humanity*. Grand Rapids: Baker Academic, 2016.

McDaniel, Michael D. "Salvation as Justification and Theosis." In *Salvation in Christ: A Lutheran-Orthodox Dialogue*, edited by John Meyendorff and Robert Tobias, 67–83. Minneapolis: Augsburg Fortress, 1992.

McEwan, David. "'A Continual Enjoyment of the Three-One God': John Wesley and the Life of God in the Soul." *Phronema* 33 (2018) 49–72.

McFarlane, Graham. *Christ and the Spirit: The Doctrine of the Incarnation according to Edward Irving*. Carlisle: Paternoster, 1996.

———. *Why Do You Believe What You Believe about the Holy Spirit?* Theological Foundations. Carlisle: Paternoster, 1998.

McGuckin, John A. "The Book of Revelation and Orthodox Eschatology: The Theodrama of Judgment." In *The Last Things: Biblical & Theological Perspectives on Eschatology*, edited by Carl E. Braaten and Robert W. Jenson, 113–34. Grand Rapids: Eerdmans, 2002.

———. "Introduction." In *On the Unity of Christ*, by Cyril of Alexandria, translated by John Anthony McGuckin, 9–48. Popular Patristics 13. Crestwood, NY: St. Vladimir's Seminary Press, 1995.

———. *The Orthodox Church: An Introduction to Its History, Doctrine, and Spiritual Culture*. Chichester: Wiley-Blackwell, 2011.

———. *Saint Cyril of Alexandria and the Christological Controversy: Its History, Theology, and Texts*. Crestwood, NY: St. Vladimir's Seminary Press, 2004.

———. "Tradition." In *CEOC* 487–89.

McKnight, Scot. "Covenant and Spirit: The Origin of the New Covenant Hermeneutic." In *The Holy Spirit and Christian Origins: Essays in Honor of James D. G. Dunn*, edited by Graham N. Stanton et al., 41–54. Grand Rapids: Eerdmans, 2004.

———. *Open to the Spirit: God in Us, God with Us, God Transforming Us*. New York: Waterbrook, 2018.

McIntyre, John. *The Shape of Pneumatology: Studies in the Doctrine of the Holy Spirit*. Edinburgh: T. & T. Clark, 1997.

McManners, John, ed. *The Oxford History of Christianity*. New York: Oxford University Press, 2002.

Menzies, Robert P. *Empowered for Witness: The Spirit in Luke-Acts*. New York: T. & T. Clark International, 2004.

Merritt, Timothy. *The Christian's Manual: A Treatise of Christian Perfection: With Directions for Obtaining that State*. Salem, OH: Schmul, 1998.

Meyendorff, John. *The Orthodox Church: Its Past and Its Role in the World Today*. Translated by John Chapin. New York: Pantheon, 1962.

———. *St. Gregory of Palamas and Orthodox Spirituality*. Translated by Adele Fiske. Crestwood, NY: St. Vladimir's Seminary Press, 1974.

Meyendorff, John, and Robert Tobias, eds. *Salvation in Christ: A Lutheran-Orthodox Dialogue*. Minneapolis: Augsburg Fortress, 1992.

Michel, Otto. "οἶκος, οἰκία, οἰκεῖος, οἰκέω, οἰκοδόμος, οἰκοδομέω, οἰκοδομή, ἐποικοδομέω, συνοικοδομέω, οἰκονόμος, οἰκονομία, κατοικέω, οἰκητήριον, κατοικητήριον, κατοικίζω, οἰκουμένη." In *TDNT* 5:119–58.

Middleton, J. Richard. *The Liberating Image: The Imago Dei in Genesis 1*. Grand Rapids: Brazos, 2005.

———. *A New Heaven and a New Earth: Reclaiming Biblical Eschatology*. Grand Rapids: Baker Academic, 2014.

Migliore, Daniel L. "The Missionary God and the Missionary Church." *Princeton Seminary Bulletin* 19 (1998) 14–25.

Molnar, Paul D. "Classical Trinity: Catholic Perspective." In *Two Views on the Doctrine of the Trinity*, edited by Jason S. Sexton, 69–95, 109–12. Counterpoints Bible & Theology. Grand Rapids: Zondervan, 2014.

Moltmann, Jürgen. *The Trinity and the Kingdom of God: The Doctrine of God*. Minneapolis: Fortress, 1993.

Moravcsik, Julius. *Plato and Platonism: Plato's Conception of Appearance and Reality in Ontology, Epistemology, and Ethics, and Its Modern Echoes*. Malden, MA: Blackwell, 2000.

Morgan, Christopher W. "Sin in the Biblical Story." In *Fallen: A Theology of Sin*, edited by Christopher W. Morgan and Robert A. Peterson, 131–62. Wheaton, IL: Crossway, 2013.

Morris, Leon. *The Gospel according to John*. Rev. ed. New International Commentary on the New Testament. Grand Rapids: Eerdmans, 1995.

Mueller, David L. *Karl Barth*. Makers of the Modern Theological Mind. Waco, TX: Word, 1979.

Muffs, Yochanan. *The Personhood of God: Biblical Theology, Human Faith, and the Divine Image*. Woodstock, VT: Jewish Lights, 2005.

Munteanu, Dana LaCourse. *Tragic Pathos: Pity and Fear in Greek Philosophy and Tragedy*. New York: Cambridge University Press, 2012.

Mure, G. R. G. *Aristotle*. New York: Oxford University Press, 1964.

Murphree, Jon Tal. *Divine Paradoxes: A Finite View of an Infinite God: A Response to Process and Openness Theologies*. Camp Hill, PA: Christian, 1998.

Murphy, Desmond. *A Return to Spirit after the Mythic Church*. New York: Crossroad, 1997.

Mursell, Gordon. *English Spirituality: From Earliest Times to 1700*. Louisville: Westminster John Knox, 2001.

Nassif, Bradley, et al. *Three Views on Eastern Orthodoxy and Evangelicalism*. Counterpoints: Exploring Theology. Grand Rapids: Zondervan, 2004.

Neteruk, Alexei V. *Light from the East: Theology, Science, and the Eastern Orthodox Tradition*. Minneapolis: Fortress, 2003.

Neusner, Jacob, and Alan J. Avery-Peck, eds. *The Blackwell Reader in Judaism*. Malden, MA: Blackwell, 2001.

Newbigin, Lesslie. *The Gospel in a Pluralist Society*. Grand Rapids: Eerdmans 2002.

Noebel, David A. *Understanding the Times*. 2nd ed. Manitou Springs, CO: Summit, 2006.

Nygren, Anders. *Agape and Eros*. Translated by Philip S. Watson. London: SPCK, 1953.

O'Day, Gail R. *The Gospel of John: Introduction, Commentary, and Reflections*. In vol. 9 of *The New Interpreter's Bible*, edited by Leander E. Keck, 491–865. Nashville: Abingdon, 1995.

O'Donovan, Oliver. *Resurrection and Moral Order: An Outline for Evangelical Ethics*. 2nd ed. Grand Rapids: Eerdmans, 1994.

O'Malley, J. Steven, and Jason E. Vickers, eds. *Methodist and Pietist: Retrieving the Evangelical United Brethren Tradition*. Nashville: Kingswood, 2011.

Oden, Thomas C. *John Wesley's Scriptural Christianity: A Plain Exposition of His Teaching on Christian Doctrine*. Grand Rapids: Zondervan, 1994.

———. *The Justification Reader*. Classic Christian Readers. Grand Rapids: Eerdmans, 2002.

———. *Life in the Spirit*. Systematic Theology 3. Peabody, MA: Prince, 1998.

———. *The Living God*. Systematic Theology 1. Peabody, MA: Prince, 1998.

Olson, Roger E. *The Story of Christian Theology: Centuries of Tradition & Reform*. Downers Grove, IL: InterVarsity, 1999.

———. "Wolfhart Pannenberg's Doctrine of the Trinity." *Scottish Journal of Theology* 43 (1990) 175–206.

Olson, Roger E., and Christopher A. Hall. *The Trinity*. Guides to Theology. Grand Rapids: Eerdmans, 2002.

Onah, Godfrey Igwebuike. *Self-Transcendence and Human History in Wolfhart Pannenberg*. Lanham, MD: University Press of America, 1999.

Origen. *Against Celsus*. In vol. 4 of *Ante-Nicene Fathers*, edited by Alexander Roberts and James Donaldson, translated by Frederick Crombie, 395–669. Peabody, MA: Hendrickson, 2004.

———. *Commentary on the Gospel of John*. In vol. 9 of *Ante-Nicene Fathers*, edited by Alexander Roberts and James Donaldson, translated by Allan Menzies, 297–408. Peabody, MA: Hendrickson, 2004.

———. *De Principiis*. In vol. 4 of *Ante-Nicene Fathers*, edited by Alexander Roberts and James Donaldson, translated by Frederick Crombie, 239–384. Peabody, MA: Hendrickson, 2004.

———. *On First Principles*. Translated by G. W. Butterworth. Notre Dame: Ave Maria, 2013.

———. *Treatise on the Passover and Dialogue of Origen with Heraclides and His Fellow Bishops on the Father, the Son, and the Soul.* Translated by Robert J. Daly. Ancient Christian Writers 54. New York: Paulist, 1992.

Osborn, Eric. *Tertullian: First Theologian of the West.* Cambridge: Cambridge University Press, 1997.

Osborne, Robin. *Greek History: The Basics.* London: Routledge, 2014.

Oswalt, John N. *The Bible among the Myths: Unique Revelation or Just Ancient Literature?* Grand Rapids: Zondervan, 2009.

———. *The Book of Isaiah: Chapters 1–39.* The New International Commentary on the Old Testament. Grand Rapids: Eerdmans, 1986.

———. *The Book of Isaiah: Chapters 40–66.* The New International Commentary on the Old Testament. Grand Rapids: Eerdmans, 1998.

———. *Called to Be Holy: A Biblical Perspective.* Nappanee, IN: Evangel, 1999.

———. "John Wesley and the Old Testament Concept of the Holy Spirit." *Religion in Life* 48 (1979) 283–91.

Outler, Albert C. "A Focus on the Holy Spirit: Spirit and Spirituality in John Wesley." In *The Wesleyan Theological Heritage: Essays of Albert C. Outler,* edited by Thomas C. Oden and Leichster R. Longden, 159–73. Grand Rapids: Zondervan, 1991.

———. "Introduction." In vol. 1 of *The Works of John Wesley,* edited by Albert C. Outler, 1–102. Nashville: Abingdon, 1984.

———. "The Wesleyan Quadrilateral in John Wesley." *The Wesleyan Theological Journal* 20 (1985) 7–18.

Owen, John. *The Holy Spirit.* East Peoria, IL: Versa, 2017.

———. *The Holy Spirit: His Gifts and Power: Exposition of the Spirit's Name, Nature, Personality, Dispensation, Operations, and Effects.* Grand Rapids: Kregel, 1960.

Palamas, Gregory. *The Triads.* Edited by John Meyendorff. Translated by Nicholas Gendle. Mahwah, NJ: Paulist, 1983.

Pannenberg, Wolfhart. *Anthropology in Theological Perspective.* Translated by Matthew J. O'Connell. Edinburgh: T. & T. Clark, 1985.

———. "Divine Economy and Eternal Trinity." In *The Theology of John Zizioulas: Personhood and the Church,* edited by Douglas H. Knight, 79–86. Burlington, VT: Ashgate, 2007.

———. *Jesus, God and Man.* Translated by Lewis L. Wilkens and Duane A. Priebe. 2nd ed. Philadelphia: Westminster, 1977.

———. *Systematic Theology.* Vol. 1. Translated by Geoffrey W. Bromiley. Grand Rapids: Eerdmans, 1991.

———. *Theology and the Kingdom of God.* Edited by Richard John Neuhaus. Philadelphia: Westminster, 1977.

Papadopoulos, Gerasimos. "The Revelatory Character of the New Testament and Holy Tradition in the Orthodox Church." In vol. 1 of *The Orthodox Ethos: Studies in Orthodoxy,* edited by A. J. Philippou, 98–111. Oxford: Holywell, 1964.

Papanikolaou, Aristotle. *Being with God: Trinity, Apophaticism, and Divine-Human Communion.* Notre Dame: University of Notre Dame Press, 2006.

———. "Divine Energies or Divine Personhood: Vladimir Lossky and John Zizioulas on Conceiving the Transcendent and Immanent God." *Modern Theology* 19 (2003) 357–85.

———. "Is John Zizioulas an Existentialist in Disguise? Response to Lucian Turcescu." *Modern Theology* 20 (2004) 601–7.

Pedersen, Johs. *Israel: Its Life and Culture*. Vols. 1–2. Denmark: Bogtrykkeri, 1959.

Pelikan, Jaroslav. *Historical Theology: Continuity and Change in Christian Doctrine*. London: Hutchinson, 1971.

Philips, Philip Edward, and Noel Harold Kaylor. *A Companion to Boethius in the Middle Ages*. Brill's Companions to the Christian Tradition. Leiden: Brill. 2012.

Pinnock, Clark H. *Flame of Love: A Theology of the Holy Spirit*. Downers Grove, IL: InterVarsity, 1996.

Pittenger, Norman W. *The Divine Triunity*. Philadelphia: United Church, 1977.

Plantinga, Cornelius, Jr. *Not the Way It's Supposed to Be: A Breviary of Sin*. Grand Rapids: Eerdmans, 1996.

Plato. *The Dialogues of Plato*. Vol. 2, *Timaeus*. Translated by B. Jowett. London: Macmillan, 1871.

———. *Laws*. Vol. 2, *Books 7–12*. Edited by G. P. Goold. Translated by R. G. Bury. Loeb Classical Library 192. Cambridge: Harvard University Press, 1984.

———. *Parmenides*. Edited by G. P. Goold. Translated by H. N. Fowler. Loeb Classical Library 167. Cambridge: Harvard University Press, 1996.

———. *Timaeus*. Edited by G. P. Goold. Translated by R. G. Bury. Loeb Classical Library 234. Cambridge: Harvard University Press, 1989.

Pontius. *The Life and Passion of Cyprian, Bishop and Martyr*. In vol. 5 of *Ante-Nicene Fathers*, edited by Alexander Roberts and James Donaldson, translated by Ernest Wallis, 267–74. Peabody, MA: Hendrickson, 2004.

Power, David N. "Sacrament of Eucharist." In *TMCE* 735–41.

Pratt, Zane. "The Heart of Mission: Redemption." In *Theology and Practice of Mission: God, the Church, and the Nations*, edited by Bruce Riley Ashford, 48–59. Nashville: B&H Academic, 2011.

Purkiser, W. T., ed. *Exploring Our Christian Faith*. Rev. ed. Kansas City: Beacon Hill, 1978.

Purkiser, W. T., et al. *God, Man, & Salvation: A Biblical Theology*. Kansas City: Beacon Hill, 1977.

Quasten, Johannes. *Patrology: The Golden Age of Greek Patristic Literature from the Council of Nicaea to the Council of Chalcedon*. Vol. 3. Westminster, MD: Christian Classics, 1990.

Rack, Henry D., ed. "The Deed of Declaration (1784) and After." In vol. 10 of *The Works of John Wesley*, 84–101. Nashville: Abingdon, 2011.

Rad, Gerhard von. *Old Testament Theology*. Vol. 2, *The Theology of Israel's Prophetic Traditions*. Translated by D. M. G. Stalker. London: Oliver and Boyd, 1965.

Radde-Gallwitz, Andrew. "Gregory of Nyssa's Pneumatology in Context: The Spirit as Anointing and the History of the Trinitarian Controversies." *Journal of Early Christian Studies* 19 (2011) 259–85.

Rahner, Karl. *The Trinity*. Translated by Joseph Donceel. New York: Crossroads, 1997.

Ratzinger, Joseph. *Jesus of Nazareth: From the Baptism in the Jordon to the Transfiguration*. Translated by Adrian J. Walker. New York: Doubleday, 2007.

Reeves, Michael. *Delighting in the Trinity: An Introduction to the Christian Faith*. Downers Grove, IL: IVP Academic, 2012.

Richard of St. Victor. *On the Trinity*. In *Trinity and Creation: A Selection of Works of Hugh, Richard and Adam of St. Victor*, edited by Boyd Taylor Coolman and Dale M. Coulter, translated by Christopher P. Evans, 195–382. Victorine Texts in

Translation: Exegesis, Theology and Spirituality from the Abbey of St. Victor 1. Hyde Park, NY: New City, 2011.

Rogers, Eugene F., Jr. *After the Spirit: A Constructive Pneumatology from Resources outside the Modern West.* Grand Rapids: Eerdmans, 2005.

Rogerson, John W. "The Hebrew Conception of Corporate Personality: A Re-examination (1970)." In *Anthropological Approaches to the Old Testament,* edited by Bernhard Lang, 43–59. Issues in Religion and Theology 8. Philadelphia: Fortress, 1985.

Rosenthal, Stanley. *One God Or Three?: Exploring the Tri-Unity of God in the Old Testament.* West Collingwood, NJ: Spearhead, 1978.

Rowe, J. Nigel. *Origen's Doctrine of Subordination: A Study in Origen's Christology.* European University Studies 272. New York: Lang, 1987.

Rousseau, Jean Jacques. *The Social Contract and Discourses.* New York: Dutton, 1950.

Routledge, Robin. *Old Testament Theology: A Thematic Approach.* Downers Grove, IL: IVP Academic, 2008.

Rufinus. *A Commentary on the Apostles' Creed.* In vol. 3 of *Nicene and Post-Nicene Fathers, Second Series,* edited by Philip Schaff and Henry Wace, translated by William Henry Fremantle, 541–63. Peabody, MA: Hendrickson, 2004.

Sanders, Fred. *The Deep Things of God: How the Trinity Changes Everything.* 2nd ed. Wheaton, IL: Crossway, 2017.

———. "What Trinitarian Theology Is For: Placing the Doctrine of the Trinity in Christian Theology and Life." In *Advancing Trinitarian Theology: Explorations in Constructive Dogmatics,* edited by Oliver D. Crisp and Fred Sanders, 21–41. Grand Rapids: Zondervan, 2014.

Sartre, Jean Paul. *Existentialism.* Translated by Bernard Frechtman. New York: Philosophical Library, 1947.

———. *Existentialism and Humanism.* Translated by Philip Mairet. Slingsby: Methuen, 2013.

Satyavrata, Ivan. *The Holy Spirit: Lord and Life-Giver.* Carlisle: Global Christian Library, 2012.

Schaeffer, Francis A. *A Christian Manifesto.* Westchester, IL: Crossway, 1981.

———. *Escape from Reason: A Penetrating Analysis of Trends in Modern Thought.* Downers Grove, IL: InterVarsity, 1968.

Schaff, Philip. *Ante-Nicene Christianity: From the Death of John the Apostle to Constantine the Great, A.D. 100–325.* History of the Christian Church 2. Peabody, MA: Hendrickson, 2002.

———. *From Constantine the Great to Gregory the Great, A.D. 311–590.* History of Christian Church: Nicene and Post-Nicene Christianity 3. Peabody, MA: Hendrickson, 2002.

———, ed. *The Creeds of Christendom: With a History and Critical Notes.* Vol. 1, *The History of Creeds.* 6th ed. Grand Rapids: Baker, 2007.

———, ed. *The Creeds of Christendom: With a History and Critical Notes.* Vol. 2, *The Greek and Latin Creeds.* 6th ed. Grand Rapids: Baker, 2007.

Schleiermacher, Friedrich. *The Christian Faith.* Edited by H. R. Mackintosh and J. S. Stewart. 2nd ed. Edinburgh: T. & T. Clark, 1928.

———. *The Christian Faith.* Edited by H. R. Mackintosh and J. S. Stewart. Berkeley: Apocryphile, 2011.

Schmeman, Alexander. "The Missionary Imperative in the Orthodox Tradition." In *Eastern Orthodox Theology: A Contemporary Reader*, edited by Daniel B. Clendenin, 195–202. Grand Rapids: Baker, 1995.

Schnabel, Eckhard J. *Acts*. Zondervan Exegetical Commentary on the New Testament. Grand Rapids: Zondervan, 2012.

Schneider, Johannes. "παραβαίνω, παράβασις, παραβάτης, ἀπαράβατος, ὑπερβαίνω." In *TDNT* 5:736–43.

Schroeder, H. J., trans. *The Canons and Decrees of the Council of Trent*. Charlotte, NC: TAN, 1978.

Schwarz, Hans. *The Human Being: A Theological Anthropology*. Grand Rapids: Eerdmans, 2013.

Schwöbel, Christoph. "Introduction." In *Trinitarian Theology Today*, edited by Christoph Schwöbel, 1–30. Edinburgh: T. & T. Clark, 1995.

Seraphim of Sarov. *On Acquisition of the Holy Spirit*. Middletown, DE: 2019.

Sexton, Jason S. "A Confessing Trinitarian Theology for Today's Mission." In *Advancing Trinitarian Theology: Exploring Constructive Dogmatics*, edited by Oliver D. Crisp and Fred Sanders, 171–90. Grand Rapids: Zondervan, 2014.

Shear, Theodore Leslie. "The Influence of Plato on Saint Basil." PhD diss., John Hopkins University, 1906.

Shults, F. LeRon. *Reforming Theological Anthropology: After the Philosophical Turn to Relationality*. Grand Rapids: Eerdmans, 2003.

Shults, F. LeRon, and Andrea Hollingsworth. *The Holy Spirit*. Guides to Theology. Grand Rapids: Eerdmans, 2008.

Simons, Menno. *The Complete Writings of Menno Simons (1496–1561)*. Edited by J. C. Wenger. Translated by Leonard Verduin. Scottdale, PA: Herald, 1984.

Smith, D. Moody. *John*. Abingdon New Testament Commentaries. Nashville: Abingdon, 1999.

Snavely, Andréa. *Life in the Spirit: A Post-Constantinian and Trinitarian Account of the Christian Life*. Pentecostals, Peacemaking, and Social Justice 9. Eugene, OR: Pickwick, 2015.

Sokolowski, Robert. "The Revelation of the Holy Trinity: A Study in Personal Pronouns." In *Christian Faith and Human Understanding: Studies on the Eucharist, Trinity, and the Human Person*, 131–50. Washington, DC: Catholic University of America Press, 2006.

Spencer, F. Scott. "Preparing the Way of the Lord: Introducing and Interpreting Luke's Narrative: A Response to David Wenham." In *Reading Luke: Interpretation, Reflection, Formation*, edited by Craig G. Bartholomew et al., 104–24. Scripture and Hermeneutics Series 6. Grand Rapids: Zondervan, 2005.

Spencer, Herbert. *An Epitome of the Synthetic Philosophy*. Ithaca, NY: Cornell University Library, 2009.

Stanglin, Keith D., and Thomas H. McCall. *Jacob Arminius: Theologian of Grace*. New York: Oxford University Press, 2012.

St. Mary's Episcopal Cathedral, Edinburgh. "Inside the Cathedral." https://www.cathedral.net/about/a-tour-of-the-cathedral/inside-the-cathedral/.

Stead, G. Christopher. "The Concept of Divine Substance." In *Doctrines of God and Christ in the Early Church*, edited by Everett Ferguson, 29–42. Studies in Early Christianity 9. New York: Garland, 1993.

Steenberg, M. C. "Eucharist." In *CEOC* 185–89.

Stolorow, Robert D. "What Is Character and How Does It Change?" *Psychology Today*, March 21, 2012. https://www.psychologytoday.com/us/blog/feeling-relating-existing/201203/what-is-character-and-how-does-it-change.

Strong, Augustus H. *Systematic Theology*. Valley Forge, PA: Judson, 1907.

Stronstad, Roger. *The Charismatic Theology of St. Luke: Trajectories from the Old Testament to Luke-Acts*. 2nd ed. Grand Rapids: Baker Academic, 2012.

Stuart, Douglas K. *Exodus*. The New American Commentary 2. Nashville: Broadman & Holman, 2006.

Studebaker, Steven M. *From Pentecost to the Triune God: A Pentecostal Trinitarian Theology*. Pentecostal Manifestos. Grand Rapids: Eerdmans, 2012.

Sweeten, Howard W. *Sinning Saints*. Salem, OH: Schmul, 1978.

Symeon the New Theologian. *The Discourses*. Translated by C. J. de Catanzaro. The Classics of Western Spirituality. Mahwah, NJ: Paulist, 1980.

Tarnas, Richard. *The Passion of the Western Mind: Understanding the Ideas That Have Shaped Our World View*. New York: Harmony, 1991.

Taylor, Richard S. *The Theological Formulation*. Vol. 3, *Exploring Christian Holiness*. Kansas City: Beacon Hill, 1985.

The Teaching of the Twelve Apostles. In vol. 7 of *Ante-Nicene Fathers*, edited by Alexander Roberts and James Donaldson, translated by M. B. Riddle, 369–84. Peabody, MA: Hendrickson, 2004.

Tersteegen, Gerhard. *Sermons and Hymns*. Vol. 2. Shoals, IN: Old Paths Tract Society, n.d.

Tertullian. *Against Hermogenes*. In vol. 3 of *Ante-Nicene Fathers*, edited by Alexander Roberts and James Donaldson, translated by Peter Holmes, 477–502. Peabody, MA: Hendrickson, 2004.

———. *Against Marcion*. In vol. 3 of *Ante-Nicene Fathers*, edited by Alexander Roberts and James Donaldson, translated by Peter Holmes, 269–476. Peabody, MA: Hendrickson, 2004.

———. *Against Praxeas*. In vol. 3 of *Ante-Nicene Fathers*, edited by Alexander Roberts and James Donaldson, translated by Peter Holmes, 597–632. Peabody, MA: Hendrickson, 2004.

———. *Apology*. In vol. 3 of *Ante-Nicene Fathers*, edited by Alexander Roberts and James Donaldson, translated by S. Thelwall, 17–60. Peabody, MA: Hendrickson, 2004.

———. *On Baptism*. In vol. 3 of *Ante-Nicene Fathers*, edited by Alexander Roberts and James Donaldson, translated by S. Thelwall, 669–80. Peabody, MA: Hendrickson, 2004.

———. *On Fasting*. In vol. 4 of *Ante-Nicene Fathers*, edited by Alexander Roberts and James Donaldson, translated by S. Thelwall, 102–15. Peabody, MA: Hendrickson, 2004.

———. *On Prescription Against Heretics*. In vol. 3 of *Ante-Nicene Fathers*, edited by Alexander Roberts and James Donaldson, translated by Peter Holmes, 243–68. Peabody, MA: Hendrickson, 2004.

———. *On Repentance*. In vol. 3 of *Ante-Nicene Fathers*, edited by Alexander Roberts and James Donaldson, translated by S. Thelwall, 657–68. Peabody, MA: Hendrickson, 2004.

———. *On the Veiling of Virgins*. In vol. 4 of *Ante-Nicene Fathers*, edited by Alexander Roberts and James Donaldson, translated by S. Thelwall, 27–38. Peabody, MA: Hendrickson, 2004.

Theophilus of Antioch. *Theophilus to Autolycus*. In vol. 2 of *Ante-Nicene Fathers*, edited by Alexander Roberts and James Donaldson, translated by Marcus Dods, 89–121. Peabody, MA: Hendrickson, 2004.

Thiselton, Anthony C. *The Holy Spirit—In Biblical Teaching, through the Centuries, and Today*. Grand Rapids: Eerdmans, 2013.

Thompson, Marianne Meye. "The Breath of Life: John 20:22-23." In *The Holy Spirit and Christian Origins: Essays in Honor of James D. G. Dunn*, edited by Graham N. Stanton et al., 69–78. Grand Rapids: Eerdmans, 2004.

Thorsen, Donald A. D. *The Wesleyan Quadrilateral: Scripture, Tradition, Reason, & Experience as a Model of Evangelical Theology*. Edited by James E. Ruark. Nappanee, IN: Asbury, 1997.

Tillich, Paul. *Love, Power, and Justice: Ontological Analyses and Ethical Applications*. New York: Oxford University Press, 1954.

———. *Systematic Theology*. Chicago: University of Chicago Press, 1967.

Tollefsen, Torstein Theodore. *The Christocentric Cosmology of St. Maximus the Confessor*. Oxford Early Christian Studies. Oxford: Oxford University Press, 2008.

Torchia, Joseph. *Exploring Personhood: An Introduction to the Philosophy of Human Nature*. New York: Rowan & Littlefield, 2008.

Törönen, Melchisedec. *Union and Distinction in the Thought of St. Maximus the Confessor*. Oxford Early Christian Studies. Oxford: Oxford University Press, 2007.

Torrance, Alan J. *Persons in Communion: Trinitarian Description and Human Participation*. Edinburgh: T. & T. Clark, 1996.

Torrance, Thomas F. *The Christian Doctrine of God: One Being Three Persons*. New York: T. & T. Clark, 2017.

———. *The Mediation of Christ*. Colorado Springs, CO: Helmers & Howard, 1992.

———. *Space, Time, and Incarnation*. Edinburgh: T. & T. Clark, 1997.

———. *The Trinitarian Faith: The Evangelical Theology of the Ancient Catholic Church*. 2nd ed. New York: T. & T. Clark, 2006.

Torrey, R. A. *The Holy Spirit: Who He Is and What He Does and How to Know Him in All the Fullness of His Gracious and Glorious Ministry*. New York: Revell, 1927.

———. *The Person and Work of the Holy Spirit as Revealed in the Scriptures and in Personal Experience*. New York: Revell, 1910.

Toussaint, Stanley D. "The Doctrine of the Future and the Concept of Hope." In *Eschatology: Biblical, Historical, and Practical Approaches: A Volume in Honor of Craig A. Blaising*, edited by D. Jeffrey Bingham and Glenn R. Kreider, 53–70. Grand Rapids: Kregel Academic, 2016.

Tozer, A. W. *The Divine Conquest*. Westwood, NJ: Revell, 1950.

Trapp, Michael. *Philosophy in the Roman Empire: Ethics, Politics, and Society*. Ashgate Ancient Philosophy Series. Burlington, VT: Ashgate, 2008.

Trostyanskiy, Sergey. "Holy Spirit." In *CEOC* 248–50.

Tucker, Austin B. *The Preacher as Storyteller: The Power of Narrative in the Pulpit*. Nashville: B&H Academic, 2008.

Turcescu, Lucian. *Gregory of Nyssa and the Concept of Divine Persons*. American Academy of Religion Series. New York: Oxford University Press, 2005.

———. "'Person' versus 'Individual', and Other Modern Misreadings of Gregory of Nyssa.'" *Modern Theology* 18 (2002) 527–39.

Turner, Max. *The Holy Spirit and Spiritual Gifts: In the New Testament Church Today.* Rev. ed. Peabody, MA: Hendrickson, 2005.

———. "Luke and the Spirit: Renewing Theological Interpretation of Biblical Pneumatology." In *Reading Luke: Interpretation, Reflection, Formation*, edited by Craig G. Bartholomew et al., 267–93. Scripture and Hermeneutics Series 6. Grand Rapids: Zondervan, 2005.

———. *Power from on High: The Spirit in Israel's Restoration and Witness in Luke-Acts.* Journal of Pentecostal Theology Supplement Series 9. Eugene, OR: Wipf & Stock, 2015.

———. "The Spirit and Salvation in Luke-Acts." In *The Holy Spirit and Christian Origins: Essays in Honor of James D. G. Dunn*, edited by Graham N. Stanton et al., 103–16. Grand Rapids: Eerdmans, 2004.

Turner, Robert. "Eschatology and Truth." In *The Theology of John Zizioulas: Personhood and the Church*, edited by Douglas H. Knight, 15–34. Burlington, VT: Ashgate, 2007.

The United Methodist Hymnal: Book of United Methodist Worship. Nashville: United Methodist, 2001.

Ury, William. *Trinitarian Personhood: Investigating the Implications of a Relational Definition.* Eugene, OR: Wipf & Stock, 2001.

VanGemeren, Willem A. *Interpreting the Prophetic Word: An Introduction to the Prophetic Literature of the Old Testament.* Grand Rapids: Zondervan, 1990.

Vatican II. *The Documents of Vatican II.* Strathfield: St. Paul's, 2013.

Venard, Olivier-Thomas. "Sacraments." In *The Cambridge Companion to the Summa Theologiae*, edited by Philip McCosker and Denys Turner, 269–90. Cambridge: Cambridge University Press, 2016.

Volf, Miroslav. *After Our Likeness: The Church as the Image of the Trinity.* Sacra Doctrina: Christian Theology for a Postmodern Age. Grand Rapids: Eerdmans, 1998.

Volz, Carl A. "Human Participation in the Divine-Human Dialogue." In *Salvation in Christ: A Lutheran-Orthodox Dialogue*, edited by John Meyendorff and Robert Tobias, 85–104. Minneapolis: Augsburg Fortress, 1992.

Wallas, Graham. *The Art of Thought.* Kent: Solis, 2014.

Waltke, Bruce K., with Charles Yu. *An Old Testament Theology: An Exegetical, Canonical, and Thematic Approach.* Grand Rapids: Zondervan, 2007.

Ward, Julian. "Pentecostal Theology and the Charismatic Movement." In *Strange Gifts? A Guide to Charismatic Renewal*, edited by David Martin and Peter Mullen, 192–216. New York: Basil Blackwell, 1984.

Ware, Bruce A. *Father, Son, & Holy Spirit: Relationships, Roles, & Relevance.* Wheaton, IL: Crossway, 2005.

Ware, Kallistos. *The Orthodox Way.* Rev. ed. Crestwood, NY: St. Vladimir's Seminary Press, 1995.

Ware, Timothy (Kallistos). "The Earthly Heaven." In *Eastern Orthodox Theology: A Contemporary Reader*, edited by Daniel B. Clendenin, 11–20. Grand Rapids: Baker, 1995.

Webb, Eugene. *In Search of the Triune God: The Christian Paths of East and West.* Columbia: University of Missouri Press, 2014.

Webster, John. *Holiness.* Grand Rapids: Eerdmans, 2003.

Wedderburn, Alexander J. M. "Pauline Pneumatology and Pauline Theology." In *The Holy Spirit and Christian Origins: Essays in Honor of James D. G. Dunn*, edited by Graham N. Stanton et al., 144–56. Grand Rapids: Eerdmans, 2004.

Wendebourg, Dorothea. "From the Cappadocian Fathers to Gregory Palamas: The Defeat of Trinitarian Theology." *Studia Patristica* 17 (1982) 194–98.

Wenger, J. C. *God's Word Written: Essays on the Nature of Biblical Revelation, Inspiration, and Authority*. Scottdale, PA: Herald, 1968.

Wesley, John. "The Almost Christian." In vol. 1 of *The Works of John Wesley*, edited by Albert C. Outler, 131–41. Bicentennial ed. Nashville: Abingdon, 1984.

———. "Brief Thoughts on Christian Perfection." In vol. 11 of *The Works of John Wesley*, edited by Thomas Jackson, 446. 3rd ed. Grand Rapids: Baker, 1998.

———. "Catholic Spirit." In vol. 5 of *The Works of John Wesley*, edited by Thomas Jackson, 492–502. 3rd ed. Grand Rapids: Baker, 1998.

———. "The Character of a Methodist." In vol. 8 of *The Works of John Wesley*, edited by Thomas Jackson, 339–46. 3rd ed. Grand Rapids: Baker, 1998.

———. "Christian Perfection." In vol. 6 of *The Works of John Wesley*, edited by Thomas Jackson, 1–2. 3rd ed. Grand Rapids: Baker, 1998.

———. "The Circumcision of the Heart." In vol. 5 of *The Works of John Wesley*, edited by Thomas Jackson, 202–1. 3rd ed. Grand Rapids: Baker, 1998.

———. "The General Deliverance." In vol. 2 of *The Works of John Wesley*, edited by Albert C. Outler, 436–50. Bicentennial ed. Nashville: Abingdon, 1985.

———. "The Difference between Walking by Sight and Walking by Faith." In vol. 7 of *The Works of John Wesley*, edited by Thomas Jackson, 256–63. 3rd ed. Grand Rapids: Baker, 1998.

———. "A Farther Appeal to Men of Reason and Religion." In vol. 8 of *The Works of John Wesley*, edited by Thomas Jackson, 46–135. 3rd ed. Grand Rapids: Baker, 1998.

———. "The First Fruits of the Holy Spirit." In vol. 5 of *The Works of John Wesley*, edited by Thomas Jackson, 87–97. 3rd ed. Grand Rapids: Baker, 1998.

———. *The Holy Spirit and Power*. Edited by Clare Weakly. Newberry FL: Bridge-Logos, 2003.

———. "Journal: October 14, 1735—November 29, 1745." In vol. 1 of *The Works of John Wesley*, edited by Thomas Jackson, 17–532. 3rd ed. Grand Rapids: Baker, 1998.

———. "Letter to Mr. Joseph Benson." In vol. 12 of *The Works of John Wesley*, edited by Thomas Jackson, 415–17. 3rd ed. Grand Rapids: Baker, 1998.

———. "The Marks of the New Birth." In vol. 5 of *The Works of John Wesley*, edited by Thomas Jackson, 212–22. 3rd ed. Grand Rapids: Baker, 1998.

———. "The Means of Grace." In vol. 5 of *The Works of John Wesley*, edited by Thomas Jackson, 185–201. 3rd ed. Grand Rapids: Baker, 1998.

———. "Minutes of Several Conversations between the Rev. Mr. Wesley and Others; From the Year 1744, the Year 1789." In vol. 8 of *The Works of John Wesley*, edited by Thomas Jackson, 299–338. 3rd ed. Grand Rapids: Baker, 1998.

———. "Minutes of Some Late Conversations between the Rev. Mr. Wesleys and Others, in 1744." In vol. 8 of *The Works of John Wesley*, edited by Thomas Jackson, 275–89. 3rd ed. Grand Rapids: Baker, 1998.

———. "The New Birth." In vol. 2 of *The Works of John Wesley*, edited by Albert C. Outler, 186–201. Bicentennial ed. Nashville: Abingdon, 1985.

———. "On the Fall of Man." In vol. 2 of *The Works of John Wesley*, edited by Albert C. Outler, 400–412. Bicentennial ed. Nashville: Abingdon, 1985.

———. "On the Holy Spirit." In vol. 7 of *The Works of John Wesley*, edited by Thomas Jackson, 508–20. 3rd ed. Grand Rapids: Baker, 1998.

———. "On Perfection." In vol. 6 of *The Works of John Wesley*, edited by Thomas Jackson, 411–23. 3rd ed. Grand Rapids: Baker, 1998.

———. "On Sin in Believers." In vol. 5 of *The Works of John Wesley*, edited by Thomas Jackson, 144–55. 3rd ed. Grand Rapids: Baker, 1998.

———. "On the Trinity." In vol. 6 of *The Works of John Wesley*, edited by Thomas Jackson, 199–205. 3rd ed. Grand Rapids: Baker, 1998.

———. "A Plain Account of Christian Perfection, as Believed and Taught by the Reverend Mr. John Wesley, from the year 1725 to the year 1777." In vol. 11 of *The Works of John Wesley*, edited by Thomas Jackson, 366–445. 3rd ed. Grand Rapids: Baker, 1998.

———. "Scriptural Christianity." In vol. 5 of *The Works of John Wesley*, edited by Thomas Jackson, 37–52. 3rd ed. Grand Rapids: Baker, 1998.

———. "The Second Essay: A Plain Explication of the Doctrine of Imputed Sin and Imputed Righteousness." In vol. 9 of *The Works of John Wesley*, edited by Thomas Jackson, 393–96. 3rd ed. Grand Rapids: Baker, 1998.

———. "The Spirit of Bondage and of Adoption." In vol. 5 of *The Works of John Wesley*, edited by Thomas Jackson, 98–110. 3rd ed. Grand Rapids: Baker, 1998.

———. "The Unity of the Divine Being." In vol. 7 of *The Works of John Wesley*, edited by Thomas Jackson, 264–72. 3rd ed. Grand Rapids: Baker, 1998.

———. "The Way to the Kingdom." In vol. 5 of *The Works of John Wesley*, edited by Thomas Jackson, 76–86. 3rd ed. Grand Rapids: Baker, 1998.

———. "What Is Man?" In vol. 4 of *The Works of John Wesley*, edited by Albert C. Outler, 19–27. Bicentennial ed. Nashville: Abingdon, 1987.

———. "Witness of the Spirit (Discourse 1)." In vol. 5 of *The Works of John Wesley*, edited by Thomas Jackson, 111–22. 3rd ed. Grand Rapids: Baker, 1998.

———. "Witness of the Spirit (Discourse 2)." In vol. 5 of *The Works of John Wesley*, edited by Thomas Jackson, 123–33. 3rd ed. Grand Rapids: Baker, 1998.

———. "Witness of Our Own Spirit." In vol. 5 of *The Works of John Wesley*, edited by Thomas Jackson, 134–43. 3rd ed. Grand Rapids: Baker, 1998.

———. "Working Out Our Own Salvation." In vol. 6 of *The Works of John Wesley*, edited by Thomas Jackson, 506–13. 3rd ed. Grand Rapids: Baker, 1998.

White, Thomas Joseph. *Exodus*. Brazos Theological Commentary on the Bible. Grand Rapids: Brazos, 2016.

Whitfield, Keith. "The Triune God: The God of Mission." In *Theology and Practice of Mission: God, the Church, and the Nations*, edited by Bruce Riley Ashford, 17–34. Nashville: B&H Academic, 2011.

Wiley, H. Orton, and Paul T. Culbertson. *Introduction to Christian Theology*. Kansas City: Beacon Hill, 1961.

Williams, David J. *Paul's Metaphors: Their Context and Character*. Peabody, MA: Hendrickson, 1999.

Williams, Thomas. "God Who Sows the Seed and Gives the Growth: Anselm's Theology of the Holy Spirit." *Anglican Theological Review* 89 (2007) 611–27.

Wilks, John G. F. "The Trinitarian Ontology of John Zizioulas." *Vox evangelica* 25 (1995) 63–88. http://biblicalstudies.org.uk/pdf/vox/vol25/zizoulas_wilks.pdf.

Wilson, Gerald H. *Psalms: Volume 1*. The NIV Application Commentary. Grand Rapids: Zondervan, 2002.

Witherington, Ben, III. *Letters and Homilies for Jewish Christians: A Socio-Rhetorical Commentary on Hebrews, James, and Jude*. Downers Grove, IL: IVP Academic, 2007.

Wolff, Hans Walter. *Anthropology of the Old Testament*. Philadelphia: Fortress, 1973.

Wood, Laurence W. *God and History: The Dialectical Tension of Faith and History in Modern Thought*. Lexington, KY: Emeth, 2005.

———. *Theology as History and Hermeneutics: A Post-Critical Conversation with Contemporary Theology*. Lexington, KY: Emeth, 2005.

Wright, Christopher J. H. *The Mission of God's People: A Biblical Theology of the Church's Mission*. Grand Rapids: Zondervan, 2010.

Wright, G. Ernest. *God Who Acts: Biblical Theology as Recital*. Studies in Biblical Theology 8. London: SCM, 1969.

Yarnell, Malcolm B., III. *Who Is the Holy Spirit? Biblical Insights into His Divine Person*. Edited by Heath A. Thomas. Hobbs College Library. Nashville: B&H Academic, 2019.

Yong, Amos. *Spirit-Word-Community: Theological Hermeneutics in Trinitarian Perspective*. Eugene, OR: Wipf & Stock, 2002.

———. *Who Is the Holy Spirit?: A Walk With the Apostles*. Brewster, MA: Paraclete, 2011.

Zakopoulos, Athenagoras N. *Plato on Man: A Summary and Critique of His Psychology with Special Reference to Pre-Platonic, Freudian, Behavioristic, and Humanistic Psychology*. New York: Philosophical Library, 1975.

Zizioulas, John D. "Appendix: Person and Individual—A 'Misreading' of the Cappadocians?" In *Communion & Otherness: Further Studies in Personhood and the Church*, edited by Paul McPartlan, 171–77. New York: T. & T. Clark, 2006.

———. *Being as Communion: Studies in Personhood and the Church*. Crestwood, NY: St. Vladimir's Seminary Press, 2000.

———. "Come Holy Spirit, Sanctify our Lives!" *Sourozh* 44 (1991) 1–3.

———. *Communion & Otherness: Further Studies in Personhood and the Church*. Edited by Paul McPartlan. New York: T. & T. Clark, 2006.

———. "The Contribution of Cappadocia to Christian Thought." In *Sinasos in Cappadocia*, edited by Frosso Pimenides and Stelios Roïdes, 23–37. London: Agra, 1986.

———. "The Doctrine of the Holy Trinity: The Significance of the Cappadocian Contribution." In *Trinitarian Theology Today*, edited by Christoph Schwöbel, 44–60. Edinburgh: T. & T. Clark, 1995.

———. "The Early Christian Community." In *Christian Spirituality: Origins to the Twelfth Century*, edited by Bernard McGinn et al., 23–43. London: Routledge & Paul, 1986.

———. "The Ecclesiology of the Orthodox Tradition." *Search* 7 (1984) 42–53.

———. "The Eucharist and the Kingdom of God (Part 1)." *Sourozh* 58 (1994) 1–12.

———. "The Eucharist and the Kingdom of God (Part 2)." *Sourozh* 59 (1995) 22–38.

———. "The Eucharist and the Kingdom of God (Part 3)." *Sourozh* 60 (1995) 32–46.

———. *Eucharist, Bishop, Church: The Unity of the Church in the Divine Eucharist and the Bishop During the First Three Centuries*. Translated by Elizabeth Theokritoff. Brookline, MA: Holy Cross Orthodox, 2001.

———. *The Eucharistic Communion and the World.* Edited by Luke Ben Tallon. New York: T. & T. Clark International, 2011.

———. "Eucharistic Prayer and Life." *Emmanuel* 81 (1975) 462–70.

———. "Human Capacity and Human Incapacity: A Theological Exploration of Personhood." *Scottish Journal of Theology* 28 (1975) 401–48.

———. "Informal Groups in the Church: An Orthodox Viewpoint." In *Informal Groups in the Church: Papers of the Second Cerdic Colloquium, Strasbourg, May 13–15, 1971,* edited by René Metz and Jean Schlick, translated by Matthew J. O'Connell, 275–98. Pittsburgh Theological Monograph Series 7. Pittsburgh: Pickwick, 1975.

———. *Lectures in Christian Dogmatics.* Edited by Douglas H. Knight. New York: T. & T. Clark, 2008.

———. *The One and the Many: Studies on God, Man, the Church, and the World Today.* Edited by Gregory Edwards. Alhamra, CA: Sebastian, 2010.

———. "Ordination—A Sacrament? An Orthodox Reply." *Concilium* 4 (1972) 33–39.

———. "Preserving God's Creation: Three Lectures on Theology and Ecology." *King's Theological Review* 12 (1989) 41–45.

———. "Preserving God's Creation: Three Lectures on Theology and Ecology." *King's Theological Review* 13 (1989) 1–5.

Zwingli, Huldrych. *Of the Clarity and Certainty of the Word of God.* In *Zwingli and Bullinger,* edited by John Baillie et al., translated by G. W. Bromiley, 59–95. The Library of Christian Classics 24. Philadelphia: Westminster, 1953.

———. *On Providence and Other Eessays.* Edited by William John Hinke. Eugene, OR: Wipf & Stock, 1999.

Author Index

Subject Index

Scripture Index

LUKE

JOHN

ROMANS

1 CORINTHIANS

2 CORINTHIANS